Approaches to Global Sustainability, Markets, and Governance

Series Editors

David Crowther, Faculty of Business and Law, De Montfort University, Leicester, UK

Shahla Seifi, Social Responsibility Research Network, Derby, UK

Approaches to Global Sustainability, Markets, and Governance takes a fresh and global approach to issues of corporate social responsibility, regulation, governance, and sustainability. It encompasses such issues as: environmental sustainability and managing the resources of the world; geopolitics and sustainability; global markets and their regulation; governance and the role of supranational bodies; sustainable production and resource acquisition; society and sustainability.

Although primarily a business and management series, it is interdisciplinary and includes contributions from the social sciences, technology, engineering, politics, philosophy, and other disciplines. It focuses on the issues at a meta-level, and investigates the ideas, organisation, and infrastructure required to address them.

The series is grounded in the belief that any global consideration of sustainability must include such issues as governance, regulation, geopolitics, the environment, and economic activity in combination to recognise the issues and develop solutions for the planet. At present such global meta-analysis is rare as current research assumes that the identification of local best practice will lead to solutions, and individual disciplines act in isolation rather than being combined to identify truly global issues and solutions.

More information about this series at https://link.springer.com/bookseries/15778

Ninh Nguyen · Hoang Viet Nguyen ·
Clare D'Souza · Carolyn Strong
Editors

Environmental Sustainability in Emerging Markets

Consumer, Organisation and Policy Perspectives

Editors
Ninh Nguyen ⓘ
Asia Pacific College of Business and Law
Charles Darwin University
Darwin, NT, Australia

Hoang Viet Nguyen ⓘ
Board of Rectors
Thuongmai University
Hanoi, Vietnam

Clare D'Souza ⓘ
La Trobe Business School
La Trobe University
Bundoora, VIC, Australia

Carolyn Strong
Cardiff Business School
Cardiff University
Cardiff, UK

ISSN 2520-8772   ISSN 2520-8780 (electronic)
Approaches to Global Sustainability, Markets, and Governance
ISBN 978-981-19-2407-1   ISBN 978-981-19-2408-8 (eBook)
https://doi.org/10.1007/978-981-19-2408-8

© The Editor(s) (if applicable) and The Author(s), under exclusive license to Springer Nature
Singapore Pte Ltd. 2022
This work is subject to copyright. All rights are solely and exclusively licensed by the Publisher, whether
the whole or part of the material is concerned, specifically the rights of translation, reprinting, reuse
of illustrations, recitation, broadcasting, reproduction on microfilms or in any other physical way, and
transmission or information storage and retrieval, electronic adaptation, computer software, or by similar
or dissimilar methodology now known or hereafter developed.
The use of general descriptive names, registered names, trademarks, service marks, etc. in this publication
does not imply, even in the absence of a specific statement, that such names are exempt from the relevant
protective laws and regulations and therefore free for general use.
The publisher, the authors and the editors are safe to assume that the advice and information in this book
are believed to be true and accurate at the date of publication. Neither the publisher nor the authors or
the editors give a warranty, expressed or implied, with respect to the material contained herein or for any
errors or omissions that may have been made. The publisher remains neutral with regard to jurisdictional
claims in published maps and institutional affiliations.

This Springer imprint is published by the registered company Springer Nature Singapore Pte Ltd.
The registered company address is: 152 Beach Road, #21-01/04 Gateway East, Singapore 189721,
Singapore

Preface

There is a plethora of sustainability and pro-environmental behaviour evident in the developed market economies literature. While the knowledge about pro-environmental behaviour and sustainable development in emerging markets remains somewhat limited, some of these countries are growing in terms of population and production. Many multinational companies regard emerging market economies as the key locations for future development and profitable growth. These countries constitute a wealth of the world's people and land, and they are expected to continue to grow faster than their developed counterparts, which leads us to ask the question of how sustainability can improve its momentum. Notably, emerging and developing countries are major contributors to climate change and air pollution owing to their rapid economic growth, large consumer base, and unsustainable consumption. There is a widening need to research the environmental sustainability of markets within these countries; this book initiates the advancement of this imperative and necessary new research domain.

Increasing evidence of environmental deterioration in emerging markets, climate change, and consequences of environmental waste have compelled not only businesses but also consumers to reduce the environmental burden, mitigate waste, and preserve resources for future generations. What actions, strategies, practices, and policies can be developed to sustain environmental sustainability in emerging markets? This book brings together fresh insights, ideas, and new research directions. The editors of this book have thoughtfully and carefully selected eleven chapters which have undergone a stringent peer-review and editorial selection process. These chapters are contributed by emerging and eminent authors from different regions of the world including Asia, Australia, Europe, North America, and South America. These contributors have implemented a range of research methods comprising case studies, in-depth interviews, systematic literature reviews, surveys, and experiments to examine environmental sustainability issues in different emerging markets (e.g., Brazil, China, India, and Vietnam) from multiple perspectives.

The first four chapters examine pro-environmental behaviours from the consumer perspective, which include conspicuous green consumption behaviour (Chapter 1), renewable energy adoption (Chapter 2), food waste reduction (Chapter 3), and green purchase behaviour (Chapter 4). The next four chapters investigate environmental sustainability issues from organisational perspective, which include eco-friendly export business strategies of seafood processing firms (Chapter 5), CSR practices in food companies (Chapter 6), green human resource management in hotels (Chapter 7), and green multinational firms' perceptions of graduate employability (Chapter 8). The last three chapters focus on the industry and policy perspectives, which include sustainability strategies for urban mass transit (Chapter 9), sustainability-centric food supply chain practices (Chapter 10), and carbon tax policies (Chapter 11).

This book provides an insightful and valuable compendium for sustainability researchers, businesses, educators, policymakers, and readers concerned about socio-environmental issues and sustainable development. This collection offers policymakers and businesses information to assist the development of policies, strategies, and programmes which will develop and encourage environmentally sustainable behaviours and practices in emerging markets and the wider global community.

Contents

1 The Role of Green Product Pricing in Conspicuous Green Consumption Behaviour—A Brazilian Perspective 1
Manoela Costa Policarpo, Edvan Cruz Aguiar, Aitor Marcos, Patrick Hartmann, and Vanessa Apaolaza

2 Promoting Sustainable Renewable Energy Consumption: Government Policy Drives Record Rooftop Solar Adoption in Vietnam 23
Hoang Viet Nguyen, Tuan Duong Vu, Steven Greenland, Thi My Nguyet Nguyen, and Van Hung Vu

3 A Behavioural Model of Urban Household Food Waste Reduction: An Empirical Study in Beijing, China 47
Ji Lu, Wenguang Zhang, Yanbo Xiao, and Emmanuel K. Yiridoe

4 Determining Green Purchase Behaviour Towards Electronic Products in an Emerging Economy: Theory and Evidence 69
Ishani Patharia, Sanjay Rastogi, and Ravinder Vinayek

5 Implementing Eco-Friendly Export Business Strategy Towards Sustaining Supply Chain Coordination and Competitive Advantage: Evidence from Vietnam's Seafood Processing Firms 95
Binh Do, Uyen Nguyen, Clare D'Souza, Thu Hang Hoang, Quynh Hoa Le, and Ninh Nguyen

6 CSR Practices in the Vietnamese Food Companies: Evidence from an Emerging Economy 127
Lan Do and Charlie Huang

7 Green Human Resource Management in Hotels in Developing Countries: A Practices- and Benefits-Related Conceptual Framework 151
Nhat Tan Pham, Tan Vo-Thanh, and Zuzana Tučková

8 Perceptions of Graduate Employability for Green Multinationals Operating in China 177
Mehdi Taghian, Clare D'Souza, Silvia McCormack, Pam Kappelides, Nkosi Sithole, and Rachel Fuller

9 Sustainability Strategies for Urban Mass Transit—Case of Pakistan 197
Muhammad Abid Saleem, Ghulam Murtaza, Rao Akmal Ali, and Syed Usman Qadri

10 Sustainable Development Practices for SDGs: A Systematic Review of Food Supply Chains in Developing Economies 213
Jubin Jacob-John, Clare D'Souza, Timothy Marjoribanks, and Stephen Singaraju

11 Carbon Taxes Beyond Emissions' Reduction: Co-benefits and Behavioural Failures in Emerging Markets 243
Aitor Marcos, Patrick Hartmann, Jose M. Barrutia, and Vanessa Apaolaza

About the Editors

Ninh Nguyen is a Senior Lecturer in the Asia Pacific College of Business and Law at Charles Darwin University, Australia. He is also a senior researcher at the Centre of Science and Technology Research and Development, Thuongmai University, Vietnam. His research focusses on promoting social and environmental sustainability within consumer and organisational contexts. His most recent work investigates consumer pro-environmental behaviour, food consumption, corporate social responsibility, and environmental strategies. His research has received funding from several universities and organisations in Australia and Vietnam. Ninh has published 50+ research papers in reputable marketing, management, hospitality, and tourism journals. He currently serves as an Associate Editor for the *Journal of Consumer Behaviour* and the *Journal of Strategic Marketing.*

Associate Professor Hoang Viet Nguyen is Vice President at Thuongmai University, Vietnam. He is currently leading the Business Sustainability Research Group hosted by the university. His broad research areas include consumer behaviour and strategic management. Viet has published his work in several well-known journals such as *International Journal of Bank Marketing*, *Leisure Studies*, *British Food Journal*, *Publishing Research Quarterly*, and *Social Responsibility Journal*, among others. He has also obtained several research grants at the ministry, provincial, and national levels.

Professor Clare D'Souza has a multidisciplinary background that involves environmental economics, commerce, marketing, and law; she has several years of practical experience in sustainability development. Prior to joining academia, she has held different positions at executive levels with international companies. Her research focusses on problem-solving and decision-making processes within consumer and organisational contexts. Apart from obtaining several research grants, she has appointments with international research centres to work on multidisciplinary related projects. She has published in reputable journals, for example, *Journal of Business Research, Journal of Business Ethics, Journal of Cleaner Production, Food Quality and Preference, International Journal of Consumer Studies, European Journal of*

Marketing, and *Journal of Retailing and Consumer Services*. She has won the National Award for curriculum development in education and has also acquired the Deans/La Trobe University and Faculty awards for curriculum design.

Carolyn Strong is a Professor in Marketing at Cardiff Business School where she teaches marketing with a focus on ethical, environmental, and social issues. She is currently the B.Sc. Business Management Programme Director and a Cardiff Business School Public Value Engagement Fellow. She is also Cardiff Business Schools Academic Director of Estates, a role which to date has successfully implemented sustainability and circular economy into all of the Business Schools space development and refurbishment projects. She has published in *Journal of Business Research, Marketing Letters, European Journal of Marketing*, and *Journal of Advertising*, among others and published an edited collection of ethical and social marketing contributions. Carolyn is the long-standing Editor-in-Chief of the Journal of Strategic Marketing where she strives to support publications from established academics and to encourage early career academics to develop their work from conception to publication. Her current research interests focus on marketing's contribution to society and the community; public value engagement in circular economy and branding and brand engagement. Her research is collaborative and has an impact on small businesses, policymakers, and society engaging in dialogue to improve society and the environment.

Chapter 1
The Role of Green Product Pricing in Conspicuous Green Consumption Behaviour—A Brazilian Perspective

Manoela Costa Policarpo, **Edvan Cruz Aguiar**, **Aitor Marcos**, **Patrick Hartmann**, and **Vanessa Apaolaza**

Abstract Encouraging green consumption behaviour by leveraging self-expressive benefits has increasingly attracted the attention of academics and practitioners. However, there has been limited evidence from emerging markets so far. Although spending money on green products reinforces the status of the individual, it is unclear which level of a conspicuous display of resources generates sufficient self-expressive benefits to influence the purchase decision. Drawing on Costly-Signalling Theory, this research investigated, with a sample of Brazilian consumers, how the price of green products is related to status motive and the self-expressive benefits obtained from such consumer behaviour. A 2 (high vs. low-status motives) × 2 (high price vs. low price) online experimental survey was administered to 241 participants in Brazil. The results confirmed that individuals are more inclined to buy a green product when they have a status motive. Furthermore, this process is explained by the anticipated self-expressive benefits of green purchases. As a result, when the product price was higher, consumers with a status motive perceived greater social benefits, which contributes to purchase intention. However, consumers with a low-status motive only increased their purchase intention when the product price was lower. Findings show that consumers with a status motive are more likely to buy more expensive green

---

M. C. Policarpo (✉) · A. Marcos · P. Hartmann · V. Apaolaza
Faculty of Economics and Business, University of the Basque Country
UPV/EHU, Avenida Lehendakari Agirre 83, Bilbao, Spain
e-mail: mcosta004@ikasle.ehu.eus

A. Marcos
e-mail: aitor.marcos@ehu.eus

P. Hartmann
e-mail: patrick.hartmann@ehu.eus

V. Apaolaza
e-mail: vanessa.apaolaza@ehu.eus

M. C. Policarpo · E. C. Aguiar
Faculty of Management and Accounting, Federal University of Campina Grande, Campina Grande, Brazil
e-mail: edvan.aguiar@ufcg.edu.br

© The Author(s), under exclusive license to Springer Nature Singapore Pte Ltd. 2022
N. Nguyen et al. (eds.), *Environmental Sustainability in Emerging Markets*,
Approaches to Global Sustainability, Markets, and Governance,
https://doi.org/10.1007/978-981-19-2408-8_1

products, suggesting that the product price signals access to resources and prosocial behaviour. Findings contribute to understanding how social factors influence the purchasing decision of green products in emerging markets and have significant implications for promoting more sustainable consumption attitudes and behaviours.

Keywords Green consumption · Conspicuous conservation · Costly-Signalling Theory · Status motives · Price

1.1 Introduction

Over the past decade, studies have investigated why individuals buy green products, even when these are often more expensive and sometimes underperform their non-green counterparts (Delgado et al., 2015; Furchtgott-Roth, 2012; Jaiswal & Kant, 2018; Lea & Worsley, 2008; Young et al., 2010). A growing body of research has shown that consumers with a status motive are more likely to choose more expensive green products as a means of signalling environmental concern and access to financial resources (Griskevicius et al., 2010; Park & Lee, 2016; Rahman et al., 2020). Nevertheless, in the absence of integrative efforts, isolated studies and untested propositions about green product purchases are imperative in consumer behaviour debates. Additionally, empirical results from the consumers of emerging markets are still scarce. To address this gap, we examine the circumstances under which pricing and status impact self-expressive benefits and, ultimately, conspicuous conservation, focusing on the Brazilian case as an example of an emerging market in which sustainable consumption is rapidly growing.

Brazil faces the challenge of integrating environmental sustainability within economic growth (Silva et al., 2017; Stoll et al., 2019), and green consumption is an important step in this direction. Brazilian consumers play a relevant role in driving growth, acting increasingly in choosing products that are more socially responsible in relation to environmental practices, and even willing to pay more (Alfenas et al., 2018; Gonçalves, 2018; Ritter et al., 2015). In response to this, several Brazilian companies are investing in eco-friendly programs and developing green products. Thus, it is necessary to understand this trend which affects the factors that influence the buying behaviour of Brazilian consumers. Therefore, this study will focus on understanding the social factors of this emerging market to bridge the knowledge gap between the increasing relevance of status motivation and the scarce literature exploring these factors (Lin et al., 2017; Park & Lee, 2016).

The status motive functions as a hierarchy of rewards in which individuals of higher status have greater access to desirable things, such as respect and admiration (Griskevicius et al., 2010). Regarding green consumption, studies have suggested that status appears as a motivation to purchase green products, since this type of purchase can demonstrate one's capacity to spend resources for the common good (Elliot, 2013; Sachdeva et al., 2015). Besides, the buying behaviour of green products associated with the status motive resonates with the concept of conspicuous conservation, defined by Sexton and Sexton (2014) as public and expensive actions to exhibit prosocial behaviour regarding environmental protection. We argue that conspicuous conservation and status are directly associated. As long as the expensive products are purchased in public, individuals will obtain social benefits (e.g. recognition and positive reputation in the social environment) (Elliott, 2013; Griskevicius, 2008; Hartmann & Apaolaza-Ibáñez, 2012). Such consumption behaviour is supported by Costly-Signalling Theory (CST; Grafen, 1990; Zahavi, 1977), which suggests that public forms of philanthropy and altruism are conspicuous displays of resources that reinforce the status of the individual. Thus, by spending more money, energy and time to purchase a green product, consumers signal to their social environment that they are concerned about environmental issues and have abundant resources (e.g. numerous enough to incur unnecessary costs).

Departing from this assumption, scholars argued that green consumption also involves hedonic aspects in consumers' purchasing behaviour, especially when they purchase green products to signal status and abundance of resources (Dastrup et al., 2012; Rahman et al., 2020; Sachdeva et al., 2015; Sexton & Sexton, 2014). Moreover, given that green products are generally more expensive than their non-green competitors, it is reasonable to assume that the acquisition and use of green products provide utilitarian benefits associated with the environment and social benefits.

The aforementioned social benefits arising from signalling information about an individual when purchasing a product are known as self-expressive benefits. In the green consumption literature, self-expressive benefits have been linked to an individual's prosocial reputation (Boobalan et al., 2021; Hartmann & Apaolaza-Ibáñez, 2012; Lin et al., 2017). Moreover, recent research has successfully explored the connection between the perceived self-expressive benefits of a green product and its purchase intention, showing that this operationalisation of a consumer's prosocial reputation is an attested antecedent of the intention to purchase green products (Policarpo & Aguiar, 2020).

Regarding the role of pricing, Griskevicius et al. (2010) found that increasing the price of a green product can make it more attractive to individuals motivated to achieve status once the consumer attaches importance to price as a sign of wealth (Chaudhuri & Majumdar, 2006; Garvey et al., 2017). Therefore, findings of pricing and self-expressive benefits research on green consumption point to a possible interaction between product expensiveness and the perception of self-expressive benefits, as it signals a prosocial reputation and abundance of resources. However, despite evidence that consumers with a status motive opt for more expensive green products (Dastrup et al., 2012; Delgado et al., 2015; Griskevicius et al., 2010; Sexton & Sexton, 2014), no integrative model explains the interplay between status motive and product price regarding green buying behaviour. Therefore, as a novel integrative exercise, our work examines whether and to what extent self-expressive benefits mediate the relationship between the desire for status and green buying behaviour, exploring the moderating role of product prices as they interact with consumers' desire for status. As a result, in this article, we aim to understand (for the case of the Brazilian consumer) how the price of a green product is related to the status motive and the self-expressive benefits obtained from green consumer behaviour.

1.2 Theoretical Framework

1.2.1 Green Consumption Behaviour

Green consumption behaviour comprises the consumer's decision-making process that considers the public consequences of their private consumption and tries to use their purchasing power to generate social change (Moisander, 2007). This behaviour is often measured as the consumers' willingness to buy products with a lower environmental impact. In other words, it refers to the motivational factors that influence the consumption behaviour of this type of product (Ramayah et al., 2010).

As Joshi and Rahman (2015) interpret it, green consumption behaviour is considered a category of environmental conservation. It represents a form of ethical decision-making behaviour in which consumers are conscious of the environmental damage caused by their consumption decisions. Thus, consumers increasingly opt for green products since they satisfy their needs without harming the environment and also contribute to a more sustainable world (Shamdasani et al., 1993). These products are safer for the environment because they have a low environmental impact (Chen & Chai, 2010).

The literature suggests that green consumption behaviour is associated with sustainable development principles for two main reasons. Firstly, the consumption of green goods and services has a lower environmental impact across their lifecycle, namely in production and distribution, consumption and final disposal (Moisander, 2007; Peattie, 2010). The second principle that green consumption appeals to is self-concept: Consumers who choose green products usually have a certain level of knowledge and environmental awareness and expect their purchasing behaviour to be in line with their personal commitment to the environment. Environmental knowledge and responsibility reinforce and may alter consumer behaviour in other environmental conservation practices (Han & Yoon, 2015; Lin & Niu, 2018).

Factors that influence green consumption in developed countries such as educational level, income, culture, public policies, values and environmental awareness do not necessarily apply to the context of emerging countries (Ester et al., 2004; Vicente-Molina et al., 2013). Therefore, understanding the factors that influence the green purchasing behaviour of emerging countries provides practical implications for the promotion of sustainable behaviour in Brazil, especially within a scenario of rapid industrialisation and insertion into the consumer society. Advancing knowledge in this area is crucial since providing green products to the growing market of emerging countries can be a way to minimise the environmental impacts of increasing consumption (Mont & Plepys, 2008).

In an attempt to explain consumer behaviour, many theories have been used to understand green buying behaviour. Recently, CST has been used to examine the relationship between conspicuous conservation and green consumption behaviour, specifically in what people signal to others when choosing green products (McGuire & Beattie, 2016; Palomo-Vélez et al., 2021). Thus, advancing this research line, our work uses CST to substantiate the theoretical arguments defended here.

1.2.2 Costly-Signalling Theory

CST provides the necessary background to understand the relationship between conspicuous conservation and green consumption behaviour. It postulates that individuals often engage in expensive behaviours but benefit others to signal honest information about themselves (McAndrew, 2002; Zahavi, 1995). Regarding green consumption, CST explains the costly sign behind green products (generally more expensive than their counterparts), as consumers spend money to communicate their desirable characteristics, like environmental awareness and access to resources (Delgado et al., 2015; Griskevicius et al., 2010; Palomo-Vélez et al., 2021). In this regard, Griskevicius et al. (2010) suggested that when consumers opt for a green product, they seek to use their consumption practices to signal prosocial behaviour to their social environment. Therefore, this consumption practice meets the concept of conspicuous conservation, defined by these researchers as public prosocial actions. Similarly, Sexton and Sexton (2014) identified a positive relationship between conspicuous conservation and the purchase of hybrid vehicles, drawing on the costly signal characterised by the price of the green product (e.g. paying more for a green product) and by the desire to display status. More broadly, green consumption has been re-evaluated as a way to exhibit prosocial behaviour and achieve self-interest benefits through gaining status.

1.2.3 The Effect of Status Motives

The notion of the need to build status in a consumption context stems from the work of Veblen (1899), who postulated that people strive to achieve social status by competing with each other for material resources and comparing their status to other individuals. In other words, consumption brings status to the consumer, as it can provide signs of wealth and differentiation. Individuals of higher status receive excessive rewards, including positive social attention, rights and privileges, in addition to influencing and controlling joint decisions and better access to scarce resources (Berger et al., 1972; Henrich & Gil-White, 2001). Choi and Seo (2017) identified that status seekers exhibited a high level of prosocial behaviour when others recognised their behaviour compared to those who did not seek status. This relationship also tends to occur in green consumption. Thus, the demand for green products is driven partly by social desires in search of status, as these products can signal buyers' characteristics for their social group (Dastrup et al., 2012; Delgado et al., 2015; Sachdeva et al., 2015).

Similarly, when considering the various benefits resulting from status signalling, consumers tend to spend resources (such as time or money) to achieve their personal goals through the consumption of goods and services (Anderson et al., 2015; Kenrick et al., 2010). Thus, the desire for status can be understood as motivation to achieve a high status in the social hierarchy (Anderson et al., 2015). Individuals grant status to others when they appear to have valuable characteristics and seem willing to use those characteristics to contribute to the common good (Ridgeway, 1982). From this assumption, Delgado et al. (2015) found that individuals attribute status to consumers of green products. Purchases like these indicate that buyers are willing to pay more for a product that benefits others.

Therefore, consumers with a greater status motive can strive to achieve social status by displaying their environmental concern to others through the purchase of comparatively more costly environmentally friendly products (Griskevicius et al., 2010; Sexton & Sexton, 2014):

H1 The activation of status motives has a positive effect on (a) attitude and (b) purchase intention towards green products.

Yang et al. (2016) affirmed that the search for status increases the satisfaction not only of the attributes of the goods or services that are being consumed but also of the people's reaction to the displayed wealth and the social acceptance obtained. Thus, the benefits resulting from the process of signalling information about oneself (i.e. self-expressive benefits) may be greater when purchasing green products because they reveal prosocial traits and preferences.

From the perspective of conspicuous conservation, consumers are motivated to achieve social status via green consumption because they understand that purchasing green products can provide them with social benefits, which in turn emit socially relevant underlying qualities associated with green consumption. For example, Palomo-Vélez et al. (2021) identified that green buying could communicate characteristics valued in romantic partners, such as trustworthiness and altruism. Consequently, the benefits arising from conspicuous conservation are likely to drive the intention to purchase green products (Policarpo & Aguiar, 2020). Therefore, we suggest that self-expressive benefits mediate the relationship between status motives and the propensity to purchase green products.

H2 The effect of status motives on (a) attitude and (b) purchase intention towards green products can be explained by the mediating influence of environmental self-expressive benefits.

1.2.4 Green Product Pricing

The price of a product is considered an important determinant of green consumption behaviour (Aschemann-Witzel & Zielke, 2017); however, the relevance of this factor depends on the role that consumers attribute to it. On its negative side, a high price means a sacrifice (i.e., spending more resources on a product favouring environmental issues) (Lin & Chang, 2012). While in its positive role, a high price can signal status (Delgado et al., 2015; Griskevicius et al., 2010; Lichtenstein et al., 1993) and quality (Van Doorn & Verhoef, 2011; Völckner & Hofmann, 2007; Zeithaml, 1988).

For instance, Delgado et al. (2015) showed in an econometrical analysis that the status signal value of the Toyota Prius corresponded to 4.5% of the hybrid car's total price. Their findings suggested that policymakers interested in increasing the adoption of hybrid vehicles can exploit the status signal through pricing as a means of stimulating consumer interest in this type of product. Conversely, green consumers interpret lower prices as inferior quality, even though they want lower prices (Hughner et al., 2007). Thus, the purchase of green products is seen as a multifaceted and even paradoxical issue because even if the willingness to pay is low, the price in purchasing behaviour is strongly related to the perception of quality and status (Aschemann-Witzel & Zielke, 2017; Delgado et al., 2015; Hughner et al., 2007; Van Doorn & Verhoef, 2011).

The literature states that green goods and services tend to have a higher price than conventional competitors (Furchtgott-Roth, 2012; Lea & Worsley, 2008; Young et al., 2010). Consumer responses to green products differ from regular ones in that they tend to pay a higher price for products with a lower environmental impact (Aertsens et al., 2011; Eze & Ndubisi, 2013; Okada & Mais, 2010). Despite some scholars considering pricing as the main reason for a low level of green purchasing (Hughner et al., 2007; Padel & Foster, 2005; Zanoli & Naspetti, 2002), findings are still inconclusive. For example, Chekima et al. (2016) found that the higher price of a green product has no negative effect on the purchase intention. Their results served to corroborate that high prices do not necessarily constitute a barrier to green consumption. This study follows the findings of Roe et al. (2001), who found that groups of people concerned about the environment are willing to pay significantly more for green electricity when emission reductions result from increased renewable fuel dependence.

CTS can explain this last perspective because people concerned with the environment can signal their altruism linked to wealth by purchasing a more expensive product in favour of the environment (Griskevicius et al., 2010; Sexton & Sexton, 2014). Thus, self-expressive benefits may be greater when purchasing more expensive green products because they reveal wealth and prosocial behaviour. In this regard, we propose the following:

H3 Product price (high vs. low) has a positive moderating influence on the effect of status motives on self-expressive benefits. For a high (vs. low) price, the effect of status motives on self-expressive benefits is strengthened (vs. attenuated).

Several studies have examined the role of price and status variables in the consumers' decision-making process, as they are associated with attitudes and behaviours of green purchasing (Delgado et al., 2015; Elliott, 2013; Griskevicius et al., 2010; Sachdeva et al., 2015). Eze and Ndubisi (2013) and Griskevicius et al. (2010) showed that price is not necessarily negatively related to consumers' purchase intentions of green products, especially when such acquisition facilitates status signalling. In addition, Chekima et al. (2016) found that high prices do not have a negative effect on the purchase intentions of green products but that attitudinal and cultural variables are important motivating factors in this consumption context. Thus, the price of the product associated with the status motive influences the perception of self-expressive benefits of the consumer since the high price of the product may signal excess resources and the willingness to incur higher costs when acquiring a product for the common good. Furthermore, consumers with a status motive can perceive a greater value in green products, as these allow them to communicate a prosocial image and a higher status. Based on these considerations, the following hypotheses were formulated:

H4a The indirect effect of status motives on (a) attitude and (b) purchase intention towards green products, mediated by self-expressive benefits, is moderated by product price (high vs. low). For a high (vs. low) price, the indirect effect of status motives is strengthened (vs. attenuated).

1.3 Method

1.3.1 Participants and Procedure

The hypotheses were tested with a convenience sample of $N = 250$ Brazilian consumers recruited from universities throughout the country. The sample comprised undergraduate and graduate students (48.13% undergraduate) and was 72.19% female, 74.27% single and with an average age of 28 years. Regarding family income, 61.82% had up to four Brazilian minimum wages (R$ 3992.00) and 29.46% between four and ten (R$ 3992.01–R$ 9980.00). As for the region of residence, 47.72% were from Brazil's southeast region, and 36.92% were from the northeast region.

An experimental study with a 2 (status motive: high vs. low) × 2 (green product price: high vs. low) between-subjects factorial design was conducted. The two independent variables manipulated in this study correspond to the status motive and the price of the green product. Griskevicius et al.'s (2006, 2010) manipulation was used to manipulate the status motives. They successfully used a 700-character text to motivate participants to achieve a higher status after reading it. In the "high-status motives" story, the participants imagined themselves as graduates and on the first day of work. The story ends when readers consider that they are rising in status in relation to their peers. In the low-status condition, the scenario did not present any element that stimulated the respondent's motivation to seek superior status. Based on the information obtained from the website of the Brazilian company RecicleUse®, which specialised in the sale of sustainable shirts (it has less environmental impact in its production process and uses organic raw materials), shirt prices were defined as low price (R$ 39.99) and high price (R$ 74.99). In this regard, the experimental design resulted in four scenarios corresponding to the combination of the levels of each of the factors (status motive and price of the green product).

1 The Role of Green Product Pricing … 9

Participants were randomly assigned to one of the scenarios. The data were collected through an online questionnaire made available from the academic community of Brazilian universities across wide-ranging student social networks. The link to access the questionnaire was distributed to each university group, and each participant was then randomly assigned to a scenario depending on the link they received. Participants could only take the survey once in order to ensure that respondents were influenced just by the stimuli of their corresponding experimental group. After a brief presentation of the research objective, participants were instructed to read the text referring to the scenario in which they were allocated (high vs. low-status motive) and to place themselves as the main character. Second, respondents were informed that questions about the story would be asked at the end of the procedure. Subsequently, the participants read the purchase context (a sustainable organic cotton t-shirt for R$ 39.99 or 74.99) and completed the survey containing the measurement scales of the constructs. Finally, the participants answered the following questions (which are related to the text read in the first step) to assess the experiment's internal validity regarding the manipulation of the status motive: (1) Besides you, how many employees were hired in the company? (2) How many months after your arrival would there be an internal promotion? This practice has been used as one of the means to guarantee the reliability of the experiment (Wu et al., 2014).

1.3.2 Measures

All variables were measured on seven-point Likert scales, ranging from strongly disagree (1) to strongly agree (7). The self-expressive benefits were measured with three items adapted from the scale used by Hartmann and Apaolaza-Ibáñez (2012). Three indicators based on Chan (2001) were used to measure attitude, and three items adapted from Grewal et al. (2003) assessed the purchase intention of the green product. All items were translated into Brazilian Portuguese using back-translation.

Additionally, Griskevicius et al.'s (2010) measure was used to check the manipulation of status motives, and the item "this price is likely higher than average market prices for this kind of product" (Kukar-Kinney & Grewal, 2007) was used to verify the price perception according to the corresponding price scenario. All scale properties and their corresponding items are shown in Table 1.1.

1.3.3 Data Analysis

After an inspection of the dataset, some cases were excluded due to inconsistent responses, lack of attention and missing data, resulting in a final sample of 241 respondents. The student's T-test was applied to verify the manipulation of the status motive (activated vs. not activated) and the price of the green product (high vs. low)

Table 1.1 Variables and measurement items

Constructs and items	Mean	Std. Dev	Cronbach's α
Attitude (Chan, 2001; Taylor & Todd, 1995)	5.61	1.43	0.907
I have a favourable opinion regarding the purchase of this product			
I like the idea of buying this product			
Buying this product seems like a good idea			
Product purchase intention (Grewal et al., 2003)	5.78	1.53	0.925
Most likely, I would buy this product if I had the resources			
I would be willing to buy this product if I had the resources			
I would consider purchasing this product if I had the resources			
Self-expressive benefits (Hartmann & Apaolaza-Ibáñez, 2012)	4.29	1.80	0.908
With this product, I can express my environmental concern			
With this product, I can demonstrate to myself and my friends that I care about environmental conservation			
In possession of this product, my friends would realise that I am concerned with the environment			
Manipulation check: status (Griskevicius et al., 2010)	7.80	4.05	0.836
Did you wish to have a higher social status in the company?			
Were you motivated to achieve greater prestige?			
Manipulation check: pricing (Kukar-Kinney & Grewal, 2007)	3.77	1.87	–
This price is likely higher than average market prices for this kind of product			

to validate the experiment. This test was also used to analyse hypotheses H1a and H1b.

The moderated mediation model was computed with Hayes PROCESS (Hayes, 2017; models 4 and 7) and SPSS 25. Initially, the relationship between the independent variable (status) and the dependent variables (attitude and purchase intention) was examined to ensure whether this relationship was significant before we performed the mediation analysis. In the second stage, the mediating variable (self-expressive benefits) was introduced into the regression to verify whether the predictor variable was related to the mediating variable and dependent variables. According to Hayes (2017), the model will be considered a mediation model if there is a reduction in the strength of the relationship between the predictor variables and the dependent variable with the entry of the mediator variable. Moreover, the indirect effect of the independent variable on the dependent variable is significant. When testing the indirect effect, the standard error of the indirect effect on the mediator variable in the relationship between the independent variables and the dependent variables was estimated using bootstrap confidence intervals with 10,000 samples. The bootstrap

1 The Role of Green Product Pricing …

Table 1.2 Manipulation check

Independent variable	Group	N	Mean	SD	Mean difference	t	p
Status motive	High	130	4.68	1.79	1.69	−7.07	< 0.001
	Low	111	2.99	1.91			
Product price	High	142	4.39	1.78	1.52	6.91	< 0.001
	Low	99	2.87	1.61			

interval indicates the lower and upper limits of the bootstrap confidence interval (Boot LLCI: bootstrap lower limit confidence interval, Boot ULCI: bootstrap upper limit confidence interval). When the corresponding bootstrap confidence interval does not contain zero, the significance of the mediation index is confirmed. In turn, in the analysis of moderation and moderated mediation, model 7 was used. This analysis verified the moderating effect of price on the relationship between status motives and green buying behaviour. All further analyses were performed using R version 4.1.0 for Windows.

1.4 Results

1.4.1 Manipulation Checks

Before testing the hypotheses, a T-test was performed to verify the effectiveness of the manipulation of the two independent variables: status motive and price of the product. As shown in Table 1.2, the average value of the items that measured the status motive was higher for the activated group than for the control group (M = 4.68 for activated status, M = 2.99 for not activated, t = −7.07, p < 0.001). The verification of price manipulation indicated significant differences between the group that received the product at a high price and a low price. The high price group obtained a higher mean in the product price perception than the low price group (M = 4.39 for the high price product, M = 2.87 for the low price product, t = 6.91, p < 0.001). Thus, we confirmed that the two variables were successfully manipulated.

1.4.2 Main Effect of Status Motives

A T-test was performed to investigate the effect of the status motive manipulation on both dependent variables: attitude and purchase intention. There was a significant effect of the status motive manipulation on the consumer's attitude towards the

Table 1.3 Test of hypotheses of the effect of the status motive

Hypothesis	Group	Mean	SD	Df	Cohen's d	t	p	Result
H1a. Attitude	High	5.83	1.29	214.59	0.33	−2.55	0.01	Supported
	Low	5.36	1.55					
H1b. Purchase intention	High	5.97	1.38	213.25	0.26	−2.00	0.04	Supported
	Low	5.57	1.67					

product ($M = 5.83$ for the activated status motive, $M = 5.36$ for the control, $t = -2.55$, $p = 0.01$) and on the purchase intention ($M = 5.97$ for the activated status motive, $M = 5.57$ for the control, $t = -2.00$, $p = 0.04$), as shown in Table 1.3. The activation of status motives had a positive effect on attitude and purchase intention towards green products, supporting hypotheses H1a and H1b.

1.4.3 The Mediating Effect of Self-Expressive Benefits

The SPSS PROCESS macro (Hayes, 2017; Model 4) was used to explore the mediating effect of self-expressive benefits on the relationship between status motive and green consumption behaviour (attitude and purchase intention). The significance of the direct and indirect effects was evaluated using 10,000 bootstrap samples to create bias-corrected confidence intervals (CIs; 95%). The total effect of the impact of status desire on attitude, without the mediator, was found to be positive and statistically significant ($\beta = 0.47$, 95% CI [0.11; 0.83], $t = 2.59$, $p = 0.01$). However, without the mediator, the model explains only 2.73% ($R^2 = 0.03$), as shown in Fig. 1.1. When introducing the mediator, the variables desire for status and self-expressive benefits together explain the variance of attitude towards the purchase of green products to 24.66% ($R^2 = 0.25$). With the mediator, the direct effect of status motive impacting attitude, controlled by self-expressive benefits, was not statistically significant ($\beta = 0.27$, 95% CI [−0.05; 0.59], $t = 1.68$, $p = 0.09$). This result implies that the status motive effect on attitude is indirect and occurs through self-expressive benefits. Thus, the mediation effect is significant ($\beta = 0.20$, 95% CI [0.02; 0.39]), which supports H2a.

Likewise, the relationship between status motive and purchase intention, without the mediator, is positive and significant ($\beta = 0.40$, 95% CI [0.01; 0.79], $t = 2.03$, $p = 0.04$). The mediation effect is significant ($\beta = 0.22$, 95% CI [0.04; 0.43]), and self-expressive benefits mediate approximately 54.57% of the relationship between status motive and purchase intent, supporting H2b.

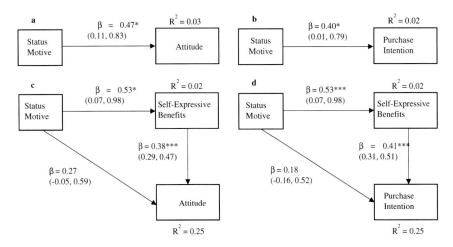

Fig. 1.1 The influence of status motive on attitude (a, c) and purchase intention (b, d) (*Note* The relationship between status motive and attitude/purchase intention without [**a, b**] and with [**c, d**] the mediating effect of self-expressive benefits; Bootstrapped 95% confidence intervals are provided in parentheses; *p < 0.05, **p < 0.01, ***p < 0.001; N = 241)

1.4.4 The Moderating Effect of Price

We used Hayes PROCESS Model 7 to analyse H3. The analysis confirmed a significant positive interaction of the effect of the status motive with the product price on self-expressive benefits ($\beta_{\text{status} \times \text{price}} = 0.91$; SE = 0.47, $t = 1.94$, $p = 0.05$, 95% CI $[-0.02, 1.83]$). However, H3 is supported only at the 10% significance level (Table 1.4). In this case, the product price has a positive moderating influence on the effect of status motives on self-expressive benefits.

Table 1.4 Results of the moderated mediation model

	β	SE	P	Boot LLCI	Boot ULCI
Constant	4.47	0.28	0.00	3.92	5.03
Status	−0.03	0.36	0.92	−0.75	0.68
Price	−0.73	0.35	0.04	−1.42	−0.39
Status × price	0.91	0.47	0.05	−0.02	1.83

Note 10,000 bootstrap samples for 95% bootstrap confidence intervals, boot LLCI = bootstrap lower limit confidence interval, boot ULCI = bootstrap upper limit confidence interval

1.4.5 Moderated-Mediation Relationship

Next, we tested the moderated mediation model to analyse hypotheses H4a and H4b. The objective was to identify whether the indirect effect of status motives on the dependent variables (attitude and purchase intention), mediated by self-expressive benefits, was moderated by the product price. As shown in Table 1.5, the moderated mediation index was significant for the dependent variables, verifying that the status motive effect is strengthened as price increases.

A conditional indirect effect analysis showed that the indirect effect of the status motive on attitude mediated by self-expressive benefits was positive and significant in the high price ($\beta_{ind} = 0.33$, SE $= 0.13$, 95% CI [0.09, 0.61]) but not significant and close to zero in the low price group ($\beta_{ind} = -0.01$, SE $= 0.13$, 95% CI [−0.26, 0.23]), providing support for H4a.

As shown in Fig. 1.2, there was a significant effect on the interaction between status motive, self-expressive benefits and price on the consumer's attitude towards the green product. This result highlights that consumers with a status motive show

Table 1.5 Moderated-mediation analysis and indirect effects

Dependent variable	Mod. med. Index (Moderator: Price)	SE	LLCI	ULCI
Attitude	0.34	0.18	0.00	0.72
Intention	0.37	0.20	0.01	0.79

Note Ten thousand bootstrap samples for 95% bootstrap confidence intervals, boot LLCI = bootstrap lower limit confidence interval, boot ULCI = bootstrap upper limit confidence interval

Fig. 1.2 Effects of interaction on consumer's attitude

Fig. 1.3 Effects of interaction on consumer's purchase intention

a greater attitude towards the green product, especially when its price is higher, supporting H4a. In comparison with the low-status scenario, the attitude was higher for the green product with a lower price. In other words, a high price boosts the indirect effect of the status motive on the attitude; consumers with status motives will perceive a heightened sense of self-expressive benefits in the purchase of the green product and, consequently, their attitude towards this product will be greater. The opposite is true for a low price, resulting in a non-significant indirect effect of the status manipulation.

Regarding purchase intention, this indirect effect of the status motive occurs in a similar way. It is even more evident when the price of the product is higher ($\beta_{ind} = 0.36$, SE $= 0.14$, 95% CI [0.10, 0.66]); that is, the purchase intention of the group with a high price was higher for those who presented an activated status motive. In contrast, a low price did not change the status effect on green buying behaviour ($\beta_{ind} = -0.01$, SE $= 0.14$, 95% CI [$-0.29, 0.24$]). Thus, H4b was also supported (Fig. 1.3).

Therefore, it is clear that the search for status implies a more positive perception of the consumer regarding the traits and preferences that the product will reveal to observers, especially when it is more expensive. This result confirms that the status signal when purchasing green products is linked to the product price.

1.5 Discussion

Our research corroborated (the case of Brazilian consumers) that the status motive is an important driver of green consumption. The novel aspect of our study comprised identifying an indirect effect of the status motive as responsible for increasing consumers' attitudes and purchase intentions. Specifically, green consumption was linked to conspicuous consumption since its demand was motivated partly by the reach of consumer signalling benefits. Thus, the status motive can also be an effective strategy to promote green purchasing in emerging markets. However, research had provided evidence for these effects only for consumers in developed countries.

In addition, we identified that self-expressive benefits mediate the relationship between status and green buying behaviour. When they perceived the benefits arising from the signalling of this purchase, consumers with status motives were more likely to buy. Thus, we argue that achieving superior status in their social environment explains consumer attitudes and purchase intentions towards green products and the need for social signalling the purchase. Therefore, signalling prosocial reputation through green buying leads consumers to demonstrate prosocial behaviour and fulfil their needs for social approval.

Furthermore, we found that consumers are price-sensitive when it comes to green products. When the product price is higher, status seekers have a greater intention to purchase than those who are not status-motivated. For participants with high-status motives, buying the most expensive green product generates more positive responses because the price contributes to the signalling of access to resources and evident prosocial behaviour. Additionally, the findings of this research are in line with studies that showed that the price of green products could negatively affect consumers' purchasing behaviour (Hsu et al., 2017; Li et al., 2016).

The findings also showed that the price of the green product is a relevant moderating variable in green purchasing decisions. Specifically, the price of a green product moderates the indirect effect of status motives on purchase intention, mediated by self-expressive benefits. Thus, for a high price, the indirect effect of the status motive is strengthened as the consumer perceives the purchase of the green product as a means of achieving superior status. Moreover, since the green product requires the sacrifice of spending more resources to obtain it, consumers with high-status motives construe it as a way of showing their desired image to their social environment.

1.6 Conclusions

Our study examined to what extent self-expressive benefits mediate the relationship between the desire for status and green buying behaviour, exploring the moderating role of product prices as they interact with consumers' desire for status. In this article, we verified the case of the Brazilian consumer and how the cost of green products is related to status motives and self-expressive benefits obtained from the purchase of green products. This study has significant theoretical and managerial implications. From a theoretical perspective, the study provides empirical evidence that substantiates an association between green consumption and conspicuous conservation (Lin et al., 2017; Park & Lee, 2016). In particular, CST proved to be adequate to explain the role that social factors play in green consumption behaviour. The study found that status motives are an important antecedent of perceptions, attitudes and purchasing behaviour related to green products. This variable explains why more expensive products are often chosen over more accessible options, especially in the case of green products, as this type of product allows consumers to signal to their peers' access to resources and environmental concerns. The success in manipulating the price variable also made it possible to substantiate Berger's (2019) assumption when stating that consumers in search of status are willing to pay up to 50% more for a green product.

As for managerial implications, marketers should use communication strategies that enhance the social benefits (prosocial reputation) of consumers who purchase green products when they're more expensive. This way, green consumers may be persuaded with the benefit of social acceptance, thus stimulating the search for status through the acquisition of this type of product. Marketing professionals can leverage advertising campaigns that label green purchases as altruistic, conferring positive attributes to the consumer, such as being an environmentally friendly person, a conscious consumer or altruistic individual who does good to society. Regarding its communication potential, buying green as a sign of prestige can easily be associated with high-status contexts such as celebrity events, because green products seem to be able to blend luxurious and altruistic contexts to signal both environmental concern and higher social status.

Furthermore, the differentiation effect of green products can be reinforced through pricing strategies. Thus, this research supports studies such as those by Delgado et al. (2015), Sexton and Sexton (2014) and Griskevicius et al. (2010) in suggesting that policymakers and marketers can exploit status signals through pricing to increase interest in green products. Our study shows that this effect, so far mostly evidenced through research conducted in developed countries, is also valid in emerging markets.

In summary, in order to enhance our knowledge of consumer behaviour involving green products, it is necessary to have a greater understanding of other factors of conspicuous conservation, such as visibility, type of product and consumer environmental awareness. So far, the status activation strategy in the purchase of green products associated with a higher price is a promising research line, but it needs to be developed further to avoid stagnating in unproductive debates around how sustainable it is to direct sales strategies along this path, since this strategy may be ineffective in certain contexts (Li, 2014; Li & Gong, 2005).

Sample homogeneity could constitute a limitation to this research since our sample comprises mainly undergraduate and post-graduate students. Therefore, caution is recommended regarding the generalisability of the results found in this study. This research also focused only on one type of green product. Future research should use a more diverse consumer sample. In addition, the role of status motives in green consumption behaviour should be studied under the influence of social presence or absence at the time of purchase (e.g., other consumers or family and friends). Future research should also analyse the role of status motives and self-expressive benefits in the purchase of green products of different categories (e.g., high visibility vs. low visibility). Furthermore, this research should be extended to the study of other prosocial behaviours, such as donations to charity and other forms of philanthropy, in which costly signalling and status motives may also play a significant role.

Acknowledgements This work was supported by the Brazilian National Council for the Improvement of Higher Education (CAPES) and FESIDE foundation.

References

Aertsens, J., Mondelaers, K., Verbeke, W., Buysse, J., & Van Huylenbroeck, G. (2011). The influence of subjective and objective knowledge on attitude, motivations and consumption of organic food. *British Food Journal, 113*(11), 1353–1378.

Ahmad, A. N. E. E. S., & Thyagaraj, K. S. (2015). Consumer's intention to purchase green brands: The roles of environmental concern, environmental knowledge and self expressive benefits. *Current World Environment, 10*, 879–889.

Alfenas, L. T., Moura, L. R. C., & da Silveira Cunha, N. R. (2018). Green brand: A percepção dos jovens consumidores sobre as marcas verdes. *Revista Estudo & Debate, 25*(2).

Anderson, C., Hildreth, J. A. D., & Howland, L. (2015). Is the desire for status a fundamental human motive? A review of the empirical literature. *Psychological Bulletin, 141*(3), 574.

Aschemann-Witzel, J., & Zielke, S. (2017). Can't buy me green? A review of consumer perceptions of and behaviour toward the price of organic food. *Journal of Consumer Affairs, 51*(1), 211–251.

Berger, J. (2019). Signaling can increase consumers' willingness to pay for green products: Theoretical model and experimental evidence. *Journal of Consumer Behaviour, 18*(3), 233–246.

Berger, J., Cohen, B. P., & Zelditch, M., Jr. (1972). Status characteristics and social interaction. *American Sociological Review, 37*(3), 241–255.

Boobalan, K., Nachimuthu, G. S., & Sivakumaran, B. (2021). Understanding the psychological benefits in organic consumerism: An empirical exploration. *Food Quality and Preference, 87*, 104070.

Chan, R. Y. (2001). Determinants of Chinese consumers' green purchase behaviour. *Psychology & Marketing, 18*(4), 389–413.

Chaudhuri, H. R., & Majumdar, S. (2006). Of diamonds and desires: Understanding conspicuous consumption from a contemporary marketing perspective. *Academy of Marketing Science Review, 11*, 1–18.

Chekima, B., Wafa, S. A. W. S. K., Igau, O. A., Chekima, S., & Sondoh, S. L., Jr. (2016). Examining green consumerism motivational drivers: Does premium price and demographics matter to green purchasing? *Journal of Cleaner Production, 112*, 3436–3450.

Chen, T. B., & Chai, L. T. (2010). Attitude towards the environment and green products: Consumers' perspective. *Management Science and Engineering, 4*(2), 27.

Choi, J., & Seo, S. (2017). Goodwill intended for whom? Examining factors influencing conspicuous prosocial behaviour on social media. *International Journal of Hospitality Management, 60*, 23–32.

Dastrup, S. R., Zivin, J. G., Costa, D. L., & Kahn, M. E. (2012). Understanding the Solar Home price premium: Electricity generation and "Green" social status. *European Economic Review, 56*(5), 961–973.

Delgado, M. S., Harriger, J. L., & Khanna, N. (2015). The value of environmental status signaling. *Ecological Economics, 111*, 1–11.

Elliott, R. (2013). The taste for green: The possibilities and dynamics of status differentiation through "green" consumption. *Poetics, 41*(3), 294–322.

Ester, P., Simões, S., & Vinken, H. (2004). Cultural change and environmentalism: A cross-national approach of mass publics and decision makers. *Ambiente & Sociedade, 7*, 45–66.

Eze, U. C., & Ndubisi, N. O. (2013). Green buyer behaviour: Evidence from Asia consumers. *Journal of Asian and African Studies, 48*(4), 413–426.

Furchtgott-Roth, D. (2012). The elusive and expensive green job. *Energy Economics, 34*, S43–S52.

Garvey, A. M., Blanchard, S. J., & Winterich, K. P. (2017). Turning unplanned overpayment into a status signal: How mentioning the price paid repairs satisfaction. *Marketing Letters, 28*(1), 71–83.

Gonçalves, F. F. (2018). A Importância do Marketing Verde Nas Organizações. *Revista de Estudos Interdisciplinares do Vale do Araguaia-REIVA, 1*(03), 14–14.

Grafen, A. (1990). Biological signals as handicaps. *Journal of Theoretical Biology, 144*(4), 517–546.

Grewal, D., Baker, J., Levy, M., & Voss, G. B. (2003). The effects of wait expectations and store atmosphere evaluations on patronage intentions in service-intensive retail stores. *Journal of Retailing, 79*(4), 259–268.

Griskevicius, V. (2008). *Conspicuous conservation: Pro-environmental consumption and status competition.* Arizona State University.

Griskevicius, V., Cialdini, R. B., & Kenrick, D. T. (2006). Peacocks, Picasso, and parental investment: The effects of romantic motives on creativity. *Journal of Personality and Social Psychology, 91*(1), 63.

Griskevicius, V., Tybur, J. M., & Van den Bergh, B. (2010). Going green to be seen: Status, reputation, and conspicuous conservation. *Journal of Personality and Social Psychology, 98*(3), 392.

Han, H., & Yoon, H. J. (2015). Hotel customers' environmentally responsible behavioural intention: Impact of key constructs on decision in green consumerism. *International Journal of Hospitality Management, 45*, 22–33.

Hartmann, P., & Apaolaza-Ibáñez, V. (2012). Consumer attitude and purchase intention toward green energy brands: The roles of psychological benefits and environmental concern. *Journal of Business Research, 65*(9), 1254–1263.

Hayes, A. F. (2017). *Introduction to mediation, moderation, and conditional process analysis: A regression-based approach.* Guilford Publications.

Henrich, J., & Gil-White, F. J. (2001). The evolution of prestige: Freely conferred deference as a mechanism for enhancing the benefits of cultural transmission. *Evolution and Human Behaviour, 22*(3), 165–196.

Hsu, C. L., Chang, C. Y., & Yansritakul, C. (2017). Exploring purchase intention of green skincare products using the theory of planned behaviour: Testing the moderating effects of country of origin and price sensitivity. *Journal of Retailing and Consumer Services, 34*, 145–152.

Hughner, R. S., McDonagh, P., Prothero, A., Shultz, C. J., & Stanton, J. (2007). Who are organic food consumers? A compilation and review of why people purchase organic food. *Journal of Consumer Behaviour: An International Research Review, 6*(2–3), 94–110.

Jaiswal, D., & Kant, R. (2018). Green purchasing behaviour: A conceptual framework and empirical investigation of Indian consumers. *Journal of Retailing and Consumer Services, 41*, 60–69.

Joshi, Y., & Rahman, Z. (2015). Factors affecting green purchase behaviour and future research directions. *International Strategic Management Review, 3*(1–2), 128–143.

Kenrick, D. T., Griskevicius, V., Neuberg, S. L., & Schaller, M. (2010). Renovating the pyramid of needs: Contemporary extensions built upon ancient foundations. *Perspectives on Psychological Science, 5*(3), 292–314.

Kukar-Kinney, M., & Grewal, D. (2007). Comparison of consumer reactions to price-matching guarantees in Internet and bricks-and-mortar retail environments. *Journal of the Academy of Marketing Science, 35*(2), 197–207.

Lea, E., & Worsley, A. (2008). Australian consumers' food-related environmental beliefs and behaviours. *Appetite, 50*(2–3), 207–214.

Li, H. M. (2014). Ecological criticism of conspicuous consumption? *Journal of Wuhan University of Technology (Social Sciences Edition), 6*, 1113–1118.

Li, S. H., & Gong, Z. M. (2005). Conspicuous consumption from the perspective of sustainable development strategy. *Consumer Economics, 21*(5), 65–68.

Li, Y., Lu, Y., Zhang, X., Liu, L., Wang, M., & Jiang, X. (2016). Propensity of green consumption behaviours in representative cities in China. *Journal of Cleaner Production, 133*, 1328–1336.

Lichtenstein, D. R., Ridgway, N. M., & Netemeyer, R. G. (1993). Price perceptions and consumer shopping behaviour: A field study. *Journal of Marketing Research, 30*(2), 234–245.

Lin, J., Lobo, A., & Leckie, C. (2017). Green brand benefits and their influence on brand loyalty. *Marketing Intelligence & Planning, 35*(3), 425–440.

Lin, S. T., & Niu, H. J. (2018). Green consumption: Environmental knowledge, environmental consciousness, social norms, and purchasing behaviour. *Business Strategy and the Environment, 27*(8), 1679–1688.

Lin, Y. C., & Chang, C. C. A. (2012). Double standard: The role of environmental consciousness in green product usage. *Journal of Marketing, 76*(5), 125–134.

McAndrew, F. T. (2002). New evolutionary perspectives on altruism: Multilevel-selection and costly-signaling theories. *Current Directions in Psychological Science, 11*(2), 79–82.

McGuire, L., & Beattie, G. (2016). Consumers and climate change: Can the presence of others promote more sustainable consumer choice? *The International Journal of Environmental Sustainability, 12*(2), 33–56.

Moisander, J. (2007). Motivational complexity of green consumerism. *International Journal of Consumer Studies, 31*(4), 404–409.

Mont, O., & Plepys, A. (2008). Sustainable consumption progress: Should we be proud or alarmed? *Journal of Cleaner Production, 16*(4), 531–537. https://doi.org/10.1016/j.jclepro.2007.01.009

Okada, E. M., & Mais, E. L. (2010). Framing the "green" alternative for environmentally conscious consumers. *Sustainability Accounting, Management and Policy Journal, 1*(2), 222–234.

Padel, S., & Foster, C. (2005). Exploring the gap between attitudes and behaviour: Understanding why consumers buy or do not buy organic food. *British Food Journal, 107*(8), 606–625.

Palomo-Vélez, G., Tybur, J. M., & Van Vugt, M. (2021). Is green the new sexy? Romantic of conspicuous conservation. *Journal of Environmental Psychology, 73*, 101530.

Park, K., & Lee, K. (2016). Is green product purchasing an innovative or conspicuous behaviour? *Social Behaviour and Personality, 44*, 29–44.

Peattie, K. (2010). Green consumption: Behaviour and norms. *Annual Review of Environment and Resources, 35*, 195–228.

Policarpo, M. C., & Aguiar, E. C. (2020). How self-expressive benefits relate to buying a hybrid car as a green product. *Journal of Cleaner Production, 252*, 119859.

Rahman, I., Chen, H., & Reynolds, D. (2020). Evidence of green signaling in green hotels. *International Journal of Hospitality Management, 85*, 102444.

Ramayah, T., Lee, J. W. C., & Mohamad, O. (2010). Green product purchase intention: Some insights from a developing country. *Resources, Conservation and Recycling, 54*(12), 1419–1427.

Ridgeway, C. L. (1982). Status in groups: The importance of motivation. *American Sociological Review, 47*(1), 76–88.

Ritter, A. M., Borchardt, M., Vaccaro, G. L., & Pereira, G. M. (2015). Motivations for promoting the consumption of green products in an emerging country: Exploring attitudes of Brazilian consumers. *Journal of Cleaner Production, 106*(2015), 507–520.

Roe, B., Teisl, M. F., Levy, A., & Russell, M. (2001). US consumers' willingness to pay for green electricity. *Energy Policy, 29*(11), 917–925.

Sachdeva, S., Jordan, J., & Mazar, N. (2015). Green consumerism: Moral motivations to a sustainable future. *Current Opinion in Psychology, 6*, 60–65.

Sexton, S. E., & Sexton, A. L. (2014). Conspicuous conservation: The Prius halo and willingness to pay for environmental bona fides. *Journal of Environmental Economics and Management, 67*(3), 303–317.

Shamdasani, P., Chon-Lin, G. O., & Richmond, D. (1993). Exploring green consumers in an oriental culture: Role of personal and marketing mix factors. *Advances in Consumer Research, 20*, 488–493.

Silva, S. Z., Bortoluzzi, F., & Bertolini, G. R. F. (2017). Gestão Ambiental e Viabilidade para Obtenção de Certificação Ambiental. *Revista de Administração IMED, 7*(1), 3–28.

Stoll, R. G., da Rosa Borges, G., & Buron, T. A. (2019). The influence of sustainable consumption in the decision to purchase organic products. *Amazônia, Organizações e Sustentabilidade, 8*(1), 129–144.

Taylor, S., & Todd, P. (1995). An integrated model of waste management behaviour: A test of household recycling and composting intentions. *Environment and Behaviour, 27*(5), 603–630.

Van Doorn, J., & Verhoef, P. C. (2011). Willingness to pay for organic products: Differences between virtue and vice foods. *International Journal of Research in Marketing, 28*(3), 167–180.

Veblen, V. (1899). *The theory of leisure class.* McMillan.

Vicente-Molina, M. A., Fernández-Sáinz, A., & Izagirre-Olaizola, J. (2013). Environmental knowledge and other variables affecting pro-environmental behaviour: Comparison of university students from emerging and advanced countries. *Journal of Cleaner Production, 61*, 130–138.

Völckner, F., & Hofmann, J. (2007). The price-perceived quality relationship: A meta-analytic review and assessment of its determinants. *Marketing Letters, 18*(3), 181–196.

Wu, L. L., Mattila, A. S., & Han, J. R. (2014). Territoriality revisited: Other customer's perspective. *International Journal of Hospitality Management, 38*, 48–56.

Yang, W., Zhang, L., & Mattila, A. S. (2016). Luxe for less: How do consumers react to luxury hotel price promotions? The moderating role of consumers' need for status. *Cornell Hospitality Quarterly, 57*(1), 82–92.

Young, W., Hwang, K., McDonald, S., & Oates, C. J. (2010). Sustainable consumption: Green consumer behaviour when purchasing products. *Sustainable Development, 18*(1), 20–31.

Zahavi, A. (1977). Reliability in communication systems and the evolution of altruism. In *Evolutionary ecology* (pp. 253–259). Palgrave.

Zahavi, A. (1995). Altruism as a handicap: The limitations of kin selection and reciprocity. *Journal of Avian Biology, 26*(1), 1–3.

Zanoli, R., & Naspetti, S. (2002). Consumer motivations in the purchase of organic food. *British Food Journal, 104*(8), 643–653.

Zeithaml, V. A. (1988). Consumer perceptions of price, quality, and value: A means-end model and synthesis of evidence. *Journal of Marketing, 52*(3), 2–22.

Chapter 2
Promoting Sustainable Renewable Energy Consumption: Government Policy Drives Record Rooftop Solar Adoption in Vietnam

Hoang Viet Nguyen[ID]**, Tuan Duong Vu**[ID]**, Steven Greenland, Thi My Nguyet Nguyen, and Van Hung Vu**

Abstract Renewable energy is critical for combatting climate change and the global sustainability crisis. Rooftop solar panels offer one of the cleanest forms of renewable energy, with residential installations particularly effective in reducing household carbon dioxide emissions. The Vietnamese government recently implemented a renewable energy strategy involving the launch of a rooftop solar initiative. This has led to the highest level of rooftop solar uptake in Southeast Asia, with generous feed-in tariff (FiT) rebates that greatly exceed those provided by neighbouring countries including Australia. This study is one of the first to investigate the factors influencing the adoption of household rooftop solar in Vietnam, including the impact of the government's feed-in tariff initiative. In summary, this research has applied the theory of planned behaviour (TPB) and used structural equation modelling (SEM) to investigate the attitudes and intentions of 296 Vietnamese households towards rooftop solar installation. The analysis reveals the significant impact of the Vietnamese government's solar incentive scheme and the motivating role of innovativeness, expectations and environmental knowledge, as well as the impact of subjective

---

H. V. Nguyen
Board of Rectors, Thuongmai University, Hanoi, Vietnam
e-mail: nhviet@tmu.edu.vn

T. D. Vu (✉) · T. M. N. Nguyen
Department of Strategic Management, Faculty of Business Administration,
Thuongmai University, Hanoi, Vietnam
e-mail: vutuanduong@tmu.edu.vn

T. M. N. Nguyen
e-mail: mynguyet@tmu.edu.vn

S. Greenland
Asia Pacific College of Business and Law, Charles Darwin University, Darwin, Australia
e-mail: steven.greenland@cdu.edu.au

V. H. Vu
Faculty of Political Theory, Thuongmai University, Hanoi, Vietnam
e-mail: hungvvu@tmu.edu.vn

© The Author(s), under exclusive license to Springer Nature Singapore Pte Ltd. 2022
N. Nguyen et al. (eds.), *Environmental Sustainability in Emerging Markets*,
Approaches to Global Sustainability, Markets, and Governance,
https://doi.org/10.1007/978-981-19-2408-8_2

norms on solar panel uptake. As anticipated, monetary barriers restricted installation intentions. Although, unlike some other consumer TPB studies this research found that brand trust does not play a predictive role in intentions to install rooftop solar, perhaps due to lack of familiarity with solar energy product brands. These findings will likely inform future government policies and support businesses trading in solar energy products. This study will also be of interest to academics and policymakers in other countries seeking to understand and promote the adoption of rooftop solar.

Keywords Future sustainability · Renewable energy · Rooftop solar · Feed-in tariff FiT · Theory of planned behaviour · Innovativeness · Environmental knowledge · Perceived monetary barriers · Government renewable energy policy · Brand trust

2.1 Introduction

Climate change driven by greenhouse gas (GHG) emissions is recognised as the most urgent global sustainability issue (United Nations Environment Programme, 2021). It is causing environmental crises in many countries, including sea level and temperature rises, as well as increasing drought frequency that is severely hindering agricultural output (O'Mahony et al., 2016). The United Nations predicts that water and food insecurity will become the leading cause of future global conflicts (CDP, 2016).

Innovations and technologies already exist that can ameliorate global warming, yet uptake has been slow; future sustainability is dependent on acceleration of their adoption (Greenland, 2019). Solar energy is one technology that will help to combat climate change (Butturi et al., 2019). The installation of photovoltaic rooftop solar panels can reduce a country's GHG emissions by more than 50% over 10 years, and help to achieve a carbon–neutral status in around 30 years (Marchi et al., 2018, p. 829).

Balancing economic development while minimising negative environmental and social impacts is a sustainability challenge confronting most countries. This especially applies in emerging markets where environmental and consumer protection is often constrained due to a range of factors including limited financial resources, lower levels of consumer awareness, corporate irresponsibility and poor governance (Nguyen, Nguyen, et al., 2019).

Vietnam is typical of many emerging markets in Southeast (SE) Asia, based on its burgeoning population and corresponding GHG emissions driven by expanding industrial activity and rapidly rising household power consumption (Nguyen, Greenland, et al., 2019). In such markets, renewable energy is a particularly viable solution for long-term energy security, reducing GHG emissions and other environmental pollution and promoting future sustainable development. Due to its geographical location, extensive coastline, tropical monsoon climate and stable agricultural economy, Vietnam is an emerging market in SE Asia that has diverse renewable energy options, including hydropower, wind power, solar power, geothermal and biofuels (Government of Vietnam, 2019). At the end of 2020, Vietnam's total power capacity was 69,300 MW; an increase of nearly 14,000 MW from 2019, with renewable energy (excluding hydropower) contributing 17,430 MW of total power capacity. There was an increase of 11,780 MW in renewables between 2019 and 2020, with this energy option comprising close to 25% of Vietnam's total power supply. Solar power generated 8550 MW or over half of all the renewable energy, with 90% of this from rooftop solar (Ministry of Industry & Trade of the Socialist Republic of Vietnam, 2021).

To reduce GHG emissions, many countries have adopted sustainable energy policies that support both households and businesses (Zander et al., 2019). For example, some governments have implemented rooftop solar energy schemes with subsidised installation fees, as well as feed-in tariff (FiT) incentives, which pay both businesses and households for any electricity generated by their solar system that is surplus to their needs (Nelson et al., 2011; Zahedi, 2010). Globally, such policies and incentives have encouraged the uptake of rooftop solar and have increased its competitiveness with traditional energy sources.

In 2019, the Vietnamese government introduced a new solar power FiT policy and guidelines (Prime Minister of Vietnam, 2020). The terms of the FiT attracted consumers and investors, in that households could sell excess electricity to the state-owned EVN and its subsidiaries at a rate of US$93.5/MWh for 20 years, along with other supporting policies such as tax exemptions (Do et al., 2020). These included households selling electricity to EVN below VND 100,000,000 not required to declare and pay personal income tax on this revenue (Ministry of Finance of the Socialist Republic of Vietnam, 2019). The FiT rate was also particularly high compared with other SE Asian and Asia Pacific countries (including developed markets). For example, in Australia, some solar FiT schemes pay around US$61.5/MWh (Northern Territory Government, 2020). This region-leading rate explains why the number of households in Vietnam with rooftop solar surpassed 100,000 by the end of 2020, and why it has had the highest solar uptake rate in SE Asia (Do & Burke, 2021).

While many former studies have investigated the effects of incentive schemes on the installation of rooftop solar (e.g., Schelly, 2014; Sun et al., 2020), there has been limited focus on emerging markets like Vietnam. Furthermore, most of the previous emerging market studies have only assessed the potential of solar power, without any detailed investigation of consumer decision-making behaviour. This study has consequently assessed the influence of both customer perceptions (internal elements—knowledge, perceptions and expectations) and contextual factors (external elements—government incentive policies) on attitudes and intentions towards rooftop solar. It therefore makes an important contribution to existing knowledge and will likely inform future government solar initiatives while supporting businesses trading in solar energy. This study should also be of interest to academics and policymakers in other countries seeking to understand and promote renewable energy.

2.2 Theoretical Background, Research Model and Hypotheses Development

2.2.1 Theoretical Background

The relationship between consumer attitude and behaviour is widely recognised in the literature. That is customers with a positive attitude towards particular products/services are more likely to buy them (Ajzen, 1991, 2002). In the context of this research, many studies focussed on customer attitude and behaviour towards environmentally friendly products have developed models based on this relationship (e.g., Nguyen, Greenland, et al., 2019). Similarly, this study has proposed a research model that is an extension of the theory of planned behaviour (TPB), involving the common elements of intention, attitude, subjective norm and perceived behaviour control.

Other empirical studies of consumer behaviour towards solar energy products have often combined relevant theories and added more specific components based on the characteristics of the research context. For example, Sun et al. (2020) proposed a model with two groups of factors relating to personal traits and psychological benefits, combined with attitude and intention, to explain the behaviour of using rooftop solar energy in the Taiwanese market.

In this study in addition to the key TPB items, additional components were: government incentive policies based on the financial benefits they can deliver to targeted users (Parker, 2008); perceived monetary barriers that can significantly impact on the intention to choose environmentally friendly products (Tanner & Wölfing Kast, 2003); brand trust based on its impact on customer perceptions, intentions and levels of loyalty (Alan & Kabadayı, 2014) and environmental knowledge based on its positive contributions to consumer decision-making in the context of environmentally friendly products (Mostafa, 2007). Furthermore, as expectation has been found to significantly influence customer's attitudes (Fornell et al., 1996), this was also included. This is in addition to the inclusion of a household innovativeness component that reflects attitudes towards new technologies (Sun et al., 2020), based on rooftop solar being a relatively new product in the Vietnam market. A summary of these components is illustrated in the proposed research model below (see Fig. 2.1).

2.2.2 Hypotheses Development

2.2.2.1 Attitude and Intention

Attitude towards a behaviour is "formed from beliefs about the likely positive or negative consequences of a behaviour" (Rai & Beck, 2015, p. 2), while purchase intention can indicate "an individual's readiness to buy a preferred product following evaluations on the basis of personal experience, perception, attitude, subjective norm,

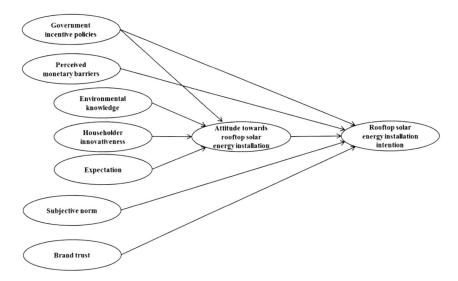

Fig. 2.1 Research model

external environment and perceived behavioural control related to that product" (Hai et al., 2017, p. 319).

According to Ajzen (1991), attitude determines an individual's intention to act. Sreen et al. (2018) emphasised that attitude, sustainability practices and purchase intention relationships are essential components in green product consumption behaviour studies. Numerous empirical studies have confirmed the relationship between positive attitudes towards green products and intention to uptake (e.g., Nguyen, Nguyen, et al., 2019; ElHaffar et al., 2020). Furthermore, the relationship between attitude and intention towards rooftop solar installation has been verified in other studies (e.g., Rai & Beck, 2015; Sun et al., 2020). Thus, the following research hypothesis was proposed here:

H₁ Attitude has a positive impact on intention toward rooftop solar energy installation.

2.2.2.2 Environmental Knowledge

Environmental knowledge generally refers to facts, concepts or relationships in the surrounding environment, including sustainability challenges (e.g., Chan & Lau, 2000; Fryxell & Lo, 2003). Most former studies have concluded that environmental knowledge or perceptions have a positive impact on consumer behaviour towards environmentally friendly products (e.g., Mostafa, 2007; Smith & Paladino, 2010). On a global scale, sustainability problems have become the responsibility of many stakeholders, including consumers, and are of particular concern in developing countries including SE Asia due to rapid population growth (Indriani et al., 2019). In Vietnam, former research has recognised that customers with higher awareness of environmental issues are more likely to choose environmentally friendly products (Nguyen et al., 2016; Nguyen, Greenland, et al., 2019). Thus, the following research hypothesis H_2 was proposed in this study:

H_2 Environmental knowledge has a positive impact on attitude towards household rooftop solar installation.

2.2.2.3 Householder Innovativeness

Innovativeness has been recognised as the driving force behind innovative consumption behaviour (Roehrich, 2004). Rogers and Shoemaker (1971, p. 27) defined such innovativeness as "the degree a person may be the first one who adopts innovation compared to the other members of the social system they belong to". Venkatraman (1991) similarly argued that innovativeness is a latent feature expressed in consumer preference for novel and unique experiences. Thus, innovativeness is related to customers' receptiveness to trial new product lines. Several studies have identified a positive relationship between innovativeness and customer attitude (Hwang et al., 2021; Sun et al., 2020; Truong, 2013), including towards rooftop solar products in Vietnam (Jirakiattikul et al., 2021). Thus, the following research hypothesis H_3 was proposed here:

H_3 Householder innovativeness has a positive impact on attitude towards rooftop solar installation.

2.2.2.4 Expectation

According to Fornell et al. (1996), expectation considers the relationship between prior consumer experiences, which can be generated through personal consumption, or advertising or observations, and the perceived ability of the product or service to meet customer needs. Expectation has therefore been identified as an important determinant affecting customer perceptions and levels of satisfaction (Hsu & Lin, 2015). Consideration of the relationship between expectation and attitude has often been incorporated into service quality and consumer satisfaction studies, such as Hsu et al. (2010) where a positive connection was identified. In the context of this study, it has been found that the success or failure of renewable energy often depends on the beliefs and/or expectations of customers (Larson & Krannich, 2016). Thus, the following research hypothesis H_4 was proposed here:

H_4 Expectation has a positive impact on the attitude towards rooftop solar installation.

2.2.2.5 Government Incentive Policies

Replacing fossil fuels with renewable energy sources has been identified as critical for reducing carbon emissions (United Nations Environment Programme, 2021). Recognised by many governments as a viable solution, solar energy has often been supported through policy (Martinot et al., 2002). Other studies have shown the reliance of rooftop solar adoption on financial support and incentive schemes (e.g., Parker, 2008; Rai & McAndrews, 2012). In line with this, the Vietnamese government has implemented policies to support renewable energy including rooftop solar installation. This includes both households and businesses selling their excess electricity back to Viet Nam Electricity Corporation (EVN) at a generous rate, along with capped access to free electricity for the first four years (Lan et al., 2020). Jirakiattikul et al. (2021) has highlighted the positive effect of these government incentives on Vietnamese householder attitudes towards rooftop solar products. Sun et al. (2020) has also demonstrated their positive influence on rooftop solar installation intention in Vietnam. The following hypotheses H_5 and H_6 were therefore proposed in this study:

H_5 Government incentive policies has a positive effect on the attitude towards rooftop solar installation.

H_6 Government incentive policies has a positive effect on the intention towards rooftop solar installation.

2.2.2.6 Perceived Monetary Barriers

Perceived monetary barriers relates to customer perceptions of high-priced products and their inability to purchase them (Tanner & Wölfing Kast, 2003). In line with this, willingness to pay relates to perceived value based on anticipated customer satisfaction (Cronin et al., 2000; Sweeny & Soutar, 2001; Zeithaml, 1988). In the context of this study, high price perceptions are widely recognised as a major barrier to customer attitudes and intention towards purchasing environmentally friendly products (Nguyen et al., 2021; Nguyen, Nguyen, et al., 2019; Soler et al., 2002; Xie et al., 2015). Indeed, in developing countries researchers have concluded that difficulties implementing renewable energy policy are largely due to customers' limited financial resources to cover installation costs (Reddy & Painuly, 2004). The following research hypothesis H_7 was subsequently proposed in this study:

H_7 Perceived monetary barriers has a negative impact on intention towards rooftop solar installation.

2.2.2.7 Subjective Norm

Subjective norm has been identified as an important determinant of customer purchase intentions (Ajzen, 1991, 2002). Rai and Beck (2015, p. 2) defined subjective norm as "perception of how a particular behaviour will be viewed by others important to the subject". Many former buyer behaviour models have factored in subjective norm, including the theory of reasoned action (Fishbein & Ajzen, 1975) and the theory of planned behaviour (Ajzen, 1991). The significant impact of the subjective norm on purchase intention has been confirmed by many researchers (e.g., Chan & Lau, 2002). More recently, Nguyen et al. (2020) demonstrated the critical role of the subjective norm in determining customer behaviour in Vietnamese setting where collectivist culture is highly regarded (i.e., relatives' views and social pressure often influence individual behaviours). In the context of this study, Korcaj et al. (2015), Liobikienė et al. (2021) and Ru et al. (2018) have reported the positive impact of subjective norms on renewable energy usage intentions. Thus, the following research hypothesis H_8 was proposed in this study:

H_8 Subjective norm has a positive impact on intention towards rooftop solar installation.

2.2.2.8 Brand Trust

Brand trust is a concept that has received attention from scholars across various disciplines including economics, sociology, psychology, management and marketing (Delgado-Ballester et al., 2003). It has been defined as a customer's commitment to a brand based on expectations of its perceived benefits (Lau & Lee, 1999). As the importance of brand has increased along with growing consumer choices, the establishment of brand trust has become an increasingly important goal for providers (e.g., Keller, 1993). Numerous studies have also proven the direct effect of brand trust on customer purchase intention (e.g., Alan & Kabadayı, 2014; Punyatoya, 2014). Thus, research hypothesis H_9 was proposed in this study:

H_9 Brand trust has a positive impact on intention towards rooftop solar installation.

2.3 Research Methodology and Data Collection

2.3.1 Methodology

This study adopted a two-phase research approach. First, qualitative research in the form of in-depth interviews were conducted to pilot the questionnaire items and research scales and to adapt where necessary in the context of the Vietnamese rooftop solar market. In-depth interviews are used widely in qualitative research and are effective for providing deeper insights to the subject of investigation (e.g., Greenland & Moore, 2021). The qualitative phase comprised five one-on-one interviews with industry experts, as well as ten with potential rooftop solar customers.

The second research phase comprised an online quantitative survey to capture the item ratings and demographic data, to facilitate statistical analysis and scale reliability testing, as well as research hypotheses testing. IBM SPSS 20 software was used to conduct the descriptive analysis and reliability coefficient tests (i.e., Cronbach Alpha and Harman's single factor test). IBM AMOS 20 software was then used for confirmatory factor analysis (CFA) and structural equation modelling (SEM) to test the proposed research model and hypotheses. The key fit indices used for the model evaluation, based on the recommendations of Hair et al. (2009) and Baumgartner and Homburg (1996), included Chi-square corrected for degrees of freedom (CMIN/df), as well as CFI (Comparative Fit Index), TLI (Tucker & Lewis Index), GFI (Goodness of Fit Index) and RMSEA (root mean square error approximation) coefficients.

2.3.2 Measures

The questionnaire design was adapted from previously established scales and items, such as TPB items for attitude and intention from Ajzen (1991). The question responses relied mainly on a 7-point Likert scale, ranging from 1 = strongly disagree to 7 = strongly agree. Further detail of the number of items selected and their original sources are presented in Table 2.1.

Two language experts ensured accurate translation of item wording and scales from English to Vietnamese. They initially worked independently and then conducted cross-checking to ensure consistency of the translated content.

Appropriate adaptation as well as pretesting were deemed important given the potential challenges of applying research approaches established in developed

Table 2.1 Summary research dimensions and sources

Dimensions	Number of items	Source
Attitude	3	Ajzen (1991)
Intention	3	Ajzen (1991)
Environmental knowledge	5	Mostafa (2007)
Householder innovativeness	4	Truong (2013)
Expectation	3	Fornell et al. (1996)
Government incentive policies	4	Sun et al. (2020)
Perceived monetary barriers	3	Tanner and Wölfing Kast (2003)
Subjective norm	3	Korcaj et al. (2015)
Brand trust	5	Chen (2010), Delgado-Ballester (2004)

western markets without due modification to the developing country context (Greenland & Rayman-Bacchus, 2014). In line with this, five consumers were first invited to participate in a detailed pilot testing exercise, to ensure clear and accurate comprehension of the statements and questionnaire wording.

To further ensure appropriate adaptation, a further five in-depth interviews involving detailed piloting of the questionnaire were conducted with five industry experts, which included three directors of companies distributing rooftop solar products in the Vietnamese market, a Doctor of Marketing and a Doctor of Business Administration. The feedback from this expert panel was analysed and discussed by the research team, to modify the questionnaire as relevant. A final check of the items in the revised questionnaire was then undertaken, via five post-survey depth interviews with consumers to ensure respondent ratings matched their intended meaning.

2.3.3 Survey Data Collection and Sample

This study used a convenience sample targeting consumers in Vietnam that had expressed interest in installing rooftop solar. Due to COVID-19, data collection was conducted via an online survey rather than face-to face-interviews, which facilitated the swift collection of information from respondents across geographically distant areas. Also, given the Coronavirus pandemic the online survey method was selected as it helped reduce the risk of disease transmission.

Six hundred personal emails with the survey link were sent to potential consumers that rooftop solar suppliers provided contact details for. The data collection was conducted over a two-month period (February 2021–April 2021), as contact details for prospective rooftop solar customers accumulated, with a total of 326 responses received. After removing invalid and incomplete surveys, 296 valid questionnaires remained, representing a response rate of 49%. Demographic details of the respondent sample are presented in Table 2.2.

2.4 Results and Analysis

2.4.1 Construct Reliability, Convergent and Discriminant Validity

To test scale reliability and convergent validity, CFA was used in conjunction with the Cronbach Alpha reliability coefficient test. The results in Table 2.3 show that the factor loadings ranged from 0.659 to 0.863 (all > 0.6), the CR (composite reliability) values ranged from 0.784 to 0.886 (all > 0.7), the AVE (average variance extracted) values ranged from 0.556 to 0.682 (all > 0.5) and the Cronbach Alpha coefficient values ranged from 0.784 to 0.878 (all > 0.7). In addition, the measurement model

Table 2.2 Demographic profile of survey respondents

Demographic characteristic	Frequency	%
Gender		
Male	159	53.72
Female	137	46.28
Age (years)		
18–29	32	10.81
30–39	78	26.35
40–49	89	30.07
50 and above	97	32.77
Education level		
High school or lesser	3	1.01
Professional degree	8	2.70
College degree	55	18.58
University undergraduate	163	55.07
Postgraduate	67	22.64
Marital status		
Single/never married	42	14.19
Currently married	225	76.01
Widowed	8	2.70
Divorced/separated	21	7.09
Household monthly income		
Under VND 10,000,000	2	0.68
VND 10,000,000–20,000,000	34	11.49
VND 20,000,000–30,000,000	76	25.68
VND 30,000,000–40,000,000	97	32.77
Over 50,000,000	87	29.39

Note 1 USD $= 23{,}770$ VND at the time of the survey

had 453 degrees of freedom, Chi-square/df $= 1.232$ (< 3) and p-value $= 0.001$ (< 0.05), and values GFI $= 0.902$, TLI $= 0.975$, CFI $= 0.979$ (> 0.9) and RMSEA $= 0.028$ (< 0.06). According to Hair et al. (2009), these results demonstrate a reliable model, with convergent validity guaranteed.

As presented in Table 2.4, the descriptive analysis showed that the mean values of perceived monetary barrier had the lowest (3.536) and the installation intention had the highest mean (4.723), with standard deviation ranging from 0.659 to 1.075. The analysis used to evaluate discriminant validity revealed that MSV (maximum shared variance) was less than AVE, and the square root of the AVE of each construct was higher than its correlation coefficients with other constructs, indicating that discriminant validity is ensured. In addition, all the correlation coefficients were less than 0.6, indicating that multicollinearity did not occur in this study (Byrne, 2010; Grewal et al., 2004; Hair et al., 2009).

Table 2.3 Items, reliability and convergent validity

Items	FLs	CR	AVE	α
Attitude (ATT)				
Installing the rooftop solar energy product is a good idea	0.826	0.877	0.704	0.878
Installing the rooftop solar energy product is a smart solution	0.863			
I enjoy using rooftop solar energy product	0.828			
Intention (INT)				
I intend to install rooftop solar energy product	0.749	0.784	0.547	0.784
I have a plan to install rooftop solar energy product	0.724			
I expect to install rooftop solar energy product in the future	0.746			
Environmental knowledge (KNO)				
I know that installing rooftop solar energy offers environmental protection	0.659	0.861	0.556	0.866
I have more knowledge than most about recycling	0.834			
I know how to choose products that reduce waste for the environment	0.803			
I know the symbols and characters of eco-friendly products	0.690			
I have much knowledge about environmental issues	0.727			
Householder innovativeness (INNO)				
Overall, I like modern, innovative technology products and want to use them	0.830	0.875	0.636	0.874
I often search for information about modern environmental protection technologies	0.784			
I know a lot about advanced solar products	0.768			
I look forward to using products with the most advanced technology	0.807			
Expectation (EXP)				
I believe that rooftop solar energy products will meet my expectations well	0.782	0.866	0.683	0.864
I believe the product will have good quality and stable performance	0.837			
I believe the product will bring me many benefits	0.859			
Government incentive policies (GOV)				
Government incentives policies on solar energy attract me	0.843	0.873	0.633	0.856
The policies to buy back electricity from rooftop solar energy are very meaningful to households in terms of benefits	0.852			
I believe government policies will create an incentive for many people to install rooftop solar energy	0.762			
I think the government's promotion policies will be continued for a long time	0.718			

(continued)

Table 2.3 (continued)

Items	FLs	CR	AVE	α
Perceived monetary barriers (MB)				
I can't pay too much for rooftop solar energy product	0.825	0.866	0.682	0.866
Rooftop solar energy product is too expensive	0.829			
Everyone should install rooftop solar energy even though it is more expensive than other products (reverse in coding)	0.824			
Subjective norm (SUBN)				
People important to me feel good about installing rooftop solar energy products	0.820	0.848	0.650	0.847
People expect me to install a rooftop solar energy product	0.809			
For people in my situation, it is common to install rooftop solar energy products	0.789			
Brand trust (BRAT)				
The brand's environmental commitments are generally reliable	0.752	0.885	0.608	0.877
The brand of the rooftop solar energy product meets my expectation	0.748			
The brand's environmental argument is generally trustworthy	0.758			
The brand name guarantees satisfaction	0.805			
The brand keeps its promises and commitments for environmental protection	0.831			

Note FLs = factor loadings; AVE = average variance extracted; CR = composite reliability; α = Cronbach Alpha coefficient

2.4.2 Common Method Variance

The construction of scales used in other studies can lead to the likelihood of common method variance (CMV), which can cause negative effects on the performance measurement of the research model (Podsakoff et al., 2012). This study therefore applied several measures to test for and limit the occurrence of CMV. For example, the order of questions was changed, and Harman's single factor test and common latent factor were used to assess the likelihood of CMV. The Harman's single factor test showed that the single factor explained 23.06% (less than 50%) of the variance. In addition, the common latent factor in the CFA accounted for 24.01% (less than 25%) of the total variance. According to Malhotra et al. (2006), these results indicate that CMV was unlikely to have occurred in this study.

Table 2.4 Descriptive statistics, correlations and discriminant validity

	Mean	SD	MSV	MaxR(H)	INT	ATT	KNOW	INNO	EXP	GOV	MB	SUBN	BRAT
INT	4.723	0.659	0.246	0.784	**0.740**								
ATT	4.324	0.831	0.269	0.879	0.494	**0.839**							
KNOW	4.518	0.881	0.238	0.873	0.488	0.437	**0.746**						
INNO	4.518	0.881	0.238	0.873	0.416	0.411	0.352	**0.798**					
EXP	3.751	0.987	0.246	0.871	0.496	0.407	0.321	0.315	**0.827**				
GOV	4.416	0.921	0.269	0.883	0.478	0.519	0.362	0.323	0.379	**0.795**			
MB	3.536	0.990	0.073	0.866	−0.270	−0.248	−0.193	−0.078	−0.180	−0.085	**0.826**		
SUBN	4.420	0.747	0.049	0.848	0.221	0.150	0.116	0.168	0.122	0.052	−0.130	**0.806**	
BRAT	4.350	1.075	0.014	0.889	0.071	−0.037	0.098	0.093	0.078	0.088	−0.119	0.078	**0.780**

Note Diagonal values that are bolded indicate the square root of AVE of construct; SD = standard deviation

2.4.3 Hypotheses Testing and Path Analysis

SEM was applied to test the research hypotheses and assess the impact of independent variables on the dependent variable. The results showed that the model has 460 degrees of freedom, Chi-square/df value $= 1.335$, p-value $= 0.000$, RMSEA $= 0.034$ and values of CFI $= 0.969$, TLI $= 0.964$, GFI $= 0.893$. According to Bagozzi and Yi (1988), Baumgartner and Homburg (1996) and Hair et al. (2009), this research model showed a good fit to the data.

The results of the hypothesis testing are presented in Table 2.5 and showed that, with the exception of H_9 (the relationship between brand trust and intention), all other hypotheses were accepted based on p-value below the 95% significance level (<0.05).

Government incentive policies most strongly influenced both attitude and intention, with β of 0.314 and 0.308, respectively. Environmental knowledge, householder innovativeness and expectation also positively affected the attitude towards rooftop solar installation, with β values of 0.210, 0.185 and 0.177, respectively. Perceived monetary barriers had adverse effects on intention towards rooftop solar installation, with $\beta = -0.162$. Lastly, subjective norm and attitude also positively affected intention, with β of 0.149 and 0.301, respectively.

The independent variables explained 41% of the variation in attitude to adopt and 37% of the intention to install rooftop solar. A more detailed description of these path analyses and hypotheses results is shown in Fig. 2.2.

Table 2.5 Hypotheses testing and path analysis results

Hypotheses			β (standardised)	t-value	p-value	Result
H_1 Attitude	$\rightarrow$	Intention	0.301	3.978	***	Accepted
H_2 Environmental knowledge	$\rightarrow$	Attitude	0.210	3.268	0.001	Accepted
H_3 Householder innovativeness	$\rightarrow$	Attitude	0.185	2.975	0.003	Accepted
H_4 Expectation	$\rightarrow$	Attitude	0.177	2.819	0.005	Accepted
H_5 Government motivation	$\rightarrow$	Attitude	0.314	4.951	***	Accepted
H_6 Government motivation	$\rightarrow$	Intention	0.308	4.175	***	Accepted
H_7 Perceived monetary barriers	$\rightarrow$	Intention	-0.162	-2.584	0.010	Accepted
H_8 Subjective norm	$\rightarrow$	Intention	0.149	2.373	0.018	Accepted
H_9 Brand trust	$\rightarrow$	Intention	0.018	0.312	0.755	Rejected

Note ***p-value < 0.001; $n = 296$

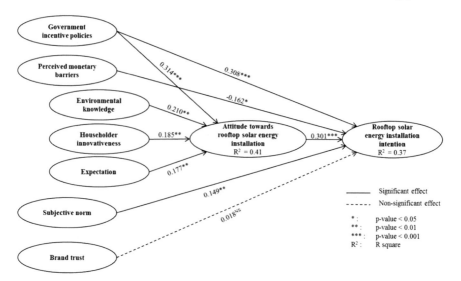

Fig. 2.2 Hypothesis testing and path analysis results

2.5 Discussion

Climate change is an urgent global sustainability issue (United Nations Environment Programme, 2021). Renewable energy can ameliorate global warming and rooftop solar is particularly effective for reducing household GHG emissions. However, its uptake has been slow and understanding household solar installation decision-making is an important research area.

This study is one of the first to apply the TPB to explain attitude and intention towards rooftop solar installation in Vietnam. The research incorporated TPB attitude and subjective norm measures (Ajzen, 1991), as well as dimensions adapted from several other green purchase behaviour studies (Chen, 2010; Delgado-Ballester, 2004; Fornell et al., 1996; Korcaj et al., 2015; Mostafa, 2007; Sun et al., 2020; Tanner & Wölfing Kast, 2003; Truong, 2013).

The analysis revealed that customers' innovativeness, expectations and environmental knowledge, and in particular their understanding of government incentives, can have a significant impact on attitudes towards rooftop solar installation. The notable influence of government incentives on positive consumer attitude highlights that widespread adoption of renewable energy such as rooftop solar relies on effective government support. This finding provides statistical evidence that supports similar observations of others regarding the importance of government incentives (e.g., Do et al., 2020; Phap et al., 2020; Sun et al., 2020).

Understanding the key influencers of consumer attitudes towards renewable energy is important for marketing. As indicated by this study's findings, promotional campaigns could be improved by clearly communicating the environmentally friendly attributes of rooftop solar energy systems, including their role in climate change mitigation. Such communication will help raise public awareness of sustainability issues and the direct benefits of renewable energy.

This study's results also indicate that overall attitude towards rooftop solar has a strong and positive impact upon adoption intentions, which is consistent with many TPB studies in other consumption contexts (e.g., Ajzen, 1991). The results also highlight that government incentives are likely to have the greatest impact on rooftop solar intentions, further reinforcing the need for effective government support in the promotion of renewable energy.

The analysis also found that subjective norms (i.e. influence of others on purchase behaviour) can also have a positive and significant impact on solar installation intentions, which concurs with other similar investigations into consumer behaviour in the context of renewable energy (e.g., Korcaj et al., 2015; Ru et al., 2018). More effective, widespread communications regarding the environmental benefits of rooftop solar should therefore strengthen the impact of a subject norm on purchase intent.

As in many other emerging markets, rooftop solar has been unaffordable for many Vietnamese, with the high cost of installation a key barrier to uptake. Access to capital has previously been recognised as a key challenge for renewable energy implementation in developing countries (Reddy & Painuly, 2004), where there are no government incentives. As shown in Vietnam, financial incentives such as installation discounts and payment programmes can help to overcome such price barriers. Further post-purchase support considerations might include support for re-purchasing solar panels and system upgrades. Manufacturing efficiency improvements would also lead to more affordable pricing, as well as having a positive impact on product quality.

Lastly, while brand trust has been identified as a key driver of adoption intention in other green purchase studies (e.g., Punyatoya, 2014), it does not appear to be as relevant in the context of rooftop solar in Vietnam. This could be due to a lack of consumer familiarity with solar products and brands, with rooftop solar only entering the Vietnamese market in the last five years, and the range of products limited (and controlled) by the authorities (e.g., Ministry of Industry & Trade of the Socialist Republic of Vietnam, 2021). It has previously been recognised that a lack of detailed rooftop solar information, such as product specifications and standards, is likely to hinder customer knowledge including quality perceptions, and thereby deter investment (Nguyên, 2021). To further support the adoption of rooftop solar, policymakers should enforce quality standards that will satisfy customer expectations.

2.6 Conclusion and Future Research

Renewable energy has been deemed critical for mitigating climate change, and rooftop solar offers an effective solution for reducing household GHG emissions. At the time of writing this paper, the 26th UN Climate Change Conference of the Parties (COP26) in Glasgow reported that "all countries need to speed up the transition away from all fossil fuel sources, and switch to renewable sources" (United Nations, 2021). Understanding customer decision-making processes associated with adopting renewable energy is therefore beneficial, so that both policymakers and suppliers can design offerings and incentives that maximise uptake (while minimising barriers to adoption).

This research makes a contribution to existing knowledge by improving understanding of the reasons for purchasing renewable energy systems. It has focussed on the factors influencing Vietnamese household decision-making in relation to rooftop solar installation, applying the TPB and using CFA and SEM to investigate attitude and intention. The findings have highlighted the positive influence of government incentives, such as the scheme used in Vietnam to increase uptake of rooftop solar. They also validate the motivating roles of perceived innovativeness, customer expectation and environmental knowledge, as well as the influence of subjective norms. Furthermore, in line with other consumer studies, these results highlight how unsubsidised costs can restrict rooftop solar installation intention. Although unlike other studies, it demonstrates that brand trust does not always play a role when it comes to rooftop solar decision-making, perhaps due to a lack of familiarity with products and brands (particularly in emerging markets).

This study is one of the first to statistically validate the effectiveness of government rooftop solar incentives, with Vietnamese uptake rates exceeding other regional markets including Australia. Such findings can be used to inform future promotions and initiatives in relation to the adoption of renewable energy such as rooftop solar. This includes countries like Australia, where climate mitigation initiatives need to be escalated. Australia was recently ranked 52 out of 63 countries in the global Renewable Energy Index, with a "very low" overall performance rating (Burck et al., 2022). While Australia's comparatively small population and large geographic size somewhat compensates for its high per capita energy consumption rates, its comparatively poor performance in renewable energy needs to be addressed. While Australia has one of the highest proportions of houses with rooftop solar (around 20%), it's incentive schemes are not as generous as Vietnam's, and its regulators and suppliers could gain beneficial insights from what has been done in the emerging market of Vietnam to kick start further progress with its renewable energy adoption.

Several limitations have been recognised in this study. First, the relatively small sample from Vietnam and the convenience sampling method that was used means the results may not be as generalisable as they could be. Second, the sample did not facilitate any detailed exploration of differences in the opinions, attitudes and behaviours of different types of consumers in Vietnam. Future research could use larger, more geographically diverse respondent groups to overcome such shortcomings. Lastly, attitude and intention towards rooftop solar were examined via a finite number of factors that have emerged as influencers in previous studies, and these authors acknowledge that there are likely to be other relevant determinants as identified in the qualitative research phase. For example, unpredictable and insufficient weather (e.g., lack of sunshine) to operate the system, as well as installation maintenance. Incorporating a wider range of attitude and intention dimensions has been recognised as worthwhile for future investigations.

Finally, although Vietnam's growth in rooftop solar uptake is noteworthy, it was still ranked 32 in the Renewable Energy Index, with a mid-range overall performance rating (Burck et al., 2022). This suggests there is still room for improvement in Vietnam, with more research needed to better inform future initiatives. More detailed investigation of renewable energy customer decision-making offers an important avenue for future research.

References

Ajzen, I. (1991). The theory of planned behavior. *Organizational Behavior and Human Decision Processes, 50*(2), 179–211.

Ajzen, I. (2002). Perceived behavioral control, self-efficacy, locus of control, and the theory of planned behavior. *Journal of Applied Social Psychology, 32*(4), 665–683.

Alan, A. K., & Kabadayı, E. T. (2014). Quality antecedents of brand trust and behavioral intention. *Procedia-Social and Behavioral Sciences, 150*, 619–627.

Bagozzi, R. P., & Yi, Y. (1988). On the evaluation of structural equation models. *Journal of the Academy of Marketing Science, 16*(1), 74–94.

Baumgartner, H., & Homburg, C. (1996). Applications of structural equation modelling in marketing and consumer research: A review. *International Journal of Research in Marketing, 13*(2), 139–161.

Burck, J., Uhlich, T., Bals, C., Höhne, N., & Nascimento, L. (2022). *Monitoring climate mitigation efforts of 60 countries plus the EU—Covering 92% of the Global Greenhouse Gas Emissions, annual report from Climate Change Performance Index (CCPI)*. https://ccpi.org/wp-content/upl oads/CCPI-2022-Results_2021-11-07_A4-1.pdf

Butturi, M. A., Lolli, F., Sellitto, M. A., Balugani, E., Gamberini, R., & Rimini, B. (2019). Renewable energy in eco-industrial parks and urban-industrial symbiosis: A literature review and a conceptual synthesis. *Applied Energy, 255*, 113825.

Byrne, B. M. (2010). *Structural equation modeling with Amos: Basic concepts, applications, and programming* (2nd ed.). New York.

CDP. (2016). *Thirsty business: Why water is vital to climate action, 2016*. Annual Report of Corporate Water Disclosure. https://www.cdp.net/en/research/global-reports/global-water-report-2016. Accessed 6 Mar 2018.

Chan, R. Y., & Lau, L. B. (2000). Antecedents of green purchases: A survey in China. *Journal of Consumer Marketing, 17*(4), 338–357.

Chan, R. Y., & Lau, L. B. (2002). Explaining green purchasing behavior: A cross-cultural study on American and Chinese consumers. *Journal of International Consumer Marketing, 14*(2–3), 9–40.

Chen, Y. S. (2010). The drivers of green brand equity: Green brand image, green satisfaction, and green trust. *Journal of Business Ethics, 93*(2), 307–319.

Cronin Jr, J. J., Brady, M. K., & Hult, G. T. M. (2000). Assessing the effects of quality, value, and customer satisfaction on consumer behavioral intentions in service environments. *Journal of Retailing, 76*(2), 193–218.

Delgado-Ballester, E. (2004). Applicability of a brand trust scale across product categories: A multigroup invariance analysis. *European Journal of Marketing, 38*(5/6), 573–592.

Delgado-Ballester, E., Munuera-Aleman, J. L., & Yague-Guillen, M. J. (2003). Development and validation of a brand trust scale. *International Journal of Market Research, 45*(1), 35–54.

Do, T. N., & Burke, P. J. (2021, March). Vietnam's solar power boom: Policy implications for other ASEAN member states. *SEAS Perspective, 28*(11). https://www.iseas.edu.sg/articles-commentar ies/iseas-perspective/2021-28-vietnams-solar-power-boom-policy-implications-for-other-asean-member-states-by-thang-nam-do-and-paul-j-burke/

Do, T. N., Burke, P. J., Baldwin, K. G., & Nguyen, C. T. (2020). Underlying drivers and barriers for solar photovoltaics diffusion: The case of Vietnam. *Energy Policy, 144*, 111561. https://doi.org/10.1016/j.enpol.2020.111561

ElHaffar, G., Durif, F., & Dubé, L. (2020). Towards closing the attitude-intention-behavior gap in green consumption: A narrative review of the literature and an overview of future research directions. *Journal of Cleaner Production, 275*, 122556.

Fishbein, M., & Ajzen, I. (1975). *Belief, attitude, intention, and behavior: An introduction to theory and research*. Addison-Wesley.

Fornell, C., Johnson, M. D., Anderson, E. W., Cha, J., & Bryant, B. E. (1996). The American customer satisfaction index: Nature, purpose, and findings. *Journal of Marketing, 60*(4), 7–18. https://doi.org/10.1177/002224299606000403

Fryxell, G. E., & Lo, C. W. (2003). The influence of environmental knowledge and values on managerial behaviours on behalf of the environment: An empirical examination of managers in China. *Journal of Business Ethics, 46*(1), 45–69.

Government of Vietnam. (2019). Solar power potential in Vietnam. *Online Newspaper of the Government of the Socialist Republic of Vietnam*. http://baochinhphu.vn/Khoa-hoc-Cong-nghe/Tiem-nang-dien-mat-troi-tai-Viet-Nam/373594.vgp

Greenland, S. J. (2019). Future sustainability, innovation and marketing: A framework for understanding impediments to sustainable innovation adoption and corporate social responsibility. In D. Crowther, S. Seifi, & A. Moyeen (Eds.), *The components of sustainable development*. Springer Nature.

Greenland, S. J., & Moore, C. (2021). Large qualitative sample and thematic analysis to redefine student dropout and retention strategy in open online education. *British Journal of Educational Technology*. Online first, 1–21. https://doi.org/10.1111/bjet.13173

Greenland, S. J., & Rayman-Bacchus, L. (2014). Ethnography-photography: A visual approach to segmentation and living standard evaluation in emerging markets. *Market and Social Research, 22*(1), 9–21.

Grewal, R., Cote, J. A., & Baumgartner, H. (2004). Multicollinearity and measurement error in structural equation models: Implications for theory testing. *Marketing Science, 23*, 519–529.

Hai, M. A., Moula, M. M. E., & Seppälä, U. (2017). Results of intention-behaviour gap for solar energy in regular residential buildings in Finland. *International Journal of Sustainable Built Environment, 6*(2), 317–329.

Hair, J. F., Black, W. C., Babin, B. J., & Anderson, R. E. (2009). *Multivariate data analysis: A global perspective* (7th ed.). Upper Saddle River.

Hsu, C. H., Cai, L. A., & Li, M. (2010). Expectation, motivation, and attitude: A tourist behavioral model. *Journal of Travel Research, 49*(3), 282–296.

Hsu, C. L., & Lin, J. C. C. (2015). What drives purchase intention for paid mobile apps?—An expectation confirmation model with perceived value. *Electronic Commerce Research and Applications, 14*(1), 46–57.

Hwang, J., Kim, J. J., & Lee, K. W. (2021). Investigating consumer innovativeness in the context of drone food delivery services: Its impact on attitude and behavioral intentions. *Technological Forecasting and Social Change, 163*, 120433.

Indriani, I. A. D., Rahayu, M., & Hadiwidjojo, D. (2019). The influence of environmental knowledge on green purchase intention: The role of attitude as mediating variable. *International Journal of Multicultural and Multireligious Understanding, 6*(2), 627–635.

Jirakiattikul, S., Lan, T. T., & Techato, K. (2021). Advancing households' sustainable energy through gender attitudes towards rooftop PV installations: A case of the Central Highlands, Vietnam. *Sustainability, 13*(2), 942.

Keller, K. L. (1993). Conceptualizing, measuring, and managing customer-based brand equity. *Journal of Marketing, 57*(1), 1–22. https://doi.org/10.1177/002224299305700101

Korcaj, L., Hahnel, U. J., & Spada, H. (2015). Intentions to adopt photovoltaic systems depend on homeowners' expected personal gains and behavior of peers. *Renewable Energy, 75*, 407–415.

Lan, T. T., Jirakiattikul, S., Chowdhury, M. S., Ali, D., Niem, L. D., & Techato, K. (2020). The effect of retail electricity price levels on the FI values of smart-grid rooftop solar power systems: A case study in the central highlands of Vietnam. *Sustainability, 12*(21), 9209.

Larson, E. C., & Krannich, R. S. (2016). "A great idea, just not near me!" Understanding public attitudes about renewable energy facilities. *Society & Natural Resources, 29*(12), 1436–1451.

Lau, G. T., & Lee, S. H. (1999). Consumers' trust in a brand and the link to brand loyalty. *Journal of Market-Focused Management, 4*(4), 341–370.

Liobikienė, G., Dagiliūtė, R., & Juknys, R. (2021). The determinants of renewable energy usage intentions using theory of planned behaviour approach. *Renewable Energy, 170*, 587–594.

Malhotra, N. K., Kim, S. S., & Patil, A. (2006). Common method variance in research: A comparison of alternative approaches and a reanalysis of past research. *Management Science, 52*, 1865–1883.

Marchi, N. V., Pulselli, R. M., & Marchettini, N. (2018). Environmental policies for GHG emissions reduction and energy transition in the medieval historic centre of Siena (Italy): The role of solar energy. *Journal of Cleaner Production, 185*, 829–840. https://doi.org/10.1016/j.jclepro.2018.03.068

Martinot, E., Chaurey, A., Lew, D., Moreira, J. R., & Wamukonya, N. (2002). Renewable energy markets in developing countries. *Annual Review of Energy and the Environment, 27*(1), 309–348.

Ministry of Finance of the Socialist Republic of Vietnam. (2019). *Incentive policies for rooftop solar power projects with installed capacity of not exceeding 50kw*. https://thuvienphapluat.vn/cong-van/Tai-chinh-nha-nuoc/Cong-van-1534-BTC-CST-2019-chinh-sach-uu-dai-doi-voi-du-an-dien-mat-troi-duoi-50kw-410737.aspx

Ministry of Industry & Trade of the Socialist Republic of Vietnam. (2021). *Improve the ability to absorb renewable energy sources to ensure safe and efficient operation of the power system*. https://moit.gov.vn/phat-trien-ben-vung/nang-cao-kha-nang-hap-thu-nguon-dien-nang-luong-tai-tao-de-d2.html

Mostafa, M. M. (2007). Gender differences in Egyptian consumers' green purchase behaviour: The effects of environmental knowledge, concern and attitude. *International Journal of Consumer Studies, 31*(3), 220–229.

Nelson, T., Simshauser, P., & Kelley, S. (2011). Australian residential solar feed-in tariffs: Industry stimulus or regressive form of taxation? *Economic Analysis and Policy, 41*(2), 113–129.

Nguyên, N. (2021). Tấm pin điện mặt trời trôi nổi quá nhiều. *Báo Thanh Niên.* https://thanhnien.vn/tai-chinh-kinh-doanh/tam-pin-dien-mat-troi-troi-noi-qua-nhieu-1353287.html

Nguyen, N., Greenland, S. J., Lobo, A., & Nguyen, H. V. (2019). Demographics of sustainable technology consumption in an emerging market: The significance of education to energy efficient appliance adoption. *Social Responsibility Journal, 15*(6), 803–818.

Nguyen, T. N., Lobo, A., Nguyen, H. L., Phan, T. T. H., & Cao, T. K. (2016). Determinants influencing conservation behaviour: Perceptions of Vietnamese consumers. *Journal of Consumer Behaviour, 15*(6), 560–570.

Nguyen, N., Nguyen, H. V., Nguyen, P. T., Tran, V. T., Nguyen, H. N., Nguyen, T. M. N., ... Nguyen, T. H. (2020). Some key factors affecting consumers' intentions to purchase functional foods: A case study of functional yogurts in Vietnam. *Foods, 9*(1), 24.

Nguyen, H. V., Nguyen, N., Nguyen, B. K., & Greenland, S. (2021). Sustainable food consumption: Investigating organic meat purchase intention by Vietnamese consumers. *Sustainability, 13*(2), 953.

Nguyen, H. V., Nguyen, N., Nguyen, B. K., Lobo, A., & Vu, P. A. (2019). Organic food purchases in an emerging market: The influence of consumers' personal factors and green marketing practices of food stores. *International Journal of Environmental Research and Public Health, 16*(6), 1037.

Northern Territory Government. (2020). *More batteries, more renewables, more local jobs*. https://industry.nt.gov.au/news/2020/april/more-batteries,-more-renewables,-more-local-jobs

O'Mahony, B., Dalrymple, J., Levin, E., & Greenland, S. J. (2016). The role of information communications technology (ICT) in sustainable water management practice. *International Journal of Sustainable Agricultural Management and Informatics, 2*(1), 79–92.

Parker, P. (2008). Residential solar photovoltaic market stimulation: Japanese and Australian lessons for Canada. *Renewable and Sustainable Energy Reviews, 12*(7), 1944–1958.

Phap, V. M., Huong, N. T. T., Hanh, P. T., Van Duy, P., & Van Binh, D. (2020). Assessment of rooftop solar power technical potential in Hanoi city, Vietnam. *Journal of Building Engineering, 32*, 101528.

Podsakoff, P. M., Mackenzie, S. B., & Podsakoff, N. P. (2012). Sources of method bias in social science research and recommendations on how to control it. *Annual Review of Psychology, 63*(1), 539–569. https://doi.org/10.1146/annurev-psych-120710-100452

Prime Minister of Vietnam. (2020). *Decision on mechanisms to promote development of solar power in Vietnam.* http://vanban.chinhphu.vn/portal/page/portal/chinhphu/hethongvanban?class_id=1&_page=19&mode=detail&document_id=199694

Punyatoya, P. (2014). Linking environmental awareness and perceived brand eco-friendliness to brand trust and purchase intention. *Global Business Review, 15*(2), 279–289.

Rai, V., & Beck, A. L. (2015). Public perceptions and information gaps in solar energy in Texas. *Environmental Research Letters, 10*(7), 074011.

Rai, V., & McAndrews, K. (2012). Decision-making and behavior change in residential adopters of solar PV. In *Proceedings of the World Renewable Energy Forum.*

Reddy, S., & Painuly, J. P. (2004). Diffusion of renewable energy technologies—Barriers and stakeholders' perspectives. *Renewable Energy, 29*(9), 1431–1447.

Roehrich, G. (2004). Consumer innovativeness: Concepts and measurements. *Journal of Business Research, 57*(6), 671–677.

Rogers, E. M., & Shoemaker, F. F. (1971). *Communication of innovations: A cross-cultural approach.* Free Press.

Ru, X., Wang, S., & Yan, S. (2018). Exploring the effects of normative factors and perceived behavioral control on individual's energy-saving intention: An empirical study in Eastern China. *Resources, Conservation and Recycling, 134*, 91–99.

Schelly, C. (2014). Residential solar electricity adoption: What motivates, and what matters? A case study of early adopters. *Energy Research & Social Science, 2*, 183–191.

Smith, S., & Paladino, A. (2010). Eating clean and green? Investigating consumer motivations towards the purchase of organic food. *Australasian Marketing Journal, 18*(2), 93–104.

Soler, F., Gil, J. M., & Sanchez, M. (2002). Consumers' acceptability of organic food in Spain: Results from an experimental auction market. *British Food Journal, 104*(8–9), 670–687.

Sreen, N., Purbey, S., & Sadarangani, P. (2018). Impact of culture, behavior and gender on green purchase intention. *Journal of Retailing and Consumer Services, 41*, 177–189.

Sun, P. C., Wang, H. M., Huang, H. L., & Ho, C. W. (2020). Consumer attitude and purchase intention toward rooftop photovoltaic installation: The roles of personal trait, psychological benefit, and government incentives. *Energy & Environment, 31*(1), 21–39.

Sweeney, J. C., & Soutar, G. N. (2001). Consumer perceived value: The development of a multiple item scale. *Journal of Retailing, 77*(2), 203–220.

Tanner, C., & Wölfing Kast, S. (2003). Promoting sustainable consumption: Determinants of green purchases by Swiss consumers. *Psychology & Marketing, 20*(10), 883–902.

Truong, Y. (2013). A cross-country study of consumer innovativeness and technological service innovation. *Journal of Retailing and Consumer Services, 20*(1), 130–137.

United Nations. (2021). *Special coverage of COP26 31 October–12 November 2021 | Glasgow, UK PODCAST: Off-grid, power on; energy day at COP26, 4 November, The lid is on.* https://news.un.org/en/audio/2021/11/1104892

United Nations Environment Programme. (2021). *Emissions gap report 2021: The heat is on—A world of climate promises not yet delivered.* Nairobi.

Venkatraman, M. P. (1991). The impact of innovativeness and innovation type on adoption. *Journal of Retailing, 67*(1), 51.

Xie, B., Wang, L., Yang, H., Wang, Y., & Zhang, M. (2015). Consumer perceptions and attitudes of organic food products in Eastern China. *British Food Journal, 117*(3), 1105–1121.

Zahedi, A. (2010). Australian renewable energy progress. *Renewable and Sustainable Energy Reviews, 14*(8), 2208–2213.

Zander, K. K., Simpson, G., Mathew, S., Nepal, R., & Garnett, S. T. (2019). Preferences for and potential impacts of financial incentives to install residential rooftop solar photovoltaic systems in Australia. *Journal of Cleaner Production, 230*, 328–338.

Zeithaml, V. A. (1988). Consumer perceptions of price, quality, and value: A means-end model and synthesis of evidence. *Journal of Marketing, 52*(3), 2–22.

Chapter 3
A Behavioural Model of Urban Household Food Waste Reduction: An Empirical Study in Beijing, China

Ji Lu, Wenguang Zhang, Yanbo Xiao, and Emmanuel K. Yiridoe

Abstract China is the largest emerging market experiencing rapid growth but challenged by sustainability issues. Economic development and urbanization have tremendously improved living standards, but household food waste is becoming a growing environmental and social problem. This study explored demographic and psychological factors that influence urban household food waste. The analysis is based on food behaviour and responses from a sample of $N = 475$ primary grocery shoppers in Beijing, China. The results indicate that family income and household size are positively related to food waste, whereas education is associated with a higher intention to reduce food waste. A structural equation model reveals that attitude towards food waste, social norms, and health consciousness are positively related to the intention of reducing waste; a strong intention is associated with less food waste. The analyses further demonstrate that participants with better household food-related skills and fewer concerns over the risk of consuming leftover foods generally feel having more control over food-related activities—such perceived behavioural control links to a strong intention of reducing food waste. This study contributes to a better understanding of food waste behaviours in China. In addition to increasing environmental awareness, the findings of this study shed light on strategies and practical household issues to reduce food waste.

Keywords Food waste · China · Ethical self-identity · Household skills · Health consciousness · TPB

J. Lu (✉) · E. K. Yiridoe
Dalhousie University, Truro, Canada
e-mail: Ji.Lu@Dal.Ca

E. K. Yiridoe
e-mail: Emmanuel.Yiridoe@Dal.Ca

W. Zhang
Beijing Normal University, Beijing, China
e-mail: zhangwenguang@bnu.edu.cn

Y. Xiao
Beijing University of Chinese Medicine, Beijing, China
e-mail: bnuxiaoyanbo@163.com

© The Author(s), under exclusive license to Springer Nature Singapore Pte Ltd. 2022
N. Nguyen et al. (eds.), *Environmental Sustainability in Emerging Markets*,
Approaches to Global Sustainability, Markets, and Governance,
https://doi.org/10.1007/978-981-19-2408-8_3

3.1 Introduction

Globally, about one-third (or 1.3 billion tonnes per year) of total edible parts of food production are wasted or lost in production, distribution, and consumption (Food & Agriculture Organization of the United Nations, 2013). Food loss along the food supply chain and food wasted in consumption can result in high economic, environmental, and social costs. The cost includes wasted natural resources, such as fresh water and energy used in the production, transportation, and preparation of the wasted food (Gentil et al., 2011). In addition, while most of the food losses and waste are end up in landfills, a large amount of greenhouse gas is generated each year (Food & Agriculture Organization of the United Nations, 2013). Furthermore, a large amount of food products wasted also tends to drive up global food prices, making food less accessible and less affordable, particularly in developing economies (Kummu et al., 2012). In recognition of this importance, the United Nations set a Sustainable Development Goal of reducing global per capita food waste and food loss by 50% by 2030 (United Nations Sustainable Development Goal 12.3).

China's economic development and urbanization have tremendously improved living standards in the past decades, while further development is challenged by many environmental problems (Bai et al., 2014). To tackle these problems, China has been progressively integrating environmental sustainability into national strategic goals, by explicitly including an ecological civilization (生态文明) to guide infrastructure development and construction (Hansen et al., 2018). Other relevant initiatives include "greenization" as a component of modernization (Zhang et al., 2019), and a carbon neutral pledge (Koondhar et al., 2021). As a greener production-consumption system is important for sustainable development, food loss and waste issues are also gaining attention from governments, businesses, and consumers in China (Mak et al., 2020). In China, the most significant portion of total food loss and waste occurs in households (Liu et al., 2013). It is estimated that Chinese consumers waste between 12 and 33 kg per capita of food each year, equivalent to 33–96 kg of carbon footprint (Song et al., 2018). The food waste and food loss challenges are particularly concerning in major cities, as more than half of municipal solid waste is household food waste (Clercq et al., 2016; Gu et al., 2017). In China, 53% of municipal waste goes to landfills and 44% to incineration contributing to air pollution and greenhouse gas emissions (Zhang et al., 2018). With nearly a 1.4 billion population, China is the largest emerging economy. Reducing household food waste in China could potentially contribute to the United Nation's Sustainable Development Goals related to climate change and food security (Wang et al., 2017; Xue et al., 2017).

China's cities are growing bigger and more urbanized, and the residents becoming wealthier (Bai et al., 2014). For example, the 2020 National Population Census reports a 902 million urban population in China. This is equivalent to an urbanization rate of 63%, which tripled from the 1980s and doubled from the mid-1990s. The profound socio-economic transitions, lifestyle transformations, and dietary changes have reshaped the food supply system (Seto & Ramankutty, 2016). Meanwhile, the emerging Chinese businesses and consumers are increasingly aware of environmental sustainability issues and the impacts, such as the deteriorating air and water quality in major cities (Ministry of Ecology and Environment, 2020). As a result, Chinese enterprises and families are seeking solutions to engage in healthier and greener consumption and lifestyles (Jin et al., 2020; Xu et al., 2020). Given the importance of the food waste issue, China adopted an Anti-food Waste Law on April 29, 2021. Under this law, the state attempts to establish "a civilized, healthy, resource-saving and environmentally friendly consumption pattern, and advocates a simple, moderate, green and low carbon lifestyle" (Anti-food Waste Law of the People's Republic of China, 2021).

A solution to reducing household food waste and food loss should be based on insights from relevant consumer behavioural models that fit empirical data. However, psychosocial research on consumer food waste issues in China is limited. In the context of rapid urbanization in China, this study explores demographic and psychological factors that may influence urban household food waste. Beijing is the capital city of China with a total population of approximately 20 million people, and the average per capita annual disposable income was more than 10,000 USD (694,300 yuan) in 2020. Beijing is also one of the cultural centres and leader in the country's trends in lifestyle and consumption patterns. Thus, this study uses Beijing as a case study to better understand the psychological mechanisms behind urban households' food waste reduction behaviour in China.

3.2 Theoretical Framework and Hypotheses

The Theory of Planned Behaviour (TPB) is a widely accepted analytical framework to explain the relationship between behaviour, intention, and beliefs (Ajzen, 1992). TPB provides a psychological model to analyze behaviours and is applied to behavioural changing interventions, such as promoting healthy eating, sustainable consumption, and active lifestyle (Stefan et al., 2013). Built on the theory of reasoned action (Fishbein & Ajzen, 1977), TPB argues that behavioural intention is an essential determinant of behaviour, while the intention is influenced by a set of beliefs, including attitude towards the behaviour (behavioural beliefs), social norms (normative beliefs), and perceived behavioural control (control beliefs). Generally, a strong intention is anticipated if the attitude towards the behaviour is positive and consistent with social norms (Ajzen, 1992). TPB further argues that a favourable attitude and social approvals are not necessarily sufficient to drive strong intentions due to circumstantial constraints. Perceived behavioural control should be included as another determinant of behavioural intention. Perceived behavioural control refers to the degree to which an individual believes that they can successfully execute a given behaviour to attain a goal. The theory suggests that people are more likely to undertake a specific behaviour (e.g., quit smoking) if they feel the behaviour is, at least, not too difficult (e.g., the belief that quitting smoking is easy).

While TPB is often employed as a behavioural model in explaining food waste behaviours (e.g., Stancu et al., 2016; Stefan et al., 2013), the model is often modified to accommodate more relevant psychosocial factors. Some studies added daily routines and habits into the model as predictors of food waste reduction intention and behaviour (Ouellette & Wood, 1998). Food-related habits and routines provide a structure for families to arrange their daily activities, which may have influence food waste. In developed countries, families without a good grocery shopping routine tend to purchase more food than they can consume and generate excessive food waste (Chandon & Wansink, 2006). Recent literature further found that health beliefs may also influence food waste. For instance, consumers who have health concerns related to leftover or expired products may hesitate to use food that may still be consumable (Aschemann-Witzel et al., 2015; Visschers et al., 2016).

In the context of urban China, this study aims to use a behavioural model based on TPB to explore psychosocial factors influencing Chinese consumers' food waste reduction behaviour. According to the TPB, individuals with stronger intentions to reduce food waste tend to produce less food waste, and the intention is influenced by consumers' attitudes, social norms, and perceived behavioural control related to food waste (Stancu et al., 2016; Stefan et al., 2013). Figure 3.1 illustrates the theoretical framework, where attitudes are a general judgement on the favourability of an object, a person, or a behaviour. Consumers generally have negative attitudes

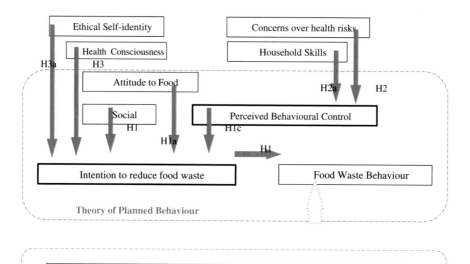

Fig. 3.1 Theoretical framework and hypotheses

towards food waste (Graham-Rowe et al., 2014; Neff et al., 2015), and such attitude is associated with the intention to avoid food waste (Leverenz et al., 2019). Social norms are shared rules or standards of behaviour that are considered acceptable in a group or society. They represent a person's beliefs of what others think one should do (Lapinski & Rimal, 2005). Social norms influence behaviour because people tend to act in socially (and morally) acceptable ways (Chung & Rimal, 2016; Schultz et al., 2018) and are associated with motivation to manage household waste responsibly.

Perceived Behavioural Control (PBC) refers to an individual's perceptions of their ability to carry out a specific behaviour (Ajzen, 1992). A high degree of perceived control reflects confidence and can reinforce the intention to perform the behaviour (Ajzen, 2002). Prior research suggests that a stronger PBC is associated with a stronger intention of minimizing food waste, and such intention can contribute to less food waste (Graham-Rowe et al., 2015; Stancu et al., 2016; Stefan et al., 2013). This study applies the TPB framework to examine how a set of psychological factors, such as attitude, social norm, and perceived behavioural control, can influence Beijing households' food waste behaviour, and such influence is mediated by the intention to reduce food waste. The related hypotheses include:

H1 Households with strong intention to reduce food waste tend to waste less food.

H1a Negative attitudes towards food waste is associated with strong intention to reduce food waste.

H1b Social norms related to food waste is associated with strong intention to reduce food waste.

H1c Perceived behavioural control is positively associated with intention to reduce food waste.

Household food waste sometimes is generated because of poor household skills, such as spoilage, lack of preparation, and food label confusion (Chu et al., 2020; Gunders et al., 2017). In addition, consumers who do not have the food-related household skills associated with planning meals and storing food tend to over-purchase food and generate more food waste (Aschemann-Witzel et al., 2017; Bell et al., 2011; Chandon & Wansink, 2006). This study conceptualizes food-related household skills as an individual's ability to perform food-provision activities, including planning, shopping, cooking, and disposing (or reusing) meals for the family. Evidence suggests that low food waste is associated with good household skills, such as planning meals ahead (Stefan et al., 2013), checking inventory and assessing food needs before shopping (Lyndhurst et al., 2007), and cooking the right amount of food for the family (Stancu et al., 2016). The behavioural model proposed in this paper further argues that household skills may impact an individual's confidence to reduce food waste. Households with poor food-provision skills may feel less confident in controlling the daily behaviours and routines and, therefore, may be unwilling to reduce food waste.

Besides household skills, prior research suggests that individuals concerned about the health risk of leftover food or packaged food close to expiration date tend to reject reusing such foods (Aschemann-Witzel et al., 2015; Visschers et al., 2016). The health risk concerns often negate the intention to reduce food waste mainly because of the food safety concerns. Consumers with significant concerns regarding food safety tend to misinterpret the meaning of "best before date" of packaged food and avoid using food product that is close to the "expiration" date (Williams et al., 2012). Households may also dispose of cooked leftover food stored for an extended period (Parizeau et al., 2015). This study argues that PBC may mediate the influence of household skills and health concerns on intention. The perceived capacity to control food waste depends on one's skill to plan the types and amount of food purchased, prepared, and consumed, and the confidence to consume stored food in case over purchase happens.

H2a Poor household skills are associated with less perceived behavioural control.

H2c Concerns over the health risk of food are associated with less perceived behavioural control.

Ethical consumption and a healthy lifestyle are two emerging consumer trends in China (Jin et al., 2020; Xu et al., 2020) that may influence one's intention to reduce food waste. Ethically conscious individuals have concerns about the impacts of human activities on the natural environment and society (Harper & Makatouni, 2002; Laroche et al., 2001). Ethical consciousness is one of the primary motivations behind socially responsible consumption and environmentally friendly product choices (Honkanen et al., 2006; McEachern & Schröder, 2002). It has been shown that some individuals' motivations to reduce food waste are rooted in environmental concerns and ethical considerations (Schmidt, 2016). A strong ethical consciousness may be considered as part of one's self-identity that represents internalized beliefs about ethical standards (Shaw et al., 2000). Such self-identity has been included as an additional factor in TPB, as beliefs regarding ethical conduct can potentially influence one's behavioural intention in a profound way. Ethical consciousness may drive the ethical consumers' food waste reduction behaviours because taking actions to reduce waste is consistent with their ethical self-identity (Shaw et al., 2000). As such, this paper hypothesizes that:

H3a Ethical consciousness is associated with a strong intention to reduce food waste.

Health consciousness indicates individuals' self-awareness about their well-being and health status (Becker et al., 1977), and is associated with a strong intention to engage in healthy lifestyle behaviours (Kraft & Goodell, 1993; Newsom et al., 2005). In food consumption, health-conscious consumers tend to favour a nutritious and balanced diet, such as fresh, natural, and organic foods (Lockie, 2002; Magnusson et al., 2003; Yiridoe et al., 2005). Previous literature has found that food-related health concerns are associated with more food waste (Barone et al., 2019; Farr-Wharton et al., 2014). Because a healthy diet relies on diversified, fresh, and perishable food products, it brings logistic challenges to everyday food preparation and links to more food waste:

H3b Health consciousness is negatively associated with the intention of food waste reduction.

The present study primarily aims to explore psychosocial factors influencing food waste reduction behaviour. Besides describing a psychological mechanism behind food waste reduction, this study also explores demographic factors, such as family structure and socio-economic status, that may associate with food waste reduction intention and behaviour.

3.3 Method

3.3.1 Participants and Procedure

Primary data for this study was obtained from an online survey coordinated by Wenjuanxing (wjx.cn), one of China's largest online survey platforms. The study participants were recruited through sampling service provided by Wenjuanxing. This online recruitment platform offered quick and reliable access to a representative sample with specific inclusion criteria for this study. Specifically, participants were randomly selected from a representative consumer panel managed by Wenjuanxing. The study required that participants must currently live in urban and suburban areas of Beijing and be the primary grocery shopper for their households. The first part of the survey included an information letter outlining the purpose of the study, procedure, and potential risks. In the following part, a question asked participants to indicate how often they do grocery shopping for their family (coded 1–7 representing never to 100% of the time). Among the 534 participants who completed the questionnaire, 43 respondents indicated that their answer is less than 50% of the time. Therefore, the data for these participants were excluded from further analyses. In another question asking for the location of their residence, 16 of the remaining participants indicated that they lived in rural areas of Beijing. After removing these responses, further analyses were based on data from 475 participants. The survey was completed in July 2021.

The second part of the questionnaire collected information regarding a set of demographic variables, including age, gender, socio-economic status, and family structure (see Table 3.1 for a detailed demographic profile of the sample).

3.3.2 Measurements

The third part of the questionnaire included questions to measure psychological constructs and behaviour related to household food waste. Food waste behaviour was measured using a 5-item scale to ask participants to recall the percentage of

Table 3.1 Demographic characteristics of participants

Variable	Options	Frequency	per cent
Gender	Male	185	38.9
	Female	290	61.1
Location	Urban	427	89.9
	Suburban	48	10.1
Education	Elementary	1	0.2
	Secondary	5	1.1
	Vocational Training	23	4.8
	Undergraduate	377	79.4
	Graduate	69	14.5
Family Income	<¥100 k	51	10.7
	¥100 k–200 k	137	28.8
	¥200 k–300 k	141	29.7
	¥300 k–400 k	73	15.4
	¥400 k–500 k	38	8
	¥500 k–600 k	8	1.7
	¥600 k–700 k	10	2.1
	¥700 k–800 k	2	0.4
	¥800 k–900 k	4	0.8
	¥900 k–1 million	5	1.1
	>¥1 million	6	1.3
Family Living Situation (Select all that applies)	Alone	54	11.4
	with Spouse/common law	316	66.5
	with Children	223	46.9
	with Parents	149	31.4
Age		Mean = 32.05	SD = 8.76
Family size (# of people in a household)		Mean = 3.17	SD = 1.07
Frequency of grocery shopping for family (1 never—7 100% of the time)		Mean = 5.99	SD = 0.99

food wasted in the previous week. Each question covered one of four food categories (milk and dairy products, fresh fruits and vegetables, meat and fish, and cereal/grain products) and total food waste (Stancu et al., 2016; Stefan et al., 2013). The estimation of food waste was used as an indicator of food waste behaviour. The intention to reduce food waste was measured by a single-item scale (Stancu et al., 2016). All other constructs were measured in multiple-item scales and based on prior literature. Most of the items were coded on a seven-point Likert scale (1: strongly disagree and 7: strongly agree). See Table 3.2 for a complete list of items. Other questions elicited

3 A Behavioural Model of Urban Household Food Waste …

Table 3.2 Confirmatory factor analysis results ($n = 475$)

Factors and items	Factor loadings	AVE*	Cronbach's Alpha
Ethical self-identity		0.53	0.68
I think of myself as someone who is concerned about ethical issues	0.67		
I think of myself as an ethical consumer	0.78		
Household skills		0.39	0.75
Planning the meals	0.69		
Planning the shopping (making shopping lists, checking inventories, etc.)	0.65		
Buying the right food in right amounts to prepare the meals and for household consumption in general	0.68		
Cooking/preparing the food	0.57		
Storing and reusing leftover food	0.53		
Scale: very poor (1) to very good (7)			
Health consciousness		0.42	0.81
I reflect about my health a lot	0.68		
I am very self-conscious about my health	0.73		
I am alert to changes in my health	0.56		
I am usually aware of my health	0.65		
I take responsibility for the state of my health	0.67		
I am aware of the state of my health as I go through the day	0.59		
Perceived behavioural control		0.46	0.64
It is very difficult for me to predict exactly how much food is going to be eaten in my household over a regular week (this item was reversed for analyses)	0.33		
I am able to cook and prepare exactly the amount of food that my household needs	0.78		
I am able to buy exactly the amount of food that my household needs	0.81		
Social norms		0.55	0.78
Make me feel guilty about people who do not have enough food	0.73		
Make me feel guilty about the environment	0.76		
Give me a bad conscience	0.74		
Concerns over possible health risks		0.48	0.72
I believe that the risk of becoming ill as a result of eating food past its use-by date is high	0.70		

(continued)

Table 3.2 (continued)

Factors and items	Factor loadings	AVE*	Cronbach's Alpha
I believe that one can't safely eat food products whose use-by dates expired a few days ago	0.69		
I am worried that eating leftovers results in adverse health effects	0.68		
Attitude towards food waste		0.29	0.61
Wasting food is negative	0.61		
Wasting food is not right	0.61		
Unconsumed food should be reused to avoid waste	0.55		
Wasting food is harmful to the environment	0.36		

All scales (except household skills): strongly disagree (1) to strongly agree (7)
Goodness-of-fit: chi-sq = 475.79, df = 194, $p < 0.001$, CFI = 0.92, RMSEA = 0.06
*AVE: Average Variance Extracted

information used to measure Theory of Planned Behaviour concepts, including attitude towards food waste, social norms, and perceived behavioural control (Ajzen, 1992; Stancu et al., 2016; Stefan et al., 2013). Household skills were measured on a 5-item scale that asks participants to assess their skills in shopping, planning, preparing, and storing food (Stefan et al., 2013). Measurement of concerns with the health risk of leftover food asked participants about their health beliefs regarding leftover and expired food (Visschers et al., 2016). Ethical consumption was measured by ethical self-identity, i.e., a pertinent part of an individual's self that is related to environmentally and socially responsible consumption behaviours (Shaw & Shiu, 2003; Shaw et al., 2000). Health consciousness was measured using a scale that asks participants' self-awareness and vigilance to their health status (Gould, 1988).

3.4   Results

A descriptive analysis of the sample (see Table 3.1) indicated that most of the participants were well-educated (94% with undergraduate education or higher), women (61%), living in an urban area (90%) in a household with child(ren) (47%) and spouse (67%). The average family size is slightly over 3 (SD = 0.99), typical for urban Chinese households. In addition, a large percentage of participants (31%) live in a household with their parents, which is not uncommon for families living in major cities (three-generation families).

A confirmatory factor analysis (CFA) was conducted to test the measurements of attitude, social norms, perceived behavioural control, household skills, risk concerns, ethical self-identity, and health consciousness. The goodness-of-fit of the CFA model was acceptable (CFI = 0.92; RMSEA = 0.06). The estimated factor loadings for items for their respective factors were higher than 0.50, except for one item related to PBC. The factor loading of this item was also found lower than 0.50 in another study (Stefan et al., 2013). All measurements' reliability (Cronbach's Alpha) was acceptable or slightly below 0.70 (see Table 3.2). Table 3.3 lists the means and standard deviations of the measurements and correlations between them. The correlation coefficients of most pairs of measurements are significant with moderate ($r > 0.3$) to strong ($r > 0.5$) associations. This result suggests that the convergent validity of the measurements is acceptable. The Average Variance Extracted (AVE) for each measurement is listed in Table 3.2. The discriminant validity is acceptable as indicated by the relatively higher square root of the AVE (the smallest AVE is 0.54) compared to the correlation among variables.

A structural equation model was used to test the hypotheses (CFI $= 0.98$; R MSEA $= 0.07$; see Table 3.4 for the model specification and estimations). Endogenous variables investigated include self-reported percentage of food wasted (FW behaviour), intention to reduce food waste (intention), and perceived behavioural control (PBC). The intention and PBC were specified as two of the predictors for the FW behaviour. Furthermore, to test the mediating effect of intention, a path from PBC to intention was specified. The model included a set of psychological and demographic variables, and all these variables were specified to predict both intention and FW behaviour. The psychological factors included attitude towards food waste, social norms, ethical self-identity, health consciousness, concerns over possible health risks, and household skills. Demographic variables investigated included age, gender, education level, family income, location (urban vs. suburban), family size, number of children in the household, and the presence of parent(s)/grandparent(s). The PBC model also included two predictors of PBC, namely, concerns over health risks and household skills.

The results reveal a clear pattern that psychological factors and demographic factors influence food waste behaviour mainly mediated by the intention to reduce food waste (see Fig. 3.2). The estimated parameters indicate that participants who had stronger intention tended to waste less food ($b = -4.10$, SE $= 1.30$, $p < 0.001$). The PBC did not have a significant direct effect on the FW behaviour ($p > 0.1$). None of the psychological factors directly affected the FW behaviour ($p > 0.13$).

A set of psychological factors predicted the intention to reduce food waste. The attitude was significantly associated with increased intention to reduce food waste ($b = 0.17$, SE $= 0.08$, $p = 0.03$). Participants with higher PBC tended to have stronger intention ($b = 0.17$, SE $= 0.06$, $p < 0.001$). Social norm was also a significant positive predictor of intention ($b = 0.31$, SE $= 0.06$, $p < 0.001$). Participants with higher health consciousness were more likely to report higher intention ($b = 0.15$, SE $= 0.07$, $p = 0.04$).

The results also reveal that PBC mediates the effect of some psychological factors on intention to reduce food waste. PBC was significantly predicted by household skills and concerns over possible health risks. Participants with better household skills generally reported higher PBC ($b = 0.69$, SE $= 0.05$, $p < 0.001$), while

Table 3.3 Correlations between major psychological measurements

		Mean	S.D	1	2	3	4	5	6	7	8
1.	Food waste (%)	27.61	28.39								
2.	Intention to reduce waste	6.11	1.15	−0.15*							
3.	Attitude to food waste	5.81	0.76	−0.02	0.36*						
4..	Social Norm	5.75	1.00	−0.07	0.44*	0.55*					
5.	PBC	4.63	1.10	−0.08	0.32*	0.25*	0.27*				
6.	Household skills	5.17	0.92	0.03	0.29*	0.36*	0.32*	0.57*			
7.	Risk Concerns	5.50	1.13	0.05	0.05	0.16*	0.07	−0.09*	0.03		
8.	Health consciousness	5.68	0.95	0.02	0.28*	0.42*	0.44*	0.31*	0.43*	0.15*	
9.	Ethical self-identity	5.56	0.83	0.03	0.31*	0.36*	0.36*	0.40*	0.48*	0.23*	0.51*

*Correlation is significant at 0.01 level

PBC: Perceived behavioural control

3 A Behavioural Model of Urban Household Food Waste …

Table 3.4 Structural equation model results

Endogenous variables	Predictors	Parameter estimate	S.E	P
Food Waste Behaviour	Intention	−4.10	1.30	<0.01
	Attitude	0.36	2.14	0.87
	Social Norm	−0.85	1.65	0.61
	PBC	−2.16	1.43	0.13
	Risk Concerns	0.63	1.19	0.59
	Household Skills	3.02	1.94	0.12
	Ethical Self-identity	0.56	1.72	0.74
	Health Consciousness	2.70	1.97	0.17
	Gender	2.55	2.62	0.33
	Age	−0.16	0.16	0.30
	Education	−2.47	2.68	0.36
	Family Income	−0.30	0.74	0.69
	Family Size	3.46	1.52	0.02
	Children @ home (Y/N)	−4.13	3.07	0.18
	Parents @ home (Y/N)	−2.11	3.48	0.54
	Location (urban vs. sub)	4.65	4.35	0.29
Intention to reduce food waste (Intention)	Attitude	0.17	0.08	0.03
	Social Norm	0.31	0.06	<0.001
	PBC	0.17	0.05	<0.001
	Risk Concerns	0.01	0.04	0.88
	Household Skills	0.06	0.07	0.36
	Ethical Self-identity	0.02	0.06	0.76
	Health Consciousness	0.15	0.07	0.04
	Gender	0.07	0.09	0.48
	Age	0.00	0.01	0.42
	Education	0.20	0.10	0.03
	Family Income	−0.07	0.03	0.01
	Family Size	−0.04	0.05	0.47
	Children @ home (Y/N)	−0.16	0.11	0.15
	Parents @ home (Y/N)	0.01	0.12	0.95
	Location (urban vs. sub)	0.06	0.15	0.69
Perceived Behavioural Control (PBC)	Risk Concerns	−0.11	0.04	<0.01
	Household Skills	0.69	0.05	<0.001

Goodness-of-fit: chi-sq $= 41.99$, df $= 12$, $p < 0.001$, CFI $= 0.98$, RMSEA $= 0.07$

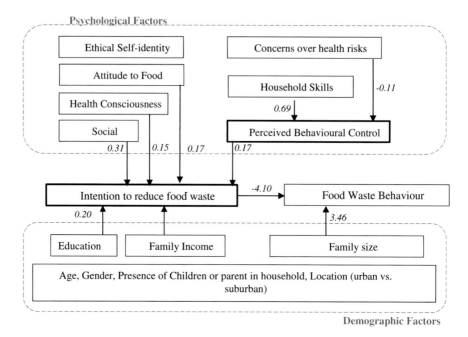

Fig. 3.2 Highlighted results of structural equation mode (*Note* • Only significant [$p < 0.05$] direct effect is presented in this figure. The numbers on lines indicate the estimated parameter coefficients [unstandardized]. • In the model presented in this paper [see Table 3.4], all psychological factors and demographic factors were included to predict both the Intention to reduce food waste and the Food waste behaviour)

respondents who were concerned over health risks had lower PBC ($b = -0.11$, SE $= 0.04$, $p < 0.01$). None of these two predictors of PBC had a significant direct effect on intention or FW behaviour.

In terms of demographic variables, only family income and education level were significant in predicting (direct effect) the intention to reduce food waste. Participants' education level was positively associated with intention; participants with higher education levels tended to report stronger intention to reduce food waste ($b = 0.20$, SE $= 0.10$, $p = 0.03$). In addition, families with lower income tended to have a stronger intention to reduce food waste than higher-income families ($b = -0.07$, SE $= 0.03$, $p = 0.01$). None of the demographic variables, except family size, had a significant direct effect on FW behaviour ($p > 0.5$). Family size was a positive predictor of FW behaviour ($b = 3.46$, SE $= 1.52$, $p = 0.02$), indicating that larger families tended to waste a larger percentage of food. Figures 3.3, 3.4, and 3.5 further demonstrates how food waste and intention of reduction are associated with family size, income, and education. Figures 3.3 and 3.4 show that the intention of reducing waste increased with education level and decreased with family income. Table 3.5 further highlights that education was positively correlated with intention to reduce, attitude, and social norm ($p < 0.01$).

3 A Behavioural Model of Urban Household Food Waste … 61

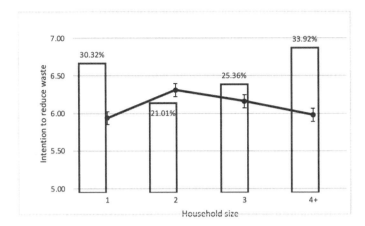

Fig. 3.3 Household waste (Colum with %) and intention to reduce waste (line with markers), according to household size (i.e., number of household members) (*Note* Columns indicate percentages of food wasted as reported by the participants. Line and markers indicate the intention to reduce food waste [anchored 1–7])

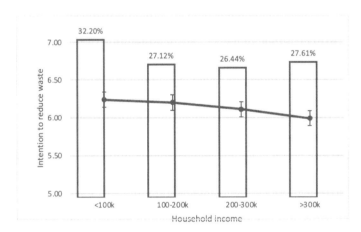

Fig. 3.4 Household waste (Colum with %) and intention to reduce waste (line with markers) separated for household income (in Chinese Yuan) (*Note* Columns indicate reported percentages of food wasted. Line and markers indicate the intention to reduce food waste [anchored 1–7])

3.5 Discussion

This study investigated food waste behaviour for a sample of Beijing urban households. On average, the participants reported that they discarded 28% of all purchased foods. This estimation is consistent with a recent study in a south China metropolitan city (Zhang et al., 2018), in which 46% of the participants reported 10–30% food waste, and 31% participants reported 30–50% waste. In this study, the number of

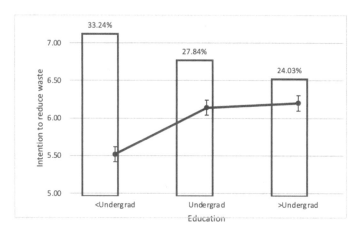

Fig. 3.5 Household waste (Colum with %) and intention to reduce waste (line with markers) according to education level (*Note* Columns indicate the percentages of food being wasted reported by the participants. Line and markers indicate the intention to reduce food waste [anchored 1–7])

Table 3.5 Correlations between psychological and demographic measurements

	Age	Education	Income	Family size
Food waste (%)	−0.05	−0.07	0.00	0.12*
Intention to reduce waste	−0.03	0.13*	−0.07	−0.07
Attitude to food waste	0.03	0.15*	0.08	0.07
Social Norm	0.03	0.10*	0.02	−0.04
PBC	0.11*	0.06	0.07	−0.02
Household skills	0.10*	0.08	0.17*	0.07
Risk Concerns	−0.07	−0.03	0.03	0.04
Health consciousness	0.03	0.02	0.09	0.13*
Ethical self-identity	0.04	0.10*	0.14*	0.08
Age		−0.08	0.04	−0.03
Education			0.24*	−0.03
Income				0.13*

*Correlation is significant at 0.01 level
PBC: Perceived behavioural control

family members is positively associated with food waste. A similar pattern was found in a Finland study (Koivupuro et al., 2012) where family size was consistently associated with the amount of household food waste. In some prior research in European and North American countries, the age and gender of primary household shoppers are associated with food waste; young and female shoppers tend to generate more waste (e.g., Koivupuro et al., 2012; Lee & Willis, 2010; Schneider & Obersteiner, 2007), while this study did not find such pattern among Beijing shoppers. This study identified some demographic factors influencing food waste behaviour but mediated by the intention of reduction. Family income is found to be negatively associated with motivation to reduce food waste. This is in line with studies in developed countries which found that financial considerations tend to decrease food waste (e.g., Aschemann-Witzel et al., 2017; Barone et al., 2019; Setti et al., 2018). The education level of primary grocery shoppers of the households is found to positively contribute to the motivation of reducing food waste, which is probably driven by attitude and perceived social norm regarding food waste, as these are associated with education (see Table 3.5).

This study also examined how psychological factors influence household intention and behaviour related to food waste. The results depict a psychological mechanism that is clearly consistent with the TPB framework, similar to studies in developed countries (e.g., Stefan et al., 2013). The results show that the effect of intention not to waste food on behaviour was significant, and attitudes, social norms, and perceived behavioural control were significant predictors of intention. It is noteworthy that the structural equation model reveals a pattern that supports a complete mediation through the intention. Most of the prior studies reveal some direct effects of attitude, social norms, and PBC on food waste behaviour (e.g., Stancu et al., 2016; Russell et al., 2017), while this study finds that the direct effects of all psychological factors on behaviour were not significant.

Prior research shows that poor food preparation and storage skills and health concerns over leftover food may cause more food waste in household consumption (e.g., Aschemann-Witzel et al., 2017; Barone et al., 2019; Farr-Wharton et al., 2014; Parizeau et al., 2015). This study found that such an effect of household skills and concerns is mediated by perceived behavioural control. Individuals with a strong sense of control tend to reduce household food waste, and household skills and risk concerns influence the perceived control. In this study, individuals with poor household skills or those who worry about the health risk of leftover/expiring food are more likely to have a strong sense of control over the waste reduction practice at home.

The study finds that health consciousness is positively associated with the intention to avoid food waste. This result contrasts with prior research conducted in Europe (Barone et al., 2019), in which healthy eating conflicts with the reduction of food waste. Barone et al. (2019) argued that healthy food, such as fresh produce, generally has a short shelf life and challenges the effort to save food (Aschemann-Witzel, 2015; Conrad et al., 2018). The contrasting pattern found in Beijing is probably because the grocery shopping habit among the respondents in China is different from European countries. Chinese diet heavily relies on leafy vegetables and plant-based protein (Batis et al., 2014). As Chinese households are well-adapted to preparing, storing, and consuming such healthy food for generations, a health-conscious diet does not necessarily impose extra logistic challenges to reduce waste. Furthermore, online grocery shopping in China (32.5% of total grocery expenditure in 2018) is more prevalent than in Europe and North America (5–7% of total grocery expenditure) (Van Ewijk et al., 2020). Since online food distribution is associated with greater convenience and accessibility of healthy foods (Maimaiti et al., 2018), health-conscious consumers in China may not find barriers to avoiding food waste as European consumers do.

Tackling food loss and waste issues is important for global sustainable development. This study has implications specifically for the food waste issues in emerging economies. Some psychosocial factors explored in this study indicate that food waste may be a growing problem with economic development and urbanization. First, the intention to reduce food waste declines with increasing household income. Economic growth in developing countries may bring higher income and better quality of life to families, but at the same time, bring more challenges to the ever-growing food waste problem. Second, declining household skills among young generations is another phenomenon observed in developing countries, while the lack of household skills is associated with less intention to reduce food waste (mediated by the perceived behavioural control). In the same token, the food safety concerns related to leftover food typically grow with family income, while the health risk concern is another factor associated with a decreased intention to save food.

Businesses in China face policy ambiguity, cultural challenges, and financial barriers to implement strategies to take environmental responsibilities (Liu et al., 2021). It is proposed that the lack of awareness of environmental protection is one of the barriers to waste reduction and reuse (Zhang et al., 2019), and this is consistent with the results of the study that changing attitude and social norm would be a viable strategy to encourage saving food. Studies suggest that increasing awareness and knowledge regarding the negative consequences of food waste may be one of the keys to reducing household waste. Consumers with environmental protection awareness and knowledge generally have strong intentions to avoid food spoilage and engage in food-saving behaviours (Schmidt, 2016). Furthermore, the study highlights a set of variables related to practical barriers to food waste reduction, such as poor household skills, less confidence in consuming expiring food, and financial considerations. Meanwhile, this study found that a relatively more ideological consideration, ethical self-identity, has no impact on household food waste. This finding suggests that besides ecological education, alternative strategies may also help Chinese consumers avoid food waste. For example, food retailers can offer smart tools to help consumers plan meals, teach appropriate storage methods, and provide more useful expiration date labels.

3.6 Conclusions and Future Research

China is the largest emerging market in the world. Food loss and waste are sustainability issues and connect to food security problems. The Chinese government has legislated anti-food waste as part of its national development policy, and businesses and consumers are eager to find solutions to reduce food waste. The primary contribution of this study is to understand the psychosocial mechanism of food waste reduction behaviour. Specifically situated in China, the behavioural model and empirical data are among the first attempts to take a holistic view analyzing the psychological barriers to reducing food waste. Moving beyond the theory of planned behaviour, this study identified household skills and food safety concerns as factors influencing urban Chinese families' intention to reduce food waste. These findings shed light on public policy and intervention strategy.

The study is based on a sample of Beijing households, whereas China is a large country with significant social, cultural, and economic differences among its 687 cities (in 2020). Also, the sample of this study is recruited from an online survey platform, which may have bias to certain demographic groups who are well-educated and have convenient access to the internet. Further study may benefit from exploring more demographic groups, geographic areas, and cities of various sizes. Furthermore, the measurement of food waste behaviour is based on self-reporting, while more objective measurements would reveal a more accurate estimation. Finally, smart technology, social media, and online food delivery platforms are rapidly changing China's food supply system (Si & Scott, 2019). Further study needs to take an analytical approach to investigate the impacts of these innovations on household food waste.

References

Ajzen, I. (1992). A comparison of the theory of planned behavior and the theory of reasoned action. *Personality and Social Psychology Bulletin, 18*, 3–9.

Ajzen, I. (2002). Perceived behavioral control, self-efficacy, locus of control, and the theory of planned behavior. *Journal of Applied Social Psychology, 32*(4), 665–683.

Aschemann-Witzel, J. (2015). Consumer perception and trends about health and sustainability: Trade-offs and synergies of two pivotal issues. *Current Opinion in Food Science, 3*, 6–10.

Aschemann-Witzel, J., Hooge, I. D., Amani, P., Bech-Larsen, T., & Oostindjer, M. (2015). Consumer-related food waste: Causes and potential for action. *Sustainability, 7*(6), 6457–6477.

Aschemann-Witzel, J., Jensen, J. H., Jensen, M. H., & Kulikovskaja, V. (2017). Consumer behaviour towards price-reduced suboptimal foods in the supermarket and the relation to food waste in households. *Appetite, 116*, 246–258.

Bai, X., Shi, P., & Liu, Y. (2014). Society: Realizing China's urban dream. *Nature News, 509*(7499), 158.

Barone, A. M., Grappi, S., & Romani, S. (2019, June). "The road to food waste is paved with good intentions": When consumers' goals inhibit the minimization of household food waste. *Resources, Conservation and Recycling, 149*, 97–105.

Batis, C., Sotres-Alvarez, D., Gordon-Larsen, P., Mendez, M. A., Adair, L., & Popkin, B. (2014). Longitudinal analysis of dietary patterns in Chinese adults from 1991 to 2009. *British Journal of Nutrition, 111*(8), 1441–1451.

Becker, M. H., Maiman, L. A., Kirscht, J. P., Haefner, D. P., & Drachman, R. H. (1977). The health belief model and prediction of dietary compliance: A field experiment. *Journal of Health and Social Behavior, 18*, 348–366.

Bell, D. R., Corsten, D., & Knox, G. (2011). From point of purchase to path to purchase: How preshopping factors drive unplanned buying. *Journal of Marketing, 75*(1), 31–45.

Chandon, P., & Wansink, B. (2006). How biased household inventory estimates distort shopping and storage decisions. *Journal of Marketing, 70*(4), 118–135.

Chu, W., Williams, H., Verghese, K., Wever, R., & Glad, W. (2020). Tensions and opportunities: An activity theory perspective on date and storage label design through a literature review and co-creation sessions. *Sustainability, 12*(3), 1–40.

Chung, A., & Rimal, R. N. (2016). Social norms: A review. *Review of Communication Research, 4*, 1–29.

Clercq, D. D., Wen, Z., Fan, F., & Caicedo, L. (2016). Biomethane production potential from restaurant food waste in megacities and project level-bottlenecks: A case study in Beijing. *Renewable and Sustainable Energy Reviews, 59*, 1676–1685.

Conrad, Z., Niles, M. T., Neher, D. A., Roy, E. D., Tichenor, N. E., & Jahns, L. (2018). Relationship between food waste, diet quality, and environmental sustainability. *PLoS One, 13*(4), e0195405.

Farr-Wharton, G., Foth, M., & Choi, J. H. (2014). Identifying factors that promote consumer behaviours causing expired domestic food waste. *Journal of Consumer Behaviour, 13*(6), 393–402.

Fishbein, M., & Ajzen, I. (1977). Belief, attitude, intention, and behaviour: An introduction to theory and research. *Philosophy and Rhetoric, 10*(2), 177–188.

Food & Agriculture Organization of the United Nations. (2013). *Food wastage footprint: Impacts on natural resources: Summary report.* https://www.fao.org/3/i3347e/i3347e.pdf. Retrieved November 2021.

Gentil, E. C., Gallo, D., & Christensen, T. H. (2011). Environmental evaluation of municipal waste prevention. *Waste Management, 31*(12), 2371–2379.

Gould, S. J. (1988). Consumer attitudes and health and health care: A differential perspective. *The Journal of Consumer Affairs, 22*(1), 96–118.

Graham-Rowe, E., Jessop, D. C., & Sparks, P. (2014). Identifying motivations and barriers to minimizing household food waste. *Resources, Conservation and Recycling, 84*, 15–23.

Graham-Rowe, E., Jessop, D. C., & Sparks, P. (2015). Predicting household food waste reduction using an extended theory of planned behaviour. *Resources, Conservation and Recycling, 101*, 194–202.

Gu, B., Fujiwara, T., Jia, R., Duan, R., & Gu, A. (2017). Methodological aspects of modeling household solid waste generation in Japan: Evidence from Okayama and Otsu cities. *Waste Management & Research: The Journal for a Sustainable Circular Economy, 35*(12), 1237–1246.

Gunders, D., Bloom, J., & Natural Resources Defense Council, issuing body. (2017). *Wasted: How America is losing up to 40 percent of its food from farm to fork to landfill* (2nd ed.). Natural Resources Defense Council.

Hansen, M. H., Li, H., & Svarverud, R. (2018). Ecological civilization: Interpreting the Chinese past, projecting the global future. *Global Environmental Change, 53*, 195–203.

Harper, G. C., & Makatouni, A. (2002). Consumer perception of organic food production and farm animal welfare. *British Food Journal, 104*(3/4/5), 287–299.

Honkanen, P., Verplanken, B., & Olsen, S. O. (2006). Ethical values and motives driving organic food choice. *Journal of Consumer Behaviour, 5*(5), 420–430.

Jin, H., Lin, Z., & McLeay, F. (2020). Negative emotions, positive actions: Food safety and consumer intentions to purchase ethical food in China. *Food Quality and Preference, 85*, 103981.

Koivupuro, H. K., Hartikainen, H., Silvennoinen, K., Katajajuuri, J. M., Heikintalo, N., Reinikainen, A., & Jalkanen, L. (2012). Influence of socio-demographical, behavioural and attitudinal factors on the amount of avoidable food waste generated in Finnish households. *International Journal of Consumer Studies, 36*(2), 183–191.

Koondhar, M. A., Tan, Z., Alam, G. M., Khan, Z. A., Wang, L., & Kong, R. (2021). Bioenergy consumption, carbon emissions, and agricultural bioeconomic growth: A systematic approach to carbon neutrality in China. *Journal of Environmental Management, 296*, 113–242.

Kraft, F. B., & Goodell, P. W. (1993). Identifying the health conscious consumer. *Journal of Health Care Marketing, 13*(3), 18–25.

Kummu, M., De Moel, H., Porkka, M., Siebert, S., Varis, O., & Ward, P. J. (2012). Lost food, wasted resources: Global food supply chain losses and their impacts on freshwater, cropland, and fertiliser use. *Science of the Total Environment, 438*, 477–489.

Lapinski, M. K., & Rimal, R. N. (2005). An explication of social norms. *Communication Theory, 15*(2), 127–147.

Laroche, M., Bergeron, J., & Barbaro-Forleo, G. (2001). Targeting consumers who are willing to pay more for environmentally friendly products. *Journal of Consumer Marketing, 18*(6), 503–520.

Lee, P., & Willis, P. (2010). *Waste arisings in the supply of food and drink to households in the UK*. Waste & Resources Action Programme (WRAP), Oakdene Hollins Research and Consulting. https://www.oakdenehollins.com/reports/2010/3/1/waste-arisings-in-the-supply-of-food-and-drink-to-households-in-the-uk. Accessed November 2021.

Leverenz, D., Moussawel, S., Maurer, C., Hafner, G., Schneider, F., Schmidt, T., & Kranert, M. (2019). Quantifying the prevention potential of avoidable food waste in households using a self-reporting approach. *Resources, Conservation and Recycling, 150*, 1–10.

Liu, G., Liu, X., & Cheng, S. (2013). Food security: Curb China's rising food wastage. *Nature (London), 498*(7453), 170–170.

Liu, Y., Wood, L. C., Venkatesh, V. G., Zhang, A., & Farooque, M. (2021). Barriers to sustainable food consumption and production in China: A fuzzy DEMATEL analysis from a circular economy perspective. *Sustainable Production and Consumption, 28*, 1114–1129.

Lockie, S. (2002). 'The invisible mouth': Mobilizing 'the consumer' in food production-consumption networks. *Sociologia Ruralis, 42*(4), 278–294.

Lyndhurst, B., Cox, J., & Downing, P. (2007). *Food behaviour consumer research: Quantitative phase*. Waste & Resources Action Programme (WRAP). https://wrap.org.uk/resources/report/food-behaviour-consumer-research-quantitative-phase. Accessed November 2021.

Magnusson, M. K., Arvolaa, A., Hurstia, U. K., Abergb, L., & Sjödén, P. (2003). Choice of organic foods is related to perceived consequences for human health and to environmentally friendly behaviour. *Appetite, 40*(2), 109–117.

Maimaiti, M., Zhao, X., Jia, M., Ru, Y., & Zhu, S. (2018). How we eat determines what we become: Opportunities and challenges brought by food delivery industry in a changing world in China. *European Journal of Clinical Nutrition, 72*(9), 1282–1286.

Mak, T. M., Xiong, X., Tsang, D. C., Iris, K. M., & Poon, C. S. (2020). Sustainable food waste management towards circular bioeconomy: Policy review, limitations and opportunities. *Bioresource Technology, 297*, 122497.

McEachern, M. G., & Schröder, M. J. A. (2002). The role of livestock production ethics in consumer values towards meat. *Journal of Agricultural and Environmental Ethics, 15*(2), 221–237.

Ministry of Ecology and Environment, The People's Republic of China. (2020). *Report on the state of the ecology and environment in China 2019*.

Neff, R., Spiker, M., & Truant, P. (2015). Wasted Food: U.S. consumers' reported awareness, attitudes, and behaviors. *PloS One, 10*(6), E0127881.

Newsom, J. T., McFarlandb, B. H., Kaplanc, M. S., Huguetc, N., & Zani, B. (2005). The health consciousness myth: Implications of the near independence of major health behaviours in the North American population. *Social Science & Medicine, 60*(2), 433–437.

Ouellette, J. A., & Wood, W. (1998). Habit and intention in everyday life: The multiple processes by which past behaviour predicts future behaviour. *Psychological Bulletin, 124*(1), 54.

Parizeau, K., von Massow, M., & Martin, R. (2015). Household-level dynamics of food waste production and related beliefs, attitudes, and behaviours in Guelph, Ontario. *Waste Management, 35*, 207–217.

People's Republic of China. (2021). Anti-food Waste Law of the People's Republic of China. Adopted at the 28th session of the Standing Committee of the Thirteenth National People's Congress of the People's Republic of China on April 29, 2021.

Russell, S. V., Younga, C. W., Unswortha, K. L., & Robinson, C. (2017). Bringing habits and emotions into food waste behaviour. *Resources, Conservation and Recycling, 125*, 107–114.

Schmidt, K. (2016). Explaining and promoting household food waste-prevention by an environmental psychological based intervention study. *Resources, Conservation and Recycling, 111*, 53–66.

Schneider, F., & Obersteiner, G. (2007). Food waste in residual waste of households—Regional and socio-economic differences. *Proceedings of the Eleventh International Waste Management and Landfill Symposium, Sardinia, Italy, 2007*, 469–470.

Schultz, P. W., Nolan, J. M., Cialdini, R. B., Goldstein, N. J., & Griskevicius, V. (2018). The constructive, destructive, and reconstructive power of social norms: Reprise. *Perspectives on Psychological Science, 13*(2), 249–254.

Seto, K. C., & Ramankutty, N. (2016). Hidden linkages between urbanization and food systems. *Science, 352*(6288), 943–945.

Setti, M., Banchelli, F., Falasconi, L., Segre, A., & Vittuari, M. (2018). Consumers' food cycle and household waste: When behaviors matter. *Journal of Cleaner Production, 185*, 694–706.

Shaw, D., & Shiu, E. (2003). Ethics in consumer choice: A multivariate modelling approach. *European Journal of Marketing, 37*(10), 1485–1498.

Shaw, D., Shiu, E., & Clarke, I. (2000). The contribution of ethical obligation and self-identity to the theory of planned behaviour: An exploration of ethical consumers. *Journal of Marketing Management, 16*(8), 879–894.

Si, Z., & Scott, S. (2019). China's changing food system: Top-down and bottom-up forces in food system transformations. *Canadian Journal of Development Studies, 40*(1), 1–11.

Song, G., Semakula, H. M., & Fullana-i-Palmer, P. (2018). Chinese household food waste and its' climatic burden driven by urbanization: A Bayesian Belief Network modelling for reduction possibilities in the context of global efforts. *Journal of Cleaner Production, 202*, 916–924.

Stancu, V., Haugaard, P., & Lähteenmäki, L. (2016). Determinants of consumer food waste behaviour: Two routes to food waste. *Appetite, 96*, 7–17.

Stefan, V., van Herpen, E., Tudoran, A. A., & Lähteenmäki, L. (2013). Avoiding food waste by Romanian consumers: The importance of planning and shopping routines. *Food Quality and Preference, 28*(1), 375–381.

Van Ewijk, B. J., Steenkamp, J. B. E., & Gijsbrechts, E. (2020). The rise of online grocery shopping in China: Which brands will benefit? *Journal of International Marketing, 28*(2), 20–39.

Visschers, V. H. M., Wickli, N., & Siegrist, M. (2016). Sorting out food waste behaviour: A survey on the motivators and barriers of self-reported amounts of food waste in households. *Journal of Environmental Psychology, 45*, 66–78.

Wang, L. E., Liu, G., Liu, X., Liu, Y., Gao, J., Zhou, B., & Cheng, S. (2017). The weight of unfinished plate: A survey based characterization of restaurant food waste in Chinese cities. *Waste Management, 66*, 3–12.

Williams, H., Wikström, F., Otterbring, T., Löfgren, M., & Gustafsson, A. (2012). Reasons for household food waste with special attention to packaging. *Journal of Cleaner Production, 24*, 141–148.

Xu, X., Wang, S., & Yu, Y. (2020). Consumer's intention to purchase green furniture: Do health consciousness and environmental awareness matter? *Science of the Total Environment, 704*, 135275.

Xue, L., Liu, G., Parfitt, J., Liu, X., Van Herpen, E., Stenmarck, Å., O'Connor, C., Östergren, K., & Cheng, S. (2017). Missing food, missing data? A critical review of global food losses and food waste data. *Environmental Science & Technology, 51*(12), 6618–6633.

Yiridoe, E. K., Bonti-Ankomah, S., & Martin, R. C. (2005). Comparison of consumer perceptions and preference toward organic versus conventionally produced foods: A review and update of the literature. *Renewable Agriculture and Food Systems, 20*(4), 193–205.

Zhang, H., Duan, H., Andric, J. M., Song, M., & Yang, B. (2018). Characterization of household food waste and strategies for its reduction: A Shenzhen City case study. *Waste Management, 78*, 426–433.

Zhang, P., Yuan, H., & Tian, X. (2019). Sustainable development in China: Trends, patterns, and determinants of the "Five Modernizations" in Chinese cities. *Journal of Cleaner Production, 214*, 685–695.

Chapter 4
Determining Green Purchase Behaviour Towards Electronic Products in an Emerging Economy: Theory and Evidence

Ishani Patharia, **Sanjay Rastogi**, and **Ravinder Vinayek**

Abstract The growing concern for environment sustainability has increased the importance of thoughtful consumption behaviour. This research integrates the theory of planned behaviour with some important psycho-demographic factors to understand the customers' purchase behaviour towards the environmental-friendly electronic products. Data was collected using the snowball sampling technique from 577 Indian customers. The results reveal that perceived behavioural control, perceived consumer effectiveness, knowledge about the products and perceived government's efforts towards supporting green initiatives can improve green purchase intention. Attitude towards green products partially mediates the relationship between knowledge about such products and green purchase intention. Environmental knowledge and awareness partially mediate the relationship between perceived government's efforts supporting green initiatives and green purchase intention. Green purchase intention is strongly related to green purchase behaviour towards environment-friendly electronic products. Age and income are positively related to green purchase behaviour. The study's major theoretical contribution is incorporating perceived government efforts, environmental knowledge and attitude and demographic variables into the theory of planned behaviour to predict green purchase behaviour. Empirically, it conceptualizes and tests an integrated model of green purchase behaviour with new insights from an emerging market which is also the test market in the Asian region. Implications for government and managers have been discussed.

I. Patharia (✉)
Department of Commerce, BPS Women University, Haryana, India
e-mail: ishani@bpswomenuniversity.ac.in

S. Rastogi
Indian Institute of Foreign Trade, New Delhi, India
e-mail: srastogi@iift.edu

R. Vinayek
Delhi School of Professional Studies and Research, New Delhi, India
e-mail: rvinayek@dspsr.in

© The Author(s), under exclusive license to Springer Nature Singapore Pte Ltd. 2022
N. Nguyen et al. (eds.), *Environmental Sustainability in Emerging Markets*,
Approaches to Global Sustainability, Markets, and Governance,
https://doi.org/10.1007/978-981-19-2408-8_4

Keywords Electronic products · Emerging economies · Green purchase behaviour · Perceived government efforts · Psycho-demographic variables · Theory of planned behaviour

4.1 Introduction

The world is facing major challenges for maintaining sustainable development. With the rapid technological development and adoption, there has been a rapid upsurge in consumption of energy, greenhouse gas emissions and waste-waste generation. The United Nations Organization has declared that energy is the dominant contributor to climate change because it accounts for more than 60 per cent of total global greenhouse gas emissions (United Nations Organization, 2021a). Consumption behaviour has an enduring impact on the environment. Therefore, there is a greater need for solicitous human activities for environmental sustainability (Liu et al., 2020; United Nations Organization, 2021b). The importance of this issue can be realized by the fact that the United Nations Sustainable Development Goals encompass responsible consumption and production as one of its important goals (United Nations Organization, 2015). There is a growing concern to curb household greenhouse gas emissions and research in this domain at micro level in developing countries (Liu et al., 2020). A recent report on environment and climate change reveals that recent pandemic closures have resulted in a reduction of greenhouse gases, but it is insufficient to substantially slow global warming (Forster et al., 2020). Therefore, it is pertinent to adopt environment-friendly strategies to harness the benefits of reduced emissions and environmental sustainability.

Environment-friendly purchase behaviour or green purchase behaviour (GPB) is an important parameter of responsible consumerism that can be defined as the purchasing or procurement efforts that give preference to products or services which are least harmful to the environment and human health (Lee, 2008). The spending on products that are not harmful to the environment; recyclable or conservable and sensitive or responsive to ecological concerns is also termed as GPB (Mostafa, 2007).

With the ever-increasing concern for the environment, a plethora of research studies come from all around the world to understand and develop a customer environment-friendly purchase behaviour model (Amoako et al., 2020; Kumar et al., 2019; Sadiq et al., 2021; Testa et al., 2019). Understanding the environment-friendly purchase behaviour of customers is very complex because it varies across geographic regions, time zones and products (Sadiq et al., 2021; Testa et al., 2019). Therefore, there is a need to conduct product-specific research in emerging economies to add new insights to this domain of knowledge (Amoako et al., 2020; Kumar et al., 2019; Patel et al., 2020).

India is one of the fastest-growing, emerging economies with a huge customer base. The research on GPB in the context of India is of primary interest due to several reasons. Firstly, many multinational companies often consider India as a test market before launching any product in the Asian region (Mitter, 2017 in Kulshreshtha et al., 2019). Secondly, India is a lucrative market for many global firms (Govindarajan & Venkatesan, 2018; Ravi, 2020). Thirdly, according to the IQAir world air quality report (2020), India was ranked the third most polluted country in the world which calls for urgent action in terms of green consumerism. Research on specific product categories is very limited in India (Khare, 2019; Khare & Sadachar, 2017; Patel et al., 2020) and the recent research studies have highlighted the need to conduct more product-specific research because diverse pro-environmental behaviours in a study may affect the results of GPB model (Amoako et al., 2020; Arli et al., 2018).

The study of consumer electronic products such as air conditioners, laptops, washing machines, mobiles, refrigerators and kitchen appliances is important because such products have greater potential for energy conservation and reducing the dreadful impact on the environment (Kulshreshtha, et al., 2019; Nguyen et al., 2017). According to a report by India Brand Equity Foundation (2020), the Indian appliance and consumer electronics (ACE) market has already touched US$10.93 billion in 2019 and it is expected to reach US$21.18 billion by 2025. The electronic products with lesser carbon emission levels, lesser energy consumption and recyclable with take-back possibilities are environment-friendly electronic products. Electronic companies are putting great efforts into the research and manufacture of environment-friendly electronic products and practices (Kulshreshtha et al., 2019). But the customer response in terms of GPB is still very low and it is a complex process of improving it because of diverse demographic profiles and several other unexplored reasons (Kulshreshtha et al., 2019). This calls for exploring and understanding the factors that affect the GPB towards electronic products in India. Therefore, the present research study focusses on developing an integrative model of GPB using psycho-demographic variables in the above context.

The present study has many implications for academics, industry and government. Firstly, the study aims to cover the gaps in the existing literature by studying the factors which have not been researched extensively so far (like environment knowledge and awareness, environment attitude, perceived consumer effectiveness, social influence, perceived government efforts, demographic variables as control variables and perceived behavioural control). This study contributes to green purchase behaviour literature by providing a better understanding of customer purchase behaviour towards environment-friendly electronic products in an emerging economy. This will give way to avenues for future research in the related areas. Secondly, the results have implications for the industry policymakers for developing focussed strategies to improve the desired green purchase behaviour in emerging markets with huge future potentials. Thirdly, the research outcomes will be useful in understanding whether government initiatives are impactful in improving GPB and refining the government efforts towards sustainability.

This article starts with a brief discussion of the review of the factors which affect GPB followed by the proposed hypotheses that are tested for significance with the use of Structural Equation Modelling (SEM). The interpretations derived from the results of SEM have been discussed and elaborated which finally percolate into some pragmatic suggestions.

4.2 Literature Review

4.2.1 Theory of Planned Behaviour

The underpinning of 'Green Purchase Behaviour' (GPB) can be related to the 'Theory of Planned Behaviour' (TPB) propounded by Ajzen (1991), which suggests that a person's attitude towards a particular behaviour, their subjective norms (social influence on product purchase decision) and perceived behavioural control (commitment towards environment-friendly purchase under situational constraints which defines ease in performing GPB) affects intentions to perform the desired behaviour which in turn affect the actual behaviour.

The claims of strong views on environmental issues, pro-environmental attitudes, intention to recycle, concern about air pollution and willingness to pay more for environment-friendly products are rarely translated into GPB (Jaiswal & Singh, 2018). Recent studies suggest that some additional variables must be used with TPB variables to understand GPB (Chen, 2020). Factors such as environmental knowledge and awareness, knowledge and awareness about the environment-friendly products, perceived government efforts and demographic variables (such as gender, age and income) may affect GPB (Chopra & Vinayek, 2013; Dhir et al., 2021; Testa et al., 2019). Therefore, the present study has used the extended theory of planned behaviour with knowledge about the product (as the antecedent of attitude towards environment-friendly electronic products), perceived government efforts, environment knowledge, environment attitude and demographic variables (as control variables) to explore the factors affecting GPB towards electronic products.

4.2.2 Psychographic Variables

For marketers of environment-friendly products, the gap between pro-environmental attitudes and green purchase behaviour is a daunting challenge where research in environmental consumerism has produced indecisive evidence in support of consumer attitude–behaviour theory. It is very important that the attitude and behaviours should not be measured in the general but specific context and should be confounded with other personal and situational factors (Ajzen, 2020; Nguyen et al., 2017). Therefore, the present study attempts to explore the pro-environmental attitude in the specific context of electronic products, i.e., attitude towards environment-friendly electronic products and perceived consumer effectiveness, whereas environmental attitude represents the general attitude towards environmental protection in the present study.

4.2.2.1 Knowledge About the Products (KAP) and Attitude Towards Green Electronic Products (AGP)

Consumers often purchase products and services with a mix of attributes including environmental attributes so that their utility is maximized. They derive extra utility from the perceived economy (price) and quality attributes rather than the environmental attributes alone. Indian customers are often price-sensitive (Manaktola & Jauhari, 2007) but while buying an environment-friendly electronic product (such as a washing machine), they may be ready to pay a premium price for quality and lower power consumption denoted by the energy-efficient star rating on the label. This reveals that they have a positive attitude and intention to purchase such a product after having knowledge about it (Kulshreshtha et al., 2019; Testa et al., 2019).

The relationship between knowledge about environment-friendly apparel and its purchase by Indian youth is highly inconsistent (Khare, 2019; Khare & Sadachar, 2017). Prakash and Pathak (2017) found that youth in India who have a positive attitude towards environment-friendly packaged products prefer to buy such products, but the researchers have highlighted the need to explore this relationship in context to other products and customers in other age groups. Therefore, it would be interesting to explore the significance of these relationships in the context of electronic products.

H_{1a} Knowledge about environment-friendly electronic products (KAP) has a positive influence on the intention to purchase environment-friendly electronic products (GPI).

Nguyen et al. (2017) found that knowledge about environment-friendly electronic appliances plays a significant role in developing a positive attitude towards the purchase of such products that has a significant positive influence on intention to purchase such products. Thus, a positive attitude towards environment-friendly electronic products may enhance the intention to purchase such products (Arli et al., 2018; Chen, 2020).

H_{1b} Knowledge about environment-friendly electronic products (KAP) has a positive influence on attitude towards environment-friendly electronic products (AGP).

H_{1c} Attitude towards environment-friendly electronic products (AGP) mediates the relationship between knowledge about environment-friendly electronic products (KAP) and intention to purchase environment-friendly electronic products (GPI).

4.2.3 Perceived Consumer Effectiveness (PCE)

Perceived consumer effectiveness in context to GPB represents the belief that adopting GPB can contribute towards environmental protection (Jaiswal & Singh, 2018). It is an important value that is significant in developing environmental preferences, intentions and behaviours by an individual (Brochado et al., 2017; Jaiswal & Singh, 2018). If the customers are convinced that their GPB may contribute towards improving environmental conditions, they are more likely to purchase environment-friendly products (Paul et al., 2016). But this belief may or may not result in the intention to purchase environment-friendly electronic products. Therefore, the following hypothesis is proposed:

H_2 Perceived Consumer Effectiveness (PCE) has a positive influence on the intention to purchase environment-friendly electronic products (GPI).

4.2.3.1 Social Influence (SI)

The theory of planned behaviour (TPB) posits that subjective norm (social influence) plays an important role in forming intentions to perform any desired behaviour (Ajzen, 2020). It comprises the belief of individuals about how the important people in their lives will view their specific behaviour or whether they adopt the specific behaviour. Social influence is usually positively related to green purchase intention and behaviour (Arli et al., 2018; Chen, 2020; Khare, 2019; Sadiqet al., 2021). Testa et al. (2019) found that social influence had no significant relation with intention to purchase organic food, but it negatively affects the actual purchase behaviour towards organic food.

Nguyen et al. (2018) found that it had no significant impact on purchase of energy-efficient appliances among young consumers in Vietnam. Many Indian studies have not considered this variable while studying GPB (Jaiswal & Singh, 2018; Prakash & Pathak, 2017). Whereas some other research studies on GPB found conflicting results in this context, i.e., it may (Khare et al., 2013) or may not (Khare & Sadachar, 2017; Patel et al., 2020; Patharia et al., 2020) influence green purchase intention. Therefore, to test the above-discussed argument the following hypothesis is proposed:

H_3 Social influence (SI) has a positive influence on the intention to purchase environment-friendly electronic products (GPI).

4.2.4 Perceived Behavioural Control (PBC)

The theory of planned behaviour posits perceived behavioural control as a proxy of actual behavioural control to measure an individual's perception of ease or difficulty in performing the desired behaviour. It is a product of control belief strength and perceived power over all accessible control factors (Ajzen, 2020). Therefore, it represents the firm belief of an individual to utilize the facilitating conditions and combating the inhibiting factors for performing a specific behaviour. In context to the present study, PCE means that an individual believes that he/she can contribute towards environment protection by purchasing an environment-friendly electronic product. Whereas PBC means that the person is ready to put in efforts to search for such products, wait for their availability, compromise with quality or pay some premium price to purchase such products.

The effect of perceived behavioural control on the intention to adopt environment-friendly practices has been found to be important and significant (Chen, 2020; Patel et al., 2020; Testa et al., 2019). But some of the research studies on GPB in India have ignored this factor inadvertently (Jaiswal & Singh, 2018; Khare, 2019; Khare et al., 2013). Therefore, the following hypothesis is proposed to test the relationship in context to environment-friendly electronic products:

H₄ Perceived Behavioural Control (PBC) has a positive influence on intention to purchase environment-friendly electronic products (GPI).

4.2.5 Perceived Government Efforts (GEF), Environmental Knowledge and Awareness (EKA) and Environmental Attitude (EA)

Government often undertakes programmes for promoting sustainability by imposing checks on production and consumption of products that may harm the environment, conducting environment-friendly awareness drives or promoting the idea of switching over to environment-friendly substitutes in several ways (Ministry of Electronics and Information Technology, 2020). The Ministry of Power, Government of India, promotes production and consumption of environment-friendly electronic products by initiatives such as standards and labelling guidelines, national mission for enhanced energy efficiency, school education programmes, etc. (Bureau of Energy Efficiency, 2020). The role of the government in enhancing green purchase behaviour has not been explored much in the context of GPB. The customers' perception of the initiatives taken by the government towards promoting environment-friendly electronic products may have a positive impact on their intention to purchase environment-friendly electronic products, environmental awareness/knowledge and attitude towards environmental protection.

H₅ₐ Perceived government efforts supporting environment-friendly initiatives (GEF) has a positive influence on intention to purchase environment-friendly electronic products (GPI).

H$_{5b}$ Perceived government efforts supporting environment-friendly initiatives (GEF) has a positive influence on increasing environmental knowledge and awareness (EKA).

H$_{5c}$ Perceived government efforts supporting environment-friendly initiatives (GEF) has a positive influence on environmental attitude (EA).

In recent research by Kumar et al. (2019) on Indian youth (20–25 years of age), it was explored that government efforts have a significant impact on environmental knowledge and concern which affects their GPI. Therefore, it is pertinent to test this relationship in a specific context to the intention to purchase environment-friendly electronic products to test whether it holds good for this product category too.

Higher knowledge and awareness about environmental conditions have a positive impact on the intention to adopt environment-friendly practices and prefer environment-friendly products over conventional products (Kumar et al., 2019; Lee, 2010). But it has also been found that knowledge about the environment may not have any significant impact on environment-friendly behaviour (Brochado et al., 2017; Jaiswal & Singh, 2018). It will be interesting to explore this relationship in context to environment-friendly electronic products. Thus, the following hypothesis is proposed:

H$_{5d}$ Environmental knowledge and awareness (EKA) mediate the relationship between perceived government efforts supporting environment-friendly initiatives (GEF) and intention to purchase environment-friendly electronic products (GPI).

The environmental concern depicts the attitude of an individual towards the protection of the environment that gives a sense of responsibility to protect the environment through their general behaviour. Such concern is commonly known as environmental attitude. Consumers function in an increasingly globalized market due to which attitudes towards environmental issues, the associated behaviours and knowledge may differ across cultures and product categories (Chen, 2020; Dhir et al., 2021; Testa et al., 2019). In India, people have a growing concern for the depletion of the ozone layer and global warming which has resulted in a preference towards environment-friendly products (Patharia et al., 2020; Sadiq et al., 2021). Previous research studies reveal a conflicting relationship between environmental attitude and GPB (Chen, 2020; Lee, 2008; Prakash & Pathak, 2017). Thus, the following hypothesis is proposed:

H$_{5e}$ Environmental attitude (EA) mediates the relationship between perceived government efforts supporting environment-friendly initiatives (GEF) and intention to purchase environment-friendly electronic products (GPI).

4.2.6 Green Purchase Intention (GPI) and Green Purchase Behaviour (GPB)

Green purchase intention refers to the readiness expressed by the individuals to behave in an environment-friendly manner (Akehurst et al., 2012). Hence, in the present context, it will be the intention to purchase environment-friendly electronic products. GPI is strongly related to GPB but sometimes a gap between intention and purchase may exist (Testa et al., 2019). Recent research in Vietnam reveals that the intention to purchase energy-efficient household appliances has a positive influence on customers' purchase behaviour (Nguyen et al., 2017, 2018). Therefore, the following hypothesis is proposed:

H₆ Intention to purchase environment-friendly electronic products (GPI) has a positive influence on the purchase of environment-friendly electronic products (GPB).

4.2.7 Demographic Variables

The study of behaviour should be confounded with other personal and situational factors (Ajzen, 1991; Nguyen et al., 2017). The socio-demographic characteristics are imperative in determining market segments for the purpose of designing appropriate green marketing strategies (Jain & Kaur, 2006). But the psychographic variables have been found to be more effective in explaining environment-friendly behaviour as compared to demographic variables (Akehurst et al., 2012). Therefore, as recommended by Dhir et al. (2021), demographic variables have been used as control variables in the present study.

The results of the research studies that have evaluated the relationship between demographic variables and environment-friendly behaviour are highly inconsistent. No significant difference was found in environment-friendly behaviour of males and females in many countries including India (Akehurst et al., 2012; Jain & Kaur, 2006). But males were found to have a more positive outlook towards environment-friendly purchases in Egypt (Mostafa, 2007).

H₇ₐ Gender has a significant influence on green purchase behaviour towards electronic products (GPB).

The influence of age on GPB has been found to differ across countries (Akehurst et al., 2012; Jain & Kaur, 2006). Most of the recent studies in India have been conducted on youth only (Jaiswal & Singh, 2018; Khare & Sadachar, 2017; Kumar et al., 2019; Prakash & Pathak, 2017) or apparel buying (Khare, 2019; Khare & Sadachar, 2017). These studies have not studied the influence of age on GPB. Gender and age are the important demographic variables that should not be ignored in research studies on GPB (Dhir et al., 2021).

H7b Age has a significant influence on green purchase behaviour towards electronic products (GPB).

Indian customers are often considered to be price sensitive (Jain & Kaur, 2006; Manaktola & Jauhari, 2007), and environment-friendly electronic products are usually more expensive than conventional products. Therefore, it can be assumed that an increase in income may contribute towards improved GPB. It will be interesting to measure the relationship between income and GPB towards environment-friendly electronic products. Thus, the following hypothesis is proposed:

H7c Income has a positive influence on green purchase behaviour towards electronic products (GPB).

4.2.8 Proposed Model

The major constructs investigated in this study on determining GPB towards environment-friendly electronic products include psychographic factors: Indian customers' environmental attitude, perceived consumer effectiveness while purchasing environment-friendly electronic products, knowledge about environment-friendly electronic products, attitude towards such products, perceived government efforts supporting environment-friendly initiatives, environmental knowledge and awareness, social influence, perceived behavioural control and GPI along with demographic factors: gender, age and income. The relationships have been explored as depicted in Fig. 4.1.

4.3 Research Methodology

4.3.1 Measures and Survey Instrument

The factors that emerged from the review of literature were conceptualized with the help of variables that envelope their definitions and the validated scales used in previous research (Arli et al., 2018; Brochado et al., 2017; Jaiswal & Singh, 2018; Khare & Sadachar, 2017; Nguyen et al., 2017; Prakash & Pathak, 2017). Furthermore, two focus groups consisting of ten customers each were organized for testing and adapting the existing validated scales in reference to the Indian context (see Table 4.2). All the variables used in the study were measured using Likert type 5-point scales (1 representing strongly disagree to 5 representing strongly agree except for GPB with 1 representing never to 5 representing always). The survey instrument was designed to appropriately meet the objectives of the study. It was pretested on a selective sample of 150 customers.

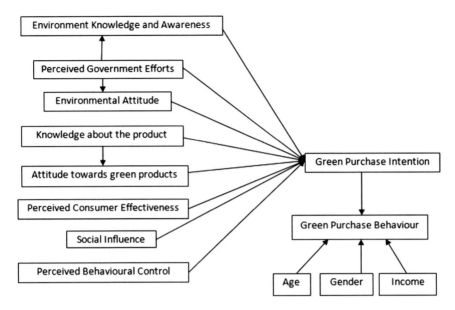

Fig. 4.1 Proposed model of green purchase behaviour (*Source* Author's Compilation)

4.3.2 Sampling Procedures and Data Collection

The target population was educated Indian citizens above 20 years of age who had purchased an electronic product (such as air conditioner, laptop, refrigerator, kitchen appliance, television and mobile phones) two years prior to the collection of data. This ensured their interest in electronic products, thus improving the prediction of purchase behaviour. Data was collected from educated adults because such respondents understand the green phenomenon and can answer the questionnaire properly.

The target population could not be identified directly without the help of middlemen. Therefore, the snowball sampling method was used for the purpose of this study. This method helps in choosing the appropriate sample where there are limited subjects in the target population (like customers who might have purchased an electronic product two years prior to the collection of data). This technique is often criticized for sampling bias because the subjects are nominated through reference. But in the present study, the subjects were approached as per the data provided by the retailers of electronic products. It was also confirmed that the respondent had purchased an electronic product in the recent past before administering the questionnaire. The retail outlets in New Delhi and the national capital region (NCR) of Delhi, India, were approached to get the contact details of the customers who were relevant to the purpose of the present research study. Researchers chose this geographical

Table 4.1 Demographic profile of the respondents

Demographic variables		%
Gender	Male	53.2
	Female	46.8
Age (Measured on ratio scale)	20–34	53.7
	35–49	32.1
	50–64	14.2
Family income per month (Measured on ratio scale)	Less than Rs. 75,000	39.2
	Rs. 75,001–Rs. 150,000	42.1
	Rs. 150,001–Rs. 225,000	11.6
	Above Rs. 225,000	7.1
Highest education qualification	Graduation	32.9
	Post-Graduation	53.4
	Doctorate	9.9
	Any other	3.8

area because it is one of the most polluted regions in the world. Four (Ghaziabad, Noida, Greater Noida and Delhi) out of the top ten most polluted cities of the world are located in this region (IQAir, 2020), and the people in NCR are expected to be receptive to more environmental challenges. Respondents were assured that the confidentiality of their responses will be maintained to overcome evaluation hesitation. They were also informed that there were no right or wrong responses to minimize biased responses due to social desirability while giving responses.

The questionnaire was either personally administered or sent via e-mail/WhatsApp to 600 respondents who were willing to participate in the survey. But, 16 responses were removed due to invalid responses or missing values and 7 responses were removed as multivariate outliers. Hence, the final effective sample was 577 responses. Table 4.1 depicts the demographic profile of the respondents.

The sample is fairly representative of the population in Delhi—NCR as per the demographic distribution of population mentioned in Statistical Yearbook India (2018) released by the Office of Registrar General of India, Ministry of Home Affairs.

4.4 Data Analysis and Results

To verify the hypothesized relationships, the two-stage process of SEM was adopted: the measurement model followed by the structural model. For the measurement model, CFA was performed using AMOS. Table 4.2 summarizes the measures of

4 Determining Green Purchase Behaviour Towards Electronic Products … 81

Table 4.2 Standardized factor loadings and reliability

Constructs and variables	Sources	Loadings	Cronbach α
Environment Knowledge and Awareness (EKA)			
I am aware of the depletion of the ozone layer	Jaiswal and Singh (2018)	0.949	**0.960**
There is a rapid depletion of non-renewable resources		0.934	
Electronic product emissions harm the environment		0.949	
Environmental Attitude (EA)			
Environmental protection more important than economic growth	Prakash and Pathak (2017)	0.821	**0.911**
Maintaining harmony with nature by conserving natural resources		0.910	
Environmental conservation is my responsibility		0.922	
Perceived Consumer Effectiveness (related to green electronic products) (PCE)			
When I purchase electronic products, I try to evaluate the consequences of this decision on the environment	Brochado et al. (2017)	0.889	**0.952**
I am ready to face inconvenience if it reduces carbon emissions		0.903	
My decision to buy green electronic products can protect the environment		0.946	
I can share the responsibility of environmental organizations and others in protecting the environment		0.857	
I think if I buy green electronic products, I would contribute a lot to our environment		0.903	
I can't do anything about environmental issues like emissions, radiation etc. from electronic products		0.766	
Knowledge about Products (KAP)			
I am aware of the environment-friendly electronic products in the market	Nguyen et al. (2017)	0.917	**0.941**
I can identify the environment-friendly electronic products		0.906	

(continued)

Table 4.2 (continued)

Constructs and variables	Sources	Loadings	Cronbach α
I check for energy-saving stars before buying electronic products		0.898	
I check for bio-safe emissions before buying electronic products		0.906	
Attitude towards green electronic products (AGP)			
Environment-friendly electronic products help in reducing the harmful impact on nature	Khare and Sadachar (2017)	0.845	**0.879**
Environment-friendly electronic products are only a sales promotion strategy of the companies, the products are actually not so		0.669	
Environment-friendly electronic products can be easily reused or recycled, without any harmful impact on nature		0.852	
Environment-friendly electronic products are cost-effective, as the use of such products reduces electricity bills		0.858	
Social Influence (SI)			
When buying products, I generally purchase those electronic products and brands that I think others will approve of	Khare and Sadachar (2017)	0.710	**0.913**
I buy only those electronic products that others buy		0.885	
It is important that others like the electronic products and brands that I buy		0.925	
I purchase such electronic products that are recommended by others		0.896	
Perceived Government Efforts (GEF)			
Increased government efforts can improve the purchase rate of environment-friendly electronic products		0.880	**0.943**
The government should subsidize research on technology for recycling waste products		0.940	

(continued)

4 Determining Green Purchase Behaviour Towards Electronic Products …   83

Table 4.2 (continued)

Constructs and variables	Sources	Loadings	Cronbach α
The government should enforce strict rules and regulations regarding the environmental impact of electronic products		0.932	
I will support government control to check harmful effluents from electronic products as they can promote the sale of green electronic products		0.914	
Perceived Behavioural Control (PBC)			
When I purchase electronic products, I can easily make an effort to buy products that are low in pollutants	Arli et al. (2018)	0.980	**0.985**
I can wait for the green electronic product to be available in the market		0.980	
It is up to me to buy electronic products that have lesser emissions or do not emit harmful radiation		0.975	
I have control over my decision while buying electronic products		0.962	
I can access information from the internet and other media so that I can easily buy environment-friendly electronic products		0.953	
Intention to Purchase Environment-friendly Electronic Products (GPI)			
I will choose an environment-friendly electronic product over an ordinary electronic product	Nguyen et al. (2017)	0.976	**0.978**
I will prefer to switch over to other brands to avoid any potential harm to the environment		0.958	
I like the idea of purchasing environment-friendly electronic products, so I make an effort to buy them		0.971	
Green Purchase Behaviour (GPB)			
I have bought environment-friendly electronic products in previous years	Nguyen et al. (2017)	0.944	**0.971**
I buy electronic products with higher star ratings because it helps reduce the electricity bills		0.915	

(continued)

Table 4.2 (continued)

Constructs and variables	Sources	Loadings	Cronbach α
I have switched over to electronic products that consume lesser resources such as water or electricity		0.954	
I have purchased eco-friendly electronic products although they were expensive		0.940	
I have avoided buying electronic products that had a potentially harmful environmental impact		0.913	

standardized factor loadings and reliability (Cronbach's alpha). All the factor loadings were significant ($p < 0.01$) and higher than 0.7 in most of the cases. The Cronbach's alpha (α) measures of reliability were very good, ranging between 0.879 and 0.985 (Hair et al., 2010).

Table 4.3 depicts the additional measures of construct reliability and validity such as composite reliability (CR), average variance extracted (AVE), maximum shared variance (MSV) and squared correlation between variable estimates. All the CR values are ideally above 0.7, AVE > 0.5 and AVE > MSV; square root of the AVE of each measure was higher than its bivariate correlation coefficients with other constructs which reveal good convergent and discriminant validity (Hair et al., 2010; Hu & Bentler, 1999).

The overall model fit indices were CMIN/DF = 3.419, CFI = 0.950, NFI = 0.931 and RMSEA = 0.065. All these indices met acceptable levels (Hair et al., 2010). This model explained 74% of the variations in GPB towards electronic products significantly. The research model was estimated with the help of standardized regression weights (β) and p values to test the hypotheses in this empirical study as shown in Table 4.4. All the standardized regression coefficients were significant albeit at different levels except for the three hypotheses, i.e., the relationship between SI and GPB, EA and GPI and differences in GPB of males and females.

4.4.1 Mediation Effect

In the present study, three mediation effects have been examined (H_{1c}, H_{5d}, and H_{5e}). For mediation to be present, two important conditions need to be satisfied (Blunch, 2012). Firstly, there must be a significant relationship between independent and dependent variables. Both KAP ($\beta = 0.056***$) and GEF ($\beta = 0.049***$) have a significant effect on GPI (H_{1a}, H_{5a}). Secondly, there must be a significant relationship between independent and mediating variables as well as mediating and dependent variables. KAP significantly affects AGP ($\beta = 0.293****$), i.e., H_{1b} is supported and further, AGP significantly affects GPI ($\beta = 0.081****$), i.e., H_{1c} is supported. Similarly, GEF significantly affects both EKA ($\beta = 0.146****$) and EA

Table 4.3 Construct validity and correlations

	CR	AVE	MSV	MaxR (H)	EA	KAP	PCE	SI	GEF	PBC	GPI	AGP	EKA	GPB
EA	0.916	0.784	0.341	0.926	**0.885**									
KAP	0.949	0.822	0.341	0.949	0.584	**0.906**								
PCE	0.953	0.773	0.409	0.962	−0.552	−0.512	**0.879**							
SI	0.917	0.736	0.013	0.936	0.005	0.114	0.077	**0.858**						
GEF	0.955	0.841	0.409	0.958	0.399	0.312	−0.640	−0.033	**0.917**					
PBC	0.988	0.941	0.834	0.989	0.050	0.360	−0.051	0.055	−0.005	**0.970**				
GPI	0.978	0.938	0.834	0.979	0.073	0.374	−0.067	0.063	0.035	0.813	**0.968**			
AGP	0.883	0.656	0.265	0.898	0.005	0.273	0.007	−0.030	−0.038	0.471	0.490	**0.810**		
EKA	0.961	0.891	0.379	0.962	0.105	0.242	−0.204	0.025	0.141	0.568	0.615	0.272	**0.944**	
GPB	0.977	0.878	0.754	0.978	0.159	0.425	−0.174	−0.004	0.074	0.791	0.869	0.515	0.490	**0.937**

Table 4.4 Summary of hypotheses testing

Variables	β	S.E	p-value	Hypothesis	Decision
GPI ← KAP	0.056	0.027	***	H_{1a}	Supported
AGP ← KAP	0.293	0.040	****	H_{1b}	Supported
GPI ← AGP	0.081	0.021	****	H_{1c}	Supported
GPI ← PCE	0.066	0.033	****	H_2	Supported
GPI ← SI	0.012	0.025	0.48	H_3	Not supported
GPI ← PBC	0.891	0.015	****	H_4	Supported
GPI ← GEF	0.049	0.034	***	H_{5a}	Supported
EKA ← GEF	0.146	0.056	****	H_{5b}	Supported
EA ← GEF	0.422	0.034	****	H_{5c}	Supported
GPI ← EKA	0.163	0.018	****	H_{5d}	Supported
GPI ← EA	0.004	0.031	0.83	H_{5e}	Not supported
GPB ← GPI	0.858	0.021	****	H_6	Supported
GPB ← Gender	0.004	0.050	0.86	H_{7a}	Not supported
GPB ← Age	0.041	0.002	*	H_{7b}	Supported
GPB ← Income	0.047	0.000	**	H_{7c}	Supported

****$p < 0.001$, ***$p < 0.01$, **$p < 0.05$, *$p < 0.10$, β standardized regression coefficient of path estimates

Table 4.5 Mediation effect analysis

Hypotheses	Direct effect	Indirect effect	Total effect	Results
KAP → AGP → GPI	0.056**	0.024****	0.080***	Partial mediation
GEF → EKA → GPI	0.050**	0.024**	0.074***	Partial mediation
GEF → EA → GPI	-	-	-	No mediation

****$p < 0.001$, ***$p < 0.01$, **$p < 0.05$, *$p < 0.10$

($\beta = 0.422****$), and EKA also affects GPI ($\beta = 0.163****$), i.e., H_{5b}, H_{5c} and H_{5d} are supported. But no mediation effect of EA is found in the model because EA fails to affect GPI, i.e., H_{5e} is not supported. After testing these conditions, the next step is to check the type of mediation present.

The significance and nature of the indirect effect was evaluated using the bootstrapping procedure (Hayes & Scharkow, 2013). Bias-corrected bootstrapping was conducted for 2,000 resamples with a 95-per cent confidence interval to evaluate the indirect effects on GPI. The results (Table 4.5) confirm the partial mediation in the study as both direct and indirect effects have been found significant (Cheung & Lau, 2008). AGP partially mediates the relationship between KAP (direct effect = 0.056**; indirect effect = 0.024****) and GPI. The total effect of KAP on GPI is 0.080*** (0.056 + 0.024). EKA also partially mediates the relationship between

GEF (direct effect $= 0.050**$; indirect effect $= 0.024**$) and GPI. The total effect of GEF on GPI is $0.074***$ $(0.050 + 0.024)$.

It is apparent from the results that the customers who possess better knowledge about environment-friendly electronic products are more likely to develop a positive attitude towards such products ($\beta = 0.293$) and intention to purchase them ($\beta = 0.056$). Thus, the relationship between knowledge about environment-friendly electronic products and green purchase intentions towards such products is consistently and partially mediated by attitude towards such products (H_{1a}, H_{1b} and H_{1c} are supported). The results of the Sobel test ($t = 3.413$, $p < 0.001$) confirm this relationship (Sobel, 1982). Product-specific attitude is more likely to develop GPI ($\beta = 0.081$) rather than environmental attitude in general ($\beta = 0.004$) (H_{1b} is supported and H_{5e} is not supported). Similarly, perceived consumer effectiveness, which is another dimension of attitude specific to the purchase of environment-friendly electronic products, results in higher GPI ($\beta = 0.066$) (H_2 is supported). Social influence was found to be insignificant in developing GPI ($\beta = 0.012$) (H_3 is not supported). As expected, perceived behavioural control can play an important role in developing GPI ($\beta = 0.891$) (H_4 is supported). It was found to be the most important predictor of GPI. Thus, the theory of planned behaviour (TPB) is partially supported in the context of GPI towards electronic products, with SI as an insignificant predictor of GPI.

Perceived government efforts supporting environment-friendly initiatives have a significant effect on GPI ($\beta = 0.049$) (H_{5a} is supported). Perceived government efforts can also play a significant role in improving environmental knowledge and awareness ($\beta = 0.146$), which in turn leads to higher GPI ($\beta = 0.163$) (H_{5b} and H_{5d} are supported). Thus, environmental knowledge and awareness mediate the relationship between government efforts and GPI consistently and partially. The results of the Sobel test ($t = 2.505$, $p < 0.05$) confirm this relationship.

Further, the hypothesized relationship between GPI and GPB holds true ($\beta = 0.858$) (H_6 is supported). No significant difference was found in the GPB of males and females ($\beta = 0.004$) (H_{7a} is not supported). Income ($\beta = 0.047$) and age ($\beta = 0.041$) have a significant positive impact on GPB (H_{7b} and H_{7c} are supported).

4.5 Discussion

This research sought to develop an integrative model (using psychographic and demographic factors) to understand the GPB towards electronic products in India—an emerging economy in Asia that has a huge customer base and is considered a test market before launching products in the Asian region (Mitter, 2017 in Kulshreshtha et al., 2019). The extended theory of planned behaviour with variables such as perceived government efforts and demographic variables is an interesting dimension in the present study. SEM analysis on responses of 577 Indian respondents validated the hypothesized relationships among the factors that affect GPI and GPB towards electronic products.

All the factors suggested by TPB except social influence were found to have a significant effect on GPI, which in turn is a strong predictor of GPB. These results are in line with the recent studies (Khare & Sadachar, 2017; Nguyen et al., 2018; Testa et al., 2019). Thus, the customers may not be influenced to buy environment-friendly electronic products just because of the advice and expectations of family, friends and society.

Many of Indian studies had not considered the impact of perceived behavioural control (PBC) on product-specific GPI (Patel et al., 2020). But the present study attempts to cover this research gap by exploring that it is the most important predictor of GPI. These findings support the prior consumer research by Arli et al. (2018); Testa et al. (2019). The second most important factor affecting GPI was found to be environmental knowledge and awareness which can be enhanced by government efforts. These results are in sync with the recent research by Kumar et al. (2019) related to GPB among young Indian consumers.

As expected, according to the TPB, it is the attitude specific to the product and behaviour in question that significantly affects GPI and not the attitude in general. Therefore, the two dimensions of attitude, i.e., attitude towards environment-friendly electronic products and perceived consumer effectiveness were found to affect GPI significantly. The findings extend the prior consumer research investigating the role of attitude towards green products in the formulation of GPI (Paul et al., 2016; Prakash & Pathak, 2017) by validating this relationship in context to environment-friendly electronic products.

Knowledge about environment-friendly electronic products plays a significant role in improving attitudes towards such products (Kulshreshtha et al., 2019). These results validate the knowledge–attitude–intention relationship in context to energy-efficient appliances explored by Nguyen et al. (2017) in another emerging economy—Vietnam. Knowledge about the product was also found to have a significant positive direct influence on GPI. Additionally, the results of the present study verified that perceived consumer effectiveness is a significant predictor of GPI (Brochado et al., 2017; Jaiswal & Singh, 2018).

The results of the present study reveal the significance of the government's supportive initiatives in developing GPI. Interestingly, these initiatives also promote environmental knowledge and awareness and environmental attitude as it was found by Kumar et al. (2019). But only environmental knowledge and awareness were found to significantly affect GPI (Kumar et al., 2019; Lee, 2010) and not the environmental attitude (Prakash & Pathak, 2017). The theory of planned behaviour states that it is the specific attitude and not the general attitude that is more pertinent in explaining the behaviour (Ajzen, 2020). The significant influence of attitude towards green electronic products and no significant influence of environmental attitude on purchase intention of purchasing environment-friendly electronic products, further support the tenets of the theory of planned behaviour.

Finally, the most important relationship between GPI and GPB was also validated. Prior studies in context to purchase of energy-efficient appliances in emerging economies also found that GPI led to GPB (Nguyen et al., 2017, 2018). The present study further extends the prior research by considering this relationship in presence of demographic variables as control variables as suggested by Dhir et al. (2021). No significant difference was found in the GPB of males and females (Dhir et al., 2021; Jain & Kaur, 2006). Age and income were found to have a significant positive impact on GPB.

Many of the previous research studies in India and elsewhere have focussed on young consumers only. But the results of the present study reveal that with the increase in age, people make more judicious decisions, and hence, there is an increase in GPB towards electronic products. This finding is contradictory to some of the earlier research that had not considered GPB in context to a specific product category (Akehurst et al., 2012). But this contradiction is not surprising as the results may vary across samples and countries (Jain & Kaur, 2006).

As expected, income had a significant positive impact on GPB. There are two main reasons for the same. Firstly, Indian customers are price sensitive, and secondly, environment-friendly electronic products are priced higher than the conventional electronic products.

4.6 Implications of the Study

The present study has manifold implications for academics, marketers and government.

4.6.1 Implications for Academicians

This study used the extended theory of planned behaviour (TPB) as the main theoretical framework that is widely applied in the field of marketing to understand consumer behaviour. The present study contributes to the existing literature by exploring the impact of some additional factors apart from those mentioned in the TPB (such as knowledge about the product, environmental knowledge and awareness, perception towards government efforts and demographic variables) on GPI and GPB directly or indirectly. The number of product-specific research is less, especially in emerging economies (Patel et al., 2020). Therefore, the present study is very important for the academicians and researchers who are interested to conduct future research on GPI or GPB as they might consider including these factors in their research framework as they have proven to fit well in the present research framework on electronic products.

4.6.2 Implications for Marketers

The present research study offers implications to marketers of electronic products such as air conditioners, washing machines, computers, mobiles and electronic appliances. The most important implications are related to perceived behavioural control, environmental knowledge and awareness, knowledge about environment-friendly electronic products, attitude towards such products and perceived consumer effectiveness.

The most important factor that emerged from the study is perceived behavioural control (PBC). Keeping in view the operational definition of PBC as per TPB, it is often assessed by the ease or difficulty of the behaviour (Ajzen, 2020). Marketers can help in improving GPI by accommodating the customers with ample supplies, better sales offer, convenient shopping environment, simplifying the decision-making process and resolving their doubts related to efficacy, purchase and use of such products. Secondly, the marketers must work meticulously towards improving the knowledge about the various environment-friendly electronic products through rigorously focussed strategies related to awareness campaigns, effective advertising, active participation of intermediaries and eco-labelling. This will not only improve attitude towards such products but also improve GPI manifold. Thirdly, the promotion messages should be more focussed on making the customers realize that each one can contribute towards environmental protection by purchasing environment-friendly electronic products. These products help in reducing carbon emissions and reducing e-wastes to a large extent. The customers of such products can be offered certain incentives such as loyalty points for future purchases or free gifts.

Keeping in view the results of the present study related to demographic variables, the marketers must use youth-focussed marketing strategies (such as involving youth icons in promotion campaigns) to promote GPB among them. The significance of income in determining GPB hints at the price sensitivity of customers with lower income. Cheaper models of such products and affordable sales offers should be developed for the customers to improve GPB.

4.6.3 Implications for the Government

The government policymakers must realize the importance of their role in promoting GPI. Government must adopt measures to support the manufacturing and supply of environment-friendly electronic products to ensure regularity and ease of availability of such products. Rigorous efforts by the government may result in the replacement of traditional electronic products by environment-friendly electronic products models in nationwide markets. Government must subsidize research on technological innovations, promote technology exchange programmes to gain access to international technology advancements and give tax incentives for green initiatives by electronic companies. Further, the government must regulate the profit margin charged on environment-friendly electronic products to bring down the out-of-pocket cost for customers. Government should propagate schemes related to exchange of old electronic products for the latest models of environment-friendly electronic products. These enduring efforts towards environmental protection can really play an important role in enhancing intention to purchase environment-friendly electronic products.

Government must organize awareness campaigns related to deteriorating air quality, the harmful impact of electronic products, such as excessive consumption of electricity and harmful greenhouse gas emissions. Awareness programmes must highlight the measures taken by the government for supporting manufacture, sale and disposal of environment-friendly electronic products through various communication platforms for various strata of society. This will increase the knowledge of customers regarding the importance of availability, use and disposal of environment-friendly electronic products. Awareness programmes must also focus on making the customers realize the importance of individual efforts in environment protection through the purchase and use of environment-friendly products. The government must perform such activities rigorously and persistently.

4.7 Limitations and Future Scope for Study

This study was conducted on the customers of Delhi—NCR, India. This region has a cosmopolitan outlook and high pollution index. But the results may vary across samples of respondents from other developing nations. Future researchers may consider longitudinal studies in other emerging economies to investigate the significance and importance of the factors which have been considered in the present study and compare the results to contribute towards developing a more generalized model. The longitudinal studies may further study the satisfaction and repurchase intention of environment-friendly electronic products. The present study focusses on environment-friendly electronic products broadly. There is a future scope to explore the relevance of the proposed model in context to white and grey electronic product categories specifically. The demographic variables have been used as control variables in the present study. The significance of age and income may further be evaluated across different age and income groups through moderation effects for various significant relationships.

References

Ajzen, I. (1991). The theory of planned behavior. *Organizational Behavior and Human Decision Processes, 50*(2), 179–211.

Ajzen, I. (2020). The theory of planned behavior: Frequently asked questions. *Human Behavior and Emerging Technologies, 2*(4), 314–324.

Akehurst, G., Afonso, C., & Gonçalves, H. M. (2012). Re-examining green purchase behaviour and the green consumer profile: New evidences. *Management Decision, 50*(5), 972–988. https://doi.org/10.1108/00251741211227726

Amoako, G. K., Dzogbenuku, R. K., & Abubakari, A. (2020). Do green knowledge and attitude influence the youth's green purchasing? Theory of planned behavior. *International Journal of*

Productivity and Performance Management, 69(8), 1609–1626. https://doi.org/10.1108/IJPPM-12-2019-0595

Arli, D., Tan, L. P., Tjiptono, F., & Yang, L. (2018). Exploring consumers' purchase intention towards green products in an emerging market: The role of consumers' perceived readiness. *International Journal of Consumer Studies, 42*(4), 389–401.

Blunch, N. (2012). *Introduction to structural equation modeling using IBM SPSS statistics and AMOS*. Sage.

Brochado, A., Teiga, N., & Oliveira-Brochado, F. (2017). The ecological conscious consumer behaviour: Are the activists different? *International Journal of Consumer Studies, 41*(2), 138–146.

Bureau of Energy Efficiency. (2020). Government of India, Ministry of Power. https://beeindia.gov.in/

Chen, M. F. (2020). The impacts of perceived moral obligation and sustainability self-identity on sustainability development: A theory of planned behavior purchase intention model of sustainability-labeled coffee and the moderating effect of climate change skepticism. *Business Strategy and the Environment, 29*(6), 2404–2417. https://doi.org/10.1002/bse.2510

Cheung, G. W., & Lau, R. S. (2008). Testing mediation and suppression effects of latent variables: Bootstrapping with structural equation models. *Organizational Research Methods, 11*(2), 296–325.

Chopra, I. P., & Vinayek, R. (2013). Global developments in conceptual framework of green purchase behaviour. *Abhigyan, 31*(3), 64–76.

Dhir, A., Talwar, S., Sadiq, M., Sakashita, M., & Kaur, P. (2021). Green apparel buying behaviour: A Stimulus–Organism–Behaviour–Consequence (SOBC) perspective on sustainability-oriented consumption in Japan. *Business Strategy and the Environment*, 1–17. https://doi.org/10.1002/bse.282

Forster, P. M., Forster, H. I., Evans, M. J., Gidden, M. J., Jones, C. D., Keller, C. A., Lamboll, R. D., Quéré, C. L., Rogelj, J., Rosen, D., Schleussner, C. F., Richardson, T. B., Smith, C. J., & Turnock, S. T. (2020). Current and future global climate impacts resulting from COVID-19. *Nature Climate Change*. https://doi.org/10.1038/s41558-020-0883-0

Govindarajan, V., & Venkatesan R. (2018). 3 reasons global firms should keep investing in India. Emerging markets. *Harvard Business Review*. https://hbr.org/2018/02/3-reasons-global-firms-should-keep-investing-in-india

Hair, J. F., Black, W. C., Babin, B. J., & Anderson, R. E. (2010). *Multivariate data analysis* (7th ed.). Pearson Education.

Hayes, A. F., & Scharkow, M. (2013). The relative trustworthiness of inferential tests of the indirect effect in statistical mediation analysis: Does method really matter? *Psychological Science, 24*(10), 1918–1927. https://doi.org/10.1177/0956797613480187

Hu, L. T., & Bentler, P. M. (1999). Cutoff criteria for fit indexes in covariance structure analysis: Conventional criteria versus new alternatives. *Structural Equation Modeling: A Multidisciplinary Journal, 6*(1), 1–55.

India Brand Equity Foundation. (2020). *Indian consumer durables industry analysis*. https://www.ibef.org/industry/consumer-durables-presentation/. Accessed 10 Jan 2020.

IQAir. (2020). *World's most polluted countries 2020* (PM2.5). https://www.iqair.com/world-most-polluted-countries

Jain, S. K., & Kaur, G. (2006). Role of socio-demographics in segmenting and profiling green consumers: An exploratory study of consumers in India. *Journal of International Consumer Marketing, 18*(3), 107–146.

Jaiswal, D., & Singh, B. (2018). Toward sustainable consumption: Investigating the determinants of green buying behaviour of Indian consumers. *Business Strategy and Development, 1*(1), 64–73.

Khare, A. (2019). Green apparel buying: Role of past behavior, knowledge and peer influence in the assessment of green apparel perceived benefits. *Journal of International Consumer Marketing*, 1–17. https://doi.org/10.1080/08961530.2019.1635553

Khare, A., Mukerjee, S., & Goyal, T. (2013). Social influence and green marketing: An exploratory study on Indian consumers. *Journal of Customer Behavior, 12*(4), 361–381.

Khare, A., & Sadachar, A. (2017). Green apparel buying behaviour: A study on Indian youth. *International Journal of Consumer Studies, 41*(5), 558–569.

Kulshreshtha, K., Bajpai, N., Tripathi, V., & Sharma, G. (2019). Consumer preference for eco-friendly appliances in trade-off: A conjoint analysis approach. *International Journal of Product Development, 23*(2–3), 212–243.

Kumar, R., Saha, R., Sekar, P. C., & Dahiya, R. (2019). Examining the role of external factors in influencing green behaviour among young Indian consumers. *Young Consumers, 20*(4), 380–398. https://doi.org/10.1108/YC-12-2018-0921

Lee, K. (2008). Opportunities for green marketing: Young consumers. *Marketing Intelligence & Planning, 26*, 573–586.

Lee, K. (2010). The green purchase behavior of Hong Kong young consumers: The role of peer influence, local environmental involvement, and concrete environmental knowledge. *Journal of International Consumer Marketing, 23*(1), 21–44.

Liu, L., Qu, J., Maraseni, T. N., Niu, Y., Zeng, J., Zhang, L., & Xu, L. (2020). Household CO_2 emissions: Current status and future perspectives. *International Journal of Environmental Research and Public Health, 17*(19), 7077. https://www.mdpi.com/1660-4601/17/19/7077

Manaktola, K., & Jauhari, V. (2007). Exploring consumer attitude and behaviour towards green practices in the lodging industry in India. *International Journal of Contemporary Hospitality Management, 19*(5), 364–377. https://doi.org/10.1108/09596110710757534

Ministry of Electronics and Information Technology. (2020). *Welcome to the launch of Electronics Manufacturing Schemes PLI, SPECS & EMC2.0.* https://www.meity.gov.in/writereaddata/files/Presentation-Electronics_Manufacturing_Schemes.pdf

Mitter, S. (2017). *Google CEO: If Google products work in India, they work elsewhere too.* https://mashable.com/2017/01/05/sundar-pichai-google-tests-globalproducts-india/#roBBCk6zWiqy. Accessed 8 Jan 2019.

Mostafa, M. M. (2007). Gender differences in Egyptian consumers' green purchase behaviour: The effects of environmental knowledge, concern and attitude. *International Journal of Consumer Studies, 31*(3), 220–229.

Nguyen, T. N., Lobo, A., & Greenland, S. (2017). Energy efficient household appliances in emerging markets: The influence of consumers' values and knowledge on their attitudes and purchase behaviour. *International Journal of Consumer Studies, 41*(2), 167–177.

Nguyen, T. N., Lobo, A., & Nguyen, B. K. (2018). Young consumers' green purchase behaviour in an emerging market. *Journal of Strategic Marketing, 26*(7), 583–600.

Patel, J. D., Trivedi, R. H., & Yagnik, A. (2020). Self-identity and internal environmental locus of control: Comparing their influences on green purchase intentions in high-context versus low-context cultures. *Journal of Retailing and Consumer Services, 53*, 102003. https://bradscholars.brad.ac.uk/bitstream/handle/10454/17524/Tivedi_Journal_of_Retailing_and_Consumer_Services.pdf?sequence=5&isAllowed=y

Patharia, I., Rastogi, S., Vinayek, R., & Malik, S. (2020). A fresh look at environment friendly customer's profile: Evidence from India. *International Journal of Economics and Business Research, 20*(3), 310–321.

Paul, J., Modi, A., & Patel, J. (2016). Predicting green product consumption using theory of planned behavior and reasoned action. *Journal of Retailing and Consumer Services, 29*, 123–134.

Prakash, G., & Pathak, P. (2017). Intention to buy eco-friendly packaged products among young consumers of India: A study on developing nation. *Journal of Cleaner Production, 141*, 385–393. https://doi.org/10.1016/j.jclepro.2016.09.116

Ravi S. (2020). How India is important for international market in terms of business. *Business World.* http://www.businessworld.in/article/How-India-Is-Important-For-International-Market-In-Terms-Of-Business/30-06-2020-292490/

Sadiq, M., Adil, M., & Paul, J. (2021). Does social influence turn pessimistic consumers green? *Business Strategy and the Environment, 1*–14. https://doi.org/10.1002/bse.2780

Sobel, M. E. (1982). Asymptotic intervals for indirect effects in structural equations models. In S. Leinhart (Ed.), *Sociological methodology 1982*, 290–312.

Testa, F., Sarti, S., & Frey, M. (2019). Are green consumers really green? Exploring the factors behind the actual consumption of organic food products. *Business Strategy and the Environment, 28*(2), 327–338. https://doi.org/10.1002/bse.2234

United Nations Organization. (2015). *The UN Sustainable Development Goals.* www.un.org/sustainabledevelopment/summit/. Accessed 22 Dec 2019.

United Nations Organization. (2021a). 7 affordable and clean energy. *Sustainable Development Goals.* https://www.un.org/sustainabledevelopment/energy/

United Nations Organization. (2021b). 12 responsible consumption and production. *Sustainable Development Goals.* https://www.un.org/sustainabledevelopment/sustainable-consumption-production/

Chapter 5
Implementing Eco-Friendly Export Business Strategy Towards Sustaining Supply Chain Coordination and Competitive Advantage: Evidence from Vietnam's Seafood Processing Firms

Binh Do, **Uyen Nguyen**, **Clare D'Souza**, **Thu Hang Hoang, Quynh Hoa Le, and Ninh Nguyen**

Abstract Given that the seafood market is globally increasing, there is a need for eco-friendly business strategies to improve sustainability and achieve a competitive advantage. The study aims to investigate how managers' perceptions of stakeholder and institutional pressures influence eco-friendly export business strategy and consequently impact supply chain coordination and competitive advantage. Data were obtained from 238 managers of Vietnam's seafood processing exporters and analysed using structural equation modelling that employed partial least squares. The findings show that the top manager's sensitivity to environmental problems transforms the

---

B. Do (✉) · U. Nguyen
Centre of Science and Technology Research and Development, Thuongmai University, Hanoi, Vietnam
e-mail: binhdt@tmu.edu.vn

U. Nguyen
e-mail: uyennguyen@tmu.edu.vn

C. D'Souza
Department of Economics, Finance and Marketing, La Trobe Business School, La Trobe University, Melbourne, VIC, Australia
e-mail: C.DSouza@latrobe.edu.au

T. H. Hoang
School of International Business—Marketing,
University of Economics Ho Chi Minh City, Ho Chi Minh City, Vietnam
e-mail: hanght@ueh.edu.vn

Q. H. Le
Thu Dau Mot University, Binh Duong, Vietnam
e-mail: hoalq@tdmu.edu.vn

N. Nguyen
Asia Pacific College of Business and Law, Charles Darwin University, Darwin City, NT, Australia
e-mail: ninh.nguyen@cdu.edu.au

© The Author(s), under exclusive license to Springer Nature Singapore Pte Ltd. 2022
N. Nguyen et al. (eds.), *Environmental Sustainability in Emerging Markets*,
Approaches to Global Sustainability, Markets, and Governance,
https://doi.org/10.1007/978-981-19-2408-8_5

firm's market pressure, regulatory pressure and competitive pressure into the firm's eco-friendly export business strategy. Importantly, this strategy leads to supply chain coordination, which in turn helps the firm obtain a competitive advantage. This study sheds new insights and contributes to the theory and practice of eco-friendly business strategies and supply chain coordination. Managerial and policy implications are highlighted.

Keywords Eco-friendly export business strategy · Competitive advantage · Seafood processing · Supply chain coordination · Sustainable development · Vietnam

5.1 Introduction

The seafood market has become highly globalized with an ever-increasing demand for seafood (Cullen-Knox et al., 2020). A limited capacity of wild fisheries and the subsequent consequences of overfishing of endangered species, increasing waste materials, water pollution, and ecological disruption (FAO, 2018) provokes a need to bring greater attention to eco-friendly export business strategies. Emerging countries have fewer sustainable strategies, and find them difficult to implement, thus encouraging strategies in the seafood industry in developing countries such as Vietnam can be useful not only due to their heavy reliance on the fish and aquacultural industry but the increasing volume of production and catch worldwide would necessitate this determinant. How and why eco-friendly seafood processing can be applied towards environmental sustainability is deemed essential for further investigation in improving sustainable practices.

According to the OECD's Agriculture Outlook 2019–2028, exports of seafood for human consumption are expected to be concentrated in fewer exporting countries, with Vietnam being a major exporter of products that have been sold to more than 165 countries and territories (General Statistic Office of Vietnam, 2018; OECD; FAO, 2019). Given that aquaculture has been increasingly growing in Vietnam since 2000 (Vietdata, 2019), it addresses the need for more sustainable production practices with the country specifically facing environmental problems that pose challenges for sustainable development of the seafood sector. The foreseeable environmental problems that are demanding attention are instability, wastewater, solid waste, packaging waste, air pollution and high risk. Notably, there is a lack of seafood safety standards for farmed production, and small-scale producers dominate seafood production (Binh & Moon, 2019; Thanh, 2014; Tran et al., 2013). The overarching issue of seafood processing plants causing waste streams and environmental pollution of soil and water also needs to be addressed (Anh et al., 2011). While seafood farmers' perceptions towards compliance with laws in agricultural land and water management are not supportive, their roles and collaborations with authorities towards maintaining sustainable models are poor (Nguyen et al., 2020). This regulatory issue is found to be a common problem that has underpinned emerging economies, and while many have addressed these problems, there is little one can do to enforce it. This calls for amplifying different ways to address these issues.

Boosting international economic integration and joining of bilateral, regional, and multilateral free trade agreements (FTAs) such as CPTPP (Comprehensive and Progressive Agreement for Trans-Pacific Partnership) and EVFTA (Vietnam—EU FTA) have assisted in broadening the market access conditions for Vietnam's seafood exporting. This has provided Vietnamese seafood processing firms with greater opportunities to expand their export markets to the EU and Pacific region with tariff cutoffs. Consequently, they are also confronted with stringent environmental regulations (VASEP, 2019; VCCI, 2019). These environmental regulations are not found to be conducive for exporting, as the EU political consortium has varying standards and policies that may not fit many of the non-EU countries. Hence, given these challenges associated with environmental issues and regulation compliance, a shift towards strategies founded on eco-friendly directions to achieve sustainable development is an essential requirement that will strengthen not only the application but the implementation as well.

In response to mitigating environmental risks, firms in general and seafood processing firms in particular, are being called upon to direct their goals to go far beyond economic benefits. Thus, this research proposes environmental strategies that would strengthen environmental goals at the firm level. Environmental strategies integrate environmental considerations within a firm's strategic plans and operational routines to address these issues (Aragón-Correa et al., 2008). Research into environmental strategies has been growing and it can be classified into five main streams, as illustrated in Table 5.1.

Table 5.1 Key research streams of environmental strategies

No.	Research streams	Selected references
1.	Determinants that include role of internal or/and external forces of environmental strategies	Alan and Alain (1998), Gallego-Alvarez et al. (2017), Garcés-Ayerbe et al. (2012), Kassinis and Vafeas (2006), Menguc et al. (2010), Zailani et al. (2012)
2.	Barriers to environmental strategies	Bey et al. (2013), Dahlmann et al. (2008), Ervin et al. (2013), Ghazilla et al. (2015), Murillo-Luna et al. (2011), Pinkse and Dommisse (2009)
3.	Consequences of environmental strategies as achieved competitive advantage or firm's performance	Barba-Sánchez and Atienza-Sahuquillo (2016), Junquera and Barba-Sánchez (2018), Leonidou et al. (2015), Molina-Azorín et al. (2009), Primc and Čater (2015), Ryszko (2016), Yusof et al. (2020)
4.	Levels of environmental strategies	Do et al. (2019), Lee and Rhee (2007)
5.	Determinants and consequences of proactive environmental strategies (PES)	Aragón-Correa and Rubio-López (2007), Buysse and Verbeke (2003), Darnall et al. (2010), Duque-Grisales et al. (2019), Liu et al. (2015), Sharma and Vredenburg (1998)

Despite the growing interest, research on environmental strategies has several major research gaps. First, previous research has primarily focused on one of the five research streams aforementioned; thus, a comprehensive model that explores both forces that drive firms to deploy eco-friendly strategies and their consequences is limited and raises a call for further investigation (Leonidou et al., 2015). Second, despite several significant attempts to analyse determinants and consequences derived from environmental strategies, they are mainly conducted at the domestic level, which significantly differs from the international level. There is scant information in the literature regarding export firms in Vietnam and their environmental approaches. Third, it becomes indeed more essential to put the research of eco-friendly business strategy (thereafter EBS) in the same regulatory context to thoroughly understand the forces that drive firms to deploy such strategy within the same industry (Bıçakcıoğlu, 2018). Only a few external and internal factors that drive firms to implement EBS were investigated in previous research, and there are unexplored areas for additional research from institutional–stakeholder perspectives that are also currently limited (Bıçakcıoğlu, 2018; Zeriti et al., 2014). Fourth, until now, there have been no conclusive results about the relationship between EBS and its consequences such as a competitive advantage (thereafter CAD). Awareness of environmental problems for world ecology drives firms not only to develop EBS but also to move towards green supply chain (Aragón-Correa & Rubio-López, 2007; Wu et al., 2014). Since the supply chain plays a critical role in successfully executing the UN's Sustainable Development Goals (Amiri et al., 2020). These compounding factors lead to a need for research on environmental strategies for supply chains to address sustainable development. This helps to integrate the connections of that strategy, supply chain coordination (thereafter SCC), and consequently, CAD becomes significant. In the context of export strategy with goals for both financial and environmental performance, it is substantive for firms to understand the unique need of EBS and develop CAD to strategically integrate "green" aspects into SCC.

This study aims to contribute to the literature by conceptualizing and testing a comprehensive model of institutional—stakeholder drivers of EBS and its consequences on export markets. Specifically, the study sheds light on EBS literature streams by examining how managers' perceptions of stakeholder and institutional pressures refer to their concentration on eco-friendly export business strategies (thereafter EEBS) and consequently realize the links of EEBS, SCC, and CAD. To the best of the researchers' knowledge, the current study is the first to provide empirical evidence as to what extent a firm leverages its SCC in EEBS to pursue CAD from a strategic management perspective.

To realize these objectives, the rest of the research is organized as follows. The following section presents the theoretical approach and development of hypotheses; the third section examines the research methodology; the fourth section discusses the results; and, finally the fifth section outlines our conclusions and discussions.

5.2 Literature and Hypotheses

5.2.1 *Stakeholder and Institutional Theory*

The stakeholder and institutional perspectives are theoretical underpinnings for an environmental strategy. Stakeholders are defined as "any individual or group who can affect the firm's performance or who is affected by the achievements of the organisation's objective" (Freeman, 1984, p. 5). The firm's environmental responsibility means harmonizing the expectations of stakeholders and environmental performance (González-Benito & González-Benito, 2006). Once stakeholders are conceptualized broadly for strategic management analysis, the combination of stakeholder theory and contingency perspective provides a better explanation of the stakeholders' roles and their links to their environmental strategy. This suggests that different stakeholders compel firms to act in various ways to reduce negative externalities and to increase positive ones. Many scholars examined the impact of internal and/ or external stakeholders on the firm's environmental strategy (e.g., Buysse & Verbeke, 2003; Darnall et al., 2008; Wang et al., 2020). Findings based on stakeholder theory, indicate that a firm's stakeholders not only promote short-term goals of profit but also motivate—firms' environmental strategies (Buysse & Verbeke, 2003; Wang et al., 2020).

The institutional theory focuses on the impacts of social and cultural pressures on firms' practices and structures. DiMaggio and Powell (1983) indicated that three categories of institutional pressures (coercive, normative, and mimetic) make organizations in a field increasingly—competitive. Institutional pressure has various implications and firms respond to different stakeholders' expectations of obtaining legitimacy by following similar corporate governance and market behaviour. Regarding the connection to environmental response, Jennings and Zandbergen (1995) were the very first researchers, who introduced Di Maggio and Powell's institutional theory of isomorphic pressures on the research theme of corporate environmental strategy. Henceforth, institutional pressure extended to market pressure, competitive pressure, and regulatory pressure (Hong et al., 2009; Wang et al., 2020). Several empirical research has confirmed the positive links between institutional pressure and environmental strategy (Delmas & Toffel, 2010; Dubey et al., 2017; Galbreath, 2017; Gunarathne et al., 2021; Yang et al., 2018).

The stakeholder theory and the institutional theory inform this study in that the study considers top management sensitivity to environmental issues, regulatory pressure, market pressure, and competitive pressures as important drivers of a firm's EEBS. The implementation of that strategy expectedly enhances SCC, which in turn creates and sustains the firm's competitive advantage.

5.2.2 Drivers of Eco-Friendly Export Business Strategy

5.2.2.1 Top Management Sensitivity

Top managers are front and centre in the organization, especially in the field of strategic management (Hambrick, 1989). Top management sensitivity to environmental issues is essential to changing the firm's strategy towards green, which requires a strong investment inappropriate technologies and capabilities. According to Drumwright (1994), top managers present their key roles in formulating organizational policies that motivate eco-initiatives by proactively investing in new resources and capabilities. Their attitudes have a significant impact on innovation that fosters eco-oriented organizational values (Stone et al., 2004). Furthermore, in reaction to introducing environmental initiatives, top managers are also responsible for training and promoting employees to become more green-conscious and to pay more attention to ecological issues, appointing appropriate people to observe the firm's environmental procedures (Banerjee et al., 2003). Notably, the top management support is one of the antecedents of the firm's environmental responsiveness (Haldorai et al., 2022), as they are the initiators for incorporating green factors into the firm's new product development (Haldorai et al., 2022; Pujari et al., 2004).

The responsibility of top managers in EBS in international markets is rather vital than in the domestic market (Leonidou et al., 2015) since they are dealing with stricter regulations and standards that firms are required to follow while trading. The more complicated the environmental differences between the domestic and foreign markets are, the higher the motivation of top managers to adjust their export strategies (Leonidou et al., 2015; Stone et al., 2004). Thus, a successful EEBS is unlikely without the significant support of top managers. Previous studies show that top management's sensitivity to environmental issues is a key driver for the adoption of EBS in general and EEBS in particular (Banerjee et al., 2003; Leonidou et al., 2015; Haldorai et al., 2022). Thus, it is proposed that:

H1 Top management sensitivity to environmental problems is related positively to the firm's EEBS.

5.2.2.2 Regulatory Pressure

According to (Scott, 2001), the coercive isomorphic of the institutional pressures could be attained by regulations. Regulatory pressure is emphasized by regulatory stakeholders, who are involved in or contribute to public policy (Schmitz et al., 2019; Zameer et al., 2021). The more stringent regulations of both home and host countries regarding environmental issues the greater will be the significant role of regulatory pressure on environmental strategies. In the face of environmental preservation worldwide, many countries, environmental protection groups, non-profit or non-governmental organizations (NGOs), or retailers have introduced environmental regulations or standards (e.g., eco-labels and certifications). From a national perspective, different countries enact different environment-related laws or regulations. For example, Vietnam's government enacted the law of environmental protection; the EU enacted REACH focusing on improving the protection of the environment and human health.

Regarding environmental standards, there are many types of eco-labels and certification schemes set up by NGOs, industry bodies, public eco-labelling schemes, or retailers. Examples of fisheries certifications from NGOs include Friend of the Sea (FOS), Aquaculture Stewardship Council (ASC), Marine Stewardship Council (MSC), and Dolphin Safe. National and regional industry bodies have also launched seafood certification schemes. For example, UK's Seafish Industry Authority developed a scheme covering all features of vessel operations, containing ecological considerations and traceability; or the Japan Fisheries Association set up the Marine Eco-Label (MEL). Currently, many retailers have also announced their environmental labels. For example, Germany's Edeka (the country's biggest supermarket chain)—stated that it would source only fisheries certified by MSC; or Swiss Manor Switzerland has a commitment to FOS. This regulatory pressure demonstrates that seafood exporters must pay attention to environmental requirements to limit the use of harmful materials or processes. Hence, to export to different markets, seafood exporters including those in Vietnam are compelled to comply with these regulations or standards. Hence, the following is hypothesized:

H2 Regulatory pressure is related positively to the firm's EEBS.

5.2.2.3 Market Pressure

Market pressure comes from market stakeholders (Wang et al., 2020). For a specific market, market pressure represents the market's trends thus, the market pressure of an export company reflects the requirements of international customers. Over the last 20 years, global demand for sustainable seafood has grown (The Seafood Certification & Ratings Collaboration, 2015). Vietnam is among the main seafood exporters worldwide as it ranked 4th in 2019 seafood export value (Statista, 2020). However, according to Lebailly (2017), Vietnam's seafood exports confront many obstacles as food safety and lack of certifications related to eco and environmental issues. In the global natural environmental preservation trend, seafood processing exporter not only has to meet the domestic market's environmental protection requirements to preserve the firm's eco-friendly image but also must adapt to the green purchasing trend of international buyers.

To strengthen their competitive edge, firms need to understand the significant role of responding to customer pressure (Freeman, 1984). As the customer is a key market stakeholder, it can put pressure on lawsuits or collective boycotts (Wang et al., 2020) and has been recognized as an important driver of environmental strategies (Dai et al., 2017). Moreover, Menguc et al. (2010) stressed that market pressure on the preservation of the environment would encourage top managers' commitment towards green, thus stimulating firms to adopt environmental strategies (Dai et al., 2017). Therefore, it is reasonable to expect that market pressure leads to EEBS and thus it is proposed that:

H3 Market pressure is positively related to the firm's EEBS.

5.2.2.4 Competitive Pressure

Previous research conceptualized that competitive pressure generates mimetic isomorphism (Daddi et al., 2015; Zhu & Sarkis, 2007). Mimetic isomorphism refers to the imitation or copying of competitors' successful practices and strategies under competitive pressure (DiMaggio & Powell, 1983). Thus, competitive pressure comes from competitors or organizations. Several empirical studies show how a firm responds to competitive pressure. For companies that decided to enter into new markets, Brouthers et al. (2005) and Haveman (1993) encouraged them to follow the leaders, who are similar and successful organizations. Furthermore, by investigating 1361 foreign joint-venture firms in China from 23 different countries, Li and Parboteeah (2015) found evidence to support that the home country culture significantly affects a firm's mimetic behaviour in reaction to competitive pressure. For firms with limited resources like small and medium companies, copying competitors' activities is the best choice (Cheng & Yu, 2008). In the case of Vietnam seafood exports, recently some of Vietnam seafood exporters have globally become famous, for example, the world biggest export shrimp processing—Minh Phu corporation; the leading catfish company—Hung Vuong corporation are a few of the top companies. In response to international customers with high sensitivity to food safety and ecological issues, both Minh Phu Corp. and Hung Vuong Corp. invested much in global certifications and had the strong leading edge on EEBS. They became a typical successful reputed organization for imitation from other seafood processing exporters in Vietnam. Therefore, based on the discourse above, it is proposed that:

H4 Competitive pressure is positively related to the firm's EEBS.

5.2.3 The Links of EEBS, SCC and CAD

Since "eco-friendly", "environmentally friendly", "ecologically friendly", "green" and "nature friendly" are the terms that have identical meanings and are synonymous (Leonidou et al., 2015), "eco-friendly export strategy" can be considered to be similar to "ecologically friendly export strategy", "environmentally friendly export strategy", "green export strategy" and "environmental export strategy". In line with previous studies, an EEBS in this study can be defined as a strategy that reflects how managers encompass eco-issues in different areas (e.g., R&D, product development, manufacturing, marketing, purchasing, human resources and supply chain) and harmonize the costs and benefits of applying greening technologies and procedures for export (Banerjee, 2001; Hart, 1995; Yang et al., 2018). The fundamental of an EEBS should direct a firm to make decisions based on a positive impact on the natural environment (Olson, 2008).

To emphasize the environmental friendliness of green strategy, Lee and Rhee (2007, p. 197) emphasized that "the environmental decision areas that firms have to consider in their environmental management include product, process, organisation and systems, supply chain and recovery, and the external relationship-related decision area". Thus, adopting EEBS requires not only cross-functional efforts towards green within a firm and each of its suppliers but also collaborative efforts among the entire supply chain's actors in response to eco-issues (Hong et al., 2009). The focal firm's final products incorporate various elements and components from either one or a series of suppliers. In Vietnam, the most common export seafood products are frozen shrimp, of which, frozen processing includes four phases as pre-treatment, de-heading, trimming and freezing, and packing and storage (Anh et al., 2011). EEBS for leading firms such as seafood processing products is possible through the integrative commitment of seed suppliers, grow-out farms, processors, traders, etc. Hence, it requires the effective collaboration of all tiers of suppliers, processors, traders, distributors, and manufacturing processes of the supply value chain to be integrated if the firm's strategic objective is to go green. That's why it is reasonable to propose that:

H5 The firm's EEBS is positively related to SCC.

Defined as an equilibrium strategy, SCC is not only a coordinative attempt with suppliers but also integrative efforts with distributors, customers, and other actors in the supply chain (Hong et al., 2009; Liu & Yi, 2018). It leans on the readiness for unhesitating and precise information that is visible to all supply chain participants (Holweg & Pil, 2008). With coordinative attempts with suppliers, a seafood processing exporter can better supervise the backward integrated supply of seed or raw materials, improve its inventory management system, optimize seafood processing, and decrease the processing costs. In addition to integrative efforts with distributors and customers, a seafood processing exporter can understand more about the market; thus, it can provide the more suitable products to the market. These factors can help the firm develop more effective eco-friendly products and strategies. A firm can gain a competitive advantage by establishing cooperation with upstream and downstream members in their supply chain. Other studies also demonstrated that SCC could help the improvement of CAD (Liao et al., 2017; Mellat-Parast & Spillan, 2014). Thus, the last hypothesis is proposed as follows:

H6 SCC is positively related to the firm's CAD.

Figure 5.1 summarises the proposed conceptual model. Firm size and firm age are included as control variables that may have an impact on EEBS.

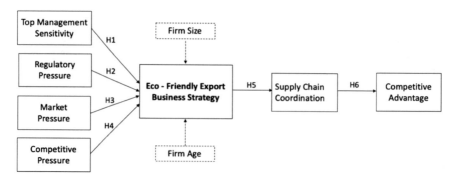

Fig. 5.1 The proposed research model

5.3 Research Methodology

5.3.1 Measurement

All the constructs and variables in the proposed model were obtained and adapted from prior studies. They were all measured with a 7-point Likert continuous scale. Specifically, six items measuring "top management sensitivity" were adapted from (Leonidou et al., 2015). The measures of "regulatory pressure", "market pressure", "competitive pressure" and "Supply chain coordination" were adapted from Hong et al. (2009). "Eco-friendly export business strategy" is a second-order construct that includes five first-order constructs of "marketing", "research and development", "production", "human resources" and "purchasing". these measures were adapted from Leonidou et al. (2015). Finally, six items measuring "competitive advantage" were adapted from the research of Banerjee et al. (2003).

Two control variables were examined in this study. From the firm's perspective, the strained resources of small and medium firms may denote environmental problems (Yang et al., 2018), hence, firm size was included in the model as a control variable that may have an impact on EEBS. The logarithm of firm size was as small, medium and large ones based on Vietnam's Decree 39/128/NĐ-CP, using three combined criteria of a number of employees, total assets and firm age was also treated as a control variable for the firm's EEBS since older firms with their better experiences might better pursue sustain growth and commit to environmental strategy than younger firms (Autio et al., 2000; Leonidou et al., 2015). The logarithm of firm age was in years, which will be further discussed in the following section.

5.3.2 Data Collection and Sample

Originally, the survey was written in English. It was then back-translated into Vietnamese and converted back into English (Harkness et al., 2004). Two bilingual researchers compared two versions of the survey to confirm that the English and Vietnamese questions transferred the same meaning. Before the official survey, in-depth interviews were conducted with five CEOs of Vietnam seafood processing exporters to collect their comments on the appropriateness, clarity, comprehensibility, and correct understanding of the survey questions, The participants confirmed that the questions were clear and easy to understand and the target group of the survey as the CEO is completely appropriate.

Due to the nature of the surveyed variables being at the strategic level, this study focused on CEOs and directors of Vietnam seafood processing exporters, who were employed in firms that were more than five years in operation. As suggested by Dillman (2007), the study used a mixed mode of paper and online collection approach to make sure that all target populations could participate in the survey. A list of seafood processing exporters was obtained from the Vietnam Association of Seafood Exporters and Producers (VASEP) and the Departments of Industry and Trade of major cities in Vietnam. The researchers contacted these exporters to request their participation in the survey and their preferred mode of questionnaire distribution. Paper-based based surveys were distributed to respondents through VASEP and the Departments. The electronic version of the survey was emailed to the respondents who preferred the online method.

To reduce the common method bias, the respondents were informed that the survey was just used for academic purposes, and their anonymity and confidentiality were ensured. This helped to decrease the respondents' apprehension (Podsakoff et al., 2003). In addition, the researchers shuffled the order of the constructs and items in the survey questionnaires. The different order of the constructs can dilute respondents' perceptions of any direct links of the constructs (Podsakoff et al., 2003).

A total of 261 responses were received, including 116 paper-based and 145 online surveys. Following the guidelines of Hair et al. (2017), 21 responses were excluded because of unanswered questions. In addition, 2 other responses were also excluded because their years of operation were less than 5 full years. Finally, the total valid responses were 238. To determine whether the sample size was sufficient for data analysis, G*Power 3.1 software was applied (Faul et al., 2007). According to the rigorous standards from G*Power, the current research model needs a sample size of 184 to ensure the analysis's reliability reaches 95%. Therefore, the sample size of 238 in this study is well enough to make sure the robustness of the results of the statistical method (Hair et al., 2017). The sample characteristics are depicted in Table 5.2.

Table 5.2 Profile of respondents

		Frequency	Percentage			Frequency	Percentage
Firm Age	5–10 years	73	30.67	**Firm Size**	Small	12	5.04
	10–15 years	79	33.19		Medium	146	61.34
	15–20 years	34	14.29		Big	80	33.62
Gender of respondents	Male	137	57.56	**Position of respondents**	Director	128	53.78
	Female	59	24.79		Chairman	77	32.35
	Unspecified	42	17.65		Department Managers	33	13.87

5.3.3 Data Analysis Procedure

Survey data were transferred to SPSS 23.0 software to check incorrect entries, detecting and removing differences. To detect for nonresponse bias and common method bias, t-test and Average block VIF were used (Armstrong & Overton, 1977; Kock, 2015). The proposed model was then examined by applying Structural Equation Modelling (SEM) that employed partial least squares (PLS) with SmartPLS 3.2.9. The SEM procedure included assessment of measurement model and structural model. According to Hair et al. (2017), PLS is appropriate and fitting for a study with a unique theoretically accepted model and it permits the combinations of formative and reflective constructs in the same model, which is the case in the current research. Furthermore, the sample responses of this study are 238 (less than 250), so making PLS is an appropriate method (Reinartz et al., 2009). Parametric bootstrapping is used to verify the hypotheses and evaluate the research model due to the complexity of the model with many variables, especially with the second-order construct of EEBS (Hair et al., 2017).

5.4 Results

5.4.1 Nonresponse Bias and Common Method Bias

To detect for nonresponse bias's issue, the researchers compared the first 20 paper-based responses and the last 20 online responses by using the independent samples t-test as suggested by Armstrong and Overton (1977). The t-test's results indicated that there was no significant difference in terms of EEBS variables. Hence, nonresponse bias was not a major concern. Following the suggestion of Kock (2015), the average block variance inflation factor (AVIF) was used to check the issue of common method bias. The AVIF value was 1.968 (much less than the recommended threshold of 3.3) and therefore, within acceptable limits.

5.4.2 Assessment of the Measurement Model

The measurement model includes the relationships between the latent and the corresponding observed variables (Hair et al., 2017). Assessing the measurement model helps us to ensure the proposed model's validity and reliability, criteria on internal consistency, convergent validity, and discriminant validity. Key results of descriptive statistics and assessing the measurement model are depicted in Table 5.3.

The results showed that all loadings, Cronbach's α values, and composite reliability (CR) all reached 0.693 or more, while none of the variables had average variance extracted (AVE) values less than 0.5 (Table 5.3). This ensured the internal

Table 5.3 Constructs, items and properties

Constructs	Items	Mean	Std. deviation	Loadings	Reliability and validity
Top management sensitivity (Leonidou et al., 2015)	MGS1. Our managers help us stay away from the risks associated with environmental problems	4.53	1.480	0.92	Cronbach's $\alpha = 0.927$ CR $= 0.943$ AVE $= 0.733$
	MGS2. Our managers are interested in environmental issues	4.26	1.247	0.817	
	MGS3. Our managers guide us clearly to reach environmental goals	4.46	1.494	0.893	
	MGS4. Our managers deeply understand the role of green issues in foreign markets	4.38	1.372	0.79	
	MGS5. Our managers confident in maintaining and operating our equipment in green way	4.40	1.469	0.861	
	MGS6. Our managers strive to understand eco-friendly aspects of the firm's operations	4.39	1.468	0.848	
Market Pressure (Wu et al., 2012)	MP1. In reaction to the ecological protection tendency, our firm will deem the influence on exportation	5.09	1.294	0.776	Cronbach's $\alpha = 0.709$ CR $= 0.838$ AVE $= 0.633$
	MP2. In reaction to the ecological protection tendency, our firm will deem the influence on sales of foreign customers	4.89	1.300	0.765	
	MP3. In reaction the ecological tendency, our firm will deem the influence on green awareness of international customers	5.12	1.320	0.843	
Regulatory Pressure (Wu et al., 2012)	RP1. Our firm's eco-friendly management (EFM) is affected by home government's eco regulations	5.20	1.232	0.845	Cronbach's $\alpha = 0.768$ CR $= 0.852$ AVE $= 0.591$
	RP2. Our firm's EFM is affected by regional and NGOs' ecological regulations	4.95	1.277	0.778	
	RP3. Potential gaps between our products and ecological regulations will influence our firm's EFM	5.14	1.198	0.713	

(continued)

5 Implementing Eco-Friendly Export Business ...   109

Table 5.3 (continued)

Constructs	Items		Mean	Std. deviation	Loadings	Reliability and validity
	RP4. Our firm's EFM is affected by buyers' ecological regulations		5.02	1.234	0.733	
	RP5. Our firm's EFM is affected by cost of environmental preserve		5.08	1.261	0.742	
Competitive Pressure (Wu et al., 2012)	CP1. Our firm's EFM is influenced by competitors' ecological protection strategy		4.83	1.097	0.835	Cronbach's $\alpha = 0.693$ CR $= 0.831$ AVE $= 0.623$
	CP2. Our firm's EFM is influenced by professional groups of environmental protection		4.79	1.151	0.697	
	CP3. Preserving the competitive edge of eco-friendly seafood will affect our firm's EFM		4.75	1.145	0.829	
Eco- Friendly Export Business Strategy, EEBS, Cronbach's $\alpha =$ 0.975, CR = 0.981, AVE = 0.911 (Leonidou et al., 2015)	Marketing	MKT1. Our firm develops eco-friendly seafood products for the foreign markets	4.55	1.323	0.851	Cronbach's $\alpha = 0.871$ CR $= 0.907$ AVE $= 0.66$
		MKT2. Our firm offers price incentives to motivate our foreign customers to our eco-friendly seafood	4.49	1.318	0.791	
		MKT3. Our firm co-operates with distribution channels in export markets towards green issues	4.59	1.272	0.776	
		MKT4. Our firm's logistics used in export seafood are eco-friendly responsible	4.45	1.352	0.807	

(continued)

Table 5.3 (continued)

Constructs	Items		Mean	Std. deviation	Loadings	Reliability and validity
		MKT5. Our firm's promotion programs in export markets convey our commitment to eco-issues	4.47	1.352	0.836	
	R&D	RD1. Our firm invests in cleaner technologies and development of cleaner seafood for export markets	4.45	1.317	0.835	Cronbach's $\alpha = 0.887$ CR $= 0.917$ AVE $= 0.69$
		RD2. Our firm focusses on ecological protection when developing technologies for exporting seafood	4.53	1.365	0.809	
		RD3. Our firm has internal environmental experts for the development of eco-friendly seafood for export	4.41	1.262	0.859	
		RD4. Our firm is consulted by external environmental experts for exporting eco-friendly seafood	4.53	1.298	0.81	
		RD5. Our firm collaborates with other organisations for the development of eco-friendly seafood for export markets	4.44	1.323	0.839	

(continued)

5 Implementing Eco-Friendly Export Business …   111

Table 5.3 (continued)

Constructs	Items		Mean	Std. deviation	Loadings	Reliability and validity
	Production	PR1. Our firm applies eco-friendly approaches for processing seafood for export markets	4.49	1.359	0.855	Cronbach's $\alpha = 0.869$ CR $= 0.911$ AVE $= 0.719$
		PR2. Our firm pays attention to deceasing effects to environment during our seafood processing for export markets	4.50	1.337	0.83	
		PR3. Eco-friendly management systems are adopted in our seafood processing for export markets	4.64	1.367	0.833	
		PR4. Non-ecological materials are systematically limited in in our seafood processing for export markets	4.32	1.371	0.873	
	Human Resources	HM1. Our firm has training programs on environmental issues for employees engaged in exports	4.55	1.345	0.808	Cronbach's $\alpha = 0.908$ CR $= 0.929$ AVE $= 0.684$
		HM2. Our firm supports employees who adopt environmental stance	4.49	1.289	0.825	

(continued)

Table 5.3 (continued)

Constructs	Items		Mean	Std. deviation	Loadings	Reliability and validity
		HM3. Our firm rewards exporting staffs who solve environmental problems	4.52	1.346	0.815	
		HM4. Our firm has special award systems to merit exporting staffs based on environmental performance	4.53	1.333	0.84	
		HM5. Our firm offers financial reward to exporting staffs who achieve ecological goals	4.53	1.355	0.83	
		HM6. The ecological goals and responsibilities are clearly assigned to exporting staffs in our firm	4.47	1.374	0.844	
	Purchase	PS1. Purchasing eco-friendly inputs for exporting processing seafood are our priority	4.39	1.354	0.858	Cronbach's $\alpha = 0.898$ CR $= 0.924$ AVE $= 0.71$
		PS2. Eco-friendly approaches are applied in our purchasing decisions for exporting seafood	4.60	1.281	0.828	
		PS3. Our firm prefers to collaborate with green suppliers when exporting seafood	4.48	1.337	0.833	

(continued)

5 Implementing Eco-Friendly Export Business … 113

Table 5.3 (continued)

Constructs	Items	Mean	Std. deviation	Loadings	Reliability and validity
	PS4. All input suppliers need to conform to eco-friendly characteristics of our seafood	4.53	1.361	0.844	
	PS5. Our firm collaborates with suppliers who can help to achieve our ecological goals for exporting seafood	4.52	1.259	0.85	
Supply Chain Coordination (Hong et al., 2009)	SCC1. Our firm implement and develop evaluating programs for suppliers	4.84	1.397	0.859	Cronbach's $\alpha = 0.768$ CR $= 0.868$ AVE $= 0.687$
	SCC2. Our firm raises collaborating level of formulating decisions and flow of goods with suppliers together with dedicated investments	4.62	1.354	0.742	
	SCC3. Our firm raises collaborating level of formulating decisions and flow of goods with customers together with dedicated investments	4.95	1.400	0.879	
Competitive Advantage (Banerjee et al., 2003)	CAD1. Being ecological conscious can result in our significant cost advantages	3.75	1.226	0.80	Cronbach's $\alpha = 0.876$ CR $= 0.915$ AVE $= 0.729$
	CAD2. With experimental ways to improve our quality of seafood and processes towards green, our firm has saved substantial cost	4.10	1.445	0.852	
	CAD3. Our regular investment for R&D on cleaner seafood and processes can result in our leader position in the market	3.98	1.405	0.872	
	CAD4. Our firm can penetrate sensitive foreign markets by adopting eco-friendly export strategies	3.93	1.378	0.884	
	CAD5. Our firm's market share can be improved by making our current seafood more eco-friendly	3.94	1.422	0.823	

(continued)

Table 5.3 (continued)

Constructs	Items	Mean	Std. deviation	Loadings	Reliability and validity
	CAD6. Decreasing the influence of the firm's activities on natural environment will lead our quality of seafood and processes increase	3.82	1.415	0.817	

Table 5.4 Discriminant validity

Constructs	CAD	CP	EEBS	Firm age	Firm size	MGS	MP	RP	SCC
CAD	*0.854*								
CP	0.578	*0.789*							
EEBS	0.851	0.681	*0.954*						
Firm age	0.247	0.223	0.281	*1*					
Firm size	0.406	0.35	0.43	0.37	*1*				
MGS	0.656	0.57	0.772	0.264	0.411	*0.856*			
MP	0.621	0.631	0.695	0.255	0.354	0.597	*0.796*		
RP	0.625	0.639	0.692	0.265	0.325	0.536	0.757	*0.769*	
SCC	0.623	0.574	0.733	0.263	0.332	0.779	0.678	0.618	*0.829*

Note MGS top management sensitivity, RP regulatory pressure, MP market pressure, CP competitive pressure, EEBS eco-friendly export business strategy, SCC supply chain coordination, CAD competitive advantage. Square roots of AVE of all constructs are along the diagonal

consistency, indicator reliability, and convergent validity of the scales. However, there were two pairs of variables that did not reach the standard of discrimination suggested by Fornell and Larcker (1981), which were between MP and RP, and between CAD and EEBS. Therefore, after considering the cross-loading coefficient between scales, the two scales, RP2 and CAD4, were removed to meet the criteria of discriminant validity.

Table 5.3 indicates that values of loadings of all scales were higher than 0.7, except the loading of CP2 was 0.697. Composite reliability reached a value higher than 0.8. In addition, all the scales achieved AVE values from 0.591 or higher. This result confirmed the scales' consistency and convergence as well as the validity of scales use for further allometric analysis. To evaluate the discriminant validity, the Fornell–Larcker criterion was checked. The correlations and square roots of AVE presented in Table 5.4 reveal that the measurement model satisfied the criterion (Fornell & Larcker, 1981); thus, establishing the rule for discriminant validity.

5.4.3 Assessment of the Structural Model

The structural model based on one-tail Bootstrap with a sub-sample of 5000 is presented in Fig. 5.2.

The structural model was first checked for collinearity problems. As VIF values of all the constructs <3.0, multicollinearity was not the issue (Hair et al., 2019). Second, the values of R^2 were checked. The results of R^2 values of EEBS, SCC, and CAD were 0.737, 0.537, and 0.389, respectively, indicating that the endogenous construct's prognosticate power was acceptable (Cohen, 1992). After that, the prognosticate relevance of the structural model was evaluated through a blindfolding procedure (Ringle et al., 2012). Stone-Geisser's Q^2 values of EEBS, SCC and CAD were 0.664, 0.362 and 0.287, respectively. These Q^2 values demonstrated the structural model's large predictive relevance (Hair et al., 2019). Most importantly, the results of SRMR and NFI values (0.057 and 0.926, respectively) met the suggested fit criteria (Hair et al., 2017). Finally, the PLS algorithm with bootstrapping was utilized to examine the hypotheses. The results of examining proposed hypotheses with a 95% confidence level, $t > 1.6$, $p < .05$, CI (confident interval) not containing zero were shown in Table 5.5.

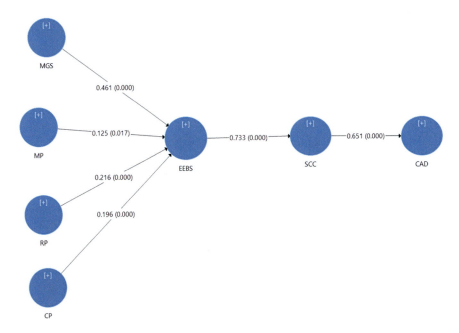

Fig. 5.2 The structural model

Table 5.5 Hypothesis testing

Hypotheses	Relationships	Std Beta	T Value	P Value	f^2	CI LL (5%)	CI UL (95%)	Findings
H1	MGS → EEBS	0.461	9.764	0	0.418	0.369	0.52	Supported
H2	RP → EEBS	0.216	4.209	0	0.069	0.127	0.315	Supported
H3	MP → EEBS	0.125	2.055	0.017	0.02	0.022	0.214	Supported
H4	CP → EEBS	0.196	3.811	0	0.065	0.112	0.259	Supported
H5	EEBS → SCC	0.733	25.114	0	1.158	0.678	0.775	Supported
H6	SCC → CAD	0.651	17.151	0	0.636	0.555	0.676	Supported

As expected, the influences of top management sensitivity ($\beta = 0.461, t = 9.764$, $p < .01$), regulatory pressure ($\beta = 0.216, t = 4.209, p < .01$), market pressure ($\beta = 0.125, t = 2.055, p < .05$) and competitive pressure ($\beta = 0.196, t = 3.811, p < .01$) on EEBS were all significant. This supported the first four hypotheses about the factors that motivate the pursuit of EEBS (H1–H4). Of which, top management sensitivity (i.e., the manager's sensitivity to environmental issues) was found to be the most important influencer with the effect size (f^2) reaching 0.418, which indicates a strong influence level (Cohen, 1988). The lowest ranking of influence on EEBS was market pressure with f^2 achieving 0.02.

The impact of EEBS on SCC was significant and strong ($\beta = 0.733, t = 25.114$, $p < 0.01, f^2 = 1.158$), confirming H5. In particular, the value of f^2 was 1.158, which far exceeded the standard of 0.35 for strong relationship affirmation given by Cohen (1988). This indicated a very close link between EEBS and SCC. This finding presented a significant demonstration of the vital role of EEBS in the collaboration among all actors in the seafood supply chain towards green.

The effect of SCC on CAD was significant ($\beta = 0.651, t = 17.151, p < .01, f^2 = 0.636$), providing support for H6. The relationship between SCC and CAD was very strong as $f^2 > 0.35$. This result was also a substantive confirmation of reaching a competitive edge from the supply chain collaboration based on pursuing EEBS.

The potential effects of firm size and firm age on EEBS were also evaluated. Results revealed that EEBS was more frequently employed in larger exporter than in smaller counterparts ($\beta = 0.64, t = 1.612, p = .054$). However, the value of f^2 was 0.011, suggesting that firm size didn't affect much EEBS. The positive effect of firm age on EEBS was also confirmed ($\beta = 0.009, t = 0.25, p = .041$). This result indicated that exporters with more years of doing business were more likely to adopt EEBS than less experienced ones. However, the influence of firm age on EEBS was minimal as the value of f^2 was almost equal to zero.

5.5 Discussion and Implications

The main purpose of this study is to examine how managers' perceptions of stakeholder and institutional pressures influence EEBS, which consequently impacts SCC and CAD. It also shows how the firm's size and the firm's age control the effects of stakeholder and institutional pressures on EEBS towards sustainable development. The study's findings offer both theoretical and practical implications.

5.5.1 Theoretical Implications

This study's findings imply four contributions to the literature. *First*, following the recent call from Testa et al. (2018), and Wei et al., (2017), this study explores how various types of stakeholder, institutional and competitive factors relate to EEBS. The research's results substantively enrich the literature on EEBS by divulging how managers' perceptions of stakeholder and institutional pressures refer to their concentration on EEBS. The extant literature is multifarious, with one—group focusing on both internal and external stakeholder–institutional pressures of EEBS (Hong et al., 2009; Leonidou et al., 2015; Stone et al., 2004; Yang et al., 2018) and the other on the consequences of that strategy (Leonidou et al., 2013, 2015, 2017; López-Gamero et al., 2009). The current research connects these two groups by bringing to the light that managers' perceptions of stakeholder and institutional pressures set off their concentration on EEBS, which in turn enhance SCC and the firm's CAD. The findings suggest that managers' perceptions of both internal and external stakeholder–institutional pressures have strong implications for the adoption of EEBS. Specifically, the top manager's sensitivity to environmental problems transforms managers' sense-making of market pressures, regulatory pressures, and competitive pressures to motivate the whole firm to pursue EEBS. As such, this research also echoes the call from Leonidou et al. (2015) for more empirical explorations on the potential influences of other types of external and internal determinants of EEBS.

Second, this research contributes to strategic management and supply chain literature by examining the links between EEBS, SCC, and CAD. Prior studies have mainly focused on environmental strategy and the green supply chain separately. Synthesizing EEBS and SCC in a comprehensive model to explore the relationships among EEBS, SCC and CAD have extended these lines of research. This study's findings show that SCC should be taken into consideration when researching EEBS. That outcome suggests that the role of SCC is associated with EEBS in transferring both internal and external stakeholder–institutional pressures into the driving forces for the firm's CAD. Materializing EEBS requires significant cooperation with all actors in the supply chain such as suppliers, distributors and consumers. Thus, SCC is a substantive element of EEBS, that management should take a holistic approach in implementing. Pursuing EEBS is not only about developing eco-friendly products and processes, but also requires firms to minimize the use of energy and materials;

minimize environmental pollution and maximize re-usability. The research model validated in this study describes the need for EEBS and SCC to achieve sources of competitive edge for sustainable development.

Third, the results indicate the positive influence of firm size on the adoption of EEBS. Extending previous studies (Autio et al., 2000; Leonidou et al., 2015; Yang et al., 2018), this research findings explicate the critical role of firm size in the adoption and implementation of firms' EEBS.

Fourth, this research enhances the EEBS literature in the rapidly changing context of the Vietnamese emerging market, where institutional environments create significant challenges to the firm (Wei et al., 2017; Yang et al., 2018). Continuing previous studies based on the context of developed countries without concentrating on a single industry with the same institutional context (e.g., Clarkson et al., 2011; Leonidou et al., 2015; López-Gamero et al., 2009), the current study reveals prominent internal and external stakeholder–institutional drivers of EEBS. Inserting to this research theme, this study suggests that managers' perceptions of stakeholder–institutional pressures refer to EEBS, which in turn create the firm's SCC and CAD. In general, these outcomes recommend the significant role of managers' sensitivity to environmental issues and institutional forces of EBS in emerging markets.

5.5.2 Practical Implications

This study conveys crucially practical implications for environmental protection and sustainable development for both export firms' managers and public policymakers in Vietnam.

5.5.2.1 Implications for Export Firms' Managers

The findings show that EEBS positively boosts SCC, which in turn results in a competitive edge. Hence, export firms' managers should aware of the substantive role of formulating and adopting EEBS to gain a source of competitive edge in international markets. Positively pursuing EEBS rather than a compliant, reactively responding to stakeholder-institutional pressures of environmental issues will help export firms achieve a sustainable competitive edge. This finding is harmonized with prior studies' results to confirm that competitive advantage is the consequence of EEBS (Ge et al., 2018; Leonidou et al., 2015, 2017).

This study also discloses the positive impacts of top managers' sensitivity to green issues on the adoption of the firm's EEBS. Firms' managers often consider solving eco-issues as a burden responsibility and inactively respond to ecological requirements (Yang et al., 2018). This situation is even worst in the case of Vietnam seafood exporters as most of them have just adopted reactive environmental strategies (Do et al., 2019). However, this study reveals that top managers' sensitivity to green issues becomes a critical factor in stimulating EEBS. Hence, top managers should introduce a green set of values and norms (e.g., materials and energy savings, sustainability, recyclable) among their staff to promote eco-thinking in the organisation. Eco-training programs and education that focus on enhancing employees' awareness and actions towards greening within the firm should also be emphasized to facilitate the adoption of eco practices and processes in each of the firm's divisions. Furthermore, appropriate incentives related to eco (e.g., best eco idea award, best eco initiative award) should be regularly considered to encourage the firm's EEBS (Leonidou et al., 2015).

The confirmation that market pressure, regulatory pressure, and competitive pressure positively affect the adoption of the firm's EEBS shows the critical role of understanding external stakeholder–institutional pressures within the firm in general and within the division of exporting in particular. Export firms' managers should regularly scan and update external stakeholder–institutional pressures in international markets to understand all market pressures, regulatory pressures, and competitive pressures related to green issues, which will help the firm to promptly convert to EEBS.

5.5.2.2 Implications for Public Policymakers

Showing that the implementation of an EEBS will help the firm enriches its competitive edge in international markets, the present study implies some suggestions for public policymakers. Importantly, they should convey to export firms' managers that the consequence of pursuing EEBS in international markets is the achievement of competitive edge; thus, export firms should formulate and implement EEBS when they decide to export their products and services. Public policymakers must create a legal corridor that encourages businesses to pursue EEBS and an emphasis on environmental reporting is imperative.

To support firms to adopt EEBS, public policymakers can organize regular export training programs that concentrate on eco programs and EEBS. In those export training programs, case studies of successful export firms in adopting EEBS should be highlighted as motivations for others. State and government agencies can also publish different country profiles that focus on environmental regulations and requirements of each foreign country. Small and young firms with limited resources for environmental solving should receive more attention. Furthermore, special schemes (e.g., tax relief or reduction for green firms, eco awards for the best eco exporters, etc.) should be considered in encouraging firms to pursue EEBS.

5.6 Conclusion and Future Research

This research examines not only the managers' perceptions of stakeholder-institutional pressures that refer to their concentration on EEBS, but also the links of EEBS, SCC and CAD. The study's findings show that top managers' sensitivity to environmental problems transforms the firm's market pressure, regulatory pressure, and competitive pressure into the firm's EEBS. Moreover, the firm's EEBS leads to SCC and in turn, SCC helps the firm reach the source of CAD. Finally, both firm size and firm age positively affected the firm's EEBS.

This study has some limitations that suggest further study directions. First, the research context just focused on a single industry based on seafood processing firms. Thus, future research could examine the interconnection links of drivers, EEBS, and its consequences in different industries or concentrate on comparing those links in different industries and/or countries. Second, a potential expansion of this study would be to employ a longitudinal study design to empirically examine the interconnection links of drivers, EEBS, and its outcomes over time. Third, given that environmental strategies can be different from reactive to proactive ones, it might also be interesting to carry out comparative research on influences of drivers of EEBS and its consequences concerning specific proactivity levels of EEBS.

References

Alan, M. R., & Alain, V. (1998). Corporate strategies and environmental regulations: An organizing framework. *Strategic Management Journal, 19*(4), 363.

Amiri, M., Hashemi-Tabatabaei, M., Ghahremanloo, M., Keshavarz-Ghorabaee, M., Zavadskas, E. K., & Banaitis, A. (2020). A new fuzzy BWM approach for evaluating and selecting a sustainable supplier in supply chain management. *International Journal of Sustainable Development and World Ecology*, 1–18. https://doi.org/10.1080/13504509.2020.1793424

Anh, P. T., My Dieu, T. T., Mol, A. P. J., Kroeze, C., & Bush, S. R. (2011). Towards eco-agro industrial clusters in aquatic production: The case of shrimp processing industry in Vietnam. *Journal of Cleaner Production, 19*(17–18), 2107–2118. https://doi.org/10.1016/j.jclepro.2011.06.002

Aragón-Correa, J. A., Hurtado-Torres, N., Sharma, S., & García-Morales, V. J. (2008). Environmental strategy and performance in small firms: A resource-based perspective. *Journal of Environmental Management, 86*(1), 88–103. https://doi.org/10.1016/j.jenvman.2006.11.022

Aragón-Correa, J. A., & Rubio-López, E. A. (2007). Proactive corporate environmental strategies: Myths and misunderstandings. *Long Range Planning, 40*(3), 357–381. https://doi.org/10.1016/j.lrp.2007.02.008

Armstrong, J. S., & Overton, T. S. (1977). Estimating nonresponse bias in mail surveys. *Journal of Marketing Research, 14*(3), 396. https://doi.org/10.2307/3150783

Autio, E., Sapienza, H. J., & Almeida, J. G. (2000). Effects of age at entry, knowledge intensity, and imitability on international growth. *Academy of Management Journal, 43*(5), 909–924. https://doi.org/10.2307/1556419

Banerjee, S. B. (2001). Corporate environmental strategies and actions. *Management Decision, 39*(1), 36–44. https://doi.org/10.1108/EUM0000000005405

Banerjee, S. B., Iyer, E. S., & Kashyap, R. K. (2003). Corporate environmentalism: Antecedents and influence of industry type. *Journal of Marketing, 67*(2), 106–122. https://doi.org/10.1509/jmkg.67.2.106.18604

Barba-Sánchez, V., & Atienza-Sahuquillo, C. (2016). Environmental proactivity and environmental and economic performance: Evidence from the winery sector. *Sustainability (Switzerland), 8*(10). https://doi.org/10.3390/su8101014

Bey, N., Hauschild, M. Z., & McAloone, T. C. (2013). Drivers and barriers for implementation of environmental strategies in manufacturing companies. *CIRP Annals—Manufacturing Technology, 62*(1), 43–46. https://doi.org/10.1016/j.cirp.2013.03.001

Bıçakcıoğlu, N. (2018). Green business strategies of exporting manufacturing firms: Antecedents, practices, and outcomes. *Journal of Global Marketing, 31*(4), 246–269. https://doi.org/10.1080/08911762.2018.1436731

Binh, D. T., & Moon, H. C. (2019). Global value chain analysis towards environmentally friendly export strategy of Vietnam seafood exporters. *Journal of Management and Economics, 41*(4), 125–144. http://tckhtm.tmu.edu.vn/uploads/tckhtm/news/2020_01/j137-138-6.pdf

Brouthers, L. E., O'Donnell, E., & Hadjimarcou, J. (2005). Generic product strategies for emerging market exports into triad nation markets: A mimetic isomorphism approach. *Journal of Management Studies, 42*(1), 225–245. https://doi.org/10.1111/j.1467-6486.2005.00495.x

Buysse, K., & Verbeke, A. (2003). Proactive environmental strategies: A stakeholder management perspective. *Strategic Management Journal, 24*(5), 453–470. https://doi.org/10.1002/smj.299

Cheng, H. L., & Yu, C. M. J. (2008). Institutional pressures and initiation of internationalization: Evidence from Taiwanese small- and medium-sized enterprises. *International Business Review, 17*(3), 331–348. https://doi.org/10.1016/j.ibusrev.2008.01.006

Clarkson, P. M., Li, Y., Richardson, G. D., & Vasvari, F. P. (2011). Does it really pay to be green? Determinants and consequences of proactive environmental strategies. *Journal of Accounting and Public Policy, 30*(2), 122–144. https://doi.org/10.1016/j.jaccpubpol.2010.09.013

Cohen, J. (1988). *Statistical power analysis for the behavioral sciences.* Routledge.

Cohen, J. (1992). A power primer. *Psychological Bulletin, 112*(1), 155–159. https://doi.org/10.1037/0033-2909.112.1.155

Cullen-Knox, C., Fleming, A., Lester, L., & Ogier, E. (2020). Tracing environmental sustainability discourses: An Australia-Asia seafood case study. *Frontiers in Marine Science, 7*, 176.

Daddi, T., Testa, F., Frey, M., & Iraldo, F. (2015). Exploring the link between institutional pressures and environmental management systems effectiveness: An empirical study. *Journal of Environmental Management, 160*(10), 120–132. https://doi.org/10.1016/j.jenvman.2016.09.025

Dahlmann, F., Brammer, S., & Millington, A. (2008). Barriers to proactive environmental management in the United Kingdom: Implications for business and public policy. *Journal of General Management, 33*(3), 1–20. https://doi.org/10.1177/030630700803300301

Dai, J., Cantor, D. E., & Montabon, F. L. (2017). Examining corporate environmental proactivity and operational performance: A strategy-structure-capabilities-performance perspective within a green context. *International Journal of Production Economics.* https://doi.org/10.1016/j.ijpe.2017.07.023

Darnall, N., Henriques, I., & Sadorsky, P. (2008). Do environmental management systems improve business performance in an international setting? *Journal of International Management, 14*(4), 364–376. https://doi.org/10.1016/j.intman.2007.09.006

Darnall, N., Henriques, I., & Sadorsky, P. (2010). Adopting proactive environmental strategy: The influence of stakeholders and firm size. *Journal of Management Studies, 47*(6), 1072–1094. https://doi.org/10.1111/j.1467-6486.2009.00873.x

Delmas, M. A., & Toffel, M. W. (2010, November 18). *Institutional pressures and organizational characteristics: Implications for environmental strategy* (Unit Working Paper No. 11-050). Harvard Business School Technology & Operations Mgt. Available at SSRN: https://ssrn.com/abstract=1711785 or http://dx.doi.org/10.2139/ssrn.1711785

Dillman, D. A. (2007). *Mail and internet surveys: The tailored design method* (2nd ed.). Wiley.

DiMaggio, P., & Powell, W. (1983). The iron cage revisited: Institutional isomorphism in organizational fields. *American Sociological Review, 48*(2), 147–160.

Do, B., Nguyen, U., Nguyen, N., & Johnson, L. W. (2019). Exploring the proactivity levels and drivers of environmental strategies adopted by Vietnamese seafood export processing firms: A qualitative approach. *Sustainability (Switzerland), 11*(14), 1–24. https://doi.org/10.3390/su1114 3964

Drumwright, M. E. (1994). Socially responsible organizational buying: Environmental concern as a noneconomic buying criterion. *Journal of Marketing, 58*(3), 1. https://doi.org/10.2307/1252307

Dubey, R., Gunasekaran, A., Childe, S. J., Papadopoulos, T., Hazen, B., Giannakis, M., & Roubaud, D. (2017). Examining the effect of external pressures and organizational culture on shaping performance measurement systems (PMS) for sustainability benchmarking: Some empirical findings. *International Journal of Production Economics, 193*, 63–76. https://doi.org/10.1016/j.ijpe.2017. 06.029

Duque-Grisales, E., Aguilera-Caracuel, J., Guerrero-Villegas, J., & García-Sánchez, E. (2019). Can proactive environmental strategy improve Multilatinas' level of internationalization? The moderating role of board independence. *Business Strategy and the Environment.* https://doi.org/ 10.1002/bse.2377

Ervin, D., Wu, J., Khanna, M., Jones, C., & Wirkkala, T. (2013). Motivations and barriers to corporate environmental management. *Business Strategy and the Environment, 22*(6), 390–409. https://doi. org/10.1002/bse.1752

FAO. (2018). The State of Fisheries and Aquaculture in the world 2018. In *Fao.Org.* http://www. fao.org/state-of-fisheries-aquaculture

Faul, F., Erdfelder, E., Lang, A. G., & Buchner, A. (2007). G*Power 3: A flexible statistical power analysis program for the social, behavioral, and biomedical sciences. *Behavior Research Methods, 39*(2), 175–191. https://doi.org/10.3758/BF03193146

Fornell, C., & Larcker, D. F. (1981). Evaluating structural equation models with unobservable variables and measurement error. *Journal of Marketing Research, 18*(1), 39–50. https://doi.org/ 10.1177/002224378101800104

Freeman, R. E. (1984). *Strategic management: A stakeholder approach* (Pitman ed.). Pitman.

Galbreath, J. (2017). Drivers of green innovations: The impact of export intensity, women leaders, and absorptive capacity. *Journal of Business Ethics, 0123456789*, 1–15. https://doi.org/10.1007/ s10551-017-3715-z

Gallego-Alvarez, I., Ortas, E., Vicente-Villardón, J. L., & Álvarez Etxeberria, I. (2017). Institutional constraints, stakeholder pressure and corporate environmental reporting policies. *Business Strategy and the Environment, 26*(6), 807–825. https://doi.org/10.1002/bse.1952

Garcés-Ayerbe, C., Rivera-Torres, P., & Murillo-Luna, J. L. (2012). Stakeholder pressure and environmental proactivity: Moderating effect of competitive advantage expectations. *Management Decision, 50*(2), 189–206. https://doi.org/10.1108/00251741211203524

Ge, B., Yang, Y., Jiang, D., Gao, Y., Du, X., & Zhou, T. (2018). An empirical study on green innovation strategy and sustainable competitive advantages: path and boundary. *Sustainability, 10*(10), 3631. https://doi.org/10.3390/su10103631

General Statistic Office of Vietnam. (2018). *Statistical summary book of Vietnam 2018.*

Ghazilla, R. A. R., Sakundarini, N., Abdul-Rashid, S. H., Ayub, N. S., Olugu, E. U., & Musa, S. N. (2015). Drivers and barriers analysis for green manufacturing practices in Malaysian smes: A preliminary findings. *Procedia CIRP, 26*, 658–663. https://doi.org/10.1016/j.procir.2015.02.085

González-Benito, J., & González-Benito, Ó. (2006). A review of determinant factors of environmental proactivity. *Business Strategy and the Environment, 15*(2), 87–102. https://doi.org/10. 1002/bse.450

Gunarathne, A. D. N., Lee, K. H., & Hitigala Kaluarachchilage, P. K. (2021). Institutional pressures, environmental management strategy, and organizational performance: The role of environmental management accounting. *Business Strategy and the Environment, 30*(2), 825–839. https://doi. org/10.1002/bse.2656

Hair, J. F., Hult, G. T. M., Ringle, C. M., & Sarstedt, M. (2017). *A primer on partial least squares structural equation modeling (PLS-SEM)* (2nd ed.). Sage.

Hair, J. F., Risher, J. J., Sarstedt, M., & Ringle, C. M. (2019). When to use and how to report the results of PLS-SEM. *European Business Review, 31*(1), 2–24. https://doi.org/10.1108/EBR-11-2018-0203

Haldorai, K., Kim, W. G., & Garcia, R. L. F. (2022, September). Top management green commitment and green intellectual capital as enablers of hotel environmental performance: The mediating role of green human resource management. *Tourism Management*, 88. https://doi.org/10.1016/j.tourman.2021.104431

Hambrick, D. C. (1989). Guest editor's introduction: Putting top managers back in the strategy pictur author(s): Donald C . Hambrick Source: *Strategic Management Journal, 10*, Special Issue: Strategic Leaders and Published by: Wiley Stable. https://www.jsto. *Strategic Management Journal, 10*, 5–15.

Harkness, J., Pennell, B.-E., & Schoua-Glusberg, A. (2004). Survey questionnaire translation and assessment. In S. Presser, J. M. Rothgeb, M. P. Couper, J. T. Lessler, E. Martin, J. Martin, & E. Singer (Eds.), *Methods for testing and evaluating survey questionnaires* (pp. 453–473). Wiley.

Hart, S. L. (1995). A natural-resource-based view of the firm. *Academy of Management Review, 20*(4), 986–1014. https://doi.org/10.5465/amr.1995.9512280033

Haveman, H. A. (1993). Follow the leader: Mimetic isomorphism and entry into new markets. *Administrative Science Quarterly, 38*(4), 593. https://doi.org/10.2307/2393338

Holweg, M., & Pil, F. K. (2008). Theoretical perspectives on the coordination of supply chains. *Journal of Operations Management, 26*(3), 389–406. https://doi.org/10.1016/j.jom.2007.08.003

Hong, P., Kwon, H. B., & Roh, J. J. (2009). Implementation of strategic green orientation in supply chain. *European Journal of Innovation Management, 12*(4), 512–532. https://doi.org/10.1108/14601060910996945

Jennings, P. D., & Zandbergen, P. A. (1995). Ecologically sustainable organizations: An institutional approach. *Academy of Management Review, 20*(4), 1015–1052. https://doi.org/10.5465/amr.1995.9512280034

Junquera, B., & Barba-Sánchez, V. (2018). Environmental proactivity and firms' performance: Mediation effect of competitive advantages in Spanish wineries. *Sustainability, 10*(7). https://doi.org/10.3390/su10072155

Kassinis, G., & Vafeas, N. (2006). Stakeholder pressures and environmental performance. *Academy of Management Journal, 49*(1), 145–159. https://doi.org/10.5465/AMJ.2006.20785799

Kock, N. (2015). Common method bias in PLS-SEM: A full collinearity assessment approach. *International Journal of E-Collaboration, 11*(4), 1–10. https://doi.org/10.4018/ijec.2015100101

Lebailly, P. (2017). Vietnam's fisheries and aquaculture development's policy: Are exports performance targets sustainable? *Oceanography & Fisheries Open Access Journal, 5*(4). https://doi.org/10.19080/ofoaj.2017.05.555667

Lee, S. Y., & Rhee, S. K. (2007). The change in corporate environmental strategies: A longitudinal empirical study. *Management Decision, 45*(2), 196–216. https://doi.org/10.1108/00251740710727241

Leonidou, L. C., Christodoulides, P., Kyrgidou, L. P., & Palihawadana, D. (2017). Internal drivers and performance consequences of small firm green business strategy: The moderating role of external forces. *Journal of Business Ethics, 140*(3), 585–606. https://doi.org/10.1007/s10551-015-2670-9

Leonidou, L. C., Fotiadis, T. A., Christodoulides, P., Spyropoulou, S., & Katsikeas, C. S. (2015). Environmentally friendly export business strategy: Its determinants and effects on competitive advantage and performance. *International Business Review, 24*(5), 798–811. https://doi.org/10.1016/j.ibusrev.2015.02.001

Leonidou, L. C., Katsikeas, C. S., Fotiadis, T. A., & Christodoulides, P. (2013). Antecedents and consequences of an eco-friendly export marketing strategy: The moderating role of foreign public concern and competitive intensity. *Journal of International Marketing, 21*(3), 22–46. https://doi.org/10.1509/jim.12.0139

Li, C., & Parboteeah, K. P. (2015). The effect of culture on the responsiveness of firms to mimetic forces: Imitative foreign joint venture entries into China, 1985–2003. *Journal of World Business, 50*(3), 465–476. https://doi.org/10.1016/j.jwb.2014.08.002

Liao, S.-H., Hu, D.-C., & Ding, L.-W. (2017). Assessing the influence of supply chain collaboration value innovation, supply chain capability and competitive advantage in Taiwan's networking communication industry. *International Journal of Production Economics, 191*, 143–153. https://doi.org/10.1016/j.ijpe.2017.06.001

Liu, P., & Yi, S. P. (2018). A study on supply chain investment decision-making and coordination in the Big Data environment. *Annals of Operations Research, 270*(1–2), 235–253. https://doi.org/10.1007/s10479-017-2424-4

Liu, Y., Guo, J., & Chi, N. (2015). The antecedents and performance consequences of proactive environmental strategy: A meta-analytic review of national contingency. *Management and Organization Review, 11*(3), 521–557. https://doi.org/10.1017/mor.2015.17

López-Gamero, M. D., Molina-Azorín, J. F., & Claver-Cortés, E. (2009). The whole relationship between environmental variables and firm performance: Competitive advantage and firm resources as mediator variables. *Journal of Environmental Management, 90*(10), 3110–3121. https://doi.org/10.1016/j.jenvman.2009.05.007

Mellat-Parast, M., & Spillan, J. E. (2014). Logistics and supply chain process integration as a source of competitive advantage: An empirical analysis. *International Journal of Logistics Management, 25*(2), 289–314. https://doi.org/10.1108/IJLM-07-2012-0066

Menguc, B., Auh, S., & Ozanne, L. (2010). The interactive effect of internal and external factors on a proactive environmental strategy and its influence on a firm's performance. *Journal of Business Ethics, 94*(2), 279–298. https://doi.org/10.1007/s10551-009-0264-0

Molina-Azorín, J. F., Claver-Cortés, E., Pereira-Moliner, J., & Tarí, J. J. (2009). Environmental practices and firm performance: An empirical analysis in the Spanish hotel industry. *Journal of Cleaner Production, 17*(5), 516–524. https://doi.org/10.1016/j.jclepro.2008.09.001

Murillo-Luna, J. L., Garcés-Ayerbe, C., & Rivera-Torres, P. (2011). Barriers to the adoption of proactive environmental strategies. *Journal of Cleaner Production, 19*(13), 1417–1425. https://doi.org/10.1016/j.jclepro.2011.05.005

Nguyen, H. Q., Tran, D. D., Luan, P. D. M. H., Ho, L. H., Loan, V. T. K., Anh Ngoc, P. T., Quang, N. D., Wyatt, A., & Sea, W. (2020). Socio-ecological resilience of mangrove-shrimp models under various threats exacerbated from salinity intrusion in coastal area of the Vietnamese Mekong Delta. *International Journal of Sustainable Development and World Ecology, 27*(7), 638–651. https://doi.org/10.1080/13504509.2020.1731859

OECD; FAO. (2019). *OECD-FAO Agricultural Outlook 2019–2028* (OECD & FAO, Eds.). OECD. https://doi.org/10.1787/agr_outlook-2015-en

Olson, E. G. (2008). Creating an enterprise-level "green" strategy. *Journal of Business Strategy, 29*(2), 22–30. https://doi.org/10.1108/02756660810858125

Pinkse, J., & Dommisse, M. (2009). Overcoming barriers to sustainability: An explanation of residential builders' reluctance to adopt clean technologies. *Business Strategy and the Environment, 18*(8), 515–527. https://doi.org/10.1002/bse.615

Podsakoff, P. M., MacKenzie, S. B., Lee, J. Y., & Podsakoff, N. P. (2003). Common method biases in behavioral research: A critical review of the literature and recommended remedies. *Journal of Applied Psychology, 88*(5), 879–903. https://doi.org/10.1037/0021-9010.88.5.879

Primc, K., & Čater, T. (2015). Environmental proactivity and firm performance: A fuzzy-set analysis. *Management Decision, 53*(3), 648–667. https://doi.org/10.1108/MD-05-2014-0288

Pujari, D., Peattie, K., & Wright, G. (2004). Organizational antecedents of environmental responsiveness in industrial new product development. *Industrial Marketing Management, 33*(5), 381–391. https://doi.org/10.1016/j.indmarman.2003.09.001

Reinartz, W., Haenlein, M., & Henseler, J. (2009). An empirical comparison of the efficacy of covariance-based and variance-based SEM. *International Journal of Research in Marketing, 26*, 332e344.

Ringle, C. M., Sarstedt, M., & Straub, D. W. (2012). Editor's comments: A critical look at the use of pls-sem in "MIS Quarterly". *MIS Quarterly, 36*(1), iii. https://doi.org/10.2307/41410402

Ryszko, A. (2016). Proactive environmental strategy, technological eco-innovation and firm performance-case of Poland. *Sustainability (Switzerland), 8*(2). https://doi.org/10.3390/su8 020156

Schmitz, E. A., Baum, M., Huett, P., & Kabst, R. (2019). The contextual role of regulatory stakeholder pressure in proactive environmental strategies: An empirical test of competing theoretical perspectives. *Organization and Environment, 32*(3), 281–308. https://doi.org/10.1177/108602 6617745992

Scott, W. R. (2001). *Institutions of and organizations.* Sage.

Sharma, S., & Vredenburg, H. (1998). Proactive corporate environmental strategy and the development of competitively valuable organizational capabilities. *Strategic Management Journal, 19*(8), 729–753. https://doi.org/10.1002/(sici)1097-0266(199808)19:8%3c729::aid-smj 967%3e3.0.co;2-4

Statista. (2020). *Leading exporting countries of fish and fishery products worldwide in 2019.* https://www.statista.com/statistics/268269/top-10-exporting-countries-of-fish-and-fis hery-products/. Accessed 10 Jan 2021.

Stone, G., Joseph, M., & Blodgett, J. (2004). Toward the creation of an eco-oriented corporate culture: A proposed model of internal and external antecedents leading to industrial firm eco-orientation. *Journal of Business and Industrial Marketing, 19*(1), 68–84. https://doi.org/10.1108/ 08858620410516754

Testa, F., Boiral, O., & Iraldo, F. (2018). Internalization of environmental practices and institutional complexity: Can stakeholders pressures encourage greenwashing? *Journal of Business Ethics, 147*(2). https://doi.org/10.1007/s10551-015-2960-2

Thanh, L. (2014). *Sustainable developement of export-orientated farmed seafood in the Mekong Delta, Vietnam* (pp. 1–305).

The Seafood Certification & Ratings Collaboration. (2015). *Sustainable seafood: A global benchmark.*

Tran, N., Bailey, C., Wilson, N., & Phillips, M. (2013). Governance of global value chains in response to food safety and certification standards: The case of shrimp from Vietnam. *World Development, 45*, 325–336. https://doi.org/10.1016/j.worlddev.2013.01.025

VASEP. (2019). *Hiˆệp định CPTPP và EVFTA: Cơ hội thuế quan và Khuyến nghị cho ngành thuỷ sản Việt Nam.*

VCCI. (2019). *CPTPP và EVFTA: Cơ hội tvà thách thức với doanh nghiệp thuỷ sản Việt Nam.*

Vietdata. (2019). *Chuyên đề Kết quả ngành thủy sản 2019 & Triển vọng 2020.*

Wang, L., Li, W., & Qi, L. (2020). Stakeholder pressures and corporate environmental strategies: A meta-analysis. *Sustainability, 12*(1172), 1–16.

Wei, Z., Shen, H., Zhou, K. Z., & Li, J. J. (2017). How does environmental corporate social responsibility matter in a dysfunctional institutional environment? Evidence from China. *Journal of Business Ethics, 140*(2), 209–223. https://doi.org/10.1007/s10551-015-2704-3

Wu, G. C., Ding, J. H., & Chen, P. S. (2012). The effects of GSCM drivers and institutional pressures on GSCM practices in Taiwan's textile and apparel industry. *International Journal of Production Economics, 135*(2), 618–636. https://doi.org/10.1016/j.ijpe.2011.05.023

Wu, T., Jim Wu, Y. C., Chen, Y. J., & Goh, M. (2014). Aligning supply chain strategy with corporate environmental strategy: A contingency approach. *International Journal of Production Economics, 147*(PART B), 220–229. https://doi.org/10.1016/j.ijpe.2013.02.027

Yang, D., Xu, A., Kevin, W., Zhou, Z., & Jiang, W. (2018). Environmental strategy, institutional force, and innovation capability: A managerial cognition perspective. *Journal of Business Ethics,* 0123456789. https://doi.org/10.1007/s10551-018-3830-5

Yusof, N., Tabassi, A. A., & Esa, M. (2020). Going beyond environmental regulations—The influence of firm size on the effect of green practices on corporate financial performance. *Corporate Social Responsibility and Environmental Management, 27*(1), 32–42. https://doi.org/10.1002/csr. 1771

Zailani, S. H. M., Eltayeb, T. K., Hsu, C. C., & Tan, K. C. (2012). The impact of external institutional drivers and internal strategy on environmental performance. *International Journal of Operations and Production Management, 32*(6), 721–745. https://doi.org/10.1108/01443571211230943

Zameer, H., Wang, Y., & Saeed, M. R. (2021, June). Net-zero emission targets and the role of managerial environmental awareness, customer pressure, and regulatory control toward environmental performance. *Business Strategy and the Environment*, 1–14. https://doi.org/10.1002/bse.2866

Zeriti, A., Robson, M. J., Spyropoulou, S., & Leonidou, C. N. (2014). Sustainable export marketing strategy fit and performance. *Journal of International Marketing, 22*(4), 44–66. https://doi.org/10.1509/jim.14.0063

Zhu, Q., & Sarkis, J. (2007). The moderating effects of institutional pressures on emergent green supply chain practices and performance. *International Journal of Production Research, 45*(18–19), 4333–4355. https://doi.org/10.1080/00207540701440345

Chapter 6
CSR Practices in the Vietnamese Food Companies: Evidence from an Emerging Economy

Lan Do⊙ and Charlie Huang⊙

Abstract Social and environmental sustainability concerns have been critical in Asian emerging economies due to their rapid economic development. Yet there is limited research into the motivations for businesses to pursue their corporate social responsibility. This study examines how food companies implement their CSR in Vietnam. Using the typology of implicit and explicit CSR proposed by (Matten and Moon, Academy of Management Review 33:404–424, 2008), we argue that this new typology not only improves our understanding of the differences of CSR practices between countries, but also those between companies within the same industry. We then investigate the antecedents of CSR practices by three companies operating in the Vietnamese food industry using a combination of institutional and stakeholder perspectives. Findings indicate that the local CSR practices primarily feature an implicit, informal and discretionary approach as a result of both institutional and stakeholder pressures. Yet, there is also evidence of more explicit and strategic CSR practices among the Vietnamese food companies in response to both external and internal influences. The study contributes to the scarce evidence addressing CSR in Vietnam and joint roles of institutional and stakeholders in promoting substantial social and environmental sustainability.

Keywords Corporate social responsibility · Institution · Stakeholder management · Emerging economy

---

L. Do (✉)
RMIT Vietnam University, Hanoi, Vietnam
e-mail: lan.dothiha@rmit.edu.vn

C. Huang
RMIT University, Melbourne, VIC, Australia
e-mail: Charlie.huang@rmit.edu.au

© The Author(s), under exclusive license to Springer Nature Singapore Pte Ltd. 2022
N. Nguyen et al. (eds.), *Environmental Sustainability in Emerging Markets*,
Approaches to Global Sustainability, Markets, and Governance,
https://doi.org/10.1007/978-981-19-2408-8_6

6.1 Introduction

Corporate Social Responsibility (CSR) has gained its prominence in public discourses in developing countries (Ji & Miao, 2020). CSR can be referred to as activities or practices which businesses adopt to address environmental and social issues in their economic activities (Aguinis & Glavas, 2012). While strong economic growth has been recorded in these emerging economies, heightened pressures to adopt more socially and environmental initiatives by businesses have been well observed especially where serious social and environmental problems have been under much public scrutiny (Pullman et al., 2009). However, there is scarce empirical research into how and why companies discharge their social responsibility (Morais & Silvestre, 2018).

The food industry has been closely linked to various social and environmental issues including water and soil pollution, waste control, customer and employee health and safety, human rights and community impact (Gangi et al., 2020). While the Vietnamese food processing industry is a significant contributor to the national economy, accounting for 26% of the GDP and creating 27.5 million jobs (Tinsley & Lambert, 2021), it is also categorized among the most polluting industries. However, there is an oversight in the literature about CSR activity in this industry and the current body of CSR research in the local context seems to focus on export-oriented firms (Vo & Arato, 2020) and the uptake of social and environmental practices has been reportedly quite limited among businesses (Nguyen et al., 2020).

While previous studies delve into CSR practices across industries, such general understanding may not be relevant to develop an insight into all industries since each industry could have its contextual peculiarities (Kim, 2017). As a results, businesses and stakeholders in such industry may have different CSR conceptualizations and institutional pressures that drive their CSR commitment (Vo & Arato, 2020). The issue this paper addresses is whether, and why, there are variations in CSR practices among companies in the same industry and within the same national institutional environments. Specifically, the paper investigates how the institutions, stakeholders and company-specific factors shape various aspects of CSR practices, thereby developing insight into how to influence firms to adopt more socially and environmentally sustainable practices.

The purpose of the paper is to identify different factors that drive companies' different forms of CSR practices (implicit versus explicit) in a seemingly similar institutional environment of the Vietnamese food industry. The main argument of the paper is that the variations in CSR practices are shaped in response to the intensity of the influences from the dismal institutional forces and the proximate internal and external stakeholders. Institutional theory and stakeholder theory are used as two theoretical approaches to explaining corporate social behaviours and reciprocal influences between the organization and its contexts (Jamali & Neville, 2011). We conducted a qualitative research study with 15 in-depth interviews with senior managers of three food companies in Vietnam in order to shed light on the following questions: (1) What type (implicit and explicit) of CSR practices are undertaken by these three companies? (2) How may national institutions, companies' stakeholders and company-specific factors influence the CSR practices among these three companies?

6.2 Literature Review

The extant literature on CSR in the developing country context has seen a nuanced conceptualization of CSR as 'complex phenomenon that is contextual and multimodal and often initiated in collaboration with others inside and outside the corporation' (Jamali & Karam, 2018, p. 13). To gain a better understanding of the nature of CSR practices in the local context, we adopt Matten and Moon (2008)'s implicit and explicit CSR categorization to discuss the variations of CSR behaviours. Explicit CSR is referred to as the company's decisions and policies to address the issues of social interests whereas implicit CSR as corporate responsibility in response to the wider formal and informal institutions. In other words, implicit CSR involves more of a 'reaction' or 'reflection' of a corporation's institutional environment, as opposed to explicit CSR which involves a deliberate, voluntary and often strategic corporate decision (Matten & Moon, 2008, p. 409). On a more specific note, implicit CSR is also investigated in terms of formal and informal practices, with the former being embedded in the regulatory systems and the latter being responses to cultural, social norms and religious issues. For example, Tran and Jeppesen (2016) highlighted the presence of informal CSR practices in the developing country context of Latin America, South Africa and Vietnam.

There has been increasing research interest in CSR practices and CSR measurements in the food industry, which is associated with numerous environmental and social issues including waste management, environmental pollution and food safety (Kim, 2017). In light of social pressure for CSR commitment, while major food brands have been quite proactive with their CSR initiatives, other food companies are still struggling to decide their CSR commitment level. Further research is needed to investigate their motivations and specific mechanisms that drive a certain approach to CSR in the food industry (Zhang et al., 2014), especially in South Asian developing country context where the institutional elements and contextual factors like cultures can be different from developed ones (Ikram et al., 2020).

The common CSR themes in the Vietnamese food industry include responsible operating practices, food quality and safety, labour rights, environmental protection and philanthropy.

While the industry is significant in terms of its contribution to the economy and its negative environmental and social impacts (Dore et al., 2008), the adoption of environmental standards and responsible practices has been hindered by low awareness and weak institutional forces (Filippini & Srinivasan, 2021). Moreover, there is limited research into the nature CSR practices of food companies as well as motivations to integrate CSR into business strategies (Vo & Arato, 2020). Thus, it is an imperative to develop an insight into the mechanisms that could drive CSR uptake among food firms towards more sustainable development.

6.2.1 Institutional and Stakeholder Theories in Organizational Studies and CSR

The institutional theory has been particularly useful in organizational studies over the past decades (Lee, 2011). It argues that the formal institutions (such as government regulations) and informal institutional (like norms, conventions, and shared values) are of equal importance and significant sources of influence in shaping organizational behaviours (North, 1991) through 'processes by which structures, schemas, rules, norms, and routines, become established as authoritative guidelines for social behavior' (Scott, 2005, p. 408). The key argument is that organizational practices change and become institutionalized because they are considered legitimate.

While the neo-institutionalism theory deals with a general environment, the stakeholder theory involves a more proximate mechanism of social relations and interactions between stakeholders and the focal companies. As Freeman maintains it, 'the stakeholder approach is about groups and individuals who can affect the organization and is about managerial behaviours taken in response to those groups and individuals' (Freeman, 1984, p. 48). A number of studies have relied on the stakeholder framework to explain corporate decisions and practices in relation to various stakeholder interests (Reynolds et al., 2006). However, while companies have a very complex set of stakeholders, they can only care about a limited number of the stakeholders (Jamali et al., 2008). Literature has provided empirical evidence that the stakeholder attributes of having power, being deemed legitimate and being able to muster urgency managers make them highly salient stakeholder groups who exert significant influence on corporate behaviours (Parent & Deephouse, 2007). In addition, several authors argue that stakeholder saliency is a function of organizational culture and commitments (Jones et al., 2007), varies by organizational lifecycle stage (Jawahar & McLaughlin, 2001), and depends on the politicizing frame of industries (Fineman & Clarke, 1996). Therefore, the understanding of which stakeholders the companies really care about and why companies choose to embark on a certain CSR practice in response to stakeholder influence can shed light on CSR in the local context.

6.2.2 Rationale for the Integration of the Two Theories

Since the central tenet of both institutional and stakeholder theories is about how institutional forces and stakeholders pressure companies to conform to social demands, it may be reasonable to expect that companies will take similar CSR strategies to gain social legitimacy (Hoffman, 1999) and to maintain their access to critical resources (Kassinis & Vafeas, 2006). However, corporate responses to different social demands regarding CSR were much more nuanced and remained quite diverse as the results of complexities and inconsistencies in external pressures as well as the identification of salient stakeholders. While some corporations adopt explicit CSR practices and become proactive in their response to external pressures 'by changing their strategies, structures, and routines' (Davis et al., 2008, p. 390), others do not. Therefore, the use of only one of the two theories may not provide adequate explanations for the variations of CSR practices (Lee, 2011).

Moreover, the two theories do have their own demerits. In terms of institutional theory, Stinchcombe (1997) maintains that it is devoid of 'clear causal substance'. In particular, despite the potential significant influence institutions have on firms, they can be ignored by companies without concrete actors as interpreters and conduits or activators of institutional mechanisms, which then result in de-coupling or rhetoric practices (Meyer & Rowan, 1977). For example, changes in regulations or social perceptions relating to environment protection in the 1970s did not automatically change the corporate environmental management practices (Ruckelshaus, 1985). There is evidence that corporate social behaviours occur as the result of the interactions between the institutional environment and the social actors (community organizations or social organizations) that transmit the institutional meaning to focal companies (Lounsbury, 2001). Similarly, as the stakeholder theory itself does not provide explanatory mechanisms of how stakeholders influence firms, the understanding of the macro-level contexts and sources of stakeholder influence allows researchers to better explain how stakeholders dictate corporate CSR practices. Specifically, the stakeholders themselves do not automatically have significant influence on the focal organization. In fact, the stakeholders that exert tangible influence on firms are salient stakeholders possessing power, legitimacy and urgency in a given institutional context.

This paper follows Lee (2011, p. 285)'s argument that 'distal institutional pressures become more effective when they are channelled and accentuated through concrete stakeholder relations' (p. 285). However, while Lee (2011) emphasizes marginal and external stakeholder groups as the salient group influencing CSR practices since they have institutional legitimacy and, along with the legitimacy, an urgent message to mobilize social support, this paper argues that the internal stakeholders (shareholders, managers or even labour unions) are also critical in the corporate CSR agenda. Several authors suggest the examination of both internal and external pressure sources to understand variances in CSR (Angus-Leppan et al., 2010; Crilly et al., 2012). In such regard, this study considers both institutional and stakeholder perspectives (internal and external) and their dynamics to examine the antecedents of various aspects of CSR behaviours in the developing country context.

6.3 Methods

A multiple case study approach was adopted in this research in order to investigate how the Vietnamese food companies implement CSR since it focuses on the "why" and "how" questions for real-life events and where the researchers have little control (Yin, 2003). This approach was chosen to enable and assist cross-case analysis and synthesis (Yin, 2003). Data were collected from three selected cases in the developing country context of Vietnam which would have rendered the comparison of cases more meaningful.

A systematic and purposive sampling method was employed for this research. Case studies were selected from the list of CSR award participants by the Vietnam Chamber of Commerce and Industry and/or based on their CSR visibility upon the consultation with sustainability government agencies. This approach allows researchers to locate all possible cases of highly specific population, maximize the depth and richness of the data to deal with the research question investigated (DiCicco-Bloom & Crabtree, 2006), thereby avoiding such sampling mistakes as conducting sampling in an improper of haphazard manner and selecting inappropriate samples.

The total number of cases was three in the Vietnamese food industry with a total of 15 in-depth interviews with senior managers and CSR managers who were involved in CSR-related decision-making and had conceptual skills and knowledge of the impacts of various factors determining CSR uptake. The key themes used for interviewing the subsidiary managers comprised the following: the scope and extent of engagement in CSR; the company's motives for engaging in CSR; and the firm's engagement with institutional actors and stakeholder and their reciprocal influence. The food industry was selected given its economic and social significance as well as their negative social impacts caused by their prevalent operation practices (Nguyen & Pham, 2011) (Table 6.1).

Several strategies were adopted to safeguard the data integrity and to address weaknesses of the qualitative research. First, we used a case protocol, multiple coders and set up a case database in order to improve reliability (Gibbert & Ruigrok, 2010; Silverman, 2010; Yin, 2003). Second, we employed triangulation of data sources, respondent validating, comprehensive data treatment and appropriate tabulation to enhance the data validity (Silverman, 2010). Three main data collection techniques of interviews, document analysis and field notes were employed, which allowed the researchers to obtain rich and complex information from interviewees (Cavana et al., 2001) and assist the researchers in interpreting interviewees' rich thoughts on the issues investigated (Ticehurst & Veal, 2000). Third, semi-structured interviews were used. The employment of the interview guide allowed the researcher to safeguard the standardization and comparability of the research and to increase the reliability of the study (Yin, 2003) while providing flexibility and autonomy to the researcher to cover many aspects of interest to the research through posing new questions during the interviews to seek additional information (Green & Browne, 2005). Moreover, it allows the researchers to use the most appropriate language to the participants without changing the meanings of the questions posed to them (Louise Barriball & While, 1994) and to build rapport with the participants for later follow-up data collection and analysis. All the interviews were then transcribed and coded in accordance with the eight-step coding guidelines suggested by Tesch (1990).

A two-stage approach for analysing the data was adopted in accordance with our research objectives: The first stage entails a single case analysis to understand the context of each Company, its CSR practices and its key stakeholders influencing

6 CSR Practices in the Vietnamese Food Companies … 133

Table 6.1 Overviews of the three case studies

	Company A	Company B	Company C
Ownership type	JV (70% foreign; 30% State)	Joint Stock	POE (100% privately)
Headquarter/ownership	Dutch cooperatives	Institutional and individuals	Individuals
Years in operations	20	7	16
Revenue (million US$)	600	400	16
Size (total employees)	1500	2000	300
Products	Dairy products	Dairy	Smallgoods
CSR-embedded strategy	CSR corporate strategy	CSR-embedded business model	CSR primarily coupled with product responsibility
CEO	Dutch CEO, headquarter appointed	Local females; ex-SOE manager; Bank group shareholder	Local Vietnamese entrepreneur
Leadership	Corporate values; leaders' local mindset	Corporate values	Leader's personal values
Core stakeholder groups identified	Employees; community; customers; local government	Government; community; customers; employees; shareholders	Customers and employees

their CSR practices. We adopted three forms of analytical activity: data management, descriptive accounts and explanatory accounts (Spencer et al., 2005). All data collected from multiple sources (e.g., interviews with the managers, official websites and corporate archives) related to the single case were analysed for comprehensive data treatment to improve internal validity (Silverman, 2010). In the second stage, cross-case analysis was conducted to account for the variations in CSR practices and possible factors explaining such variations in CSR practices (Ali, 2016; Husted & Allen, 2006) due to the differences in the institutional environment, internal and external stakeholders, the ownership, and business strategy in these three cases. Then we used a cross-case tabulation display (Miles & Huberman, 1994) in order to compare and contrast the cross-case findings and to further improve the internal validity (Silverman, 2010). For improving internal validity, we solicited feedback from the interviewees in order to validate the findings. The external validity was sought by discussing the findings with managers working in other companies and the government and non-government authorities in charge of CSR areas.

6.4 Findings

The findings suggest a mix of implicit and explicit CSR practices at the studied companies. Yet there are several variations in their explicit CSR initiatives in terms of themes, scopes, ownership and commitment. Table 6.2 captures the main implicit and explicit CSR themes identified by the respondents.

In relation to implicit CSR, we probed for CSR practices, which were either mandatory or customary and considered important by the local companies. Consistently, most of the interviewed managers provided a quick discussion of formal legal requirements in such areas as labour standards, working environment, occupational health and safety, and went on with detailed elaboration of informal responsible practices towards the employees. Company C's HR manager discussed about the legal compliance with the labour codes, '*Employee rights are clearly provided in the labour codes regarding working conditions, freedom of association, non-discrimination, mandatory insurance schemes or occupational safety and health. These are the minimum requirement that all companies have to conform to if they want to be in business*'. This indicates that the formal legal systems in the local context have codified the responsibilities of the companies in relations to employees' rights (Matten & Moon, 2008). During our interviews, we observed that many interviewed managers outlined their implicit CSR practices characterized by informal arrangements in favour of the employees' benefits and wellbeing. As one local manager put it:

> *I was challenged if we embraced CSR. I would say yes and prove it. I showed them the written decision document showing the funding of VND 8 million [3 months' salary] to an employee who was under kidney treatment. I do not know about the world standards for CSR but that what we did about it. Though the health problem was in no way associated with the occupational health and safety at our workplace, we still did that because of compelling moral motivation and the tradition of 'taking care of the weaker/poorer. (Company C)*

A living wage with other informal arrangements to help employees manage their living costs is also a common theme among both local and foreign-owned businesses. The informal practices include employee loans, travelling allowances, childcare support, support funds for those with financially difficult situations were outlined by interviewed executives. In particular, the issue of living wage has not been especially highlighted as it was in this 'southern context', where businesses are reported to suffer from economic survival pressure in the wake of global competition (Fulop & Hisrich, 2000). The significance of the living wage as a social issue is illustrated in the following quote.

> *Our immediate responsibility as we see is to make sure our employees all have enough to live on and support their families. This is the issue of utmost concern to the employees. Hence, our labour union and the management have been working on various ways to expand market and production capacity to ensure nearly 300 employees have stable jobs and increased income of VND 3.5 to 5 million per month. The nationally stipulated minimum of VND 3million [about US $14]. In fact, this is a very difficult in the current situation when maintaining a regular income for employees have become a mammoth task for local businesses. (Company C HR manager)*

6 CSR Practices in the Vietnamese Food Companies … 135

Table 6.2 Summary of Implicit/Explicit CSR practices in the food companies

	Company		Company A	Company B	Company C
	Implicit CSR				
Social dimensions	Labour (formal rules)	Recognition of right of association	1	1	1
		No-child labour or compulsory labour	1	1	1
		No-discrimination and equal employment opportunities	1	1	1
		Safe and healthy working environment	1	1	1
		Occupational health and safety training	1	1	1
		Mandatory social and health insurance contributions	1	1	1
	Labour (informal practices)	Inflation-adjusted salary increase	1		
		Living wages package	1	1	1
		13th month salary and non-performance bonuses	1	1	1
		Extra insurance schemes for employees	1	1	
		Reduced working days	1		
		Living cost subsidy (travelling, childcare, accommodation)	1	1	1
		Financial support funds (loans)	1	1	1
		Maternity leave payment	1		
		Maternity flexible work arrangement and health care	1	1	

(continued)

Table 6.2 (continued)

Company			Company A	Company B	Company C
Implicit CSR					
		Employee family counselling and support	1		
		Supportive employment relationships	1	1	1
		Family obligation leaves (funerals, wedding, sickness)	1	1	1
		Company benefits (funded holidays, sports and cultural activities)	1	1	1
	Community	Employee-led philanthropic contribution	1	1	1
Environmental dimension	Environment	Pollution control program as stipulated	1	1	1
		Total	22	18	16

Explicit CSR practices					
		Philanthropic contributions	Company A	Company B	Company C
Social dimensions	Charitable work	In-kind support for disaster-stricken provinces by the Company	1	1	
		In-kind donations for poor, disadvantaged, orphan children and patients	1	1	1
		In-kind donation for blood donors in the 'Red Sunday' programs	1	1	
	Youth development	Sponsorship of sports activities at local schools			1
		Internship programs offered to students			1

(continued)

6 CSR Practices in the Vietnamese Food Companies … 137

Table 6.2 (continued)

	Explicit CSR practices				
		Philanthropic contributions	Company A	Company B	Company C
		Scholarships for poor students	1	1	
		Sponsorship for young talent development gameshow	1	1	
	Community development	Providing funds for medical equipment at local hospital		1	
		Funding for free health care services for the poor	1	1	
		Sponsorship for house building for poor families		1	
		Poverty alleviation initiatives (providing cows or funds to farmers)		1	
		Leading sponsorship of national school milk program		1	
		Sustainable dairy farming zone development program	1		
	Culture	Sponsorship for pagoda renovations		1	
	Education	Nutrition awareness education	1	1	
		Multi-partnership education promotion program (building and renovating schools)	1		
Environmental dimensions	Environment	Private regulation (certification)	1	1	
		Energy saving and recycling scheme	1		
		Employee environmental awareness program	1		

(continued)

Table 6.2 (continued)

	Explicit CSR practices			
	Philanthropic contributions	Company A	Company B	Company C
	Use of environmental-friendly technology and/or materials	1	1	
	Sustainable dairy farming technology transfer	1		
	Total	14	14	3

Other employee benefits include flexible time arrangements for female employees, extra insurance cover, company-funded holidays, teamwork and sports activities together with supportive working relationships and spiritual and material support by labour union and management at employee's important or critical events (e.g., wedding, funerals, accidents) are the features of informal CSR practices. These initiatives have been seen as norms in the local context and have been practised long before the coming of the CSR terms (Tran & Jeppesen, 2016). This 'family-like' business management approach is reflected in the following quotes on employee–manager relationship.

> *The closest community that it needs to look after first is its employees. They form the core part of a nuclear family that needs attention and care before we go out and care for our neighbours...Our managing director ... always creates the best environment for the employees. He is willing to sit down and listen to the employees...even spends time to attend employee's wedding. That's how employees think they are respected and cared about.*

Non-performance based bonuses on important cultural events and holidays (like traditional Tet holiday, National Independence Day, Labour Day) are another example of informal CSR practice that they have accommodated. These culturally related payments were previously identified as significant issues by the interviewed managers and employees in the study by Tran and Jeppesen (2016).

> *There have been improvements in employee policies. Previously, they did not get the thirteenth month salary on Tet holiday, now they are entitled to that. As you know, the thirteenth month salary is not mandatory, but it is dependent on the manager's decision and the company performance. (Company C General Manager)*

The interviews with the senior executives also show that these informal practices were likely to be shaped by the normative system of cultural values and society's expectations from businesses and the managers' cognitive thinking (Scott, 2013).

> *For Vietnamese people, bonuses are expected on traditional Tet holidays and other cultural days. This has been unwritten laws and beyond what is regulated. That explains why new employees always ask about that. For example, on the National Independence Day, they expect to receive bonuses before they take the holiday or at least in-kind gifts. (Company C Admin Manager)*

Employee-led philanthropic contribution activities were also cited by most of the interviewed managers regarding social activities. In fact, these were initiated by the Company's labour union and contributions were made voluntarily by employees in case of support needed for natural disaster victims and poor and remote communities. They were common especially in local companies which were not financially resourceful for charitable activities. As Company C manager puts it,

We don't have a specific fund for philanthropic activities like helping natural disaster victims. However, our labour union has for years led these social activities by initiating and collecting contributions from the employees. We don't call it CSR; it is just our cultural tradition.

With regard to explicit CSR, most of the interviewed managers referred to varied types of explicit CSR activities, ranging from donations for the poor, orphans and handicapped, to sports and cultural development type activities, to educational and healthcare programs. On one hand, these social interventions reflect the local flavour of social issues. On the other hand, they are observed to be diversified in terms of themes, scope, ownership and commitment. As suggested by the joint venture company (Company A) manager, '*the focus of our CSR activity is on environment, education and rural development, which are not just issues of the society's concern but also on the State's millennium priority list*'. Similarly, one of the local Company's executives commented on their CSR themes, '*the Company's CSR initiatives revolves around the spiritual, physical and intellectual development of the Vietnamese human capital. Specifically, we have sponsored TV educational shows, School Milk programs for school children development and numerous nutrition education conferences and workshops.*' Philanthropic contributions for the disadvantaged groups (the poor, homeless, remoted or disabled people) and/or the war or disaster victims are found common among the studied companies (see Table 6.2). These charitable activities were limited in monetary value, time- and locality-specific and of discretionary nature. As one of the executives from Company C put in in these words, '*we responded well to the local request for philanthropic contributions to help people in disaster-stricken areas. We also provided meals for the local social protection and funds to support local school sports events. They were not much in value but meaningful to the people in need*'. In addition, there were several CSR programs that involved larger scale, higher degree of commitment in terms of time, resources and structure and were undertaken on an ongoing basis by all the companies. This was clearly reflected in the interviews with the executives of Company A.

During the past years, we spent 30 million VND (US$ 1.5 million) to run the School Milk programs at 17 of 19 districts of Nghe An province to provide free milk to hundreds of thousands school children. We have successful enlisted the support and participation from the Vietnam Television, Ministry of Education and Training, Ministry of Health and the Central Party as well as contributions from individuals and organization to execute the National School Milk program, in which we pledge to a funding of US$ 20 million for the 5-year period from 2016-2021.

Unlike the discretionary CSR activities, programs as such also suggest the Company's strategic focus in order to leverage the company's competitive advantage and market presence as indicated in the comments by Company B marketing manager.

Table 6.3 Illustrative quotes to indicate external institutional pressures

Most of the time, we take on CSR in order to meet the requirements set out by the competent authorities. In the old days there were no such Environmental Laws as we have today. Therefore, if we did not comply, we would be subject to penalty. When it comes to 'hard laws', we have to embrace it. (Company C General Manager)
The government at the State and provincial level is very important stakeholders as without their support, our business could be hard to achieve. For example, the State president recently met with the local businesses in a meeting called on the contribution of various investors in our ambitious national school milk Programs. Competitors may have some impact which is limited to keeping talents… and our foreign partner rarely has impact on the Company. Therefore, the CSR-related decisions are mostly in the hand of the owners/managers. (Company B HR manager)
As a matter of fact, we have to say that the changes in the competition landscapes and social issues facing businesses in each stage have pushed businesses to be more responsive, leading to revisions and adaptation on a gradual basis. Over times those that appeared to meet with the social challenge would be maintained and developed. (Compare A Legal Department Head)
We have provided meals to the local social protection center and sponsored sports activities for several years. Those contributions may be insignificant in value, but they could be valuable to those disadvantaged people, which make their lives somehow better. What I did is not for a special purpose but to satisfy my need to do something for the society for the poor. In essence it is all about what we need, that what others need and what society needs. (Company C Marketing Manager)
As a MNC with a foreign identity, we realized that we had to try hard to gain legitimacy, especially after the introduction of government policy of 'Vietnamese people buy Vietnamese products' and increasingly competitive market landscape. We selected education and rural dairy development our main focus of social activities in accordance with the cultural value of learning and the government priority of development areas. We hope we will be considered an indispensable part of Vietnamese society and Vietnamese daily life. Vietnamese people do appreciate the goodwill, good intension and genuine care for the environment and community thus we would be granted legitimacy and public recognition in the local community. (Company A, Corporate Affairs Manager)
We have signed an agreement on the development of a sustainable dairy farming zone with the Ministry of Agriculture. Sadly, such agreement was signed maybe to make us happy and only for us to keep and nothing was turned into a minister-level policy or guidelines for implementation. I present that agreement to various provincial authorities, but none except one did listen to us. How sad it is! (Company A Deputy General Manager)
As our production involves a mega-farming area, having the support from our external stakeholders being the State government, the Party, the local authorities are crucial for our success. Our community engagement programs are aimed at enhancing the life of the local people in a substantial way. (Company B)

Source Authors

Our product positioning, corporate brand and business philosophy is associated with the nature, the freshness and 'for community development' theme. Our CSR strategy is crafted in the light of the corporate strategy and the business mission of enhancing the sustainability and creating a happier life for the people. We, therefore, have been persistently undertaken various social initiatives aimed at improving the spiritual and material life of the people in different regions in the country.

Evidently, there was a shift of focus to the long-term and strategic CSR programs which exhibited more commitment and better alignment with the Company's core business and strategy (Jamali, 2007).

> During the early of operations, we were engaged in several philanthropic activities for the local disabled groups. But then, we realized that we needed to engage in something more sustainable to ensure our public presence and gain legitimacy while doing business here. (Company A Deputy General Manager)

In summary, the analysis of the three food companies reveals that CSR practices features their tendency to adopt implicit and informal labour-related CSR practices and at the same time exhibit a mix of explicit CSR activities and programs with discretionary and strategic nature.

6.4.1 Influence of Institutional and Stakeholder Interaction on CSR Practices

All three cases indicated there were complex interactions of institutional pressures and stakeholder influence which then shaped different aspects of CSR activities. While the pressure to adopt implicit CSR practices was the product of social norms, cultural values and socialist legacy as discussed above, it is evidenced that the new regulatory change and the perceived bargaining power of the employees seem to heighten the pressure to adopt better labor standards. The quotations below exemplify the degree of pressure from the interaction of the internal stakeholder (the employee) and external institutional pressure.

> The recent introduction of Unemployment Insurance Law allows contracted employees to receive a lump sum upon work termination and exposed businesses to undesired workforce fluctuation. This also means that employees, have more bargaining power and businesses facing a more competitive labor market are pressured to offer better benefits to the employees in order to attract and retain them... (Company C General Manager)

The findings also reveal that the scope of explicit CSR practices, particularly the discretionary CSR activities were not only attuned to the social issues of the context, but also shaped by the management. The following quote illustrates discretionary CSR practices at the local SME and the influence of the top management.

> We have provided meals to the local social protection center and sponsor its sports activities for several years. Those contributions may be insignificant in value, but they could be valuable to those disadvantaged people as they could make their lives somehow better. What I did is not for a special purpose but to satisfy my need to do something for the society for the poor.

The findings also reveal that the explicit CSR practices at both local and foreign-owned companies were driven by institutional pressures as well as internal and external stakeholders. This is exemplified in Company A with the foreign identity which reported the need to seek legitimacy through being responsive to the social issues in the host country market. As its executive manager indicated, the social issues that the Company addresses were determined in accordance with the institutional forces and social expectations.

As a MNC with a foreign identity, we realized that we had to try hard to gain legitimacy, especially after the introduction of government policy of 'Vietnamese people buy Vietnamese products' and increasingly competitive market landscape. We selected education (especially right to go to school) and rural dairy development our main focus of social activities in accordance with the cultural value of learning and the government priority of development areas. We hope we will be considered an indispensable part of Vietnamese society and Vietnamese daily life. Vietnamese people do appreciate the goodwill, good intention and genuine care for the environment and community thus we would be granted legitimacy and public recognition in the local community.

On one hand, the interviews with the senior managers revealed that specific external stakeholder groups (like the state government, the local governments and the media) could have direct impact on the decision of what explicit CSR practices to adopt and how to implement it.

At the national level, we have even signed an agreement on the development of a sustainable dairy farming zone with the Ministry of Agriculture. Sadly, such agreement was signed maybe to make us happy and only for us to keep and nothing was turned into a minister-level policy or guidelines for implementation. I present that agreement to various provincial authorities, but none except one did listen to us. How sad it is! (Company A Deputy General Manager)

On the other hand, the findings also highlighted the influence of the internal stakeholder groups (the shareholders and management). For example, as a result of the major shareholding group/the head quarter's centralized cost-cutting policy, Company A then had to change the governance structure of their explicit CSR practice from sole ownership to include multiple partnerships in order to sustain the project.

Over the recent years, they [headquarter] imposed tight resource allocation policy, In fact, the local management can partly localize CSR strategies and decisions whereas the major programs are determined in accordance with the headquarter overall strategic plan.

Similarly, given the seemingly same institutional environment, the other locally owned (Company B) also exhibited a strong influence from the external stakeholders as well as the top management/the owner in terms of their explicit CSR practices. The following quote illustrates the perceived salience of the local government in granting legitimacy and access to resources for the sizeable operations.

As our production involves a mega-farming area of 370 square kilometres and 45,000 cows, having the support from our external stakeholders being the State government, the Party, the local authorities are crucial for our success. Keeping that in mind, our community engagement programs are aimed at enhancing the material and spiritual life of the local people in a substantial way and on an extensive scale. The national school milk program that we initiated reflects a clear alignment with the national human capital development. (Company B CSR Manager)

This evidence suggests the influence of the owner founder/the manager in aligning explicit CSR practice with business strategy and values. Overall, the three cases provide support to the arguments that the external pressures from the institutional

6 CSR Practices in the Vietnamese Food Companies … 143

forces and external stakeholders were moderated by internal forces (internal stake-holders, the owner and the management) with regards to CSR practices. Tables 6.3 and 6.4 provide the quotes that illustrates how internal and external stakeholders directs the CSR practices at the local companies.

Table 6.4 Illustrative quotes to indicate internal stakeholder pressures

The owner/CEO's business philosophy is so strong that it drives everything else, including CSR activities. She has defined the business philosophy of 'putting the corporate interest within the interests of the wider society' right from the start. Hence, our products are promoted closely associated with freshness, nature and 'for community' and our CSR strategy goes hand in hand with that. (Company B Marketing Manager)

The recent introduction/of unemployment insurance laws allows contracted employees to receive a lump sum upon work termination and exposed businesses to undesired workforce fluctuation. This also means that employees, with the representation of the labor union have more bargaining power and businesses facing a more competitive labor market are pressured to offer better benefits to the employees in order to attract and retain them… Yet, the manager and the owner/shareholder actually determine the role of labor union and have the final decision as to how well employee are treated. (Company C General Manager)

CSR involves the laws and regulations on one side and the leaders' conscience on the other side. I think that the laws are what you must follow, and the conscience is therefore the decisive factor

Trade union, in fact, is created by the management/the owner. To be or not to be, that is the question of managerial decision. If the manager-owner supports, it thrives. Otherwise, it could not survive. I myself strongly support Trade union as it serves the interests of the employees

Our source of labor attraction and retention is greatly from our human resource policies. In reality what employees really care about is how they are paid, treated and cared about or whether the compensation and insurance entitlements are adequately provided. For example, they have been entitled to bonuses and incentives, Company-paid holidays and cultural and sports activities, particularly needy staff are given support in material and spiritual terms

Over the recent years, they [headquarter] imposed tight resource allocation policy, in fact, the local management can partly localize CSR strategies and decisions whereas the major programs are determined in accordance with the headquarter overall strategic plan. For example, our more-than—ten-year education promotion program is now no longer included in any category or budget. Therefore, we have to seek the support, both financial and non-financial from outside partners and individuals

Our adoption of international certifications or private regulations, on one hand. Improve the effectiveness and efficiency of the production. On the other hand, they help create a positive corporate image, and thereby enhance competitive advantage. (Company A HR manager)

Giving back to society programs may not be long-lived and sustainable as they depend on the CEO's 'tastes' and preferences and the Company's business performance. Different CEOs have different preferences for community programs or partners to work on such programs; one prefers to work with the Red Cross others may like to work with Women's Associations for instance, which makes it hard to maintain commitment on a continual basis. (Company A)

Source Authors

6.5 Discussion

The findings discussed in relation to the two research questions suggest that CSR Vietnam is characterized by a hybridized expression of both implicit and explicit CSR. This lends support to Jamali and Karam (2018)'s argument that CSR practices in a developing country are distinctive, heterogeneous and 'enacted in a contextually responsive manner such that expressions are shaped in reaction to multilevel socio-political and historically situated factors' (p. 17).

In relation to implicit CSR, the findings indicate that informal CSR practices were highlighted in the local companies' discourse on CSR in both foreign-owned and locally owned companies and revolved around employee-related issues. Such informal CSR arrangements as extra leaves for culturally important events (funerals, weddings, family member sickness), non-performance bonuses for religious festival or holidays, or providing financial support and loans to employees to cover urgent living costs were consistently observed in the local companies. This could be attributed to the imprints of social norms, political ideology and cultural values on local CSR expressions. Tran and Jeppesen (2016) maintain that there exists a 'social contract' or 'shared understanding' regarding social expectations about employee benefits given the fact that the official salary is not yet a living one for employees. Moreover, the socialist ideology featuring job security and equal distri-bution and cultural values regarding family relationships (Tran, 2011) also helps explain why there have long existed the social norms and expectations of a lump sum Tet bonus, flexible work arrangements and short-term leave for important family obligations (weddings and funerals). Similarly, the traditional view of the business as a 'family' also indicates the importance of informal CSR practices particularly among SMEs regarding employees–manager work relationship and attention and support for employees' life issues (Jeppesen & Azizi, 2015). Overall, the findings lend support to the extant literature on CSR in developing country positing that the long-standing social and culture norms and socialist values still permeate the local CSR practices (Jeppesen & Azizi, 2015; Tran & Jeppesen, 2016).

In relation to explicit CSR, the findings show that discretionary CSR practices adopted by the companies in Vietnam are of philanthropic nature with common themes of education promotion, community development, donations to disadvan-taged groups. This suggests that explicit CSR in developing country were largely characterized by a 'still evolving amateur type stance from corporate social respon-sibility rather than a systematic, focused, and institutionalized approach' (Jamali & Mirshak, 2007, p. 259). However, there is evidence that the strategic form of explicit CSR in two of the companies with CSR reflected in the goals, values, missions and policies of the companies. These explicit CSR expressions in the local context indi-cate that on one hand they were driven by the need to gain public acceptance and legitimacy through building a positive corporate identity and adopting global best practices in private regulation. On the other hand, they were attuned social issues of the context in question and to the values embedded in the implicit social contract. For example, the managers from both Company A and Company B stressed the alignment of their companies' strategic CSR focus with the issues of national priority and cultural significance. The findings are in consistency with previous studies on the drivers and nature of explicit CSR in the developing country context (Jamali & Karam, 2018; Matten & Moon, 2008). In addition, the presence of strategic CSR programs with multiple partnerships (the local governments, foreign government, NGOs and individuals) in the local companies also lend support to the extant literature suggesting that CSR in developing country context can be fostered through initiating a range of collaborative relationships with others inside and outside the corporation (Lund-Thomsen & Nadvi, 2010; Maloni & Brown, 2006).

The findings confirm Lee (2011)'s argument that there is a striking difference in how companies engage in CSR. On one hand, some companies display a minimal commitment to substantial CSR. There were, on the other hand, companies that exemplified their corporate citizenship very well (Waddock, 2009). The investigations of the three companies in the same industry under the same institutional environment illustrate that firms can be induced to adopt similar strategies in response to the regulative, normative and cognitive pressures from institutions (Scott, 2013). However, given the fact that institutions were distal mechanisms, they can be ignored by firms unless the institutional pressure was transmitted, reconstructed, and amplified by actors directly engaged with firms to have the intended effect on firms. For example, the Corporate Affair manager from Company A emphasized that their management of relations with the government and engagement in programs to promote education and rural dairy farming were the Company's strategic posture in response to counteract the local government's policies on 'Vietnamese people buy products made by Vietnamese company' with the aim to gain legitimacy and minimize the government price controls in the industry. This suggests that the government as a salient external stakeholder can directly shape corporate behaviour by removing the resources that the companies need (Lee, 2011). In addition to the salient external stakeholder pressure, the internal stakeholder influence such as the headquarter/foreign owner control at Company A and owner/CEO's impact in Company B were important factors that defined the nature of CSR practices. Evidently, when both institutional and stakeholder pressures were strong, the companies would be more likely to adopt a more proactive CSR approach to retain their legitimacy and gain control of their situation (Lee, 2011).

6.6 Conclusion

This paper presents an institutional and stakeholder analysis of CSR practices in a developing country context. The empirical findings demonstrate that CSR in developing country depicted to be 'more heterogeneous than merely reflecting implicit/explicit hybridity' (Jamali & Karam, 2018, p. 14). Indeed, the local CSR activities are simultaneously shaped by dismal institutional forces and the proximate internal and external stakeholders and characterized by the continued local predominance of corporate philanthropy.

This paper has some important implication for research in business–society relations. First, the paper suggests the relevance of using more comprehensive, multi-level studies to understand the complex mechanism and processes in how companies adopt certain CSR practices and how different factors drive companies' different forms of CSR practices (implicit versus explicit). Second, the paper also confirms that CSR is not only the outcome of institutional pressure but that of the amalgam of institutional, stakeholder and company interactions, which suggests practical implications for improving business–society relationship. In particular, the study contributes to the understanding of the underlying driving forces for social and environmental sustainability and suggests the importance of the multi-stakeholder involvement in addressing prevalent social and environmental issues in emerging economies as well as the proactive stance towards the social responsibility businesses should take to ensure sustainable development. Furthermore, different social actors and stakeholders such as governments, NGO, industry associations and the society at large need to exert influence through appropriate institutions and direct engagement on the stakeholder level to keep companies responsible, accountable and proactive in further social goods.

Despite some significant empirical findings on CSR practices in a developing country, this paper has some limitations. First, the findings do not allow generalizability beyond the context understudied, which is common in case study research (Yin, 2010). Second, since the study utilized data collected during a specific time period, which, therefore, may not fully reflect the nature of organizational responses and institutional pressures within a country, a longitudinal study would ideally be better to understand the research context (Mondejar & Zhao, 2013). Lastly, this paper relies on self-reported managers' perceptions and secondary CSR data, further research should employ multiple sources of data from external and internal stakeholder groups to improve research credibility. Future research should aim to investigate whether different social issues are more effectively and efficiently addressed by explicit than by implicit CSR.

References

Aguinis, H., & Glavas, A. (2012). What we know and don't know about corporate social responsibility: A review and research agenda. *Journal of Management, 38*(4), 932–968.

Ali, M. A. (2016). Stakeholder salience for stakeholder firms: An attempt to reframe an important heuristic device. *Journal of Business Ethics.* https://doi.org/10.1007/s10551-015-2819-6

Angus-Leppan, T., Metcalf, L., & Benn, S. (2010). Leadership styles and CSR practice: An examination of sensemaking, institutional drivers and CSR leadership. *Journal of Business Ethics, 93*(2), 189–213.

Cavana, R., Delahaye, B., & Sekaran, U. (2001). *Applied buisness research: Qualitative and quantative methods.* Wiley.

Crilly, D., Zollo, M., & Hansen, M. T. (2012). Faking it or muddling through? Understanding decoupling in response to stakeholder pressures. *Academy of Management Journal, 55*(6), 1429–1448.

Davis, G. F., Morrill, C., Rao, H., & Soule, S. A. (2008). Introduction: Social movements in organizations and markets. *Administrative Science Quarterly, 53*(3), 389–394.

DiCicco-Bloom, B., & Crabtree, B. F. (2006). The qualitative research interview. *Medical Education, 40*(4), 314–321.

Dore, G., Brylski, P., Nygard, J., Thi, P., & Tran, T. (2008) *Review and analysis of the pollution impacts from the Vietnamese manufacturing sectors.* EASRE, The World Bank.

Fineman, S., & Clarke, K. (1996). Green stakeholders: Industry interpretations and response. *Journal of Management Studies, 33*(6), 715–730.

Filippini, M., & Srinivasan, S. (2021). Adoption of environmental standards and a lack of awareness: Evidence from the food and beverage industry in Vietnam. *Environmental Economics and Policy Studies*, 1–34.

Freeman, E. (1984). *Strategic management: A stakeholder perspective.* Pitman.

Fulop, G., & Hisrich, R. D. (2000). Business ethics and social responsibility in transition economies. *Journal of Management Development, 19*(1), 5. http://search.ebscohost.com/login.aspx?direct=true&db=bth&AN=2965012&site=bsi-live

Gangi, F., D'Angelo, E., Daniele, L. M., & Varrone, N. (2020). The impact of corporate governance on social and environmental engagement: What effect on firm performance in the food industry? *British Food Journal, 123*(2), 610–626.

Gibbert, M., & Ruigrok, W. (2010). The "what" and "how" of case study rigor: Three strategies based on published work. *Organizational Research Methods, 13*, 710–737. https://doi.org/10.1177/1094428109351319

Green, J., & Browne, J. (2005). *Principles of social research.* McGraw-Hill International.

Hoffman, A. J. (1999). Institutional evolution and change: Environmentalism and the US chemical industry. *Academy of Management Journal, 42*(4), 351–371.

Husted, B. W., & Allen, D. B. (2006). Corporate social responsibility in the multinational enterprise: Strategic and institutional approaches. *Journal of International Business Studies, 37*(6), 838–849. http://search.ebscohost.com/login.aspx?direct=true&db=bth&AN=23189761&site=bsi-live

Ikram, M., Qayyum, A., Mehmood, O., & Haider, J. (2020). Assessment of the effectiveness and the adaption of CSR management system in food industry: The case of the South Asian versus the Western food companies. *SAGE Open, 10*(1), 2158244019901250.

Jamali, D. (2007). The Case for Strategic Corporate Social Responsibility in Developing Countries. *Business & Society Review (00453609), 112*(1), 1–27. https://doi.org/10.1111/j.1467-8594.2007.00284

Jamali, D., & Karam, C. (2018). Corporate social responsibility in developing countries as an emerging field of study. *International Journal of Management Reviews, 20*(1), 32–61.

Jamali, D., & Mirshak, R. (2007). Corporate social responsibility (CSR): Theory and practice in a developing country context. *Journal of Business Ethics, 72*(3), 243–262. https://doi.org/10.1007/s10551-006-9168-4

Jamali, D., & Neville, B. (2011). Convergence versus divergence of CSR in developing countries: An embedded multi-layered institutional lens. *Journal of Business Ethics, 102*(4), 599–621. https://doi.org/10.1007/s10551-011-0830-0

Jamali, D., Safieddine, A. M., & Rabbath, M. (2008). Corporate governance and corporate social responsibility synergies and interrelationships. *Corporate Governance: An International Review, 16*(5), 443–459. https://doi.org/10.1111/j.1467-8683.2008.00702.x

Jawahar, I., & McLaughlin, G. L. (2001). Toward a descriptive stakeholder theory: An organizational life cycle approach. *Academy of Management Review, 26*(3), 397–414.

Jeppesen, S., & Azizi, S. (2015). Avenues of rethinking CSR in development. In *Development-oriented corporate social responsibility: Volume 2: Locally led initiatives in developing economies* (p. 91). Routledge.

Ji, H., & Miao, Z. (2020). Corporate social responsibility and collaborative innovation: The role of government support. *Journal of Cleaner Production, 260*, 121028. https://doi.org/10.1016/j.jcl epro.2020.121028

Jones, T. M., Felps, W., & Bigley, G. A. (2007). Ethical theory and stakeholder-related decisions: The role of stakeholder culture. *Academy of Management Review, 32*(1), 137–155.

Kassinis, G., & Vafeas, N. (2006). Stakeholder pressures and environmental performance. *Academy of Management Journal, 49*(1), 145–159.

Kim, Y. (2017). Consumer responses to the food industry's proactive and passive environmental CSR, factoring in price as CSR tradeoff. *Journal of Business Ethics, 140*(2), 307–321.

Lee, M.-D.P. (2011). Configuration of external influences: The combined effects of institutions and stakeholders on corporate social responsibility strategies. *Journal of Business Ethics, 102*(2), 281–298. https://doi.org/10.1007/s10551-011-0814-0

Louise Barriball, K., & While, A. (1994). Collecting data using a semi-structured interview: A discussion paper. *Journal of Advanced Nursing, 19*(2), 328–335.

Lounsbury, M. (2001). Institutional sources of practice variation: Staffing college and university recycling programs. *Administrative Science Quarterly, 46*(1), 29–56.

Lund-Thomsen, P., & Nadvi, K. (2010). Clusters, chains and compliance: Corporate social responsibility and governance in football manufacturing in South Asia. *Journal of Business Ethics, 93*(2), 201–222.

Maloni, M. J., & Brown, M. E. (2006). Corporate social responsibility in the supply chain: An application in the food industry. *Journal of Business Ethics, 68*(1), 35–52.

Matten, D., & Moon, J. (2008). "Implicit" and "explicit" CSR: A conceptual framework for a comparative understanding of corporate social responsibility. *Academy of Management Review, 33*(2), 404–424.

Meyer, J. W., & Rowan, B. (1977). Institutionalized organizations: Formal structure as myth and ceremony. *American Journal of Sociology, 83*(2), 340–363.

Miles, M. B., & Huberman, A. M. (1994). *Qualitative data analysis*. Sage Publications.

Mondejar, R., & Zhao, H. (2013). Antecedents to government relationship building and the institutional contingencies in a transition economy. *Management International Review, 53*(4), 579–605.

Morais, D. O. C., & Silvestre, B. S. (2018). Advancing social sustainability in supply chain management: Lessons from multiple case studies in an emerging economy. *Journal of Cleaner Production, 199*, 222–235. https://doi.org/10.1016/j.jclepro.2018.07.097

Nguyen, H. P., & Pham, H. T. (2011). The dark side of development in Vietnam: Lessons from the Killing of the Thi vai River. *Journal of Macromarketing, 32*(1), 74–86. https://doi.org/10.1177/0276146711423666

Nguyen, P. M., Vo, N. D., Phuc Nguyen, N., & Choo, Y. (2020). Corporate social responsibilities of food processing companies in Vietnam from consumer perspective. *Sustainability, 12*(1), 71.

North, D. C. (1991). Institutions. *Journal of Economic Perspectives, 5*(1), 97–112.

Parent, M. M., & Deephouse, D. L. (2007). A case study of stakeholder identification and prioritization by managers. *Journal of Business Ethics, 75*(1), 1–23.

Pullman, M. E., Maloni, M. J., & Carter, C. R. (2009). Food for thought: Social versus environmental sustainability practices and performance outcomes. *Journal of Supply Chain Management, 45*(4), 38–54. https://doi.org/10.1111/j.1745-493X.2009.03175.x

Reynolds, S. J., Schultz, F. C., & Hekman, D. R. (2006). Stakeholder theory and managerial decision-making: Constraints and implications of balancing stakeholder interests. *Journal of Business Ethics, 64*(3), 285–301.

Ruckelshaus, W. D. (1985). Environmental guest protection: Politics and reality. *Groundwater Monitoring & Remediation, 5*(1), 4–6.

Scott, W. R. (2005). Institutional theory: Contributing to a theoretical research program. *Great Minds in Management: The Process of Theory Development, 37*(2), 460–484.

Scott, W. R. (2013). *Institutions and organizations: Ideas, interests, and identities*. Sage Publications.

Silverman, D. (2010). *Doing qualitative research: A practical handbook* (3rd ed.). Sage.

Spencer, L., Ritchie, J., & O'connor, W. (2005). Analysis: Practices, principles and processes. In J. R. J. Lewis (Ed.), *Qualitative research practice* (pp. 199–218). Sage.

Stinchcombe, A. L. (1997). On the virtues of the old institutionalism. *Annual Review of Sociology, 23*(1), 1–18.

Tesch, R. (1990). Eight steps for data analysis. In A. S. de Vos (Ed.), *Data analysis in qualitative research.* Van Schaik.

Tinsley, M., & Lambert, J. (2021). *The economic impact of the Agri-Food Sector in Southeast Asia.* Oxford Economics. Retrieved November 17, 2021, from https://www.oxfordeconomics.com/recent-releases

Ticehurst, G., & Veal, A. (2000). Business research methods: A managerial approach. *NSW Australia: Pearson Education.*

Tran, A., & Jeppesen, S. (2016). SMEs in their own right: The views of managers and workers in Vietnamese textiles, garment, and footwear companies. *Journal of Business Ethics, 137*(3), 589–608.

Tran, A. N. (2011). Corporate social responsibility in socialist Vietnam. *Labour in Vietnam, 31,* 119.

Vo, H. T. M., & Arato, M. (2020). Corporate social responsibility in a developing country context: A multi-dimensional analysis of modern food retail sector in Vietnam. *Agroecology and Sustainable Food Systems, 44*(3), 284–309.

Waddock, S. (2009). *Leading corporate citizens: Vision, values, value added-3/E.* McGraw-Hill.

Yin, R. (2010). *Qualitative research from start to finish.* Guilford Press.

Yin, R. K. (2003). *Case study research: Design and methods* (3rd ed.). Sage.

Zhang, D., Jiang, Q., Ma, X., & Li, B. (2014). Drivers for food risk management and corporate social responsibility: A case of Chinese food companies. *Journal of Cleaner Production, 66,* 520–527.

Chapter 7
Green Human Resource Management in Hotels in Developing Countries: A Practices- and Benefits-Related Conceptual Framework

Nhat Tan Pham⑩, Tan Vo-Thanh⑩, and Zuzana Tučková⑩

Abstract Owing to the recent emergence of "green" human resource management (GHRM), there is a research gap around the understanding of GHRM practices and their contribution to organisational performance. By extending the Ability-Motivation-Opportunity theory into the green context, this study aimed to build a conceptual framework for GHRM practices and their benefits in the hotel industry in developing economies in Asia. Adopting the multiple-case design, we examined three 4–5-star hotels. In terms of results, a conceptual framework capturing the relationships between GHRM practices and their benefits was proposed and enriched empirically. This study yielded two new findings: (1) a potential mediating role of employee environmental performance on the relationships between GHRM practices, green human capital, green motivation, and corporate environmental performance; and (2) a potential direct effect of external benefits of GHRM on corporate financial performance. This research also identified differences in GHRM practices and external benefits due to different top management cultures. Finally, this study contributes to the literature on environmental sustainability by investigating GHRM practices and their benefits in 4–5-star hotels in emerging markets, which remains a black box that needs to be explored.

Keywords Green human resource management · External benefits · Internal benefits · Ability · Motivation · Opportunity theory · Environmental sustainability · Emerging markets · Multiple-case design

---

N. T. Pham
School of Business, International University, Ho Chi Minh City, Vietnam
e-mail: ptnhat@hcmiu.edu.vn

Vietnam National University, Ho Chi Minh City, Vietnam

T. Vo-Thanh (✉)
Department of Marketing, Excelia Business School, La Rochelle, France
e-mail: vothanht@excelia-group.com

Z. Tučková
Faculty of Management and Economics, Tomas Bata University in Zlín, Zlín, Czech Republic
e-mail: tuckova@utb.cz

© The Author(s), under exclusive license to Springer Nature Singapore Pte Ltd. 2022
N. Nguyen et al. (eds.), *Environmental Sustainability in Emerging Markets*,
Approaches to Global Sustainability, Markets, and Governance,
https://doi.org/10.1007/978-981-19-2408-8_7

7.1 Introduction

An increase in environmental legislation and pressure from consumers have enhanced organisations' awareness of environmental issues (Chan & Hawkins, 2012). Consequently, firms have increasingly employed strategies linked to proactive environmental management (EM) to reinforce their position (Chiappetta Jabbour et al., 2010).

The role of human resource management (HRM) is essential in implementing EM practices to proactively address environmental problems (Pham, Vo-Thanh, Shahbaz et al., 2020; Ren et al., 2018). Green human resource management (GHRM), defined as the EM aspect in HRM (Renwick et al., 2013), relates to using various HRM practices to train, motivate, and involve staff in environmental issues. GHRM has an important role to play in the development of organisations' green strategies, and focus on this field has become a new trend in HRM research (Ren et al., 2018). GHRM practices can have a role to play in improving not only environmental performance (Nisar et al., 2021; Pham, Vo-Thanh, Shahbaz et al., 2020; Pham, Vo-Thanh, Tučková et al., 2020; Úbeda-García et al., 2021), but also the organisation's financial performance (Úbeda-García et al., 2021). To support this claim, it is necessary to consider empirical studies on the GHRM practices–organisational performance link. However, there are still few such studies that empirically explore how GHRM practices influence organisational performance (Pham, Vo-Thanh, Tučková et al., 2020; Úbeda-García et al., 2021). As noted by Ren et al. (2018), the factors that give rise to GHRM (including when and how it influences outcomes) are still under-explored.

Second, in the hotel industry, environmental problems have been addressed by many hotels because they often cause a negative impact on the environment as a result of using significant amounts of natural resources (Pham, Chiappetta Jabbour, Vo-Thanh et al., 2020). GHRM is thus of strategic importance for any hotel. Yet, there has been little investigation to deeply understand GHRM practices implemented in hotels and their benefits (Kim et al., 2019; Pham, Vo-Thanh, Tučková et al., 2020). Prior studies have only shed light on the connection of GHRM to green behaviour and corporate environmental performance, while contributions of GHRM application in hotels towards other aspects such as external benefits (e.g., customer satisfaction, community, competitive advantage, public image) and green human capital have been under-developed (Ansari et al., 2021; Nisar et al., 2021). Moreover, almost all of the environment-related studies in the hotel context have only emphasised general EM practices (Molina-Azorín et al., 2015).

Third, Myung et al. (2012) have identified that environment-related research in the hotel sector, especially in emerging markets, is still in its infancy. Very few recent hotel GHRM-related studies have been conducted in developing countries (e.g., in Asia—Kim et al., 2019), despite the fact that these countries depend heavily on the hospitality and tourism industry, in which environmental problems challenge the future of this industry (Singjai et al., 2018). Most existing studies have mainly focused on environmental practices in developed countries (Molina-Azorín et al., 2015). Although some strategies successfully implemented in one country may be transferable to another, the implementation of proactive environmental strategies might be affected by local factors such as local regulations, local environmental infrastructure, and local available resources (González-Benito & González-Benito, 2006). Furthermore, the environmental challenges and policy choices in developed countries are often different from those in developing countries. The latter commonly feature a large informal economy, high levels of poverty and inequality, weak capacity and resources for innovation and investment, as well as limited mechanisms for implementing environment-related incentives. Additionally, the implementation of environmental policies in HRM may not be similar in developed and developing countries because of cultural differences (Hoang et al., 2018). Finally, Ren et al. (2018) identify an urgent need to clarify the GHRM concept. Further research into GHRM in the hotel industry in developing countries is therefore required.

This paper aims to fulfil the earlier mentioned research gaps by answering the following research question:

What GHRM practices do hotels in developing countries apply, and why and how are they implemented?

This research contributes to the literature in several ways: (1) extending the Ability–Motivation–Opportunity (AMO) theory to developing a conceptual framework related to GHRM practices and their benefits, a theoretical basis for future research on this topic; (2) indicating out new contributions regarding the mediating role of employee environmental performance on the connections between GHRM practices, green human capital, green motivation, and corporate environmental performance, and the role of different culture of top management (Western vs. local) towards GHRM practices and their benefits, undeveloped by prior scholars; and (3) conducting empirical research on GHRM practices and their benefits in a new research area: the hotel industry in emerging markets.

7.2 Literature Review

7.2.1 Related Theory

Various theories (e.g., social exchange theory, social identity theory, AMO theory) have been used to investigate the role of GHRM practices in organisations. For instance, drawing upon the social exchange theory (e.g., Yusliza et al., 2019) and social identity theory (e.g., Chaudhary, 2020), previous studies state that an effective GHRM can be important to boosting employees' green behaviours. Previous research also mobilises the AMO theory to explore the relationships between GHRM practices and employees' behaviours and attitudes and organisational performance (e.g., Pham, Vo-Thanh, Tučková et al., 2020). According to the AMO theory, HRM practices could affect employees' abilities (by training and recruitment), motivations (by reward and performance management), and opportunities (by involvement and teamwork), and improve the firm's performance (Renwick et al., 2013). Thus, the AMO theory can be utilised to investigate internal benefits when implementing GHRM practices.

The AMO theory is also appropriate for seeking external benefits gained from the GHRM implementation (e.g., competitive advantage and customer satisfaction). For example, employees' green ability may be a rare and inimitable resource, which helps organisations to be competitive. Additionally, the AMO theory is primarily employed to investigate the links between GHRM practices and benefits. For example, the AMO theory has been used to define GHRM practices (Renwick et al., 2013) and explore the relationships between GHRM practices and green commitment and behaviour (Pham, Vo-Thanh, Tučková et al., 2020; Pinzone et al., 2016).

7.2.2 GHRM Practices: What and How?

In accordance with the AMO theory, according to Renwick et al. (2013), GHRM practices include three main components which aim to develop green abilities (e.g., through recruitment, training sessions), motivate green employees (e.g., by applying reward system, performance management), and create green opportunities (e.g., by using employee involvement, organisational culture).

Table 7.1 summarises GHRM practices based on the literature.

7.2.3 Why Apply GHRM Practices?

7.2.3.1 External Benefits

Anchored in the AMO theory, scholars have proposed external benefits of HRM to organisations, for example, customer relationships and competitive advantage. Customers are increasingly concerned about environmental practices, especially in the service sector (Vo-Thanh et al., 2020, 2021b). Hence, developing customer relationships based on EM is necessary to enhance customer satisfaction and loyalty, build a positive public image, and achieve sales that improve competitive advantage (Longoni & Cagliano, 2016). For the hotel industry, previous studies have indicated that EM practices boost differentiation, public image, and cost advantage (Molina-Azorín et al., 2015), providing the hotel with a competitive advantage.

Another potential benefit lies in the reduction of external stakeholders' pressure (e.g., government, community, NGOs). Stakeholders can exert pressure on organisations' environmental goals. This motivates organisations to achieve green goals to satisfy external stakeholders. Guerci et al. (2016) assume that GHRM application should be encouraged as a means of responding to stakeholders' pressure on environmental problems, increasing the organisation's social legitimacy.

7 Green Human Resource Management in Hotels ... 155

Table 7.1 GHRM practices

Green HRM practices		References
Recruitment	Firm highlights the preference to attract environment-oriented candidates	Renwick et al. (2013)
	Firm adds the environmental criteria to recruitment message	Masri and Jaaron (2017)
	The job description sheet emphasises environmental concerns and what is expected from candidates	Masri and Jaaron (2017)
Training	Firm provides environmental trainings to all employees	Daily et al. (2012), Guerci et al. (2016)
	Firm communicates environmental training and information to the workforce	Renwick et al. (2013)
	There are evaluations about performance of training programs	Daily et al. (2012)
Performance management	Firm establishes the EM information system for monitoring environmental activities	Renwick et al. (2013)
	Firm sets up green targets for managers	Renwick et al. (2013)
	Firm provides the clear green targets and responsibilities for employees	Chiappetta Jabbour et al. (2010)
	Firm translates environmental feedback (from customers or top management) to employees or teams	Govindarajulu and Daily (2004)
Reward	Firm has the monetary-based reward (e.g., bonus, cash)	Renwick et al. (2013)
	Firm sets up green initiative/performance as a part of reward system	Masri and Jaaron (2017)
	Firm establishes the non-monetary-based reward (e.g., special gifts, time off, public recognition)	Tang et al. (2018)

(continued)

Table 7.1 (continued)

Green HRM practices		References
Employee involvement	Firm allows employees to consult and suggest solutions in solving environmental issues	Tang et al. (2018)
	Employees are encouraged to make suggestions and decisions for environment improvements	Daily et al. (2012)
	Firm emphasises sharing environmental initiatives or programs with employees (e.g., green team)	Renwick et al. (2013)
	Firm gives opportunities to employees to involve and participate in green suggestion schemes and problem-solving groups	Masri and Jaaron (2017)
Green organisational culture	Vision, mission, and value consist in emphasising the environmental protection	Chiappetta Jabbour et al. (2010)
	Top management provides employees with environmental training, initiatives, and goals	Govindarajulu and Daily (2004)
	Firm has environment-oriented policies in management and specific environmental tasks	Chou (2014)
	Firm has punishment system in case of noncompliance in environmental rules	Masri and Jaaron (2017)

7.2.3.2 Internal Benefits

HRM practices can enhance employees' human capital and motivation, and improve operational and financial outcomes (Ansari et al., 2021; Nisar et al., 2021; Pham, Chiappetta Jabbour, Vo-Thanh et al., 2020). GHRM is expected to bring internal benefits to the organisation, including improvement of employees' green human capital and motivation, and organisational performance (Ansari et al., 2021; Nisar et al., 2021).

Following the AMO theory, skill and motivation-enhancing HRM practices can directly optimise employees' human capital, commitment, and behaviour (Nisar et al., 2021; Pham, Chiappetta Jabbour, Vo-Thanh et al., 2020). Effective environmental training is one of the most important tools to fill the gaps in employees' environmental awareness, knowledge, and skills (Daily et al., 2012). This helps employees understand how the environment can be influenced by their decisions, identify environmental problems, and contribute to the improvement of the organisation's environmental performance (Govindarajulu & Daily, 2004).

Additionally, in a firm that concentrates on green human resources, if employees feel satisfied with their job, they will be more willing to involve themselves voluntarily in eco-behaviour (Pham, Chiappetta Jabbour, Vo-Thanh et al., 2020). An effective GHRM strategy may promote employees' green human capital (e.g., green knowledge, skills, awareness) and green commitment and behaviour, which in turn improve the organisation's environmental performance (Ren et al., 2018).

In the hotel industry, Kim et al. (2019) also demonstrate a positive effect of GHRM on employee commitment and organisational citizenship behaviour regarding the environment, improving the hotel's environmental performance. Green practices such as training, performance management, employee involvement (Pinzone et al., 2016), and top management's involvement (Tung et al., 2014) may increase employees' motivation towards environmental issues. Thus, GHRM practices can create positive changes in employees' green attitudes and behaviours (Ren et al., 2018), helping meet the organisation's environmental requirements. GHRM practices can play a key role in raising the corporate's environmental and financial outcomes (Nisar et al., 2021; Pham, Vo-Thanh, Tučková et al., 2020; Úbeda-García et al., 2021).

Based on the AMO theory and literature outlined above, a conceptual framework summarising various GHRM practices and their benefits is proposed. Figure 7.1 explains various GHRM practices and their relationship with organisational performance. Specifically, GHRM practices can directly influence internal benefits (i.e., green human capital, green motivation, corporate environmental and financial performance) and external benefits (i.e., competitive advantage, reduction of external stakeholders' pressure). Additionally, some studies recognise the mediating roles that

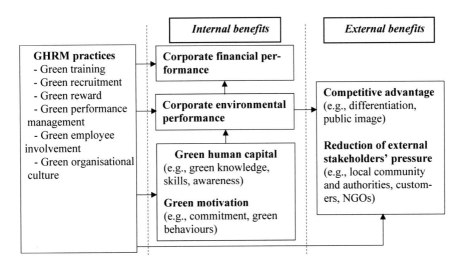

Fig. 7.1 Conceptual framework

green human capital and green motivation play in the link between GHRM practices and corporate environmental performance, and the mediating roles of corporate environmental performance between GHRM practices and corporate financial performance, competitive advantage, and reduction of external stakeholders' pressure.

7.3 Methodology

7.3.1 Method

In accordance with Saunders et al. (2009), due to the shortage of research on a deep understanding of the implementation of GHRM practices in the hotel industry in developing countries and the causal relationship between GHRM and organisational outcomes, a qualitative research method was adopted.

Moreover, we chose the case study approach because it is the most appropriate to answer our "what", "how", and "why" research questions, and to meet research objectives. According to Yin (2014), the case study strategy should be mobilised when such questions are being asked about a contemporary set of events over which the investigator has little or no control. In line with Yin (2014), Saunders et al. (2009) also recommend the use of the case study approach to answer questions, such as "what", "how", and "why". As the main objective of this research is to explore the contemporary issue of GHRM practices implemented in hotels and explain how these practices influence the hotels' performance, the case study strategy appears particularly relevant. The case study approach aims to examine an issue (e.g., GHRM) by means of case(s), illustrating the issue's complexity (Creswell, 2007). Given the current research objectives, the case study approach seems the most relevant.

7.3.2 Study Site and Sampling

In 1993, the Vietnamese government enacted environmental protection laws to encourage the development of environmentally friendly industries. In 2012, the Prime Minister of Vietnam approved the "Strategy on Green Growth for the Period of 2011–2020 and Vision to 2050" (Pham, Chiappetta Jabbour, Vo-Thanh et al., 2020). The Vietnamese government has considered the tourism industry one of the main pillars of the economy. The Vietnamese hotel industry has been expanding quickly to satisfy the increase in international and domestic tourists since the 2000s (Trung & Kumar, 2005). In 2018, there have been 28,000 tourist accommodations with 550,000 rooms. The number of 4–5-star hotels has been 306, with 51,591 rooms in 2015 (Vietnam National Administration of Tourism, 2019). However, these hotels are primarily located in major cities and famous tourism cities (e.g., Ho Chi Minh City, Hanoi, Vung Tau, Da Nang) (Vietnam National Administration of Tourism, 2019). Regarding the top-level management culture of these hotels, there are three main categories: hotels managed by Western multinational corporations, hotels managed by collaborations between Western international corporations and state-owned ones, and hotels managed by local private corporations.

Based both on the hotel category (4–5-star hotels category) and top management culture criteria, we purposefully opted for a multiple-case (holistic) design by choosing three 4–5-star hotels. Case A (hotel A) is a five-star international hotel and has been operating for five years. This hotel is managed by a multinational corporation that has a long history of operating hotels all over the world. Case B (hotel B) is a four-star joint-stock hotel. For the last 10 years, this hotel has been conjointly managed by an international hospitality corporation with many years of experience in luxury hotel management and a state-owned tourism company operating for over 25 years in Vietnam. Case C (hotel C), opened in 2010, is a four-star private hotel, owned and managed by a local private corporation operating in tourism, real estate, construction, and other sectors. The three hotels follow ISO:14001 and TCVN: 4391:2015 standards, which are strictly controlled by local authorities.

Examining 4–5-star hotels was supported by three main observations: (1) 4–5-star hotels represent an important segment of the Vietnamese hotel industry; (2) compared to hotels of inferior categories, 4–5-star hotels often adopt a GHRM approach, ensuring sufficient availability of data to answer research questions; and (3) prior studies on EM have also collected data from 4–5-star hotels, for the same reasons described (e.g., Pham, Chiappetta Jabbour et al., 2020).

We chose the three mentioned cases for several reasons: (1) as recommended by Creswell (2007), for case study research it is preferable to include no more than four or five cases in a single study; and (2) the three cases are purposefully selected. Indeed, purposeful sampling is often used in case study research, habitually requiring a very small sample, and this sampling is suitable to select cases that are particularly informative (Saunders et al., 2009).

7.3.3 Data Collection

We selected participants using the following criteria:

- Participants must have adequate knowledge and understanding of GHRM. To ensure this criterion, we chose only employees who are in charge of implementing/executing GHRM practices in the three selected hotels.
- We chose both managers and employees. The employees' answers were compared to managers' ones to ensure data reliability.
- Following Chan and Hawkins (2012), we chose only full-time employees, aged 18 years old and over, and having at least one year of experience in the hotel.

Twelve semi-structured interviews (Table 7.2) were conducted by two authors. Each author interviewed one manager and one employee separately in each hotel, but used the same interview guide and protocol (interviewing schedule, materials, etc.),

Table 7.2 Characteristics of participants

No.	Participants (Code)	Case	Age (year)	Position	Experience in hotel (year)
1	MA1	A	47	Manager of administration department	5
2	MA2	A	40	Manager of front office department	5
3	EA1	A	26	Employee of maintenance department	3
4	EA2	A	26	Employee of housekeeping department	3
5	MB1	B	51	Manager of administration department	10
6	MB2	B	52	Manager of housekeeping department	7
7	EB1	B	32	Senior employee of housekeeping department	5
8	EB2	B	26	Employee of front office department	3
9	MC1	C	49	Manager of human and training department	7
10	MC2	C	41	Manager of maintenance department	6
11	EC1	C	29	Senior employee of kitchen room	4
12	EC2	C	28	Senior employee of maintenance department	4

ensuring research reliability (Yin, 2014). After completing the interviews, the authors summarised the data of each case carefully. At this stage, to improve data reliability, the process of member checking was used, which entailed contacting interviewees via e-mail or Facebook to confirm the previously collected information. Moreover, multiple sources were integrated, including documentary information, interviews, and participant observation, which significantly enhanced the research validity (Yin, 2014).

7 Green Human Resource Management in Hotels ...   161

7.3.4 Data Analysis

First, the content of all interviews was transcribed and saved in a Microsoft Word file. Based on the conceptual framework (Fig. 7.1), a dictionary of GHRM practices and their benefits (themes) was developed. A content analysis using QSR NVivo 10 software was performed case by case and according to the category of respondents (managers or employees).

To ensure internal validity, following Vo-Thanh et al. (2021a) and Vo-Thanh and Kirova (2018), the authors together analysed the first interview. After that, each author analysed the rest of the corpus independently using the same developed dictionary of themes. The final results were compared. Divergences were discussed to reach a consensus. Moreover, the authors together cross-checked the results to examine similarities and differences in GHRM practices and their benefits, and to draw a single set of "cross-case" conclusions (Tables 7.3 and 7.4) (Creswell, 2007). The draft report for each hotel was sent to the manager of that hotel to review before compiling the full report encompassing all cases, helping increase the research validity (Yin, 2014). Finally, the full report was translated into English, using the back-translation method.

7.4 Findings

7.4.1 Applied GHRM Practices

7.4.1.1 Developing Green Abilities

Our interviews confirm that green training is one of the most important practices in the three cases. The training sessions are planned by top management and training departments, and offered adequately to employees. Training must be embedded in the hotel's essential needs (e.g., saving energy and water, classifying waste, ensuring food safety, and hygiene). Training sessions are primarily designed and delivered by foreign experts (cases A and B) and department managers and the human resources and training department (case C).

> Environmental training is required for all employees. The hotel usually invites famous experts two–three times a year for training. (MA1)
>
> I was educated about the reasons I must identify and classify waste. (EB1)
>
> Detailed guidance for saving water (e.g., avoiding thawing meat/fish using hot water) was provided to employees of my department. (EC1, Guidance Paper)

The training programs are purposely elaborated. Information before and after training is communicated by the human resources and training department via e-mails, notices, and department managers. Moreover, the hotel focuses on measuring

Table 7.3 Applied GHRM practices and environmental standards

Green practices and environmental standards		Case A	Case B	Case C
Recruitment		N	N	N
Training	Hotel provides all employees with environmental trainings	V	V	V
	Hotel communicates environmental training and information to the workforce	V	V	V
	There are evaluations about performance of training programs	V	V	V
Performance management	Hotel establishes the EM information system for monitoring environmental activities	V	V	V
	Hotel requires the report of employee's environmental performance	N	V	V
	The environmental performance is an indicator of performance management system	N	V	V
	Hotel sets up clear green targets and responsibilities for employees	N	V	V
	Supervisors monitor environmental protection activities	V	V	V
	Hotel translates environmental feedback (from customers or top management) to employees or teams	V	V	V
Reward	Hotel has a monetary-based reward (e.g., bonus)	N	V	V
	Hotel sets up green performance as a part of reward system	N	V	V
	Hotel establishes a recognition-based reward	V	V	V
Employee involvement	Employees consult and suggest solutions to solving environmental issues	V	V	N
	Employees are encouraged to make suggestions and decisions for environmental improvements	V	V	N

(continued)

7 Green Human Resource Management in Hotels … 163

Table 7.3 (continued)

Green practices and environmental standards		Case A	Case B	Case C
	Hotel emphasises sharing environmental initiatives or programs with employees (e.g., green team)	V	V	N
	Hotel gives opportunities to employees to involve and participate in green suggestion schemes	V	V	N
Green organisational culture	Vision, mission, and value consist in emphasising the environmental protection	V	V	N
	Top management provides employees with environmental training, initiatives, and goals	V	V	N
	Hotel has environment-oriented policies in management and specific environmental tasks	V	V	N
	Hotel defines punishment system in case of noncompliance in environmental rules	V	V	V
ISO: 14001		V	V	V
TCVN 4391:2015		V	V	V
A proactive green strategy		V	V	N
Top management		W	Mx	L

N: Not mentioned, V: Applied practices/criteria, W: Western, Mx: The mix of a Western and local, L: Local

the efficiency of training programs through water consumption, energy conservation, and especially the energy consumption of the ventilation and air conditioning system.

> We have to assess the cost of total annual energy usage from the ventilation and air conditioning, kitchen […]. These figures are then compared with previous years. (MA1)
>
> The performance of training programs is evaluated carefully by supervisors and the administration department through a test which includes general environmental knowledge, and related skills and activities done in employees' work. (MB1)

Green recruitment is not highlighted by the three hotels. After recruited, new employees will be carefully trained both about green and professional skills for working in the hotel.

> Candidates will be trained carefully and regularly about the environment. So, we do not worry about their environmental skills. (MB1)

Table 7.4 Benefits of applying GHRM practices

Benefits		Case A	Case B	Case C
External	Relationship with local community	H	H	N
	Relationship with local authority	P	H	N
	Customer satisfaction	H	P	N
	Attracting customer	H	P	N
	Positive public image (competitive advantage)	H	P	N
	Differentiation (competitive advantage)	H	P	N
	Relationship with partner	P	P	N
Internal	Employees' environmental knowledge, skills and awareness	H	H	H
	Employees' environmental attitudes, commitment and work behaviours in role	H	H	H
	Employees' environmental voluntary behaviour (extra role)	H	H	P
	Employee's environmental performance	H	H	H
	Environmental performance	H	H	H
	Financial performance	H	H	P

N: Not mentioned, H: High priority, P: Priority

7.4.1.2 Motivating Green Employees

Hotels undertake green performance management (GPM) by monitoring environmental protection activities, especially in cases B and C. The hotel assigns environmental targets and responsibilities to employees and uses these to evaluate their environmental performance. Environmental feedback is regularly transmitted to employees. Results of environmental performance appraisals are considered carefully. These results determine employees' bonuses, promotions, and commitment.

> Supervisors appraise employees' environmental tasks […]. Department managers help supervisors make an accurate evaluation by providing them related monthly reports. (MB1)
>
> It is difficult to encourage employees to participate actively in environmental activities without monitors' and managers' appraisals, and embedded environmental targets. (MC2)

Although case A pays less attention to GPM, monitoring employees' environmental activities is found. For instance, supervisors are responsible for monitoring these activities and for providing feedback to employees to ensure they undertake green processes.

Regarding green reward, hotels concentrate their effort on rewarding employees and teams who achieve good environmental results. Managers/supervisors recognise, in meetings, employees or staff who have excelled in environmental protection and reward them in front of others. However, monetary-based rewards are only applied in cases B and C. Employees can be rewarded or charged money based on their monthly environmental performance reports.

> The hotel has a budget for rewarding employees […]. A motivated and engaged employee is one whose performance is recognised. (MC1)
>> Staffs' environmental effectiveness is a criterion for reward system. (EB2)

7.4.1.3 Creating Green Opportunities for Employees

Both green employee involvement and organisational culture are strongly stressed in hotels A and B only.

Concerning green employee involvement, employees are always encouraged to suggest environmental solutions, and to involve themselves in environment-related activities, such as green teamwork (between and within departments). For example, the hotel created an e-mail group to communicate its environmental programs, information, notices, and more to others. Furthermore, the hotel embed environmental tasks in job description.

> […]. Employees are encouraged to undertake environmental protection activities. They must be active participants in environmental solutions, especially in solving environment-related customer complaints. (MB2)
>> I can provide feedback via a suggestion box for environmental issues. (EA1)

In terms of green organisational culture, top management always considers green strategy a part of the hotel's overall business strategy, aiming to actively develop social and environmental values.

> Social responsibility is highlighted in the hotel's vision and values […]. The hotel's staff must understand their environmental duties and responsibilities towards the community and the hotel. (MA1)

To develop a green culture, top management clearly communicates to employees the hotel's environmental goals, and establishes systems of environmental training, performance management, and punishment, which are included in the hotel's HRM strategy. The administration manager generally has overall responsibility, and each department manager undertakes the lead role in managing the environmental performance of his/her department.

7.4.2 GHRM Application and Its Benefits

7.4.2.1 Empirical External Benefits

External benefits (relationships, customer satisfaction, competitive advantage) are highlighted by cases A and B. The satisfaction of external stakeholders is an important benefit of GHRM practices. For instance, complying with environmental standards and achieving hotel green performance prevent problems in the relationships with the local community and authorities, and partners. Furthermore, competitive advantage is emphasised because rich customers and business partners tend to require high environmental standards from luxury hotels and such requirements are often not easy to assume by competitors.

> Special recognition from the local community, customers and business partners towards environmental effectiveness is the best way to build brand image and competitive position. (MA1)

The hotel also focuses on employees' environmental effectiveness as a contributor to customer satisfaction.

> Employees' environmental activities are embedded into the hotel's image and influence customers' satisfaction. (MB2)

In the long term, GHRM strategy helps improve the hotel's financial performance by not only saving electricity and water costs but also retaining current customers and attracting new ones.

> An effective GHRM strategy could help us achieve two strategic objectives: consolidate internal resources (human resources) and develop market share (retain existing customers and attract new ones). (MB2)
>
> The final goal of the green strategy is to increase profit; only customers bring to us profits. (MA2)

To obtain external benefits, concentration on green culture is central as it helps employees and managers deeply understand the hotel's core values. This sustainably boosts their commitment towards firms' environmental activities, helping develop good relationships with the local authorities and community, partners, and customers, and improving competitive advantage.

> We are fully aware of important roles in communicating the hotel's eco-culture to both internal and external stakeholders, especially customers. (MA1)
>
> We will fail our green strategy if we miss employees' eco-friendly behaviour. We should think about employees' environmental performance first […]. Honestly, the final corporate objective is financial. This objective can be obtained through a good corporate green strategy that helps improve competitive advantage, customer satisfaction, and relationships with the local community and authorities, as well as business partners. (MA2)

7.4.2.2 Empirical Internal Benefits

For all three cases, benefits of applying GHRM practices lie not only in employees' green knowledge, skills, and awareness, but also in their green behaviour, which in turn improves their environmental performance.

Concretely, green training sessions, reward system, and employee involvement provide employees with relevant green knowledge, skills, and awareness, increase their morale and enthusiasm, and improve their behaviour towards environmental issues in extra roles. For instance, a reward ceremony held in front of many other employees inspires them to engage in similar green activities.

7 Green Human Resource Management in Hotels … 167

> Training helps enhance my awareness in saving energy when using electrical devices in the hotel and at home. (EB2)
>
> Thanks to help from colleagues and the leader, I gained a lot of knowledge and skills to classify waste and so on. I also attempt to independently grasp these skills and knowledge by observing the activities of others. (EA2)

Employees can rapidly acquire skills and knowledge about environmental tasks and change their behaviour to suit the hotel's culture if they are properly guided by supervisors.

> I will be more aware of, and participate actively in, environmental tasks if I am guided by supervisors. This motivates me to learn skills and work harder to meet these tasks. (EC1)

Such environmental knowledge and skills, as well as green behaviour help employees understand how to perform successfully environmental tasks, and accordingly enhance their environmental performance. Individual's green performance is a key component to ensure the success of corporate environmental strategy.

> Employees are more aware of environmental tasks and perform them better after being adequately trained. Corporate environmental performance first rests on each employee's environmental performance. (MC1)

Finally, GRHM practices help employees improve their personal environmental performance, which in turn enhances the hotel's environmental and financial performance thanks to saving energy, water consumption, and other environment-related costs. Such benefits are found in the three hotels.

> Employees have links with many environmental activities and costs […]. Performing environmental tasks well will bring environmental and financial benefits to the hotel. (MC2)
>
> As employees' environmental activities were monitored successfully, annual energy consumption in 2018 decreased over 7% in comparison to 2013. (MB1, Energy Consumption Report)

7.4.3 Summary

Tables 7.3 and 7.4 summarise the empirical findings related to GHRM practices implemented in the three hotels and their benefits. Figure 7.2 shows the relationships between GHRM practices and their benefits. Findings almost fit the literature presented in Fig. 7.1. This research supports the GHRM practices identified in the literature, with the exception of green recruitment.

Additionally, GHRM practices can lead to internal benefits (e.g., green human capital, green motivation—not only in role but also out of role, corporate environmental and financial performance), and external benefits (e.g., competitive advantage, customer satisfaction, and relationships with local community, authorities, and business partners). The mediating effects of green human capital, green motivation, and corporate environmental performance identified in the literature are also found in the current research.

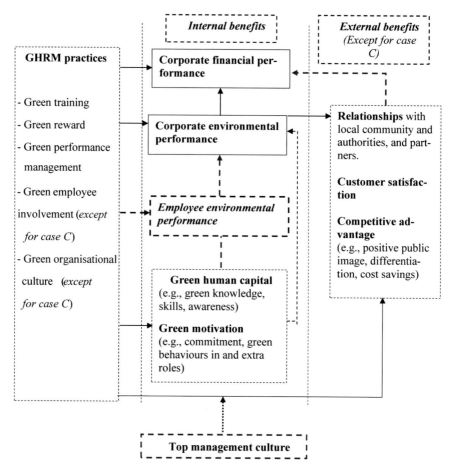

Fig. 7.2 GHRM practices and their benefits from the empirical results. Arrows and boxes expressed in broken lines reflect the new contributions of the current research ················▶ Moderating effect

However, this study suggests some new findings. First, employee environmental performance may play a mediating role between GHRM practices, green human capital, green motivation, and corporate environmental performance. Second, external benefits may directly improve financial performance, which is the final goal of hotels.

7.5 Discussion

7.5.1 Concerned GHRM Practices

Noting the omission of green recruitment, GHRM practices implemented in the hotel industry include training, performance management, reward, employee involvement, and organisational culture that are consistent with the AMO theory. Findings allow us to answer the first part of the research question.

The literature claims that organisations often develop green ability by recruiting and training. Yet, this study does not entirely support this assertion. Indeed, the three cases regard candidates' working experience more highly than their environmental skills. A manager explains that *"candidates will be trained carefully and regularly about the environment. So, we do not worry about their environmental skills."* (MB1). However, for all hotels, green training is considered a core practice to achieve environmental goals. This result corroborates earlier studies, suggesting that green training is a key factor to improve environmental effectiveness (Daily et al., 2012; Pham, Vo-Thanh, Shahbaz et al., 2020). Training programs, such as those addressing energy efficiency and waste recycling, are necessary for all employees (Renwick et al., 2013).

Previous studies indicate the need to involve employees in environmental activities (Daily et al., 2012). Green employee involvement contributes to corporate environmental performance (Pham, Vo-Thanh, Tučková et al., 2020; Pinzone et al., 2016) that is beneficial to all stakeholders (e.g., local community, customers, and business partners). This point is clearly delineated by our findings, especially in cases A and B. Furthermore, the practice of sharing environmental initiatives with others (e.g., establishing a green team, green boxes) is highlighted by hotels A and B.

A green organisational culture is revealed in both cases A and B. In fact, environmental responsibility is considered a strategic priority and translated fully by top management to employees and customers. Findings identify the important role of top management in providing environmental initiatives, goals, and customer feedback to employees. This is consistent with Pham, Chiappetta Jabbour, Vo-Thanh et al. (2020), and Tung et al. (2014) stating that top management is crucial in successfully implementing new environment-related practices, and in identifying and resolving environmental issues. Likewise, a punishment system for violating environmental rules is indispensable to develop a green culture.

Finally, the study indicates that motivating green employees by implementing GPM and green reward systems should be encouraged. Setting environmental targets for individuals and teams and providing them with environmental performance reports are productive in the three hotels. These methods help employees understand the need to change, avoid unwanted attitudes, and strengthen exemplary green behaviours (Pinzone et al., 2016). Regarding motivating employees, this research recognises the importance of implementing both monetary and non-monetary-based rewards, a point which is also described by Tang et al. (2018). Moreover, hotels stress the importance of including employees' green goals as a part of a reward system, because this affects the effectiveness of EM and employees' green motivation (Chiappetta Jabbour et al., 2010).

7.5.2 Benefits of Applying GHRM Practices

The AMO theory is employed to examine external (e.g., relationship with local authorities, competitive advantage) and internal benefits (e.g., green human capital, green motivation) of applying GHRM practices, thereby answering the second part of the research question.

Hotels A and B pay attention to developing a green brand by creating a positive relationship with not only customers but also the local community and authorities, and business partners. This can help them obtain a competitive advantage. These findings support the arguments of prior scholars, emphasising the need to develop good relationships with external stakeholders and good public image (Longoni & Cagliano, 2016), and the role of GHRM in reducing environmental pressure from stakeholders (Guerci et al., 2016). Theoretically, this study addresses external reasons why hotels should apply GHRM practices. Consequently, benefits such as customer satisfaction, relationships with the local community, authorities, and business partners, and competitive advantage are the main external benefits of applying GHRM practices. Yet, the final goal is financial performance, because developing competitive advantage is one of the main factors used to attract visitors, who will bring more revenue to hotels.

Drawing on the AMO theory, the literature explains that GHRM practices enhance employees' green awareness, knowledge, and skills (Ren et al., 2018) and attitudes, commitment, and behaviours (Ansari et al., 2021; Nisar et al., 2021; Pham, Chiappetta Jabbour, Vo-Thanh et al., 2020; Pham, Vo-Thanh, Tučková et al., 2020). These internal benefits are supported by our findings. Setting up GHRM policies seems important to increase employees' green human capital and green motivation. These policies contribute to strengthening employee environmental performance, and consequently corporate environmental performance. This finding is new in the subject's literature. Indeed, few studies have mentioned the mediating role of employee environmental performance between GHRM practices and corporate environmental performance. This finding also fits with the AMO theory underlining that GHRM practices may improve the firm's performance (Renwick et al., 2013). The findings also suggest that GHRM practices in the three hotels aim to save energy and water consumption, and reduce hazardous air and waste. Accordingly, effectively implementing these practices will increase the hotel's environmental performance, which in turn improves its financial performance. This result is supported by previous research stating that GHRM practices contribute to improving both the organisation's environmental and financial outcomes (Ansari et al., 2021; Longoni & Cagliano, 2016; Nisar et al., 2021; Pham, Vo-Thanh, Shahbaz et al., 2020; Pham, Vo-Thanh, Tučková et al., 2020; Úbeda-García et al., 2021).

7.5.3 New and Unexpected Findings

This research suggests two new findings which lie in (1) the potential mediating role that employee environmental performance may play between GHRM practices, green human capital, green motivation, and corporate environmental performance, regardless of the top management culture; and (2) the positive effect of external benefits on corporate financial performance. Moreover, two unexpected and significant findings due to differences in top management culture were found, relating to (1) applied GHRM practices, and (2) external benefits of implementing GHRM practices.

First, although previous studies have paid less attention to employee green performance, the results of this study suggest that this component may play mediating roles between GHRM practices, green human capital, green motivation, and corporate environmental performance. This pretention is consistent with the AMO theory. Based on this theory, HRM practices affect employees' outcomes, which may mediate the links between HRM practices and organisational performance.

Second, it seems that staff working in hotels A and B are more willing to voluntarily participate in environmental policies than those working in hotel C. These differences may be explained by the different cultures of top management. Hotels A and B are managed by two different international tourism corporations from Western countries and have long operation histories. This highlights the importance of environmental responsibility in their vision, mission, and values (Table 7.3). For this reason, both hotels must follow the strategy of sustainable environmental development. Naturally, their senior managers develop long-term green culture through employees' positive and active participation in achieving internal and external benefits, which in turn helps them sustain their competitive advantage and corporate financial performance. Case C is a young hotel managed by a local family group. This group places focus on Vietnamese cultural conservation. Sustainable environmental development is not its strategic priority (Table 7.3). Accordingly, green organisational culture is not its main priority. This also explains why hotel C does not pay attention to the related external benefits. This study suggests that top management culture (Western vs. local) may influence hotels' green strategy. Concretely, different cultures of top management may lead to dissimilar green policies being implemented in hotels. This result supports a study by Hoang et al. (2018) highlighting that the practices of firms operating in Vietnam may be influenced by their headquarters. Therefore, senior managers who are aware of environmental goals (cases A and B) pay attention to communicating green objectives to employees and encouraging them to actively involve themselves in green activities. Meanwhile, employees of hotel C are rather passive in participating in these tasks, even though they have been well trained and supervised, because top management seems to focus on environmental regulation and local authorities rather than building a proactive green strategy. Thus, hotel C lacks the real strategy and support from top management needed to develop a green organisational culture. Consequently, different cultures of top management may be one of the main factors explaining differences in implementing GHRM practices and interpreting their external benefits in the studied hotels. In this regard, the potential moderating role of top management culture on the relationship between GHRM practices and their external benefits may be established.

7.6 Contributions and Implications

7.6.1 Theoretical Contributions

This research contributes to the literature by several ways:

The first theoretical contribution lies in the support and enrichment of the GHRM practices and both external and internal benefits identified in the literature. Little prior research has investigated the external benefits of implementing GHRM practices. This study addresses this gap by clearly highlighting the main external benefits. This research also supports most GHRM practices identified in the literature, with the exception of green recruitment. By extension, this research offers a GHRM practices- and benefits-related conceptual framework. This conceptual framework constitutes an important theoretical basis for future research on the same topic.

Second, this study highlights the relevance of the AMO theory, which can be extended in the green context to explain the relationships between GHRM practices and organisational performance.

Third, this research shows that (1) employee environmental performance may play mediating roles between GHRM practices, green human capital, green motivation, and corporate environmental performance; and that (2) external benefits may directly improve financial performance. These new findings, under-explored by previous works, contribute to enriching the literature on GHRM.

Fourth, as unexpected findings, this research identifies that GHRM practices and strategies have been adopted by the studied hotels in different ways. For instance, hotel C does not address GHRM's external benefits as one of its strategic priorities. Meanwhile, hotels A and B consider green issues as one of their strategic areas of concern. Theoretically, this may be due to the different culture of top management (Western vs. local). This interesting finding establishes a new theoretical contribution to existing studies seeking to investigate differences related to GHRM practices and their benefits among organisations of different top management cultures.

Finally, environment-related research in the hospitality sector, especially in emerging markets, needs more attention from scholars (Myung et al., 2012). This is because of weak capacity and resources for innovation and investment, as well as limited mechanisms for implementing environment-related incentives. Thus, by clarifying GHRM practices applied in hotels and their benefits, as well as suggesting new avenues of research, this study significantly contributes to the existing literature on hotels-related environmental sustainability in the emerging markets context.

7.6.2 *Managerial Implications*

HR managers and top management should implement environmental training programs to boost green human capital and green motivation of their employees, which enhance their environmental performance, as results suggest that employees' environmental performance has a beneficial role to play in strengthening corporate environmental performance, and therefore corporate financial performance. To achieve an effective green training program, HR managers and top management need to first communicate environmental training information to the workforce, and second, to set up a performance evaluation system assessing the green training program. This evaluation system could be a test on green knowledge and skills after training and/or an assessment related to employees' green commitment and behaviour in and extra roles, a period of time after the training session (e.g., one trimester after training).

Furthermore, green employee involvement and green organisational culture also have a key role to play in attaining an effective green strategy. Thus, on the one hand, organisations need to create opportunities for employees to participate in setting up environment-related activities. For instance, organisations can encourage employees to take part in suggesting ideas. To this end, idea boxes and/or discussion groups on environmental policies could be implemented by organisations, which also need to be very clear about their vision, mission, and values in terms of environmental strategy. This strategy must be communicated to employees, discussed, and shared by them. To make the environmental strategy a real competitive advantage, in line with Tung et al. (2014), it is indispensable for organisations to install a punishment system for employees violating environmental rules.

Finally, employees' green motivation (commitment and behaviours in and extra roles) can also be enhanced by GHRM practices such as GPM and rewards. HR managers and top management can introduce clear green objectives and responsibilities for employees. They should report to employees on green feedback from customers and/or top management, and on employees' green activities. Organisations can establish a reward system (monetary and non-monetary rewards) based on objectives realised. Employees who achieve the assigned objectives will be rewarded according to this reward system.

7.7 Conclusion, Limitations, and Future Research

4–5-star hotels in Vietnam have been addressing environmental issues. Facing growing consumer awareness of and regulations related to environmental sustainability, GHRM is no longer just a concern of organisations in developed countries. Changes increasing hotels' environmental responsibility through effective GHRM policies have been becoming necessary for the hotel industry in developing countries.

In developing countries like Vietnam, implementing GHRM practices in 4–5-star hotels may be explained either by a strategic choice (e.g., cases A and B) or by a response to laws (e.g., case C). In a context where tourists' behaviour is evolving towards greater respect for the environment, GHRM is becoming a strategic tool for any international high-end hotels regardless of their location. Additionally, the research suggests that GHRM practices have a positive effect on organisational performance.

Despite its important contributions, this research suffers from some limitations. First, documentary evidence (e.g., energy and water consumption reports) were used, but these were provided in limited form by participants. Second, due to the qualitative nature of this study, the relationships between GHRM practices and organisational performance have not yet been statistically tested. This is especially relevant for the moderating and interactive roles of these practices in internal and external benefits. Bos-Nehles et al. (2013) argue that the interactive effects of practices to enhance motivation and create opportunities for employees will promote a stronger impact of ability on organisational performance. Thus, it could be interesting to examine these relationships via a quantitative study. Third, as an unexpected and significant contribution, this multiple-case research suggests differences in GHRM practices and external benefits according to the different managerial cultures (Western vs. local). It may be useful to conduct a quantitative study aiming to confirm or disprove this finding. Moreover, to increase the robustness of this finding, more cases for each type of top management culture should be included. Fourth, based on prior studies, little is known about the challenges organisations can encounter in implementing GHRM practices. Thus, further research on the challenges of implementing GHRM practices could be of interest. Finally, using the institutional theory, future research seeking to compare GHRM issues in developed economies with those in developing economies would seem to offer a pertinent contribution to the literature.

References

Ansari, N. Y., Farrukh, M., & Raza, A. (2021). Green human resource management and employees pro-environmental behaviours: Examining the underlying mechanism. *Corporate Social Responsibility and Environmental Management, 28*(1), 229–238. https://doi.org/10.1002/csr.2044

Bos-Nehles, A. C., Van Riemsdijk, M. J., & Looise, J. K. (2013). Employee perceptions of line management performance: Applying the AMO theory to explain the effectiveness of line managers' HRM implementation. *Human Resource Management, 52*(6), 861–877. https://doi.org/10.1002/hrm.21578

Chan, E. S. W., & Hawkins, R. (2012). Application of EMSs in a hotel context: A case study. *International Journal of Hospitality Management, 31*(2), 405–418. https://doi.org/10.1016/j.ijhm.2011.06.016

Chaudhary, R. (2020). Green human resource management and employee green behavior: An empirical analysis. *Corporate Social Responsibility and Environmental Management, 27*(2), 630–641. https://doi.org/10.1002/csr.1827

Chiappetta Jabbour, C. J., Santos, F. C. A., & Nagano, M. S. (2010). Contributions of HRM throughout the stages of environmental management: Methodological triangulation applied to companies in Brazil. *The International Journal of Human Resource Management, 21*(7), 1049–1089. https://doi.org/10.1080/09585191003783512

Chou, C.-J. (2014). Hotels' environmental policies and employee personal environmental beliefs: Interactions and outcomes. *Tourism Management, 40*, 436–446. https://doi.org/10.1016/j.tourman.2013.08.001

Creswell, J. W. (2007). *Qualitative inquiry and research design: Choosing among five approaches* (2nd ed.). Sage.

Daily, B. F., Bishop, J. W., & Massoud, J. A. (2012). The role of training and empowerment in environmental performance: A study of the Mexican maquiladora industry. *International Journal of Operations & Production Management, 32*(5), 631–647. https://doi.org/10.1108/01443571211226524

González-Benito, J., & González-Benito, Ó. (2006). A review of determinant factors of environmental proactivity. *Business Strategy and the Environment, 15*(2), 87–102. https://doi.org/10.1002/bse.450

Govindarajulu, N., & Daily, B. F. (2004). Motivating employees for environmental improvement. *Industrial Management & Data Systems, 104*(4), 364–372. https://doi.org/10.1108/02635570410530775

Guerci, M., Longoni, A., & Luzzini, D. (2016). Translating stakeholder pressures into environmental performance—The mediating role of green HRM practices. *The International Journal of Human Resource Management, 27*(2), 262–289. https://doi.org/10.1080/09585192.2015.1065431

Hoang, H. T., Rao Hill, S., Lu, V. N., & Freeman, S. (2018). Drivers of service climate: An emerging market perspective. *Journal of Services Marketing, 32*(4), 476–492. https://doi.org/10.1108/JSM-06-2017-0208

Kim, Y. J., Kim, W. G., Choi, H.-M., & Phetvaroon, K. (2019). The effect of green human resource management on hotel employees' eco-friendly behavior and environmental performance. *International Journal of Hospitality Management, 76*, 83–93. https://doi.org/10.1016/j.ijhm.2018.04.007

Longoni, A., & Cagliano, R. (2016). Human resource and customer benefits through sustainable operations. *International Journal of Operations & Production Management, 36*(12), 1719–1740. https://doi.org/10.1108/IJOPM-11-2014-0564

Masri, H. A., & Jaaron, A. A. M. (2017). Assessing green human resources management practices in Palestinian manufacturing context: An empirical study. *Journal of Cleaner Production, 143*, 474–489. https://doi.org/10.1016/j.jclepro.2016.12.087

Molina-Azorín, J. F., Tarí, J. J., Pereira-Moliner, J., López-Gamero, M. D., & Pertusa-Ortega, E. M. (2015). The effects of quality and environmental management on competitive advantage: A mixed methods study in the hotel industry. *Tourism Management, 50*, 41–54. https://doi.org/10.1016/j.tourman.2015.01.008

Myung, E., McClaren, A., & Li, L. (2012). Environmentally related research in scholarly hospitality journals: Current status and future opportunities. *International Journal of Hospitality Management, 31*(4), 1264–1275. https://doi.org/10.1016/j.ijhm.2012.03.006

Nisar, Q. A., Haider, S., Ali, F., Jamshed, S., Ryu, K., & Gill, S. S. (2021). Green human resource management practices and environmental performance in Malaysian green hotels: The role of green intellectual capital and pro-environmental behavior. *Journal of Cleaner Production, 311*, 127504. https://doi.org/10.1016/j.jclepro.2021.127504

Paillé, P., Amara, N., & Halilem, N. (2018). Greening the workplace through social sustainability among co-workers. *Journal of Business Research, 89*, 305–312. https://doi.org/10.1016/j.jbusres.2017.12.044

Pham, N. T., Chiappetta Jabbour, C. J., Vo-Thanh, T., Huynh, T. L. D., & Santos, C. (2020). Greening hotels: Does motivating hotel employees promote in-role green performance? The role of culture. *Journal of Sustainable Tourism, 1–20*. https://doi.org/10.1080/09669582.2020.1863972

Pham, N. T., Vo-Thanh, T., Shahbaz, M., Huynh, T. D. L., & Usman, M. (2020). Managing environmental challenges: Training as a solution to improve employee green performance. *Journal of Environmental Management, 269*, 110781. https://doi.org/10.1016/j.jenvman.2020.110781

Pham, N. T., Vo-Thanh, T., Tučková, Z., & Vo, T. N. T. (2020). The role of green human resource management in driving hotel's environmental performance: Interaction and mediation analysis. *International Journal of Hospitality Management, 88*, 102392. https://doi.org/10.1016/j.ijhm.2019.102392

Pinzone, M., Guerci, M., Lettieri, E., & Redman, T. (2016). Progressing in the change journey towards sustainability in healthcare: The role of 'Green' HRM. *Journal of Cleaner Production, 122*, 201–211. https://doi.org/10.1016/j.jclepro.2016.02.031

Ren, S., Tang, G., & Jackson, S. E. (2018). Green human resource management research in emergence: A review and future directions. *Asia Pacific Journal of Management, 35*(3), 769–803. https://doi.org/10.1007/s10490-017-9532-1

Renwick, D. W. S., Redman, T., & Maguire, S. (2013). Green human resource management: A review and research agenda. *International Journal of Management Reviews, 15*(1), 1–14. https://doi.org/10.1111/j.1468-2370.2011.00328.x

Saunders, M. N. K., Lewis, P., & Thornhill, A. (2009). *Research methods for business students* (5th ed.). Prentice Hall.

Singjai, K., Winata, L., & Kummer, T.-F. (2018). Green initiatives and their competitive advantage for the hotel industry in developing countries. *International Journal of Hospitality Management, 75*, 131–143. https://doi.org/10.1016/j.ijhm.2018.03.007

Tang, G., Chen, Y., Jiang, Y., Paillé, P., & Jia, J. (2018). Green human resource management practices: Scale development and validity. *Asia Pacific Journal of Human Resources, 56*(1), 31–55. https://doi.org/10.1111/1744-7941.12147

Trung, D. N., & Kumar, S. (2005). Resource use and waste management in Vietnam hotel industry. *Journal of Cleaner Production, 13*(2), 109–116. https://doi.org/10.1016/j.jclepro.2003.12.014

Tung, A., Baird, K., & Schoch, H. (2014). The relationship between organisational factors and the effectiveness of environmental management. *Journal of Environmental Management, 144*, 186–196. https://doi.org/10.1016/j.jenvman.2014.05.025

Úbeda-García, M., Claver-Cortés, E., Marco-Lajara, B., & Zaragoza-Sáez, P. (2021). Corporate social responsibility and firm performance in the hotel industry: The mediating role of green human resource management and environmental outcomes. *Journal of Business Research, 123*, 57–69. https://doi.org/10.1016/j.jbusres.2020.09.055

Vietnam National Administration of Tourism. (2019, June 24). *Tourist accommodation establishments (2000–2018)*. Vietnam National Administration of Tourism. https://vietnamtourism.gov.vn/english/index.php/items/10262

Vo-Thanh, T., & Kirova, V. (2018). Wine tourism experience: A netnography study. *Journal of Business Research, 83*, 30–37. https://doi.org/10.1016/j.jbusres.2017.10.008

Vo-Thanh, T., Seraphin, H., Okumus, F., & Koseoglu, M. A. (2020). Organizational ambidexterity in tourism research: A systematic review. *Tourism Analysis, 25*(1), 137–152. https://doi.org/10.3727/108354220X15758301241701

Vo-Thanh, T., Vu, T.-V., Nguyen, N. P., Nguyen, D. V., Zaman, M., & Chi, H. (2021a). COVID-19, frontline hotel employees' perceived job insecurity and emotional exhaustion: Does trade union support matter? *Journal of Sustainable Tourism*. https://doi.org/10.1080/09669582.2021.1910829

Vo-Thanh, T., Vu, T.-V., Nguyen, N. P., Nguyen, D. V., Zaman, M., & Chi, H. (2021b). How does hotel employees' satisfaction with the organization's COVID-19 responses affect job insecurity and job performance? *Journal of Sustainable Tourism, 29*(6), 907–925. https://doi.org/10.1080/09669582.2020.1850750

Yin, R. K. (2014). *Case study research: Design and methods* (5th ed.). Sage.

Yusliza, M.-Y., Norazmi, N. A., Jabbour, C. J. C., Fernando, Y., Fawehinmi, O., & Seles, B. M. R. P. (2019). Top management commitment, corporate social responsibility and green human resource management: A Malaysian study. *Benchmarking: An International Journal, 26*(6), 2051–2078. https://doi.org/10.1108/BIJ-09-2018-0283

Chapter 8
Perceptions of Graduate Employability for Green Multinationals Operating in China

Mehdi Taghian , **Clare D'Souza** , **Silvia McCormack** , **Pam Kappelides** , **Nkosi Sithole** , and **Rachel Fuller**

Abstract The present research investigates green multinational firms' perceptions of Chinese graduates' employability. China's strong economic growth has increased demand for new talent and heightened attention on graduate employability skills. In addition to desirable 'hard skills' (e.g., technical expertise and knowledge), recruiters are increasingly looking at 'soft skills' (e.g., the personal attributes, social skills, and sustainability principles that are needed for graduates to interact effectively and productively with others). Research has shown that implementing a training program for directors will improve their sustainability skills set. A survey design was used to collect data from green multinational firms operating in China ($N = 229$). Since the study was exploratory in nature, factor analysis and descriptive statistics were used to analyse the data. The findings revealed eight essential graduate employability soft skills also required for the sustainability of the MNCs: (1) perceptual and mental strengths; (2) creativity; (3) teamwork; (4) communication and presentation; (5) leadership; (6) commitment; (7) problem-solving; and (8) numeracy. Sustainability

---

M. Taghian (✉)
Department of Marketing, Deakin Business School, Deakin University, Burwood, VIC, Australia
e-mail: mehdi.taghian@deakin.edu.au

C. D'Souza · N. Sithole · R. Fuller
Department of Economics, Finance and Marketing, La Trobe Business School, La Trobe University, Melbourne, VIC, Australia
e-mail: C.DSouza@latrobe.edu.au

N. Sithole
e-mail: n.sithole@latrobe.edu.au

R. Fuller
e-mail: r.fuller@latrobe.edu.au

S. McCormack
College of Arts, Social Sciences and Commerce, La Trobe University, Melbourne, VIC, Australia
e-mail: s.mccormack@latrobe.edu.au

P. Kappelides
Department of Management, Sport and Tourism, La Trobe Business School, La Trobe University, Melbourne, VIC, Australia
e-mail: p.kappelides@latrobe.edu.au

© The Author(s), under exclusive license to Springer Nature Singapore Pte Ltd. 2022
N. Nguyen et al. (eds.), *Environmental Sustainability in Emerging Markets*,
Approaches to Global Sustainability, Markets, and Governance,
https://doi.org/10.1007/978-981-19-2408-8_8

skills were also seen as an imperative. Rather than being ranked, these characteristics are essential together. This study has implications for higher education providers and green firms alike in terms of how to redesign courses that incorporate these criteria, and how to make graduates more effective in their jobs.

Keywords Employability · Soft skills · Higher education · Graduates · Green multinational corporations · China

8.1 Introduction

The growing complexity of today's business environment, including rapidly emerging information and communication technologies (ICT), sustainability and globalisation, have led to substantial progressive changes taking place in the graduate employment market (Osmani et al., 2015; Sato et al., 2021). Such dynamics mean that graduates need to possess an ever-changing mix of attributes that industry recruiters require in terms of merging sustainability skills. Moreover, educational institutions are under increasing pressure to create dynamic learning and development programs focusing on the attributes graduates are expected to possess.

A particular set of skills that graduates are increasingly expected to hold are 'soft skills, or personal attributes, habits, attitudes, sustainability ideals, and social intelligence that make a person compatible in the workplace. Rather than being developed via formal education, soft skills are acquired via informal socialisation processes, such as in schools, families, and other social groups (Cham et al., 2020; James et al., 2013). According to Tomlinson (2012), soft skills enable the satisfactory discharge of the role's responsibilities; that is, enable an employee to interact effectively and productively with other people at work. In this sense, while candidates clearly need to have necessary "hard skills" for a position they are seeking (i.e., technical expertise and knowledge), it is soft skills that make those skills "useable"' (Mozgalova et al., 2021; Nilsson, 2010).

The present research investigates the importance of soft skills in the context of green multinational firms operating in China. A green multinational firm can be defined as a green company, operating in various countries, that claims to act in a way that minimises damage to the environment. It also requires employees to hold certain sustainability skills that will enhance the sustainability of their firm.

China at present is the world's top emitter, producing more than a quarter of the world's annual greenhouse gas emissions, which contribute to climate change. The country pledged to cut emissions under the Paris Agreement, reduce coal use, and invest in renewable energy. But its Belt and Road Initiative still finances coal-fired power plants abroad. Air pollution, water scarcity, and soil contamination remain threats to the health and livelihoods of China's people, increasing dissatisfaction with the government (Council on Foreign Relations, 2021). In recent times there have been expanded collaborations between American and Chinese companies, scientists, and experts on clean energy and carbon-capture technologies to address these problems

(Sandalow, 2009). Green multinationals can contribute to these activities to mitigate the Chinese environmental problems.

China is an important context to research given its particularly competitive employability environment. That is, in addition to an oversupply of local graduates, there is increasing number of overseas students returning home in anticipation of obtaining attractive opportunities via the strong local economy (China Daily, 2018). Moreover, the improved quality and reputation of China's local universities have attracted increasing numbers of foreign students who, since 2017, have been permitted to work in the country after graduating (ICEF, 2016). More specifically, recent findings show that implementing a training program for directors will enhance their sustainability skillset (Nguyen et al., 2021).

There are indications that sustainability engagement and positive stakeholder relationships are being managed by university management in private universities in China. However, public universities need to incorporate more sustainability-related context into the curriculum and academic projects (Wang et al., 2020).

This study specifically looks at multinational firms since they have created a heightened demand for new skills and capabilities across China. Specifically, China's economic reform, remarkable growth, and open-door policy have enabled international companies to relocate all or part of their production facilities and/or invest in the country. In turn, new skills and capabilities are needed to meet the momentum of expansion, as well as the standards and management practices set by Western countries as the key investors. Within multinational firms, there is an increasing number of 'green' firms, which refer to companies that operate in a host country (in this case China) and who have sustainability or 'green' focus. We specifically investigate the perceptions held by green multinational firms in China because universities are increasingly expected to meet the employment demands of an international economy and more importantly addressing the sustainability skills for a sustainable economy, as proposed by the UN Decade for Education for Sustainable Development. Many educational departments are using the action plan that 'all learners will need to develop the skills, knowledge and value base to be active citizens in creating a more sustainable society' (Cade & Tennant, 2005, p. 11; García-Feijoo et al., 2020).

In line with this, the study adopted a survey design, collecting data from 229 green multinational firms operating in China. Due to the exploratory nature of the study, the results were analysed using simple descriptive statistics and factor analysis to get a broader understanding of graduate employability and competence development in terms of the skills set and its impact on green multinationals.

This research forms part of a larger inquiry into sustainability in multinational firms operating in China. To the best of the authors' knowledge, there has been no prior research understanding green multinational firms' perceptions of graduate employability skills, especially about soft skills in China. The study contributes to the graduate employability literature by empirically illustrating a broad range of skills that are required to be instituted within green multinationals in China. It extends our knowledge on the link between higher education and workplace practices.

The paper is structured as follows. First, it sets the scene with the competitive Chinese higher education context, before reviewing the literature on graduate employability skills. Following that, it presents the methods and results of our survey concerning green multinational firms' perceptions of graduates' soft skills. Lastly, it discusses the results and makes suggestions to extend the findings in future research.

8.2 Background

8.2.1 Chinese Higher Education and Employment

It is estimated that around 8 million students graduated from Chinese universities in summer 2019 (International Consultants for Education and Fairs Monitor—ICEF, 2016), indicating a substantial growth in education participation over the last 20 years. Once a rare privilege enjoyed only by a small amount of urban elite within China, this continual growth took off when the national government launched a program in 1999 to expand university attendance. Many university-educated workers have since entered the Chinese job market, and while most find work, many are only in part-time or low-paid jobs (Asadullah & Xiao, 2020; Stapleton, 2017). Of the 50 most in-demand occupations in China, 30% are low-skilled positions and do not require a university degree (Stapleton, 2017).

The recent slowing of the economy has resulted in what has been termed as a 'graduate glut' in China, with high rates of unemployment and underemployment (Kapur & Perry, 2020; Wall Street Journal, 2012). Not only does the country have an oversupply of local graduates, but there is an increasing number of overseas graduates returning home in anticipation of obtaining attractive opportunities via the local economy (China Daily, 2018). While these overseas graduates enjoy some advantages over their local counterparts (e.g., due to their improved foreign language skills and international experience), they can also suffer from less developed professional networks in China and unfamiliarity with the local job market (China Daily, 2018). As reported in the online newspaper Sixth Tone (2017), foreign degrees have also become so common among Chinese job applicants that they are no longer the deciding factor for gaining a position. Moreover, there is an increasing number of foreign students studying in China's local universities (ICEF, 2016; Yang, 2020), who, due to a policy announced by the Chinese Government in 2017, is now allowed to stay and work after graduating. Collectively, these factors contribute to a highly competitive graduate marketplace.

On top of this, China's economic reforms and open-door policy continue to create the requirement for new graduate skills and capabilities. The number of multinational enterprises operating in the country has rapidly changed China's industrial landscape by bringing new technologies, management skills, and marketing networks to the country to support their investment. This has meant that new graduate skills are needed to meet the momentum of change, as well as the standards and management practices set by Western countries as the key investors. This has required close attention by business organisations to the quality of human resources and particularly the skills of graduates.

8.2.2 Graduate Employability Skills

Hillage and Pollard (1998) define graduate employability as characteristics that enable an applicant to be selected for the job, hold onto it, and can move self-sufficiently within the labour market through sustainable employment. It has similarly been defined as a set of skills, knowledge, behaviours, and personal attributes that make a graduate more likely to be successful in their chosen occupation (Hinchcliffe, 2001; Succi & Canovi, 2020).

Although there is clearly no argument that a candidate should not have the necessary 'hard skills' required for a position they are seeking (i.e., technical expertise and knowledge; Barrera-Osorio et al., 2020; Nilsson, 2010), these skills alone are increasingly seen as inadequate. In the Chinese context, some graduates are being employed in lower-skill jobs not requiring a university degree (Fareri, et al., 2020; James et al., 2013); thus, the value of having a university degree appears to have somewhat diminished. Further to this, a graduate qualification is only one factor within the recruitment decision. It has formerly been proposed that in graduate recruiting, about 20% of the weighting is given to hard skills (qualifications) and the rest involves the reputation of the degree-awarding institution, plus the type and level of the qualifications (James et al., 2013; Neiles & Mertz, 2020).

Considering this, graduate employability is increasingly being defined in terms of the personal attributes needed to obtain and maintain employment (e.g., Andrews & Higson, 2008; Atkins, 1999; Stanton & Stanton, 2020). 'Soft skills' are defined as the personal attributes, habits, attitudes, sustainability ideals, and social intelligence that make a person compatible in the workplace. These attributes are believed to have deeper and more enduring qualities than hard skills (Atkins, 1999; Hillage & Pollard, 1998; Volkova et al., 2020), which can quickly change with new technologies and efficiencies. Rather than being developed via formal education, soft skills are acquired socially throughout a graduate's life experiences (James et al., 2013; Succi & Canovi, 2020).

Soft skills have been examined from both the employer's and the graduate's perspective. From the employer's perspective, soft skills include cognitive abilities such as learning, analytical capability, problem-solving, innovation, and communication (Bikson & Law, 1995; Ṇikadimovs & Ivanchenko, 2020), and can be extended to possessing a sense of responsibility, skills for seeking and obtaining a job, ability to deduce and solve problems, health and safety usage, and personality characteristics (e.g. Ṇikadimovs & Ivanchenko, 2020; Zhong, 2005). From the graduate's perspective, soft skills are believed to comprise of three parts: (1) development—including career management and obtaining of knowledge; (2) expression—showing

Table 8.1 Employability skills (Artess et al., 2017)

Employability skills
Communication and interpersonal
Problem-solving
Using initiative and being self-motivated
Working under pressure and to deadlines
Organisational skills
Team working
Ability to learn and adapt
Numeracy
Valuing diversity and difference
Negotiation skills

employability assets to the labour market in an acceptable way; and (3) adaptation—the individual's ability to adapt to labour market environment and to practise their employability capacity (Hillage & Pollard, 1998).

Table 8.1 shows the top employability skills reported by UK companies, which demonstrates a range of skills from communication and problem-solving to the team working and numeracy. This list highlights the need for both hard and soft skills, but especially features soft skills. A similar list has been created in the context of Chinese graduates. Su and Zhang (2015) suggested a competency model with the following five main graduate employability categories: (i) practical experience and ability to solve problems, helping to achieve a goal and complete a task; (ii) professional competency—to perform a professional job; (iii) communication and personal relationship—teamwork; (iv) personality in the working process—self-confidence, sense of responsibility, ability to bear pressure, and ability to resist frustration; and (v) working attitude—taking initiatives, cultivate awareness and find solutions. The same authors (Su & Zhang, 2015) also put together a graduate employability criterion based on Chinese graduate employer's feedback, made up of the following 16 elements ranked by level of importance (see Table 8.2).

8.2.3 Employability Skills in Green Multinational Companies in China

Given that sustainable development is integrated into national and international governance and policies, it tends to impact not only human behaviour but also behaviour of the firms. There is a need to educate students with high expertise in businesses or other facets of the education sector to design, develop, deploy, and maintain systems and communication architectures for sustainable development (Klimova et al., 2016; Pop et al., 2020). Understanding hard and soft skills and the contribution

8 Perceptions of Graduate Employability for Green Multinationals … 183

Table 8.2 Graduate employability criteria (Su & Zhang, 2015)

Rank	Skills
1	Sense of responsibility
2	Teamwork
3	Professional knowledge
4	Morals quality
5	Initiative
6	Solve professional problems
7	Oral communications
8	Attractive appearance
9	Internship experience
10	Understanding other's intentions
11	Practice experience
12	Related professional certification
13	Faith
14	Interpersonal skills
15	Ability to find solutions
16	Psychological competency

that higher education institutions can make to address sustainability, more particularly, firms that transcend international borders, what types of skill competencies are demanded by them, and what contribution they can make to produce appropriate green emphasises that impact their firms (Putra et al., 2020). To date, no prior research has explored the perceptions of graduate employability (soft skills) held by green multinational firms operating in China. This leads to the primary research question that is addressed in this paper, as follows:

RQ1: What is the employability (soft skills) criteria that green multinational firms expect from graduate candidates?

RQ2: In terms of sustainable development, what types of skills do green multinationals in China expect from young graduates?

8.3 Methods

8.3.1 Data Description

The study is based on the analysis of a survey of green multinational firms operating in China. The survey was distributed by an international professional market research firm with offices in China. This project is part of a larger study. Initially, we performed a soft launch with 38 multinational companies (MNCs) in China. The questions were amended and back-translated again to ensure further clarity. The focus was to acquire responses from senior managers, directors/CEOs, and C-level executives. Thus, entry and mid-level employees were not included in this survey. A total sample of 229 MNC executives working within MNCs in China participated in the survey. This was considered an adequate sample size for the study (Hair et al., 2008). Firms operating only in China, that is Chinese firms were excluded from this study. Participants that did not belong to a green multinational firm were excluded. The market research firm performed quality checks on the quality standards, cross-referencing of the sample profile data along with survey responses and other such tasks to reduce and eliminate data errors. SPSS was used to analyse the data. To obtain broader distribution of the sample, this research also involved different states in China based on their location and concentration of industries. The sample involved demonstrated that 32% of MNCs are located in Shanghai, 20% in Beijing, 16% in Guangzhou, 7% in Shenzhen, and the remaining 2% were from Chongqing, Tianjin, Wuhan, Chengdu, Hangzhou, and a few other states in China.

8.3.2 Scale Items

The scale items for the survey were drawn from the Victorian Curriculum and Assessment Authority's (VCAA) Industry Specific Skills Standards 2014 (VCAL, 2014) and modified to suit this study's specific research questions. The VCAA is a global education provider and provides a curriculum guide for the industry-specific skills required for further learning or employment.

As this study was conducted in China, the survey was translated into Chinese and then back-translated into English to ensure language accuracy—a bilingual person compared the two original languages. The questionnaire was pre-tested using 12 English-speaking foreign companies' graduate recruiters. Some necessary minor modifications were made before proceeding with data collection. The final questionnaire included items relating to graduates' soft and hard skills attributes, organisational behavioural indicators, cognitive capabilities, sustainability skills, and graduate employability skills. All questions were measured on a 5-point Likert type scale ranging from 1 'will not consider' to 5 'always consider' and 1 'not at all important' to 5 'extremely important'.

8.3.3 Data Analyses

Quality assurance was conducted by the research firm including cross-referencing of the sample profile data with survey responses, data cleaning, data validation (edits), and eliminating data errors. The responses were then loaded into a SPSS database for statistical analysis.

Due to the descriptive nature of this study, the data were analysed using descriptive statistics (mean, standard deviation) and exploratory factor analysis (EFA). The EFA resulted in the extraction of seven factors including (1) achievement orientation; (2) self-management; (3) cognitive strength; (4) calmness under pressure; (5) perseverance; (6) dealing with adversity; and (7) reasoning. Principal components analysis was also used, to identify and compute composite scores for those seven factors (see Table 8.3). Cronbach's Alpha was then used to examine internal consistency for each of the scales (factors), which ranged from reasonable to moderately high (see Table 8.3).

8.4 Results

Table 8.4 presents the most important soft skills ranked by the study's respondents. Adaptability tops the list, closely followed by commitment. Enthusiasm, honesty, and integrity, dealing with pressure, and loyalty appear next as a group of ideal characteristics.

Table 8.5 details the recruiters' perceptions and level of importance for each employability item. As shown, the level of consideration of the employability skills varied slightly (range: 4.13–4.52; Table 8.5). In addition, the level of importance of each item is tracked at virtually the same level as consideration, indicating little preference for one attribute over the other. It appears that these attributes are all recognised as being important and are required in combination.

Further evidence that employability skills are not considered individually but viewed as a combination of various dimensions comes from the Exploratory Factor Analysis (Table 8.3). As shown, Factor 1, labelled Achievement Orientation, is the largest variable that was extracted and includes items that are mixed in terms of their contents. In classifying and summarising the items included in the Achievement Orientation factor, the following mix of soft skills, irrespective of their level of importance were identified:

1. Perceptual and mental strengths
2. Creativity
3. Teamwork
4. Communication and presentation
5. Leadership
6. Commitment
7. Problem-solving
8. Numeracy.

This suggests that a graduate needs to possess these characteristics together rather than in isolation. Furthermore, it appears that soft skills are a combination of both interpersonal (people) skills and personal (career) attributes.

Similarly, in terms of sustainability skills competence MNCs would like universities to provide students with those skills listed in Table 8.6.

Table 8.6 highlights that graduates need to be aware of and recognise the principles of sustainable development elements, environmental, social, and economic. These

Table 8.3 Exploratory factor analysis

Factor 1	Achievement orientation	
	Reliability: 0.92 – Mean 70.5 – variance – ST deviation – 7.652 – item means = 4.378	
Question	Description	Score
37	Analyse and use numbers and data accurately	0.71
36	Understand, evaluate and apply the methods, policy, theory research	0.70
32	Behave in a manner which is morally and socially responsible	0.70
39	Initiate change and add value by embracing new ideas, addressing challenges	0.68
27	Achieve prescribed goals in a timely manner	0.66
44	Understand organisational structure, operations, culture and adapt accordingly	0.66
34	Go beyond the call of duty, undertaking menial tasks as required	0.65
21	Self-confident in dealing with the challenges of employment	0.64
30	Set, maintain and act on achievable goals and realistic schedules	0.63
20	Remain committed to the core values such as honesty and integrity	0.61
14	Communicate orally in a clear and sensitive manner	0.59
16	Manage projects	0.58
22	Reflect on personal practices, strengths and weaknesses in the workplace	0.58
24	Understand and regulate emotions and demonstrate self-control	0.56
5	Develop a range of solutions using lateral and creative thinking	0.55
10	Complete group tasks through collaborative communication, problem-solving, discussion and planning	0.54
Factor 2	Self-management	
	Alpha = 0.75 – scale mean = 21.46 – var = 6.469 – std = 2.543 – item mean = 4.293	
Question	Description	Score
31	Manage their time to achieve agreed goals	0.68
45	Understand and account for local, national and global economic conditions and their influence on business success	0.61
35	Take action unprompted to achieve agreed goals	0.58
42	Participate constructively in meetings	0.56
6	Retrieve, interpret, evaluate and interactively use information in a range of different formats	0.56
Factor 3	Cognitive strength	
	Alpha = 0.63 – Item means = 4.361 – scale mean = 17.45 – variance = 3.959 – St dev = 1.99	

(continued)

8 Perceptions of Graduate Employability for Green Multinationals … 187

Table 8.3 (continued)

Factor 3	Cognitive strength	
Question	Description	Score
59	Pitching in and undertaking mental tasks when needed	0.65
29	Complete tasks in a self-directed manner in the absence of supervision	0.61
47	Being willing to face and learn from errors	0.53
11	Operate within, and contribute to, a respectful, and supportive group	0.53
Factor 4	Calmness under pressure	
	Alpha = 0.58 – Item mean = 4.185 – Scale mean = 12.55 – variance = 3.029 – std = 1.740	
Question	Description	Score
53	Able to tolerate ambiguity and uncertainty	0.64
50	Remaining calm under pressure or when things take an unexpected turn	0.52
12	Understand the complex emotions and viewpoints of others and respond sensibly and appropriately	0.51
Factor 5	Perseverance	
	Alpha = 0.50 – Item means = 4.273 – Scale mean = 8.55 – variance = 1.6 – std = 1.265	
Question	Description	Score
58	Willingness to persevere when things are not working out as anticipated	0.66
55	Having energy, passion, and enthusiasm for the profession and role	0.64
Factor 6	Dealing with adversity	
	Alpha = 0.54 – Item means = 4.271 – Scale mean = 8.54 – variance = 1.609 – std = 1.268	
Question	Description	Score
48	Bounce back from adversity	0.67
54	Being true to one's personal values and ethics	0.67
Factor 7	Reasoning	
	Alpha = 0.59 – Item mean = 4.26 – Scale mean = 8.52 – variance = 1.663 – std = 1.29	
Question	Description	Score
3	Use rational and logical reasoning to deduce appropriate and well-reasoned conclusions	0.68
1	Recognise patterns in detailed documents and scenarios to understand the bigger picture	0.53

Table 8.4 Personal characteristics ranking

Rank	Characteristic	% of total	Cumulative %
1	Adaptability	12.60	12.60
2	Commitment	10.78	23.38
3	Enthusiasm	9.98	33.36
4	Honesty and integrity	9.75	43.11
5	Dealing with pressure	9.75	52.86
6	Loyalty	9.51	62.37
7	Reliability	8.72	71.09
8	Motivation	7.92	79.01
9	Personal presentation	5.55	84.56
10	Self-esteem	5.31	89.87
11	Sense of humour	3.65	93.52
12	Balancing work and home life	3.33	96.85
13	Common sense	3.17	100.00

elements should be integral and integrated together featured in curricula to best practice in each subject and discipline offered.

8.5 Discussions, Limitations, and Conclusions

This study investigated the perceptions of graduate employability soft skills held by green multinational firms operating in China. Given the growth of the Chinese economy, the growing number of foreign businesses operating there, as well as the escalation in locally and internationally educated Chinese graduates seeking employment, the country's employment dynamics are continually evolving meaning that recruiters' selection criteria of graduate employability need to keep pace. We specifically looked at green multinational firms because graduate skills in these types of businesses have seldom been investigated.

The findings shed light on several aspects of graduate employability in China. First, the findings indicate that graduate employability is often related to personal characteristics (soft skills) that are transferrable across a range of occupations, and which are independent of knowledge qualifications (e.g., hard skills). Furthermore, the findings suggest that the absence of these soft skills could make a graduate less desirable for employment. Second, our results show that the need to introduce sustainability skills within the curriculum was considered important by these MNCs.

8 Perceptions of Graduate Employability for Green Multinationals …

Table 8.5 Employability criteria

Question	Attributes—mean values	Level of consideration	Level of importance
	Critical thinking		
Q2A	Recognise patterns in detailed documents	4.13	4.16
	Recognise and retain key points	4.30	4.27
	Problem-solving		
Q2B	Use rational and logical reasoning	4.39	4.22
	Analyse facts and ask the right questions	4.41	4.40
	Decision management		
Q2C	Develop a range of solutions and use lateral thinking	4.26	4.15
	Retrieve, interpret and interactively use information	4.25	4.55
	Make appropriate and timely decisions	4.27	4.30
	Political skills		
Q2E	Defend and assert their rights	4.15	3.97
	Address and resolve contentious issues	4.27	4.33
	Working effectively with others		
Q2F	Complete group tasks through collaborative communication	4.38	4.21
	Operate within and contribute to a respectful, supportive group	4.40	4.33
	Understand the complex emotions and viewpoints of others	4.50	4.25
	Work productively with people from diverse cultures, races, ages	4.17	4.16
	Oral communication		
Q2G	Communicate orally in a clear and sensitive manner to different audiences	4.36	4.18
	Give and receive feedback	4.31	4.31
	Leadership skills		
Q2H	Manage projects	4.30	4.14
	Motivate, support and develop others	4.29	4.14
	Facilitate meetings according to an agenda	4.33	4.20
	Instructively coach and help others	4.35	4.31

(continued)

Table 8.5 (continued)

Question	Attributes—mean values	Level of consideration	Level of importance
	Personal ethics		
Q2I	Remain consistently committed to and guided by core values and beliefs	4.52	4.52
	Confidence		
Q2J	Be self-confident in dealing with challenges of employment	4.52	4.42
	Self-awareness		
Q2K	Reflect on and evaluate personal practices, strengths, and weaknesses	4.43	4.17
	Actively seek, monitor, and manage knowledge and opportunities	4.45	4.44
	Self-discipline		
Q2L	Understand and regulate their emotions and demonstrate self-control	4.48	4.22
	Preserve and retain effectiveness under pressure	4.29	4.31
	Understand the importance of well-being and strive to maintain a balance of work and life	4.33	4.32
	Performance		
Q2M	Achieve prescribed goals in a timely and resourceful manner	4.35	4.23
	Able to multi-task	4.39	4.25
	Complete tasks in a self-directed manner in the absence of supervision	4.51	4.42
	Organisational skills		
Q2N	Set, maintain, and consistently act upon achievable goals, prioritised tasks, and plans	4.32	4.21
	Manage their time to achieve agreed goals	4.38	4.33
	Professional responsibility		
Q2P	Consistent with company policy and community	4.46	4.21
	Accept responsibility for own decisions	4.51	4.48

(continued)

Table 8.5 (continued)

Question	Attributes—mean values	Level of consideration	Level of importance
	Work ethic		
Q2Q	Go beyond the call of duty by pitching in, including undertaking menial tasks	4.31	4.17
	Take action unprompted to achieve agreed goals	4.34	4.34
	Business principles		
Q2R	Understand, evaluate and apply methods, policy, theory, research, and legislation	4.30	4.37
	Core business skills		
Q2S	Analyse and use numbers and data accurately and use into relevant information	4.33	4.23
	Select and use appropriate technology to address diverse tasks	4.39	4.41
	Innovation		
Q2T	Initiate change and add value by embracing new ideas and showing ingenuity	4.38	4.22
	Manage change and demonstrate flexibility in their approach to all aspects of work	4.41	4.37
	Formal communication		
Q2U	Speak publicly and adjust their style according to the audience	4.24	4.05
	Participate constructively in meetings	4.20	4.12
	Present knowledge, in a range of written formats, in a professional structured manner	4.38	4.28
	Environmental awareness		
Q2V	Understand organisational structure, operations, culture and systems and adapt accordingly	4.36	4.17
	Understand and account for local, national and global economic conditions and their influence	4.30	4.32

(continued)

Table 8.5 (continued)

Question	Attributes—mean values	Level of consideration	Level of importance
	Personal skills		
Q2W	Able to understand their personal strengths and limitations	4.37	4.25
	Being willing to face and learn from errors	4.29	4.30
	Bounce back from adversity	4.31	4.18
	Able to maintain a good work/life balance	4.18	4.10
	Remaining calm under pressure or when things take an unexpected turn	4.18	4.20
	Being willing to take a hard decision	4.13	4.18
	Being confident to take calculated risks	4.23	4.22
	Able to tolerate ambiguity and uncertainty	4.12	4.06
	Being true to one's personal values and ethics	4.23	4.24
	Having energy, passion and enthusiasm for the profession and role	4.34	4.28
	Wanting to produce as good as good a job as possible	4.19	4.33
	Being willing to take responsibility for projects and how they turn out	4.34	4.24
	Willingness to persevere when things are not working out as anticipated	4.21	4.15
	Pitching in and undertaking menial tasks when needed	4.15	4.24

Graduates need to be aware of sustainable development, the need to recognise sustainable development goals (SDGs) should be linked to student learning were some of the key findings.

These results contribute to the literature in two main ways: (i) the implications for graduate recruiters and companies, and (ii) the implications for educational institutions in terms of developing specific programs and courses that provide candidates with the required graduate employability skills. Proponents have proposed a set of social practices and a set of identities that are required to the social situations, which

Table 8.6 Sustainability skills set

Sustainability skills—Alpha = 0.64	Factor 1 Score	Mean	Std Dev	N
Q1—Graduates need to be aware of sustainable development as a consideration in twenty-first-century culture, and of how 'environment, society, and economics' feature in their studies. Systems thinking	0.606	4.23	0.757	229
Q2—Graduates should be able to recognise that the principles of sustainable development are the starting point to an intervention or action rather than an end product	0.571	4.22	0.661	229
Q3—The principles of sustainable development should be integral to best practice in each subject and discipline	0.433	4.28	0.712	229
Q4—The principles of sustainable development should be intimately linked to student learning within their subjects on three levels: educational; professional and personal; discipline culture and graduate capabilities	0.635	4.24	0.725	229

is an alternative to the skills agenda as an approach to graduate employability (Healy et al., 2020; Holmes, 2001), while these are useful frameworks, such initiatives to integrate graduate employability measures require a changing of the structures (i.e. curricula that better prepares students for jobs), changing the program mix (i.e. development of programs and qualifications with vocational focus), curriculum development (i.e. incorporating employability elements, sustainability skills integration), extra-curricular strategies (i.e. career and employability services), and networking strategies (i.e. involving external stakeholders in the development of student employability). Zhiwen and van der Heijden (2008) identified that higher educational institutions in China are trying to deepen students' knowledge and enhance the employability of their graduates (Jung & Li, 2021). Although some of those higher education institutions are still more teacher-centred and exam-oriented, rather than being industry focused, resulting in graduates with high exam scores, but low levels of transferrable soft skills.

It would appear that despite strong demand for graduates in China by both local and foreign firms, many graduates have been unable to find a job due to a mismatch between their capabilities and labour market demands, which highlights the need to focus on business education (hard skills), sustainability skill development and graduate employability (soft skills) (Zhiwen & van der Heijden, 2008).

8.6 Limitations and Future Research

This research comes with some limitations. A larger sample would provide a better understanding of the literature, more specifically in terms of the types of sustainability skills required. Since only MNCs were included, the results may have been varied if local Chinese businesses were also involved in the study. For example, we might expect to see local Chinese businesses also adhering to the SDGs in the same manner as most of the foreign national companies. Self-reported measures are often subjective and can cause social desirability bias.

Another possible limitation is that we didn't identify organisations' characteristics, the perception of the fitting of the candidate within the organisational culture, considerations for future promotions, and the character of the recruiting manager, particularly the chemistry between the candidate and the recruiter at the interview. Thus, even if a graduate has all the required soft skills, employment success also may still depend on other elements.

References

Andrews, J., & Higson, H. (2008). Graduate employability, 'soft skills' versus 'hard' business knowledge: A European study. *Higher Education in Europe, 33*(4), 411–422.

Artess, J., Hooley, T., & Mellors-Bourne, R. (2017). *Employability: A review of the literature 2012–2016*. Higher Education Academy.

Asadullah, M. N., & Xiao, S. (2020). The changing pattern of wage returns to education in post-reform china. *Structural Change and Economic Dynamics, 53*, 137–148.

Atkins, M. J. (1999). Oven-ready and self-basting: Taking stock of employability skills. *Teaching in Higher Education, 4*(2), 267–280.

Barrera-Osorio, F., Kugler, A. D., & Silliman, M. I. (2020). *Hard and soft skills in vocational training: Experimental evidence from Colombia* (No. w27548). National Bureau of Economic Research.

Bikson, T. K., & Law, S. A. (1995). Toward the borderless career. Corporate hiring in the '90s. RAND reprints. *International Educator, 4*(2), 2–11.

Cade, A., & Tennant, I. (2005). *Graduate employability for sustainability*. Submitted to the Institute of Environmental Management (IEMA) for publication in their December.

Cham, K. M., Gaunt, H., & Delany, C. (2020). Pilot study: Thinking outside the square in cultivating "soft skills"—Going beyond the standard optometric curriculum. *Optometry and Vision Science, 97*(11), 962–969.

China Daily. (2018). Growing number of Chinese graduates from foreign universities returning home. *Forbes*. http://www.chinadaily.com.cn/a/201801/26/WS5a6b162ca3106e7dcc1 37104.html. Accessed 14 Oct 2021.

Council on Foreign Relations. (2021). https://www.cfr.org/backgrounder/china-climate-change-pol icies-environmental-degradation

Fareri, S., Fantoni, G., Chiarello, F., Coli, E., & Binda, A. (2020). Estimating Industry 4.0 impact on job profiles and skills using text mining. *Computers in Industry, 118*, 103222.

García-Feijoo, M., Eizaguirre, A., & Rica-Aspiunza, A. (2020). Systematic review of sustainable-development-goal deployment in business schools. *Sustainability, 12*(1), 440.

Hair, J. F., Celsi, M., Ortinau, D. J., & Bush, R. P. (2008). *Essentials of marketing research* (Vol. 2). McGraw-Hill/Irwin.

Healy, M., Hammer, S., & McIlveen, P. (2020). Mapping graduate employability and career development in higher education research: A citation network analysis. *Studies in Higher Education, 47*, 1–13.

Hillage, J., & Pollard, E. (1998). *Employability: Developing a framework for policy analysis*. Department for Education and Employment.

Hinchcliffe, R. (2001). *Nice work (if you can get it): Graduate employability in the arts and humanities*. The Developing Learning Organisations Project, Preston.

Holmes, L. (2001). Reconsidering graduate employability: The 'graduate identity' approach. *Quality in Higher Education, 7*(2), 111–119.

ICEF Monitor. (2016). *Chinese universities break into top global rankings for the first time*. https://monitor.icef.com/2016/08/chinese-universities-break-top-global-rankings-first-time/. Accessed 14 Oct 2021.

James, S. C., Warhurst, C., Tholen, G., & Commander, J. (2013). What we know and what we need to know about graduate skills. *Work, Employment & Society, 27*(6), 952–963.

Jung, J., & Li, X. (2021). Exploring motivations of a master's degree pursuit in Hong Kong. *Higher Education Quarterly, 75*(2), 321–332.

Kapur, D., & Perry, E. J. (2020). Higher education reform in China and India. In *Beyond regimes: China and India compared* (p. 208).

Klimova, A., Rondeau, E., Andersson, K., Porras, J., Rybin, A., & Zaslavsky, A. (2016). An international Master's program in green ICT as a contribution to sustainable development. *Journal of Cleaner Production, 135*, 223–239.

Mozgalova, N. G., Baranovska, I. G., Hlazunova, I. K., Mikhalishen, A. V., & Kazmirchuk, N. S. (2021). Methodological foundations of soft skills of musical art teachers in pedagogical institutions of higher education. *Linguistics and Culture Review, 5*(S2), 317–327.

Neiles, K. Y., & Mertz, P. S. (2020). Professional skills in chemistry and biochemistry curricula: A call to action. In *Integrating professional skills into undergraduate chemistry curricula* (pp. 3–15). American Chemical Society.

Nguyen, T. H., Elmagrhi, M. H., Ntim, C. G., & Wu, Y. (2021). Environmental performance, sustainability, governance and financial performance: Evidence from heavily polluting industries in China. *Business Strategy and the Environment*. https://doi.org/10.1002/b23.2748

Ņikadimovs, O., & Ivanchenko, T. (2020). Soft skills gap and improving business competitiveness by managing talent in the hospitality industry. *Economics & Education, 5*(1), 36–48.

Nilsson, S. (2010). Enhancing individual employability: The perspective of engineering graduates. *Education+ Training, 52*(6/7), 540–551.

Osmani, M., Weekkody, V., Hindi, N., Al-Esmail, R., Eldabi, T., Kapoor, K., & Irani, Z. (2015). Identifying the trends and impact of graduate attributes on employability: A literature review. *Tertiary Education and Management, 21*(4), 367–379.

Pop, S., Lobonţiu, M., & Lobonţiu, G. (2020). Open innovation—The driver for a smart, sustainable and livable Europe. *Scientific Bulletin Series C: Fascicle Mechanics, Tribology, Machine Manufacturing Technology, 2020*(34).

Putra, A. S., Novitasari, D., Asbari, M., Purwanto, A., Iskandar, J., Hutagalung, D., & Cahyono, Y. (2020). Examine relationship of soft skills, hard skills, innovation and performance: The mediation effect of organizational learning. *International Journal of Science and Management Studies (IJSMS), 3*(3), 27–43.

Sandalow, D. (2009). President Obama's Energy and Climate Policy. *Remarks Delivered to Beijing Energy Club*. https://www.energy.gov/sites/prod/files/piprod/documents/SandalowBeijingSpeech06-09-09.pdf

Sato, S., Kang, T. A., Daigo, E., Matsuoka, H., & Harada, M. (2021). Graduate employability and higher education's contributions to human resource development in sport business before and after COVID-19. *Journal of Hospitality, Leisure, Sport & Tourism Education, 28*, 100306.

Sixth Tone. (2017). Newspaper fresh voices from today's China. *Sixth Tone*.

Stanton, W. W., & Stanton, A. D. A. (2020). Helping business students acquire the skills needed for a career in analytics: A comprehensive industry assessment of entry-level requirements. *Decision Sciences Journal of Innovative Education, 18*(1), 138–165.

Stapleton, K. (2017). Inside the world's largest higher education boom. *The Conversation*. http://theconversation.com/inside-the-worlds-largest-higher-education-boom-74789. Accessed 10 Mar 2018.

Su, W., & Zhang, M. (2015). An integrative model for measuring graduates' employability skills—A study in China. *Cogent Business & Management, 2*(1), 1–11.

Succi, C., & Canovi, M. (2020). Soft skills to enhance graduate employability: Comparing students and employers' perceptions. *Studies in Higher Education, 45*(9), 1834–1847.

Tomlinson, M. (2012). Graduate employability: A review of conceptual and empirical themes. *HE Policy, 25*(4), 407–421.

VCAL. (2014). *Victorian Certificate of Applied Learning.* https://www.vcaa.vic.edu.au/documents/vcal/vcal_cpg_wk_rel_skills.pdf. Accessed 2019.

Volkova, N., Zinukova, N., Vlasenko, K., & Korobeinikova, T. (2020). Soft skills, their development and mastering among post graduate students. In *SHS Web of Conferences* (Vol. 75, p. 04002). EDP Sciences.

Wall Street Journal. (2012). China's graduates face glut. *Wall Street Journal.* https://www.wsj.com/articles/SB10000872396390443545504577566752847208984. Accessed 23 Aug 2021.

Wang, J., Yang, M., & Maresova, P. (2020). Sustainable development at higher education in China: A comparative study of students' perception in public and private universities. *MPDP Open Access: Sustainability, 12*, 2158. https://doi.org/10.3390/su12062158

Yang, R. (2020). China's higher education during the COVID-19 pandemic: Some preliminary observations. *Higher Education Research & Development, 39*(7), 1317–1321.

Zhiwen, G., & van der Heijden, B. I. J. M. (2008). Employability enhancement of business graduates in China: Reacting upon challenges of globalization and labour market demands. *Education + Training, 50*(4), 289–304.

Zhong, H. (2005). *Thinking and practice of international cooperative education.* China Documentary Press.

Chapter 9
Sustainability Strategies for Urban Mass Transit—Case of Pakistan

Muhammad Abid Saleem⑩**, Ghulam Murtaza, Rao Akmal Ali, and Syed Usman Qadri**

Abstract The global transport sector causes a significant amount of emissions and is a major contributor to global warming and climate change. Particularly, the passenger transport segment, which is rapidly growing, shares a more significant proportion of emissions caused by the transport sector. Realising the importance of transport in providing access to jobs, health and education, and the contribution of the same in economic growth, many technological advancements have taken place in the sector. Specifically, focussing on the efficiencies related to the environment, society, and economy, various transport models ranging from Mass Transit to Mobility-as-a-Service have been introduced, receiving varying responses from travellers across the world. This chapter documents the sustainability impacts of the transportation sector in order to highlight the significance of the same in achieving sustainable development targets and presents case studies from a developing country, Pakistan, where four Mass Transit projects were launched to curb growing sustainability issues. In so doing, this chapter summarises and critically evaluates different modes of transportation for their sustainability performance and spatial and temporal efficiencies, which then leads to an evaluation of case study models on global efficient transport standards and their potential contribution towards achieving sustainability goals. In the end, some recommendations are provided to further improve the MassTransit strategies in order to fully harness the potential of efficient transport technology for achieving sustainability goals.

M. A. Saleem (✉) · G. Murtaza
Asia Pacific College of Business and Law, Charles Darwin University, Darwin, Australia
e-mail: muhammad.saleem@cdu.edu.au

G. Murtaza
e-mail: ghulam.murtaza@cdu.edu.au

R. A. Ali
Department of Management Sciences, National University of Modern Languages (NUML), Multan Campus, Islamabad, Pakistan
e-mail: rakali@numl.edu.pk

S. U. Qadri
Department of Management Sciences, TIMES Institute, Multan, Pakistan

© The Author(s), under exclusive license to Springer Nature Singapore Pte Ltd. 2022
N. Nguyen et al. (eds.), *Environmental Sustainability in Emerging Markets*,
Approaches to Global Sustainability, Markets, and Governance,
https://doi.org/10.1007/978-981-19-2408-8_9

Keywords Mass Transit · Sustainability strategies · Urban transport · Pakistan

9.1 Introduction

The transport sector fuels economies by supporting jobs, leveraging businesses, and satisfying mobility needs. Growing economies have been experiencing an exponential upsurge in transport demand in both freightand passenger transport sectors. Particularly, the passenger transport sector has dramatically evolved over the years, with the digital revolution that is hailed as the fourth industrial revolution. The amplification in transport demand can be attributed to economic stability, globalisation, rural–urban migration, and population growth of the emerging economies. In order to meet elevating demand for transport, various solutions have been introduced by the transport sector, in both commercial as well as individual transport segments. Synthesis of work to date on the travel behaviour of people reveals that a large majority of travellers are prone to using motorised means of transportation for personal needs, including commuting to work, shopping, and entertainment, for the reasons which are many and various (Saleem et al., 2018). This is a healthy trend in one way that it supports economic activity in the transport sector and promises growth encouraging increased investment in the sector and heightening investor confidence.

Nevertheless, an increase in personal means of motorised transport poses serious challenges to spatial and temporal efficiencies in travelling, predominantly in densely populated cities, as well as threatens environmental sustainability. In view of such challenges, a strong, efficient, reliable, and resilient public transport network can help reduce the use of personal means of motorised transport, thereby helping in reducing congestion, pollution, transport emissions, and traffic safety issues. Further sections of this chapter unpack contemporary trends in public transportation and present a case study from emerging economy Pakistan that helps understand how various modes of urban mass transit may help achieve sustainability goals without compromising travel quality and comfort. Additionally, this chapter also provides a critical evaluation of various transport modes in the passenger transport sector with regards to their sustainability performance as well as temporal and spatial efficiencies.

9.2 Transportation and Emissions

The predominant use of fossil fuels in the industry and transportation sectors is a significant cause of CO_2 emissions. Among others, carbon emissions come from burning crops' remains and solid waste and the biomass fuel used for cooking purposes. Among other agriculture practices, land use, organic waste, livestock manure, production and transport of oil, natural gas, and coal, and water treatment are also included among the anthropogenic sources of CH_4 and N_2O. While F-Gases are synthetic gases, that enter the atmosphere during industrial processes.

GHG are the primary source of global carbon emissions. For the year 2018, GHG comprised around 48.94 GtCO$_2$ globally. Furthermore, World Resources Institute's data repository has revealed that CO$_2$ (36.44 Gt of CO$_2$-equivalent) is the highest contributor to global GHG emissions, accounting for three-quarters (74%) of total global GHG emissions. Whereas CH$_4$ (8.30 Gt of CO$_2$-equivalent), N$_2$O (3.06 Gt of CO$_2$-equivalent), and F-Gases (1.14 Gt of CO$_2$-equivalent) are relatively fewer emitters, contributing 17, 6.3, and 2.3% to total global GHG emissions, respectively (World Resources Institute, 2021).

Historical data showed that since the 1750s radiative forcing (RF) of CO$_2$ has been doubled as compared to the sum of all remaining well-mixed GHGs. Since IPCC 4th Assessment Report (AR4), published in 2007, WMGHG-RF of CO$_2$ has increased nearly 10%, with an average growth rate of 0.27 W m^{-2} per decade. Thus, CO$_2$ emissions have made the most significant contribution to the increased anthropogenic forcing in every decade since the 1850s.

Identifying trends and characteristics of carbon emissions, several research studies and agencies' reports have concluded that the significant increase in carbon emissions is related to the global transport sector (for instance, Button & Rothengatter, 1993; IPCC, 2006; Mohsin et al., 2019; Saidi & Hammami, 2017; Shafique et al., 2021; Stern et al., 1996; Suhrke, 1994; Tiwari et al., 2020). Transportation has contributed 27% to total global carbon emissions during 2019—which designates it 2nd largest carbon emitter—after the industrial sector, contributing 40% to total global carbon emissions. Whereas 'buildings sector', after reallocating electricity and heat, has ranked as 3rd highest carbon emitter following industry and transportation (WRI, 2021) as shown in Fig. 9.1.

Transport-related CO$_2$ emissions are rising year on year. Since the 2000s, approximately 8.1 gigatons emissions (27% of total global carbon emissions) have been reported, demonstrating a persistent increase of 1.7% per annum—considered an

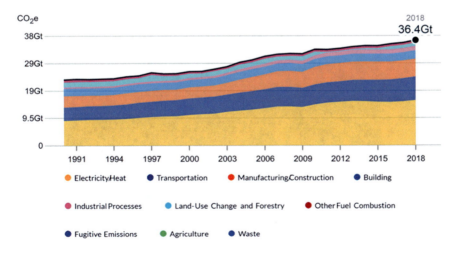

Fig. 9.1 Global emissions by sectors, 1990–2018 (*Source* Climate Watch, 2020)

important impediment to environmental sustainability. A shifting paradigm of social, economic, and demographic change, political and institutional developments, and upward trending global economic growth, characterised by free consumers' choices, have remained responsible for ratcheting transport-related carbon footprints. Under increasing global population estimated to reach 9.1 billion by the end of 2050, trade-enhanced higher growth further scaled up through the recent wave of globalisation, would further exacerbate the demand for all modes of transportation, including railways, air, water, and especially for road transportation. The transport sector is expected to increase 25% of global GDP by the year 2030, hence, posing a serious challenge to environmental resilience efforts to limit transport-related carbon emissions (Tian et al., 2018).

9.3 Urban Mass Transit and Sustainability Strategies

The climate-resilient efforts limiting transport-related carbon emissions have been undermined by an increasing trend of owning and using private cars, which dominates over other modes of passengers' mobility, including bus, cycling, and walking. Rising global per capita incomes that have increased three-fold in the last 50 years, coupled with growing travelling demand, especially in the developing countries, have remained the critical reasons for a massive increase in private car use. Figure 9.2 shows the startling facts that from 2010 (60.1 million) to 2020 (73.1 million), approximately 22% more passengers' vehicles were sold globally. Upsurge in the global car market happened primarily because of the increase in fuel-hungry sport

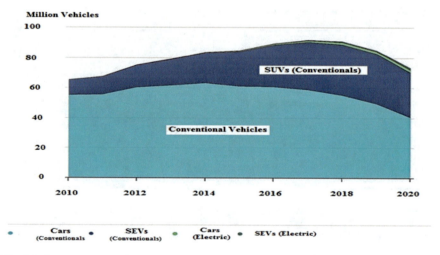

Fig. 9.2 Passengers cars sales, by size and powertrain 2010–2020 (*Source* IEA, 2020)

utility vehicles (SUVs) against the declining trend in conventional cars, which added disproportionately to the overall increase in private cars.

The growing concerns of energy use and carbon emissions in transportation have compelled the governments to rethink how the different modes of transport facilitating people mobility can work efficiently for sustainable transport with limited energy use and carbon emissions. In this regard, Clewlow (2012) argued that combined with social and economic costs in terms of traffic congestion, road mishaps, time-delayed trips, parking cost, and demand-driven rising oil prices, personal means of motorised transport have incurred an additional environmental cost since the use of private cars has increased. A major share of total global carbon emissions from the 'road passenger transport' sector comes from private car use, especially when SUVs are considered. In the case of developed countries, the changes to carbon emissions related to road passenger transport are turning negative because of a growing trend of using electric vehicles (EVs) as an alternative. However, the positive climatic impacts of EVs have not outreached the adverse effects of SUVs on the environment. A number of studies have proposed the new aspects of sustainable transportation, advocating a change in travel behaviour and endorsing the least possible use of private personal cars.

Transportation policy by various governments worldwide has focused on changing people's travel choices for a range of different travelling objectives. The target of all such policies has been reducing traffic congestion, road accidents, accommodating for space scarcity in densely populated metropolitan cities, environmental impacts of personal transport use, and sustained regional mobility (Belgiawan et al., 2013; Bocarejo et al., 2012; Cao et al., 2016). In so doing, a variety of different structural measures (regulatory mechanisms) and volunteering programmes have been introduced, all with varying degrees of effectiveness. Transport policy related to reducing travel demand of personal cars has inextricably been linked to three key issues: (1) amount of land use, (2) travel times, and (3) various environmental issues (noise, emissions, etc.), and structural measures have been accordingly designed.

Based on spatial and temporal efficiencies and environmental impacts, Hensher et al. (2020) have divided various transport modes into four different classifications: active modes, public modes, private modes, and shared modes. Active travel modes (or travel behaviour) include walking to destination and/or cycling, which are highly efficient both spatially and environmentally. However, the limitations associated with active travel modes are related to temporal efficiency. Active travel modes can only be adopted for short distance travelling, mostly limited to two miles or below (Götschi et al., 2017; Hensher et al., 2020), which includes mobility within central business districts (CBD). In addition to the temporal inefficiency of active travel modes, extreme and unpredictable weather and road safety also pose a significant threat to the adoption of active travel modes. Regions with unpredictable rain patterns, very high (or low) temperatures, and poor road safety may also impede the adoption of active transport modes of travelling even for short distances or within CBDs. Interestingly, in some societies, particularly those characterised by high power distance, psychological factors such as social status and social class attribution may also become a reason to avoid using active travel modes (Ababio-Donkor et al., 2020; Grayson et al., 2019).

Private cars may offer a potential solution to challenges facing active travel modes, undermining the spatial and environmental benefits of walking or using bicycles for short distance commuting. Private modes of travelling perform poorly on spatial efficiency and environmental performance. Particularly, when private cars are used without consideration given to carpooling, ride-sharing and maximum capacity utilisation, the scenario around spatial efficiency worsens even more. Studies on the road space use by different travel modes report that, on average, private car use performs more than ten times poorer than public transport when evaluated on space occupation-passengers transportation measure (Hoffmann et al., 2018; Li et al., 2017; Will et al., 2020) adding to mounting congestion issues in urban areas. In addition to on-road space consumption, growing parking space needs for private cars further exacerbate the space concerns associated with the use of private cars for travelling. The aforesaid issues are in addition to the environmental impacts of using private cars (or personal motorised means of transport) elaborated in the earlier section of this chapter.

Public transport modes, such as Metro, Bus Rapid Transit (BRT) systems, and heavy rails present a balanced option in terms of spatial and temporal efficiency. Public transport modes are capable of carrying more passengers per space occupied and are reliable and affordable options for travellers. However, with conventional fossil fuel-driven technology used in public transports, the environmental performance of such modes is highly contested and presents results no different than private cars. In addition, from customers' choice perspective public transport modes are inconvenient when compared with private cars. Particularly, those who rate inclusive point-to-point transportation and maintenance of privacy during commute extremely high may find public modes of transportation unattractive (Cao et al., 2016; Nadeem et al., 2021; Nguyen, 2021). The current trends in integrated transportation, characterised by shared economy, have attempted to address the concerns customers of public transport usually have regarding point-to-point transportation and the reliability of public transport modes.

9.4   Shared Economy and Transportation Trends

Ground-breaking developments in information technology, the internet of things (IoT), and smartphones and apps have ushered new trends in the transportation industry. Particularly, the rise of transport network companies (TNCs), such as Uber, Ola (Indian version of Uber), and Careem (Middle-Eastern TNC), have made integration of public transport modes with private transport services providers possible, thereby improving the viability and attractiveness of public modes of transportation for customers. From an environmental sustainability perspective, trends in the shared economy reshaping travelling choices present a unique opportunity to implement sustainability strategies for reducing emissions produced by the transportation sector.

In this context, the IPCC Special Report 2018 suggests that achieving net-zero by 2050 does not seem possible without sustained support and participation from people, including departure from using personal cars and inclination towards public transport or shared means of travelling. Furthermore, research findings of Nijland and van Meerkerk (2017); Viergutz and Schmidt (2019) also assert that, in an array of strategies to the pathway to ecologically sustained transport, a paradigm shift in travel behaviour from conventional public transport (CPT) system to demand-responsive transport (DRT) system—such as replacing car trips with carsharing and ride-sharing services, or even with more flexible public transport system particularly in developing economies—is compelling, which is estimated to reduce 4% global carbon emissions.

Demand-responsive transport (DRT) system, evolving since the 1960s, is though not a newly devised contemporary solution to currently confronted mobility problems amidst rising population and urbanisation, but a paradigm shift from fixed (trips, locations, and schedule/timetable wise) public transport to multi-modal flexible public transport system (Cole, 1968). The rising challenges, including accessibility, safety, affordability and/or cost efficiency, congestion, quality of service, and most importantly, greenhouse gases (GHG) emissions, aggregated now under the definition of 'sustainability', have replaced the CPT system with multi-modal DRT system. A well-featured issue (accessibility) of today's modern mobility, especially in remote areas where fewer users remain for mobility services, has made the CPT system cost-ineffective both financially and environmentally.

As an alternative, a real-time DRT system with fully automated dispatching started its pilot operation in the last decade, which was implemented in Helsinki (Finland) in 2012. Since then, among several others, Bridj (USA), Via (USA), UberPOOL (USA), Lyft Line (USA) or Abel (the Netherlands), are prominent DRT systems launched initially. Over time, developing demand-responsive transport (DRT) system backed up with Information and Communications Technologies (ICT) is transformed into a shared demand-responsive transport (SDRT) system. Among various SDRT system objectives, the decision to reduce private car ownership favouring alternative travel modes and carsharing has been noted as overarching. On five continents, by 2016, around 8 million people have been sharing 100,000 cars (Navigant Research, 2019). Owing to the characteristics of route flexibly, with no specific route schedule/timetable, carsharing is travellers' preference. Adaptation to such travel business models, particularly in advanced countries, has reduced private car ownership and associated carbon emissions. It appears that such new trends will now make their way to densely populated emerging economies.

9.5 Bus Rapid Transport (BRT) Systems in Pakistan—Sustainability Challenges and Opportunities

Pakistan is a densely populated country in South Asia, with a total population of over 226 million, more than 35% living in the urban areas, and a population density of $287/km^2$ (Worldometer, 2021). Due to steady economic growth, the transport needs of people in Pakistan are also growing, resulting in a constant increase in private car ownership. It is estimated that private car ownership, which currently sits at 15.4 cars per 1000 persons in Pakistan, will expand to over 50 cars per 1000 persons by 2050 (HelgiLibrary, 2019), which is a huge addition in total passenger cars on the road for such a huge population. While the data on emissions clearly argues against the use of private cars to meet global emissions reduction targets, meeting the travel needs of people is equally important to fuel economy. In addition, the need for a cost-effective, reliable, and efficient transport model for sustained growth compelled transport policy makers in Pakistan to invest in public transport infrastructure. Consequently, in 2013, the Pakistan government took a major leap towards introducing a modern sustainable Mass Transit system to provide an alternative to passenger cars, reduce road congestion and environmental pollution, and increase sustainable mobility. Starting in 2013 from the second-most densely populated city of the country, Lahore, five major mass transit infrastructure projects in three provinces have been completed so far. The following sections shed light on four of the five projects and highlight how sustainability considerations have been incorporated in the mass transit systems.

9.5.1 Lahore Metrobus System—Lahore

Lahore Metrobus System (LMS) is the first Mass Transit project of Punjab Mass Transit Authority, Govt. of the Punjab province, Pakistan, situated in Lahore. Lahore is the capital of the Punjab province of Pakistan. According to the, 2017 population census, the urban population of the Lahore district was estimated at over 10.1 million people (Pakistan Bureau of Statistics, 2017). Due to dense urban population, Lahore severely suffers from various issues related to transport, including very high road congestion, severe parking issues, constantly increasing rate of road accidents, unreliable mobility services, and, above all, poor air quality (Zaman, 2008). Because of the high number of motorised means of transport underuse in Lahore (200 cars per 1000 persons), the country's cultural capital was ranked as the worst in the world on the air quality index (Arora, 2020). Due to the growing transport needs of the city and mounting environmental issues, it was deemed inevitable to invest in public transport infrastructure.

LMS was completed in February 2013, spread over a route length of 28 km, with 28 bus stations and 66 buses operating to provide service (Transport Department

Government of the Punjab, 2021). The system was developed with the cooperation of the Turkish Government, cost a total of 30 billion Pak Rupee (around USD 167 million), provides mobility to over 140,000 commuters each day, and has led to a 24% increase in public transport use, i.e. over 35,000 commuters switching from personal means of transport to Metrobus system in Lahore (Majid et al., 2018). The system is highly subsidised with a fixed fair of PKR 30 (USD 17 cents) regardless of the trip length. That has caused a burgeoning burden of over PKR 1.64 billion in terms of Government subsidy, making the system highly competitive and unsustainable economically (The Nation, 2019).

Studies conducted on the socio-economic and environmental impacts of the LMS reveal that, in some way, the project has contributed to the social, environmental, and economic sustainability of the region. For instance, Mansoor et al. (2016) reported that in five years' time since the project became operational, there had been considerable improvement in the air quality of the city, resulting in decreased respiratory and lungs diseases, a significant decline in noise pollution and road congestion, and a substantial decrease in petroleum products consumption/energy (estimated around 61% reduction in energy use related to transport in the district) (Mansoor et al., 2016). The project has extensively improved temporal and spatial efficiencies related to travelling for many commuters. Economically, while substantial job opportunities were created for the region, the commuters also harnessed the benefits of subsidised travelling attractive, particularly for those belonging to low socio-economic segments. There has also been a significant decline in road accidents in the region covered by LMS, and people reported reduced psychological stress that was previously caused by lengthy delays during the commute (Mansoor et al., 2016).

9.5.2 Pakistan Metrobus System—Rawalpindi/Islamabad

Pakistan Metrobus System (PMS) is the second Mass Transit project of Punjab Masstransit Authority, Govt. of the Punjab province, Pakistan, located in the cities of Islamabad and Rawalpindi. Rawalpindi and Islamabad are called twin cities, with Islamabad being the capital of the country. According to the, 2017 population census, the aggregate urban population of the Rawalpindi and Islamabad districts accounted for over 1.8 million people (Pakistan Bureau of Statistics, 2017).

Completed in June 2015, PMS is spread over a route length of 24 kms, with 24 bus stations and 68 buses operating to provide service (Transport Department Government of the Punjab, 2021). Due to busy roads on the route of the PMS, 10 out of 24 bus stations are elevated. The project was completed with a cost of approximately PKR 45 billion (US$260million) funded through debt secured from the Asian Development Bank (ADB) and a contribution of the federal govt. of Pakistan and provincial govt. of the Punjab province. PMS is one of the busiest Mass Transit systems in the country, transporting around 150,000 passengers every day, with a total ridership exceeding 76 million by 2017 since its operations started (Punjab Mass Transit Authority, 2020).

PMS has contributed significantly to social sustainability in that it has provided reliable, affordable, and safe mobility options to the masses in the region, which was considered the most expensive in terms of transport cost in the country. According to one estimate, the transport cost for masses using PMS decreased by 800% for those using end-to-end service, travel time was reduced by 80% due to dedicated route for the PMS, and road congestion significantly declined due to a considerable reduction in the use of private cars (The News, 2017). This is particularly critical for maintaining the image of Islamabad city, which is considered one of the greener and most beautiful capitals of the world and providing reliable transport service for masses who were before relying on private taxi services to access job, health, and education facilities. Though the Environment Protection Agency (EPA) of Pakistan reported significant environmental pollution due to dust, roadblocks, cutting down of trees, and digging out of green belts to expand roads at the construction stage of PMS (Shaikh & Tunio, 2014), a net environmental impact after the project completed and got operational was highly positive. The Institute of Transport and Development Policy (ITDP) ranking of global BRT systems in terms of quality attributes, measuring different facets including social and environmental sustainability impacts, rank PMS in its second-most prestigious 'Silver' category (Haider et al., 2021), further testifying the sustainability impact of the system.

9.5.3 Multan Metrobus System—Multan

Multan Metrobus System (MMS) is the third Mass Transit project of Punjab Masstransit Authority, Govt. of the Punjab province, Pakistan. Multan is a major city in the south of the Punjab province of Pakistan. According to the, 2017 population census, the urban population of the Multan district was estimated at over 2.0 million people (Pakistan Bureau of Statistics, 2017). The city climate is hot, with the temperature reaching up to 50 °C during the summer seasons (May to August), with roads mostly dusty, particularly dust storms with heatwaves hitting the city in the months of May and June. The city is included in the map of those vulnerable to extreme weather, expected to face prolonged heatwaves, and may become uninhabitable in the next 50 years (Bendix, 2019).

Completed in January 2017, MMS is spread over a route length of 18.5 kms, with 21 bus stations and 35 buses operating to provide service (Transport Department Government of the Punjab, 2021). Again, due to road congestion and limited room for expansion of the existed roads, 12.5 kms of MMS route and 14 stations are elevated. The project was completed with a cost of approximately PKR 29 billion (US$167 million). As for other projects of the Punjab Mass Transit Authority, MMS is also highly subsidised with fare fixed at PKR 30 (USD 17 cents); however, unlike LMS and PMS, MMS failed to achieve its targeted ridership of 90,000 passengers per day, further exacerbating its losses and requiring more subsidies for continued operations. Since the inauguration of the MMS, several steps have been taken to increase the ridership, including expansion in connected arteries and feeder bus systems to improve the reach of passengers from the outskirts, yet little improvement has been recorded. Some downscoping was carried out in MMS to rationalise the ridership, and the additional resources were transferred to LMS. Largely, the transport experts consider MMS a failed project in that it caters to the transport needs of limited pockets of the population because of poor route planning and design of the project, intricate ticketing system, and cheaper motorised mean of transport available in the city, for instance, Qinqi Rickshaw.

While MMS is at par with LMS and PMS in terms of BRT service quality attributes as assessed by ITDP (Haider et al., 2021), the system has not received as much appreciation from passengers as LMS and PMS. The lack of attractiveness of the MMS among travellers significantly undermines its social sustainability goals (Shah et al., 2020). A study reports that MMS has contributed substantially to achieving spatial and temporal efficiency goals; however, the energy consumption efficiencies were not evident in the MMS. Because a major proportion of the low socio-income class resides in Multan city, the MMS system has been effective in providing affordable access to various facilities; however, the limited coverage has undermined its scope. On the other hand, as the city is densely populated and road system bears an overwhelming burden of transport, the MMS has contributed significantly to reducing road accidents, congestion, and travel time (Haider et al., 2021; Nadeem et al., 2021).

9.5.4 *Zu Peshawar Bus Rapid Transit System*

The Peshawar BRT (PBRT) project is the first Mass Transit project of the Khyber Pakhtunkhwa Urban Mobility Authority, Govt. of the Khyber Pakhtunkhwa (KPK) province Pakistan, located in the Peshawar city, the capital of KPK province. Peshawar is a major city situated in the northwest of Pakistan and is the capital of Khyber Pakhtunkhwa province. Peshawar is the centre of trade and commerce and, according to the, 2017 population census, has an urban population of around 2 million people (Pakistan Bureau of Statistics, 2017). Having close proximity to the borders of Afghanistan, the road infrastructure in Peshawar is overburdened with domestic transport as well as commercial vehicles.

PBRT was completed in August 2020, spread over a route length of 27 kms, with 31 bus stations and a fleet of 65 low-emission, electric hybrid buses operating to provide service (TransPeshawar, 2021). PBRT route is 100% step-free dedicated lines avoiding congestion and providing hassle-free quick mobility service to the travellers. PBRT was constructed with assistance from Asian Development Bank, costing an overall PKR 71 billion (US$46 million), making it the most expensive BRT built in the country. Managed through an automated ticketing system, PBRT fare ranges between PKR 10–50 (max 29 cents) depending on the distance travelled. The system transports over 170,000 passengers each day, with the ridership increasing sharply as more feeder buses are added to the system to increase accessibility to the outskirts of the city—ridership expected to reach up to 300,000 passengers each day when PBRT operates at full capacity. Interestingly, PBRT uses a multi-modal corridor to offer cycle lanes for those who prefer to use a non-energy-driven mode of travelling. Due to the facilities of PBRT, ITDP ranks it among some of the best BRT systems in the world in its highest Gold Category (Haider et al., 2021).

According to Asian Development Bank (2021) estimate, PBRT is expected to reduce an equivalent of 31,000 tons of carbon footprint each year due to its energy-efficient fleet and option of cycles for short distance travelling. The system has already cut usage of personal cars to half, reduced operations of pollution-generating conventional public transport busses by 75%, and travelling time up to 60% due to dedicated route lines (Asian Development Bank, 2021). The PBRT project has contributed heavily towards economic sustainability goals by providing jobs linked directly to the projects and access to jobs through reliable mobility services. By buying up old emission-spewing buses, the PBRT project resulted in significantly reducing noise and air pollution, contributing to decreasing public health issues (Mukhtar, 2021). Overall, a considerable improvement in travel time, road safety, GhG emissions, and air pollution has been reported since the inauguration of the PBRT project.

9.6 Discussion and Conclusion

Mass Transit projects are costly undertakings for providing high-quality, efficient mobility services to the masses. Such projects are mostly financed through debt. Therefore, a large amount of money is required for debt servicing over the projects' life span, making them vulnerable to economic unsustainability. The analysis of Mass Transit systems provided in the earlier sections of this chapter highlights various contributions of such systems towards economic, social, and environmental sustainability while raising challenges that need to be addressed through effective transport policy.

First, as highlighted in the discussion of the four projects, a large amount of financing was done through internal and external debts as an initial investment cost to fund the huge amounts required to build infrastructure for these projects. In addition, as fare price was fixed at the lowest possible to make it affordable for masses, particularly the low socio-economic class, projects needed additional funding in the form of subsidies by provincial and federal governments. The subsidies and loan amounts together pose the risk of the project becoming financially unviable. To overcome these issues, a significant increase in ridership is inevitable. Modern technology and trends in public transportation can be leveraged to increase ridership, leading to the financial viability of such projects.

Second, the challenge of declining ridership is associated with accessibility and traveller segments using these public transport modes. The primary purpose of such megaprojects is to provide affordable mobility services for all segments of the society, ensuring that social, economic, and environmental sustainability objectives are supported. The reduction in the use of personal cars is one primary motive in this regard. An increasing number of private cars on the road increases road congestion and adds to increasing emissions that are causing global warming. However, replacing private car use with public transport is very challenging as studies so far have concluded that personal car use is attributed not only to convenience but also considered as a means to reflect social image—this is mainly a more potent factor in societies with high power distance and social class differences (Reck et al., 2020). The recent trends in integrated mobility service as an outcome of increased TNCs and stable public transport infrastructure have made it possible to attract more travellers' segments towards using public transport. Particularly, those who were reluctant in using public transport due to a lack of door-to-door service are increasingly interested in the modern concept of mobility-as-as service (Maas)—an integrated mobility solution including various public and private transport service providers linked through technology powered by apps (Alonso-González et al., 2020; Ho et al., 2018; Loubser et al., 2020). However, MaaS is only in its nascent stage of development, and there are many unanswered questions about the development, execution, and success of MaaS, particularly in developing countries.

Finally, it is anticipated that the modern development in transport technology, such as alternative fuel vehicles, electric cars, and autonomous vehicles, will be highly considered in designing future Mass Transit projects. These technologies are expected to create massive disruptions in how modern travelling trends shape and travellers' choices evolve. Though the proliferation of such technologies into developing countries may take some time, an early appreciation of these developments would enable policymakers to keep provisions for the inclusion of these technologies in their sustainable cities and transport designs.

Permissions The material used in this chapter taken from other sources is openly available under the creative commons license. The permission where required have been taken from the authors/sources.

References

Ababio-Donkor, A., Saleh, W., & Fonzone, A. (2020). The role of personal norms in the choice of mode for commuting. *Research in Transportation Economics, 83*, 100966. https://doi.org/10.1016/j.retrec.2020.100966

Alonso-González, M. J., Hoogendoorn-Lanser, S., van Oort, N., Cats, O., & Hoogendoorn, S. (2020). Drivers and barriers in adopting Mobility as a Service (MaaS)—A latent class cluster analysis of attitudes. *Transportation Research Part a: Policy and Practice, 132*, 378–401. https://doi.org/10.1016/j.tra.2019.11.022

Arora, S. (2020). *US Air Quality Index: Lahore is world's most polluted city.* https://currentaffairs.adda247.com/us-air-quality-index-lahore-is-worlds-most-polluted-city/

Asian Development Bank. (2021). *Zu Peshawar bus rapid transit system transforming lives.* https://www.adb.org/news/videos/zu-peshawar-bus-rapid-transit-system-transforming-lives

Belgiawan, P. F., Schmöcker, J.-D., & Fujii, S. (2013). Effects of peer influence, satisfaction and regret on car purchase desire. *Procedia Environmental Sciences, 17*, 485–493. https://doi.org/10.1016/j.proenv.2013.02.063

Bendix, A. (2019). Scientists say these 11 major cities could become unlivable within 80 years. *Business Insider Australia*. https://www.businessinsider.com.au/cities-that-could-become-unliva ble-by-2100-climate-change-2019-2?r=US&IR=T

Bocarejo, J. P., Velasquez, J. M., Díaz, C. A., & Tafur, L. E. (2012). Impact of bus rapid transit systems on road safety: Lessons from Bogotá Colombia. *Transportation Research Record, 2317*(1), 1–7. https://doi.org/10.3141/2317-01

Button, K., & Rothengatter, W. (1993). Global environmental degradation: The role of transport. In K. B. D. Banister (Ed.), *Transport, the environment and sustainable development*. Routledge.

Cao, J., Cao, X., Zhang, C., & Huang, X. (2016). The gaps in satisfaction with transit services among BRT, metro, and bus riders: Evidence from Guangzhou *Journal of Transport and Land Use, 9*(3), 97–109. https://doi.org/10.5198/jtlu.2015.592

Clewlow, R. R. L. (2012). *The climate impacts of high-speed rail and air transportation: A global comparative analysis*. (PhD), Massachusetts Institute of Technology, Cambridge, Massachusetts. Retrieved from http://web.mit.edu/hsr-group/documents/Clewlow_Thesis_2012.pdf

Climate Watch. (2020). *Global emissions by sectors, 1990–2018*. https://www.climatewatchdata.org

Cole, L. M. (1968). *Tomorrow's transportation: New systems for the urban future*. U.S. Government Printing Office.

Götschi, T., de Nazelle, A., Brand, C., Gerike, R., Alasya, B., Anaya, E., . . . on behalf of the, P. C. (2017). Towards a comprehensive conceptual framework of active travel behavior: A review and synthesis of published frameworks. *Current Environmental Health Reports, 4*(3), 286–295. https://doi.org/10.1007/s40572-017-0149-9

Grayson, A., Totzkay, D. S., Walling, B. M., Ingalls, J., Viken, G., Smith, S. W., & Silk, K. J. (2019). Formative research identifying message strategies for a campus bicycle safety campaign using self-determination theory and the social norms approach. *Accident Analysis & Prevention, 133*, 105295. https://doi.org/10.1016/j.aap.2019.105295

Haider, F., Rehman, Z. U., Khan, A. H., Ilyas, M., & Khan, I. (2021). Performance evaluation of BRT standard in decision support system for integrated transportation policy. *Sustainability, 13*(4). https://doi.org/10.3390/su13041957

HelgiLibrary. (2019). *Passenger cars per 1,000 people rose 1.55% to 15.4 vehicles in Pakistan in 2019*. https://www.helgilibrary.com/charts/passenger-cars-per-1000-people-rose-155-to-154-vehicles-in-pakistan-in-2019/

Hensher, D. A., Mulley, C., Ho, C., Smith, G., Wong, Y., & Nelson, J. D. (2020). *Understanding mobility as a service (MaaS): Past, present and future*. Elsevier.

Ho, C. Q., Hensher, D. A., Mulley, C., & Wong, Y. Z. (2018). Potential uptake and willingness-to-pay for Mobility as a Service (MaaS): A stated choice study. *Transportation Research Part a: Policy and Practice, 117*, 302–318. https://doi.org/10.1016/j.tra.2018.08.025

Hoffmann, C., Abraham, C., Skippon, S. M., & White, M. P. (2018). Cognitive construction of travel modes among high-mileage car users and non-car users—A repertory grid analysis. *Transportation Research Part a: Policy and Practice, 118*, 216–233. https://doi.org/10.1016/j.tra.2018.08.031

IEA. (2020). *Passenger car sales by size and powertrain, 2010–2020*. https://www.iea.org/data-and-statistics/charts/passenger-car-sales-by-size-and-powertrain-2010-2020

IPCC. (2006). *Guidelines for National Greenhouse Gas Inventories. The National Greenhouse Gas Inventories Programme, The Intergovernmental Panel on Climate Change*. Retrieved from Hayama, Kanagawa, Japan.

Li, T., Sipe, N., & Dodson, J. (2017). Social and spatial effects of transforming the private vehicle fleet in Brisbane, Australia. *Transportation Research Part d: Transport and Environment, 51*, 43–52. https://doi.org/10.1016/j.trd.2016.12.010

Loubser, J., Marnewick, A. L., & Joseph, N. (2020). Framework for the potential userbase of mobility as a service. *Research in Transportation Business & Management*, 100583. https://doi.org/10.1016/j.rtbm.2020.100583

Majid, H., Maliky, A., & Vyborny, K. (2018). *Infrastructure investments and public transport use: Evidence from Lahore, Pakistan.* https://www.theigc.org/project/urban-transportation-labour-markets-and-access-to-economic-opportunity-evidence-from-lahores-bus-rapid-transit-system/

Mansoor, A., Zahid, I., & Shahzad. (2016). Evaluation of social and environmental aspects of Lahore metro bus transit through public opinion. *Journal of Environmental Science and Management, 19*, 27–37.

Mohsin, M., Abbas, Q., Zhang, J., Ikram, M., & Iqbal, N. (2019). Integrated effect of energy consumption, economic development, and population growth on CO_2 based environmental degradation: A case of transport sector. *Environmental Science and Pollution Research, 26*(32), 32824–32835.

Mukhtar, I. (2021). *FEATURE-In Pakistan city, green scheme for polluting bus owners inches along.* https://www.reuters.com/article/pakistan-pollution-transportation-climat-idUSL8N2ON0RQ

Nadeem, M., Azam, M., Asim, M., Al-Rashid, M. A., Puan, O. C., & Campisi, T. (2021). Does Bus Rapid Transit System (BRTS) meet the citizens' mobility needs? Evaluating performance for the case of Multan, Pakistan. *Sustainability, 13*(13), 7314. https://www.mdpi.com/2071-1050/13/13/7314

Navigant Research. (2019). *Navigant research report shows global sales of plug-in electric vehicles grew more than 70% from 2017 to 2018.* Retrieved from https://www.businesswire.com/news/home/20190312005099/en/Navigant-Research-Report-Shows-Global-Sales-of-Plug-in-Electric-Vehicles-Grew-More-Than-70-from-2017-to-2018

Nguyen, M. H. (2021/2021). *Evaluating the service quality of the first bus rapid transit corridor in Hanoi City and policy implications.* Paper presented at the Proceedings of the International Conference on Innovations for Sustainable and Responsible Mining, Cham.

Nijland, H., & van Meerkerk, J. (2017). Mobility and environmental impacts of car sharing in the Netherlands. *Environmental Innovation and Societal Transitions, 23*, 84–91.

Pakistan Bureau of Statistics. (2017). *District wise census-2017 results.* https://www.pbs.gov.pk/content/district-wise-census-2017-results

Punjab Mass Transit Authority. (2020). *State of art mass transit for all.* https://pma.punjab.gov.pk/our_services

Reck, D. J., Hensher, D. A., & Ho, C. Q. (2020). MaaS bundle design. *Transportation Research Part a: Policy and Practice, 141*, 485–501. https://doi.org/10.1016/j.tra.2020.09.021

Saidi, S., & Hammami, S. (2017). Modeling the causal linkages between transport, economic growth and environmental degradation for 75 countries. *Transportation Research Part d: Transport and Environment, 53*, 415–427.

Saleem, M. A., Eagle, L., & Low, D. (2018). Climate change behaviors related to purchase and use of personal cars: Development and validation of eco-socially conscious consumer behavior scale. *Transportation Research Part d: Transport and Environment, 59*, 68–85.

Shafique, M., Azam, A., Rafiq, M., & Luo, X. (2021). Investigating the nexus among transport, economic growth and environmental degradation: Evidence from panel ARDL approach. *Transport Policy, 109*, 61–71.

Shah, S. A. R., Shahzad, M., Ahmad, N., Zamad, A., Hussan, S., Aslam, M. A., ... Waseem, M. (2020). Performance evaluation of bus rapid transit system: A comparative analysis of alternative approaches for energy efficient eco-friendly public transport system. *Energies, 13*(6), 1–15. https://doi.org/10.3390/en13061377

Shaikh, S., & Tunio, S. (2014). It's buses versus trees in Islamabad as 'green' priorities collide. *The Guardian.* https://www.theguardian.com/global-development/2014/jun/25/buses-versus-trees-green-islamabad-pakistan

Stern, D. I., Common, M. S., & Barbier, E. B. (1996). Economic growth and environmental degradation: The environmental Kuznets curve and sustainable development. *World Development, 24*(7), 1151–1160.

Suhrke, A. (1994). Environmental degradation and population flows. *Journal of International Affairs, 47*, 473–496.

The Nation. (2019). *Lahore metro—Unsustainable?* https://nation.com.pk/11-Mar-2019/lahore-metro-unsustainable

The News. (2017). *Rawalpindi-Islamabad metro bus offers fast, affordable and convenient ride for commuters.* https://cdia.asia/2017/04/20/rawalpindi-islamabad-metro-bus-offers-fast-affordable-and-convenient-ride-for-commuters/

Tian, X., Geng, Y., Zhong, S., Wilson, J., Gao, C., Chen, W., . . . Hao, H. (2018). A bibliometric analysis on trends and characters of carbon emissions from transport sector. *Transportation Research Part D: Transport and Environment, 59*, 1–10. https://doi.org/10.1016/j.trd.2017.12.009

Tiwari, A. K., Khalfaoui, R., Saidi, S., & Shahbaz, M. (2020). Transportation and environmental degradation interplays in US: New insights based on wavelet analysis. *Environmental and Sustainability Indicators, 7*, 100051.

TransPeshawar. (2021). *BRT features.* https://zupeshawar.com/wp/brt-features/

Transport Department Government of the Punjab. (2021). *Metro bus services.* https://transport.punjab.gov.pk/metro_bus_services

Viergutz, K., & Schmidt, C. (2019). Demand responsive—Vs. conventional public transportation: A MATSim study about the rural town of Colditz Germany. *Procedia Computer Science, 151*, 69–76. https://doi.org/10.1016/j.procs.2019.04.013

Will, M.-E., Cornet, Y., & Munshi, T. (2020). Measuring road space consumption by transport modes: Toward a standard spatial efficiency assessment method and an application to the development scenarios of Rajkot City, India. *Journal of Transport and Land Use, 13*(1), 651–669. https://doi.org/10.5198/jtlu.2020.1526

World Resources Institute. (2021). *Climate Watch historical GHG emissions.* https://www.climatewatchdata.org/ghg-emissions. Retrieved August 27, 2021, from https://www.climatewatchdata.org/ghg-emissions

Worldometer. (2021). *Pakistan population.* https://www.worldometers.info/world-population/pakistan-population/

Zaman, M. Q. U. (2008). Valuing Environmental costs due to automobile pollution in Pakistan. *The Lahore Journal of Economics, 4*(1), 23–40.

Chapter 10
Sustainable Development Practices for SDGs: A Systematic Review of Food Supply Chains in Developing Economies

Jubin Jacob-John⊙, Clare D'Souza⊙, Timothy Marjoribanks⊙, and Stephen Singaraju⊙

Abstract The implementation and scope of sustainable supply chain operations vary globally, and, in developing economies, structural inefficiencies can significantly impact the sustainability orientation of Food Supply Chains (FSCs). The purpose of this paper is twofold: first, it examines the current scientific knowledge on the impact on sustainable development practices in FSCs in achieving United Nations' Sustainable Development Goals (SDGs). Secondly, it will identify the theoretical understanding of waste within FSCs and finally, provide recommendations for achieving SDGs. By focusing on two SDGs, this systematic review of 171 peer-reviewed articles addressing SDGs further analyzed and synthesized 40 academic studies that focused only on developing economies. The study identifies and describes sustainability-centric FSC practices which are trifurcated based on their economic, environmental, and social underpinnings as explicated in current FSC literature on developing economies. Further, using inhibitors and enablers to SDGs, the study developed a novel conceptual framework that identifies successful sustainable development practices that enable achievement of SDG 2 and SDG 12; thereby directing managerial interventions. Additionally, the enablers and impediments within FSCs in developing countries are further explicated which can enable future researchers to empirically evaluate the effect of these enablers and impediments.

J. Jacob-John (✉) · C. D'Souza
Department of Economics, Finance and Marketing, La Trobe Business School, La Trobe University, Melbourne, VIC, Australia
e-mail: j.jacobjohn@latrobe.edu.au

C. D'Souza
e-mail: c.dsouza@latrobe.edu.au

T. Marjoribanks
School of Business, Law, and Entrepreneurship, Swinburne University of Technology, Melbourne, VIC, Australia
e-mail: tmarjoribanks@swin.edu.au

S. Singaraju
Melbourne, VIC, Australia

© The Author(s), under exclusive license to Springer Nature Singapore Pte Ltd. 2022   213
N. Nguyen et al. (eds.), *Environmental Sustainability in Emerging Markets*,
Approaches to Global Sustainability, Markets, and Governance,
https://doi.org/10.1007/978-981-19-2408-8_10

Keywords Sustainable development goals · Food supply chains · SDG 12 · SDG 2 · Zero hunger · Responsible consumption and production

10.1 Introduction

Since the latter half of the twentieth century, the world witnessed an exponential increase in the human population; resulting in an increasing demand for food and, major shifts in dietary patterns of the global populace (Kearney, 2010). In addition to significant impacts on ecological sustainability, this increased demand for food products impacted global Food Supply Chains (FSCs) due to the increased demand for food by an ever-growing population. Feeding an increasing global population necessitated a complete revolution in agriculture in food production systems globally, albeit at the expense of sustainable food systems.

Academic literature has started paying attention to the environmental and social implications of alterations within the supply chain, thereby resulting in the evolution of Sustainable Supply Chain Management (SSCM) literature (Touboulic & Walker, 2015). This evolution in SSCM literature called for increased focus on sustainable operations within the supply chain (Cattaneo et al., 2021; Julia, 2014) and in the food context, a fundamental change in FSCs are necessitated for a sustainable future and this is addressed in the United Nations' Sustainable Development Goals (SDGs) (Govindan, 2018). Although FSCs have started implementing sustainability-centric practices, far too little attention has been paid to FSCs in developing economies and this study aims to address this gap in the literature by explicating SDG practices of FSC actors in developing economies.

The United Nations developed 17 SDGs and 169 targets that are to be achieved by 2030, thereby tracing a path for sustainability globally. As Caiado et al. (2018, p. 1284) suggest, the SDGs are a step toward "creating a more inclusive and equal society" and, achieving these goals is critical for human sustenance. Access to food and nutrition is critical to achieving sustainability and as an extension, global food systems are critical to achieving all 17 SDGs which are based on the three dimensions of sustainability—the economic, social, and environmental dimensions (UN, 2021). The social dimensions of SDGs account for People and Prosperity by aiming to end poverty and hunger and lead fulfilling lives and, this should be achieved while protecting the planet from degradation through sustainable consumption and production patterns (UN, 2015). This implies interlinkages between SDGs as explicated in Jacob-John et al. (2021) which exemplifies that SDG 2[1] aiming to eliminate hunger is linked to sustainable food production and consumption, addressed in SDG 12.[2] Altering global consumption and production systems to be more sustainable is necessary to achieve these SDGs and this requires a complete overhaul of food systems (UN, 2021).

---

[1] GOAL 2: Zero Hunger.

[2] GOAL 12: Responsible Consumption and Production.

Although the SDGs aim to be relevant globally, promoting prosperity in developing nations is pivotal to global sustainability. As an example, access to safe and quality food is a key issue in developing countries that mandate immediate attention, and therefore, the UN addressed this issue in the SDGs; thereby highlighting the importance of FSCs in achieving SDGs (UN, 2015, 2021). In developing nations, due to structural inefficiencies within the FSC, a significant portion of food is lost during various supply chain operations and the FAO (2021) estimates this loss at 400 billion US dollars a year. Such losses can be catastrophic to the disadvantaged in developing economies. However, in addition to the economic impact, due to its impact on accessibility to food and nutrition, Food Loss and Waste (FLW) translates to environmental and social impacts. From a social perspective, lost food in the supply chain translates to decreased access to food resulting in food insecurity. However, to recoup this loss and manage demand for food, there is an increased level of food production, resulting in significant environmental impacts including limiting landfill space, increasing air pollution through odor creation and, increasing leachate and GHG emissions (Lee et al., 2007; Read et al., 2020).

FSC operations can significantly influence achieving multiple SDGs as evidenced in current literature (Jacob-John et al., 2021). Govindan (2018) evidence this by evincing the impact of sustainable consumption and production patterns in achieving SDG 12. For example, improving production and consumption patterns using digital technologies that improve food quality can directly contribute to the accessibility of food which is a significant issue faced in developing economies (Govindan, 2018; Kaur, 2019). Asian et al. (2019) evidence this by modeling the effects of a Sharing-Economy (SE) based technological food system in India which improved food accessibility and food security; thereby contributing to SDGs. Lillford and Hermansson (2020) further extend this by illustrating the impact of innovative digital technologies in food sciences which contributes to an improvement in operations within food systems; thereby contributing to an improved diet. Literature evidence that improving FSCs enables food systems to achieve multiple SDGs including SDG 2 and SDG 1[3] which is crucial in developing economies (Fan et al., 2017; Nedelciu et al., 2020). However, supply chain inefficiencies and externalities can result in barriers to the achievement of SDGs in developing countries (Karki et al., 2021; Kumar et al., 2020; Magalhães et al., 2020; Raut & Gardas, 2018). For example, in developing economies, resource limitations leading to inefficient storage and handling processes can result in becoming a barrier to achieving SDG 12.3[4] which aims to halve global food waste by 2030 (Hu et al., 2019; Raut & Gardas, 2018). This is more pronounced in low-income developing countries where wastage is high in the production phase; thereby necessitating a further focus on sustainability in the FSC (Raut & Gardas, 2018).

---

[3] GOAL 1: No Poverty.

[4] SDG target 12.3—By 2030, halve per capita global food waste at the retail and consumer levels and reduce food losses along production and supply chains, including post-harvest losses.

However, far too little attention has been paid to how FSCs respond to sustainability challenges and the practices adopted to achieve SDGs and this chapter addresses this gap in the literature by focusing on sustainable FSC practices in developing economies.

Effective FSCs can contribute to improved access to healthy food and nutrition, especially in developing regions (Asian et al., 2019; Kaur, 2019) and as an extension, FSC stakeholders can significantly influence the achievement of multiple SDGs due to their impact on food quality and availability. In fact, sustainable operations within a supply chain can influence waste mitigation as evidenced in Rivera et al.'s (2019) study on food packaging's impact on shelf life and food waste. Multiple studies evidenced the impact of the supply chain in achieving SDGs including SDG 12.3 (addressing food waste) and other SDGs including SDG 12 and SDG 2 (Blesh et al., 2019; Rockström & Sukhdev, 2016; UN, 2020). These studies evidence that FSC practices can contribute to the achievement of SDGs and since the need to achieve SDGs is vital, these practices play a pivotal role in developing economies.

However, research to date has tended to focus on developed high-income countries and strategies implemented in these settings (Jacob-John et al., 2021; Michel-Villarreal et al., 2020) and, there has been little discussion on strategies implemented by FSC stakeholders in developing economies. Due to their impact on achieving SDGs, it is important to understand these strategies and practices as evidenced in the current literature; albeit, by focusing on the developing world. Against this backdrop, this study aims to address this gap in the literature and present a review of practices implemented by FSC actors in developing economies as evidenced in the literature that could contribute to the achievement of SDGs.

10.2 Methods

Paré et al. (2015) identify nine types of literature reviews in current literature including Narrative, Descriptive, Scoping/mapping, Meta-analysis, Qualitative systematic, Umbrella, Theoretical, Realist, and Critical reviews. The qualitative systematic review, as Paré et al. (2015) employs narrative and more subjective (in contrast to statistical) methods to encapsulate the findings of the identified literature. Based on this, we conducted a multi-step qualitative systematic review as illustrated in Fig. 10.1 by replicating the research process employed by other studies in FSC and SDG literature (Thomé et al., 2021; Yetkin Özbük & Coşkun, 2020).

After identifying the research question, the second stage involved the design of inclusion and exclusion criteria as illustrated in Fig. 10.1. Following the inclusion criteria, only peer-reviewed academic journal articles studying food systems were retrieved for analysis, and articles published in languages other than English,

10 Sustainable Development Practices for SDGs ...

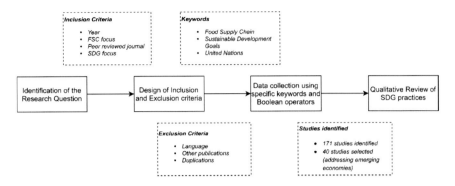

Fig. 10.1 Literature review process

nonacademic, non-peer-reviewed journal articles, and other texts (book chapters and conference proceedings) were excluded from the study.

The data collection stage involved retrieving published studies and to focus on studies addressing SDGs in sustainability literature, specific keywords were selected in line with the inclusion and exclusion criteria for a multi-step systematic review (Paré et al., 2015). The keywords that encapsulated the study included "Sustainable Development Goals", "United Nations", and "Food Supply Chain" and by limiting to these three keywords, articles published between 2015 and 2020 (inclusive) were retrieved using the inclusion and exclusion criteria and this time period is appropriate as the SDGs were introduced in 2015. The articles were sourced using four trusted and popular databases in marketing and management literature (Elsevier, ProQuest, Emerald, and WSI), and 171 peer-reviewed journal articles were retrieved.

After identifying the geographic scope of the articles, the articles were classified based on this scope into developed and developing economies based on their industrialization and per capita income levels (Table 10.1), and 40 articles addressing SDGs in the developing world were analyzed in further detail and using Microsoft Excel, a classification framework was synthesized by recording the authors, publication details, region of focus, SDGs addressed, key enablers and impediments, and practices for sustainable development. Through a comprehensive review of effective sustainable practices as explicated in current literature, this chapter will elucidate these sustainable practices employed in FSCs in the developing world as addressed in these 40 articles (Table 10.2).

Table 10.1 Number of studies based on geographic scope

Regional focus of study	Number of studies
Colombia and Mexico	1
Ethiopia	1
GCC	1
Indonesia and India	1
Mexico	1
Peru	1
Poland	1
Rwanda	1
South Africa	1
South Asia	1
Tajikistan	1
Zambia	1
Qatar	1
African countries	3
Thailand	3
Developing countries	4
Brazil	5
India	6
China and territories	6
Grand Total	**40**

10.3   Synthesis of Results

Studies in developing countries identify multiple solutions currently implemented to achieve sustainability (Adeyeye & Idowu-Adebayo, 2019; Conceição et al., 2016; Kaur, 2019; Pohlmann et al., 2020). Using a comprehensive review of 40 academic journal articles addressing SDGs within the FSC in developing economies, multiple practices were identified that enabled the achievement of SDGs and using the triple bottom line approach, these practices were trifurcated based on their direct and indirect impacts on Economic, Environmental, and Social practices. Economic practices are practices that can directly have an impact on the financial bottom line of multiple stakeholders while impacting the environment or society positively. In a similar vein, environmental practices directly impact the environment while social practices contribute to social sustainability directly.

10 Sustainable Development Practices for SDGs …

Table 10.2 Key studies reviewed

Author	Year	Title	Purpose	Key product	Country
Clark and Hobbs (2015)	2015	Innovations in International Food Assistance Strategies and Therapeutic Food Supply Chains	Discusses how changes in institutional objectives for international food assistance has influenced the organization of supply chains for innovative therapeutic foods designed to address problems of malnutrition and undernutrition	Therapeutic food	African countries
Farooque et al. (2019)	2019	Barriers to circular food supply chains in China	Identify and systematically analyze the causal-effect relationships among barriers to circular food supply chains in China	NA	China
Franklin and Oehmke (2019)	2019	Building African Agribusiness through Trust and Accountability	Analyze the social institutions of trust, accountability, and corporate shared value in creating an enabling environment for private sector investment in African agricultural and food systems	Coffee	Rwanda
Kaur (2019)	2019	Modeling internet of things driven sustainable food security system	Model the sustainable food security system using various technologies driving internet of things (IoT)	NA	India
Kowalewska and Kołłajtis-Dołowy (2018)	2018	Food, nutrient, and energy waste among school students	Estimate households' food waste and wastage-related losses of energy and nutrients among middle school students as well as assess educational intervention regarding food waste prevention	Potatoes, bread, fruits and vegetable, and meat	Poland

(continued)

Table 10.2 (continued)

Author	Year	Title	Purpose	Key product	Country
Kumar et al. (2020)	2020	Exploring the relationship between ICT, SCM practices and organizational performance in agri-food supply chain	Investigate the role of information and communication technology (ICT) in agri-food supply chain and determines the impact of supply chain management (SCM) practices on firm performance	Food grains	India
Michel-Villarreal et al. (2020)	2020	Exploring producers' motivations and challenges within a farmers' market	Explore food producers' motivations and challenges while participating in short food supply chains (SFSCs)	Organic food	Mexico
Raut and Gardas (2018)	2018	Sustainable logistics barriers of fruits and vegetables	Address the causal factors of post-harvesting losses (PHLs) occurring in the transportation phase	Fruits and vegetables	India
Sjauw-Koen-Fa et al. (2018)	2018	Exploring the integration of business and CSR perspectives in smallholder souring	Assess the impact of smallholder supply chains on sustainable sourcing to answer the question how food and agribusiness multinationals can best include smallholders in their sourcing strategies and take social responsibility for large-scale sustainable and more equitable supply	Soybean and tomato	Indonesia and India
Yawar and Kauppi (2018)	2018	Understanding the adoption of socially responsible supplier development practices using institutional theory: Dairy supply chains in India	Explain the motivations behind the adoption of similar SD strategies to address sustainability (particularly social issues) occurring in local supply chains of a developing country	Dairy	India

(continued)

10 Sustainable Development Practices for SDGs …

Table 10.2 (continued)

Author	Year	Title	Purpose	Key product	Country
Adeyeye and Idowu-Adebayo (2019)	2019	Through a comprehensive review of effective sustainable practices, this chapter will elucidate SDG centric practices employed by FSC actors in the developing world.	Critical review of genetically modified (GM) foods and the use of GM and biofortified crops for food security in developing countries where foods are not adequately available and people are not food secured	GM biofortified crops	Developing countries
do Canto et al. (2020)	2020	Supply chain collaboration for sustainability: a qualitative investigation of food supply chains in Brazil	Investigates how chain members collaborate to ensure the sustainability of supply chains through the social capital perspective	Eco-innovative products	Brazil
Fan et al. (2020)	2020	Linking agriculture to nutrition: the evolution of policy	The purpose of this paper is to summarize the evolution of global and national policies linking agriculture to nutrition in 2010–2020, and provides insights on the recent policy trajectory in China to illustrate how individual countries are addressing agriculture and nutrition	NA	China
Magalhães et al. (2020)	2020	Food loss and waste in the Brazilian beef supply chain: an empirical analysis	Identify the causes of FLW, model their interrelationships, and determine their root causes for the Brazilian beef supply chain (SC)	Beef	Brazil
Bustos and Moors (2018)	2018	Reducing post-harvest food losses through innovative collaboration: Insights from the Colombian and Mexican avocado supply chains	Explore the structural inefficiencies that lead to post-harvest losses and analyses how innovative collaboration could lead to more sustainable food supply chains (FSCs) by reducing those inefficiencies	Avocado	Colombia and Mexico

(continued)

Table 10.2 (continued)

Author	Year	Title	Purpose	Key product	Country
Cheng et al. (2017)	2017	Effects of moisture content of food waste on residue separation, larval growth and larval survival in black soldier fly bioconversion	Determine the most suitable moisture content of food waste that can improve residue separation as well as evaluate the effects of the moisture content of food waste on larval growth and survival	Waste materials	Hong Kong
Conceição et al. (2016)	2016	Toward a food secure future: Ensuring food security for sustainable human development in Sub-Saharan Africa	This paper argues that agriculture is central to improving food security and reducing poverty in Africa	NA	African Countries
Ellis et al. (2020)	2020	Economic and nutritional implications of losses and contributing factors along the bean value chain	Estimate quantitative, qualitative, and nutritional losses at the production and marketing stages of the common bean value chain in Zambia	Beans	Zambia
Feil et al. (2020)	2020	Profiles of sustainable food consumption: Consumer behavior toward organic food in southern region of Brazil	Analyze the relation between the socioeconomic and demographic profiles of organic food consumers and their motivations, perceptions, and attitudes	Organic food	Brazil
Filimonau et al. (2020)	2020	Food waste management in Shanghai full-service restaurants: A senior managers' perspective	This paper advances knowledge by exploring the food waste management practices adopted in a sample of Shanghai full service restaurants	Restaurant food	China

(continued)

Table 10.2 (continued)

Author	Year	Title	Purpose	Key product	Country
Galford et al. (2020)	2020	Agricultural development addresses food loss and waste while reducing greenhouse gas emissions	Investigate FLW interventions across multiple value chains or countries, most likely due to challenges in collecting and synthesizing data and estimates, let alone estimating greenhouse gas emissions	Various	Developing countries
Larrea-Gallegos and Vazquez-Rowe (2020)	2020	Optimization of the environmental performance of food diets in Peru combining linear programming and life cycle methods	Propose a methodology in which Life Cycle Assessment results linked to dietary patterns in Peru were combined with nutritional and economic data to optimize diets	Various	Peru
Gillespie et al. (2019)	2019	Nutrition and the governance of agri-food systems in South Asia: A systematic review	Explore how is agriculture and the wider agri-food system positioned within the constellation of factors and processes that determine nutrition outcomes in different contexts and countries and what is known about the role of enabling environments and the governance of agri-food systems in driving nutrition outcomes	NA	South Asia
Hu et al. (2018)	2018	Evaluating agricultural grey water footprint with modeled nitrogen emission data	Evaluate the GWF of food production with detailed food types and production process	Crops, livestock, aquaculture	China

(continued)

Table 10.2 (continued)

Author	Year	Title	Purpose	Key product	Country
Kawabata et al. (2020)	2020	Food security and nutrition challenges in Tajikistan: Opportunities for a systems approach	Present a food systems analysis of Tajikistan, applying the conceptual framework that has been developed by the HLPE	Various	Tajikistan
Liu et al. (2020)	2020	Food waste in Bangkok: Current situation, trends, and key challenges	Evaluate options for preventing and reducing FW in Bangkok,	NA	Thailand
Namany et al. (2020)	2020	Sustainable food security decision-making: An agent-based modeling approach	Design a novel dynamic decision-making framework considering two major components within the food production system, namely domestic production and international imports	Tomato	Qatar
Pohlmann et al. (2020)	2020	The role of the focal company in sustainable development goals: A Brazilian food poultry supply chain case study	Discuss the role of the focal company in sustainable development goals in a Brazilian food poultry supply chain	Poultry	Brazil
Thamagasorn and Pharino (2019)	2019	An analysis of food waste from a flight catering business for sustainable food waste management: A case study of halal food production process	Identify the amount of food waste generated from Halal kitchen flight catering production process in order to identify food waste hotspots by conducting a food waste composition analysis	Halal food	Thailand
Thorlakson et al. (2018)	2018	Improving environmental practices in agricultural supply chains: The role of company-led standards	Examine how Woolworths Holding Ltd.'s (Woolworths) supply chain standard affects the uptake of environmental best management practices among their fruit, vegetable, and flower growers in South Africa	Fruit, vegetable, and flower	South Africa

(continued)

10 Sustainable Development Practices for SDGs …

Table 10.2 (continued)

Author	Year	Title	Purpose	Key product	Country
Tucho and Okoth (2020)	2020	Evaluation of neglected bio-wastes potential with food-energy sanitation nexus	Assess the quantity and characteristics of food wastes and human excreta generated from Jimma University with the food-energy sanitation nexus approach	University food and waste	Ethiopia
Wang et al. (2017)	2017	The weight of unfinished plate: A survey-based characterization of restaurant food waste in Chinese cities	Investigate the amount and patterns of restaurant food waste in China in 2015	Restaurant food	China
Abulibdeh and Zaidan (2020)	2020	Managing the water-energy-food nexus on an integrated geographical scale	Develop a holistic and comprehensive systemic framework to optimize WEF resources management and to capture the integration and interactions between these resources, in order to contribute to economic development at the national, regional, and international levels	NA	GCC
Asian et al. (2019)	2019	Sharing economy in organic food supply chains: A pathway to sustainable development	Investigate the role of the sharing economy (SE) in enabling organic smallholders to overcome their specific set of challenges by sharing resources and aggregating peer-to-peer activities using an SE-based cooperative platform	Organic food	India
Kruijssen et al. (2020)	2020	Loss and waste in fish value chains: A review of the evidence from low and middle-income countries	Review literature assessing fish waste and loss in low- and middle-income countries	Fish	Multiple developing countries

(continued)

Table 10.2 (continued)

Author	Year	Title	Purpose	Key product	Country
Matzembacher et al. (2020)	2020	An analysis of multi-stakeholder initiatives to reduce food loss and waste in an emerging country—Brazil	Investigate the roles adopted by the distinct stakeholders that are engaged in a voluntary initiative to reduce food loss and waste (FLW) in the context of an emerging country	NA	Brazil
Mir et al. (2020)	2020	Realizing digital identity in government: Prioritizing design and implementation objectives for Aadhaar in India	Evaluate design and execution choices made during the tenure of the project	NA	India
Tsolakis et al. (2020)	2020	Supply network design to address United Nations Sustainable Development Goals: A case study of blockchain implementation in Thai fish industry	Evaluate data asymmetry that exists in supply chains to achieve Sustainable Development Goals and present design principles for blockchain-centric food supply chains	Fish	Thailand
Suárez II (2018)	2018	Cabotage as an External Non-tariff Measure on the Competitiveness on SIDS's Agribusinesses: The Case of Puerto Rico	Explores the multidimensional effects of an external non-tariff measure (NTM) on maritime transportation between the United States (US) and Puerto Rico (PR) trades	Agribusiness logistics	Developing regions (PR)
Adenle et al. (2017)	2018	The era of sustainable agricultural development in Africa: Understanding the benefits and constraints	Evaluate if sustainable agriculture save Africa from poverty and food insecurity	Various food	African Countries

10.3.1 Descriptive Analysis

A comprehensive analysis of the 171 studies identified a significant gap in current literature in the context of developing countries. A majority of the studies (77) focused on developed economies, compared to the 40 studies from developing economies.

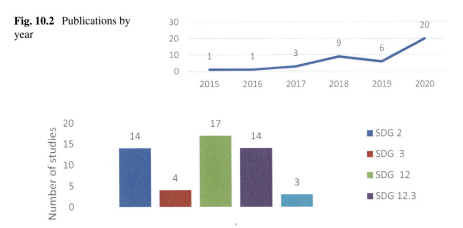

Fig. 10.2 Publications by year

Fig. 10.3 Most cited SDGs[5]

10.3.1.1 Activity Indicators

The review of existing supply chain literature focusing on SDGs within the developing world highlight the growing academic interest in SDGs, since its introduction in 2015. As illustrated in Fig. 10.2, the number of peer-reviewed academic journal articles published on SDGs in FSCs increased steadily since 2015 with a slight dip in 2019. This increase in academic interest suggests the existence of an increasing debate in supply chain literature on the FSC's role in achieving SDGs.

Analysis of papers citing specific SDGs suggests that SDG 12 is the most widely cited SDG (17 studies) in FSC research (see Fig. 10.3), followed by SDG 2 (14 studies); thereby suggesting the implications of FSCs in achieving SDG 12 and SDG 2. Specifically, SDG 12.3 is addressed in 14 studies highlighting the importance of FSC operations in minimizing FLW. Further analysis of studies focussing on SDG 2 and SDG 12 illustrates an increase in academic interest in both SDGs since 2016 (see Fig. 10.4).

Sustainable practices that directly impact the fiscal bottom line of organizations is a significant enabler to SDGs and this is evidenced in numerous studies in SDG and SCM literature (Clark & Hobbs, 2015; Fan et al., 2020; Michel-Villarreal et al., 2020). In the next section, the economic practices of FSC actors in developing economies that enable the achievement of SDGs are explicated in detail. Multiple SDGs addresses the ecological underpinning of sustainability, and the succeeding section focuses on practices that directly address the environmental variable of sustainability followed by social practices.

---

[5] Table limited to instances with more than 2 studies of SDGs cited.

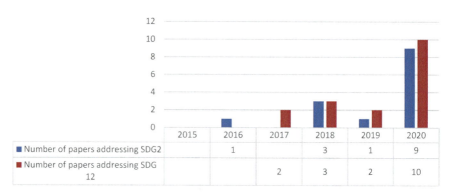

Fig. 10.4 SDG 2 and SDG 12 publications

10.3.2 Key Economic Practices Identified in the Literature

10.3.2.1 Sourcing

Sustainable sourcing strategies mandate procurement of products that satisfy specific sustainability requirements; thereby ensuring that the products procured are produced through responsible and sustainable methods. In the reviewed literature, there are multiple exemplifications of sustainable procurement strategies including regional procurement (Clark & Hobbs, 2015), Service Level Agreements (SLAs) (Bustos & Moors, 2018), certifications, and supplier compliance (Thorlakson et al., 2018), and sustainability incentives (Fan et al., 2020; Thorlakson et al., 2018) and such sourcing strategies can coerce suppliers to be sustainable.

Farmer and smallholder incentivization is a critical element in emerging economies as evidenced in the Indian and Indonesian context (Sjauw-Koen-Fa et al., 2018). This is significant due to the preponderance of smallholders in the agricultural sector in developing economies where farms in rural areas in developing countries are mostly owned and operated by smallholders (Rapsomanikis, 2015). Smallholder sourcing models through sustainable practices including guaranteed prices for smallholders, buying commitment, and standards of buyers can contribute to the overall sustainability of the supply chain.

10.3.2.2 Sustainable Supply Chain Management Practices

Practices aimed at specifically the supply chain actors using multi-stakeholder initiatives including sustainable production, logistics, collaboration for sustainability, food storage and warehousing, and other processes can contribute to various SDGs (Bustos & Moors, 2018; do Canto et al., 2020; Ellis et al., 2020; Kruijssen et al., 2020; Matzembacher et al., 2020).

10 Sustainable Development Practices for SDGs … 229

In a developing country context, Asian et al. (2019) illustrate the contribution of supply chain practices of group purchasing and operations management underpinned by a novel SE-based technological solution in achieving SDGs. In smallholder food production systems, a dominant form of food production in developing economies, individual smallholders might not possess the resources to procure specific machinery. Using an SE-based collaborative supply chain model, wherein supply chain partners share resources, issues associated with access to expensive farming tools can be mitigated; thereby contributing to multiple SDGs (Asian et al., 2019). Integrated approaches through improved supply chain collaboration and sustainable supply chain operations can mitigate several issues evidenced in FSCs in developing economies (Bustos & Moors, 2018; do Canto et al., 2020; Ellis et al., 2020). However, awareness is key and multi-stakeholder initiatives including awareness improvement campaigns and capacity building within the supply chain can result in improved efficiency and decrease losses along the supply chain while contributing to SDGs.

As FLW is a significant issue in developing economies, estimating FLW through economic and nutritional measurement within the supply chain can serve as a guideline for the development of initiatives to reduce FLW (Ellis et al., 2020). These FLW interventions for improving food quality through improved processing, testing, sorting and segregation, and other operations along the supply chain can contribute to the achievement of SDGs including target 12.3 in Africa, Asia, Latin America, and Caribbean nations (Galford et al., 2020). In addition to the operational elements of the FSC, in food retailing, food waste management practices including First In, First Out (FIFO) approaches, food rescue systems through distribution platforms, stakeholder engagement, and incentivization can contribute to minimizing food waste and achievement of SDG 12.3 (Filimonau et al., 2020; Liu et al., 2020).

10.3.2.3 Investments

Instilling sustainability within FSCs requires financial resources to enhance the nutrition sensitivity of agricultural systems. The absence of financial resources is a significant barrier to sustainability, and this is more profound in FSCs in developing economies and responsible investments from both private and public sectors can mitigate this (Franklin & Oehmke, 2019; Gillespie et al., 2019).

In developing economies, with more small and medium businesses involved in agricultural food systems, diversifying income streams is critical to smallholders, and therefore, investments for diversifying income are critical (Michel-Villarreal et al., 2020). Additionally from a public funding perspective, spending on R&D, development assistance for growers, tariff restructuring, and other such strategies are effective in developing countries (Abulibdeh & Zaidan, 2020; Franklin & Oehmke, 2019). Such investments could contribute to improving the sustainability of production systems and improve food security; thereby contributing to multiple SDGs.

In addition to FSC partnerships through improved collaboration, effective public–private partnerships are critical to the achievement of SDGs (Clark & Hobbs, 2015). In a nutshell, investments from both public and the private sector, both key stakeholders in developing nations, can contribute to the achievement of SDGs.

10.3.2.4 Technology

From a supply chain context, improvement to the technological systems can contribute to the improvement of efficiency and SDGs. Kaur (2019) illustrates this in the context of sustainable food systems in the Indian context by evidencing the impact of disruptive technologies including blockchains, robotics, and analytics in reducing FLW and improving food quality. This is critical in the developing world context due to structural inefficiencies like the absence of refrigerated logistics and storage systems within the supply chain which results in food loss (Adeyeye & Idowu-Adebayo, 2019; Kumar et al., 2020; Raut & Gardas, 2018). Technology-enabled food products, as evidenced by Adeyeye and Idowu-Adebayo (2019) in the context of genetically modified and biofortified crops can contribute to improved food security in developing countries.

10.3.3 Key Environmental Practices Identified in the Literature

10.3.3.1 Policy Reformulation

Research demonstrates that policies can drive sustainability (Ji et al., 2014; Zhu & Sarkis, 2006) and as an extension, the SDGs. The design and implementation of sustainable, resilient, and green policies can benefit the environment and assist the achievement of ecological SDGs (Tucho & Okoth, 2020). However, these policies are not limited to governmental policies as evidenced by Thorlakson et al.'s (2018) analysis of company-led standards in the South African FSC context. Through a detailed analysis of farm audits and crossmatching analysis of quantitative data, the study evidences the impact of private governance mechanisms in achieving environmental sustainability in a developing country. Additionally, Environmental Management Systems including ISO standards and other ecological third-party certifications (e.g.—Forest Stewardship Council [FSC] and the Roundtable for Sustainable Palm Oil [RSPO], ISO 14001, Rainforest Alliance, or organic standards) can improve the sustainability orientation of the supply chain (Matzembacher et al., 2020; Pohlmann et al., 2020; Thorlakson et al., 2018). Procurement strategies that necessitate supply chain partners to adhere to such standards can pressurize supply chain actors in developing economies to be sustainable by adhering to these standards.

10.3.3.2 Sustainable Agriculture

From a food production perspective, sustainable production practices including organic and sustainable agricultural practices that respect natural cycles of agriculture are pivotal in achieving SDGs (Adenle et al., 2017; Asian et al., 2019; Feil et al., 2020; Namany et al., 2020). By evidencing the case of Sub-Saharan Africa, Adenle et al. (2017) illustrate the importance of sustainable agricultural methods through minimal soil disturbance, soil coverage, and crop rotation in achieving SDGs. Feil et al. (2020) illustrate this in organic food production in the Brazilian context by citing two sides of organic food consumption: the "free" side and the "better" side. The free side illustrates that organic agriculture is free of, among others, transgenic agrochemicals; and the better side is healthier and tastier food products. This evidences that in addition to societal benefits of consuming healthier superior quality products, sustainable agricultural systems free of transgenic inputs can be beneficial to the environment and as an extension, achievement of ecological SDGs.

10.3.3.3 Green Supply Chain Management

Sustainable operations of the FSC can contribute to the achievement of ecological and societal sustainability and therefore, is pivotal in the developing world context. Through effective design for the environment improving collaboration with the supply chain, and minimising and transforming waste generated through the supply chain, supply chains can reduce pollution and achieve the SDGs (Farooque et al., 2019).

From an FLW management context, GSCM practices through the "3Rs" (i.e. Reduce, Reuse, Recycle) (Liu et al., 2020) and Prevention, Reduction, Recycling and Reuse of waste (Pohlmann et al., 2020) can contribute to sustainability. Effective operations are necessary to reduce food wastage at the source, instead of "recovery before landfill disposal" as "reduction of wastage" is environmentally sustainable than "recovery processes" similar to recycling (Thamagasorn & Pharino, 2019). For this, sustainable practices including regular waste audits can bolster the environmental performance of food supply chains as they contribute to drivers of FLW (Thamagasorn & Pharino, 2019).

10.3.3.4 Technology

Technology is a significant enabler in achieving environmental sustainability through innovative technology-aided agriculture and food processing (Cheng et al., 2017; Galford et al., 2020; Hu et al., 2018; Pohlmann et al., 2020). In the Chinese agricultural context, through an analysis of reactive nitrogen and Grey Water Footprint (GWF), Hu et al. (2018) show that due to water pollution they generate, regions in China are engaged in non-sustainable agricultural production. Such agricultural systems can adversely affect the achievement of SDGs in developing economies and technology-based solutions could contribute to the abatement of such issues (Hu et al., 2018). For example, Cheng et al. (2017) Illustrate the influence of innovative food waste management systems by exemplifying bioconversion innovations in achieving ecological sustainability.

10.3.4 Key Social Practices Identified in the Literature

10.3.4.1 Multi-Stakeholder Education

Awareness improvement mechanisms are critical in developing economies due to the lack of education and training existent in stakeholders within FSCs (Ellis et al., 2020; Kowalewska & Kołłajtis-Dołowy, 2018). This is relevant in developing economies as minimal awareness of food handling procedures and myopic perspectives on food consumption and production can result in increased food wastage and decreased food quality; thereby contributing to food insecurity. Educational practices should be multi-stakeholder initiatives as limitations in awareness among multiple stakeholders can adversely impact SDGs; thereby requiring awareness campaigns among multiple stakeholders.

From an operational perspective, Matzembacher et al. (2020) suggest that producers should be educated to refrain from discarding food products that fail to meet acceptable appearance standards. However, as a result of consumer preferences for "good-looking" food, these standards are mandated by the retailers. This requires systemic initiatives in changing the consumer mindset of "acceptable appearances" through education; thereby channelizing sustainability pressures in the supply chain.

Within the supply chain context, initiatives aimed at supply chain members in training and capacity building, educational interventions, and training of value chain members are critical to sustainable development (Ellis et al., 2020). An in-depth study on the foodservice sector of China identifies food consumption habits as a key contributor to food waste and thereby, posing a barrier to SDG 12.3 (Filimonau et al., 2020). As a solution, nationwide consumer awareness campaigns to raise public awareness were proposed in the Chinese context, evidencing the role of consumers in food waste minimization. Education about SDGs and Public Participation is also identified by Pohlmann et al. (2020) as a key contributor to sustainability and this must not be limited to the generic public, but such initiatives must be developed for purchasing employees and suppliers (Galford et al., 2020; Pohlmann et al., 2020).

10.3.4.2 Food Security Initiatives

Access to food is a significant contributor to multiple SDGs; especially SDG 2 (zero hunger) and SDG 3 (good health and wellbeing) (UN, 2021). In this context, food security initiatives are critical to the achievement of SDGs. By focusing on China, Fan et al. (2020) evidence that though developing economies have started linking agriculture and nutrition through effective policies, the progress is uneven, localized, and in early stages. Improving food security through multi-stakeholder initiatives including food fortification and the provision of micronutrient fortified products to children and pregnant women were identified as practices that can contribute to multiple SDGs as these improve food security.

Additionally, due to a preponderance of smallholder entities in the agriculture sector, developing economies must implement farmer-centric incentives, responsible agriculture, micro-credit systems, and other initiatives which could potentially contribute to improving smallholder sustenance (Adenle et al., 2017; Fan et al., 2020). In addition to the initiatives aimed at food production, food security through improved waste minimization is a critical aspect in developing economies due to structural inefficiencies that contribute to FLW in emerging economies.

10.3.4.3 Policy Reformulation

Strategies aimed at policy reformulation within organizations and supply chains, and other legislations can drive the achievement of multiple SDGs (Filimonau et al., 2020; Raut & Gardas, 2018; Wang et al., 2017). An investigation on food waste patterns in Chinese restaurants proposes the impact of government interventions and social campaigns such as the "Clean Your Plate" campaign in mitigating food waste, thereby contributing to SDG 12.3. Adhering to other social standards like the 18001 OHSAS (replaced by ISO 45001) and company-led standards can contribute to achieving social SDGs in developing economies (Raut & Gardas, 2018; Thorlakson et al., 2018).

10.3.4.4 Responsible Supply Chain Management

Responsible Supply Chain Management (RSCM) practices that improve productivity and agricultural operations from a societal perspective are pivotal to achieving social sustainability—particularly, establishing social responsibility within supply chains is critical in developing economies due to the impact of smallholders in the FSC (Thorlakson et al., 2018). RSCM, through the inclusion of smallholders in a socially responsible manner, can contribute to the sustainability orientation of Indonesian and Indian food supply chains (Sjauw-Koen-Fa et al., 2018). Inclusive stakeholder engagement, sustainable sourcing models, and equitable smallholder inclusion are effective sustainability practices evidenced in developing economies (Franklin & Oehmke, 2019; Sjauw-Koen-Fa et al., 2018). This is further explicated in the Indian context through farmer cooperatives, responsible business models, and technology-enhanced supply chain practices which result in improved sustainability orientation and food security in developing economies (Asian et al., 2019; Kaur, 2019).

Innovative supply chain practices as evidenced by Kaur (2019) in Indian FSCs using Public Distribution System (PDS) can contribute to food security, which is critical to SDG 2 and alternative approaches to supply chain management using farmers' markets (FMs), community-supported agriculture (CSA), box schemes, cooperatives, farm shops, and other initiatives to ensure food availability can enable the achievement of social SDGs in developing nations (Kawabata et al., 2020; Michel-Villarreal et al., 2020).

10.3.5 Enablers

The achievement of SDGs is dependent on economic and non-economic enablers as evidenced in current literature and this section delves into enablers as identified in the literature on developing economies. One of the key enablers for SDGs is access to financial resources and, investments from both the public and private sector can be a significant driver to the achievement of multiple SDGs (Franklin & Oehmke, 2019).

Sustainable agricultural practices can drive the achievement of SDGs due to its potential to address the challenges faced by conventional agricultural practices in developing countries as evidenced in the Sub-Saharan African region (Adenle et al., 2017). This includes Good Agriculture Practices (GAP) and other sustainable modes of farming including organic agricultural systems that are perceived to be more environmentally sustainable than conventional farming. Therefore, drivers of sustainable agricultural systems can enable SDGs.

From a supply chain context, partnerships, including collaborative supply chain partnerships could ensure the sustainability of supply chains (do Canto et al., 2020). As evidenced in the African agricultural and food systems, social institutions of trust are critical in this context (Franklin & Oehmke, 2019) and this is a significant precursor to SSCM. By redesigning supply chains through increased commitment to agriculture and production-centric sustainability issues, multiple SDGs could be achieved (Thorlakson et al., 2018; Tsolakis et al., 2020). As evidenced in the literature on the Indian context, technology-enabled food systems can contribute to the sustainability orientation of these production systems; therefore the existence of technology-enabled processes and knowledge can contribute to SDGs (Kaur, 2019; Kumar et al., 2020). Furthermore, multi-stakeholder initiatives can drive sustainable operations and this is enabled by effective policies and implementation of global and national policies (Fan et al., 2020; Liu et al., 2020); however, this is dependant on the level of awareness existent within stakeholders.

10.3.6 Impediments—Structural Inefficiencies

An analysis of Colombian and Mexican food supply chains evidence structural inefficiencies in supply chains in developing economies (Bustos & Moors, 2018), and this is typical in developing economies (Galford et al., 2020; Magalhães et al., 2020). As a result of managerial flaws, operational inefficiencies, relationships, and ineffective

10 Sustainable Development Practices for SDGs … 235

incentive management at both organizational and individual levels, these inefficiencies can contribute to compromising sustainability within a supply chain (Bustos & Moors, 2018).

Infrastructural challenges in the supply chain, a result of a lack of investment is the underlying reason for these issues in developing economies (Clark & Hobbs, 2015; Farooque et al., 2019; Kaur, 2019; Magalhães et al., 2020). This results in operational issues including ineffective storage facilities and logistics, forecasting systems, and post handling issues as evidenced in the Indian context which in turn, result in increased FLW and food insecurity (Kumar et al., 2020; Raut & Gardas, 2018). Such issues resulting in supply chain inefficiencies, as evidenced in the livestock sector in the Brazilian context can significantly contribute to food waste and food insecurity, thereby posing as a major barrier to SDGs (Magalhães et al., 2020).

Bustos and Moors (2018) classify these impediments by defining them as structural inefficiencies and classify them into corporate inefficiencies, cognitive and affective inefficiencies, and tangible inefficiencies. Corporate inefficiencies are weaknesses in the processes, corporate structures, and managerial mechanisms within the food supply chain while cognitive and affective inefficiencies are inefficiencies stemming from psycho-social presumptions of FSC participants. These cognitive and affective inefficiencies can relate to perceptions, expectations, beliefs, emotions, values, behaviors, and feelings of individuals involved in the FSC. Tangible inefficiencies, in contrast, are infrastructural or operational flaws in supply chain processes and the management of these impediments is critical to achieving SDGs. Such impediments can adversely affect the achievement of SDGs in food systems as evidenced in the model.

10.3.7 Recommendations

As demonstrated in the previous sections, the achievement of SDGs is critical in the developing world and FSCs have a pivotal role in achieving these SDGs (Adenle et al., 2017; Asian et al., 2019; Tucho & Okoth, 2020). The identified practices were trifurcated into economic, environmental, and social practices and effective implementation of these practices could contribute to the achievement of multiple SDGs. Economic practices including sustainable sourcing and operations, sustainable investments, and green tech are essential in this context. In a similar vein, environmental practices including policy formulation, GSCM, and sustainable agricultural practices can contribute to environmental sustainability while social practices including education, policy reformulation, and responsibility centric SCM can influence the overall responsibility orientation of the FSC. The chapter illustrates studies that evidence the implications of these practices in achieving multiple SDGs and therefore, propose that stakeholders including FSC managers and regulators enable the implementation of these practices in FSCs.

The achievement of these SDGs is dependent on the existence of enablers including financial resources, stakeholder commitment, access to technology, and

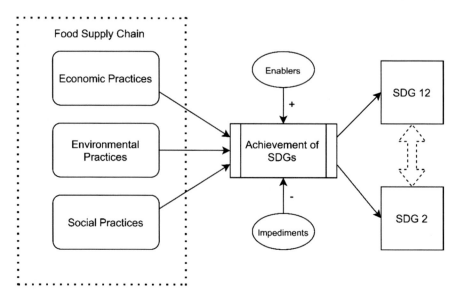

Fig. 10.5 Conceptual framework of FSC practices for SDGs

others. However, structural inefficiencies resulting in supply chain impediments can pose a significant barrier to the achievement of SDGs. Therefore, FSC managers must develop and implement strategies that could effectively mitigate these impediments to SDGs in the FSC context. The model illustrated in Fig. 10.5 encapsulates the key findings of this research and based on the literature review, illustrates the impact on SDG 2 and SDG 12.

10.3.8 Limitations and Future Research

The chapter was limited in several ways. First, the literature review is limited to papers addressing SDGs as addressed in FSC literature. Secondly, as a literature review, the study is limited to secondary data from literature and thereby, is unable to evaluate the influence of these practices in achieving SDGs in the FSC.

It is evident that literature tends to be focused on the developed world thereby requiring further research on FSCs in the developing world. In addition to mathematical modeling studies, empirical studies that address sustainability challenges along multiple tiers of the supply chain and best-practice cases should be explored in the developing world; thereby contributing to knowledge on issues existent in these supply chains.

Although some studies address SDGs besides SDG 2 and SDG 12 (Gillespie et al., 2019; Pohlmann et al., 2020; Tsolakis et al., 2020; Tucho & Okoth, 2020), there is a very limited focus on other SDGs. Future studies must address this gap in the literature and focus on FSC operations' impact on multiple SDGs.

10.4 Conclusion

Sustainable FSC strategies and practices can contribute to improved food security in developing economies and as an extension, achieve multiple SDGs. This chapter explicates the impact of sustainability practices as evidenced in FSC literature on developing economies and, effective implementation of these practices is essential for achieving SDGs. However, implementing these practices addressing economic, social, and environmental facets of sustainability is contingent on the existence of enablers and in contrast, structural inefficiencies existent in developing economies negate the effectiveness of these practices. FSC managers must address these inefficiencies in food systems, especially in developing economies, to ensure the achievement of multiple SDGs. Although the chapter conceptualizes a model for SDGs while illustrating sustainability-centric practices, there are significant gaps in current literature. Future studies should explore these gaps in literature thereby contributing to our knowledge on issues pertaining to FSC operations in developing economies. In addition to improving knowledge on SDGs, knowledge of such successful sustainability-centric strategies will bolster managerial interventions since such successful strategies can be replicated in other settings.

References

Abulibdeh, A., & Zaidan, E. (2020). Managing the water-energy-food nexus on an integrated geographical scale. *Environmental Development, 33*. https://doi.org/10.1016/j.envdev.2020.100498

Adenle, A. A., Azadi, H., & Manning, L. (2017). The era of sustainable agricultural development in Africa: Understanding the benefits and constraints. *Food Reviews International, 34*(5), 411–433. https://doi.org/10.1080/87559129.2017.1300913

Adeyeye, S. A. O., & Idowu-Adebayo, F. (2019). Genetically modified and biofortified crops and food security in developing countries. *Nutrition & Food Science, 49*(5), 978–986. https://doi.org/10.1108/nfs-12-2018-0335

Asian, S., Hafezalkotob, A., & John, J. J. (2019). Sharing economy in organic food supply chains: A pathway to sustainable development. *International Journal of Production Economics, 218*, 322–338. https://doi.org/10.1016/j.ijpe.2019.06.010

Blesh, J., Hoey, L., Jones, A. D., Friedmann, H., & Perfecto, I. (2019). Development pathways toward "zero hunger." *World Development, 118*, 1–14. https://doi.org/10.1016/j.worlddev.2019.02.004

Bustos, C., & Moors, E. H. M. (2018). Reducing post-harvest food losses through innovative collaboration: Insights from the Colombian and Mexican avocado supply chains. *Journal of Cleaner Production, 199*, 1020–1034. https://doi.org/10.1016/j.jclepro.2018.06.187

Caiado, R. G. G., Leal Filho, W., Quelhas, O. L. G., de Mattos Nascimento, D. L., & Ávila, L. V. (2018). A literature-based review on potentials and constraints in the implementation of the sustainable development goals. *Journal of Cleaner Production, 198*, 1276–1288.

Cattaneo, A., Federighi, G., & Vaz, S. (2021). The environmental impact of reducing food loss and waste: A critical assessment. *Food Policy, 98*, 101890. https://doi.org/10.1016/j.foodpol.2020.101890

Cheng, J. Y. K., Chiu, S. L. H., & Lo, I. M. C. (2017). Effects of moisture content of food waste on residue separation, larval growth and larval survival in black soldier fly bioconversion. *Waste Management, 67*, 315–323. https://doi.org/10.1016/j.wasman.2017.05.046

Clark, L. F., & Hobbs, J. E. (2015). Innovations in international food assistance strategies and therapeutic food supply chains. In *Food security in an uncertain world* (pp. 111–128). Emerald Group Publishing.

Conceição, P., Levine, S., Lipton, M., & Warren-Rodríguez, A. (2016). Toward a food secure future: Ensuring food security for sustainable human development in Sub-Saharan Africa. *Food Policy, 60*, 1–9. https://doi.org/10.1016/j.foodpol.2016.02.003

do Canto, N. R., Bossle, M. B., Vieira, L. M., & De Barcellos, M. D. (2020). Supply chain collaboration for sustainability: A qualitative investigation of food supply chains in Brazil. *Management of Environmental Quality: An International Journal, ahead-of-print* (ahead-of-print). https://doi.org/10.1108/meq-12-2019-0275

Ellis, E., Kwofie, E. M., & Ngadi, M. (2020). Economic and nutritional implications of losses and contributing factors along the bean value chain. *Journal of Stored Products Research, 87*, 101582. https://doi.org/10.1016/j.jspr.2020.101582

Fan, S., Cho, E. E., & Rue, C. (2017). Food security and nutrition in an urbanizing world. *China Agricultural Economic Review, 9*(2), 162–168. https://doi.org/10.1108/caer-02-2017-0034

Fan, S., Yosef, S., & Pandya-Lorch, R. (2020). Linking agriculture to nutrition: The evolution of policy. *China Agricultural Economic Review, 12*(4), 595–604. https://doi.org/10.1108/caer-03-2020-0040

FAO. (2021). *Sustainable development goals.* http://www.fao.org/sustainable-development-goals/indicators/1231/en/

Farooque, M., Zhang, A., & Liu, Y. (2019). Barriers to circular food supply chains in China. *Supply Chain Management: An International Journal, 24*(5), 677–696. https://doi.org/10.1108/scm-10-2018-0345

Feil, A. A., Cyrne, C. C. d. S., Sindelar, F. C. W., Barden, J. E., & Dalmoro, M. (2020). Profiles of sustainable food consumption: Consumer behavior toward organic food in southern region of Brazil. *Journal of Cleaner Production, 258*. https://doi.org/10.1016/j.jclepro.2020.120690

Filimonau, V., Zhang, H., & Wang, L.-E. (2020). Food waste management in Shanghai full-service restaurants: A senior managers' perspective. *Journal of Cleaner Production, 258*, 1–13. https://doi.org/10.1016/j.jclepro.2020.120975

Franklin, K., & Oehmke, J. (2019). Building African agribusiness through trust and accountability. *Journal of Agribusiness in Developing and Emerging Economies, 9*(1), 22–43. https://doi.org/10.1108/jadee-01-2018-0005

Galford, G. L., Peña, O., Sullivan, A. K., Nash, J., Gurwick, N., Pirolli, G., Richards, M., White, J., & Wollenberg, E. (2020). Agricultural development addresses food loss and waste while reducing greenhouse gas emissions. *Science of The Total Environment, 699*. https://doi.org/10.1016/j.scitotenv.2019.134318

Gillespie, S., van den Bold, M., & Hodge, J. (2019). Nutrition and the governance of agri-food systems in South Asia: A systematic review. *Food Policy, 82*, 13–27. https://doi.org/10.1016/j.foodpol.2018.10.013

Govindan, K. (2018). Sustainable consumption and production in the food supply chain: A conceptual framework. *International Journal of Production Economics, 195*, 419–431. https://doi.org/10.1016/j.ijpe.2017.03.003

Hu, G., Mu, X., Xu, M., & Miller, S. A. (2019). Potentials of GHG emission reductions from cold chain systems: Case studies of China and the United States. *Journal of Cleaner Production, 239*, 118053.

Hu, Y., Huang, Y., Tang, J., Gao, B., Yang, M., Meng, F., & Cui, S. (2018). Evaluating agricultural grey water footprint with modeled nitrogen emission data. *Resources, Conservation and Recycling, 138*, 64–73. https://doi.org/10.1016/j.resconrec.2018.04.020

Jacob-John, J., D'Souza, C., Marjoribanks, T., & Singaraju, S. (2021). Synergistic interactions of SDGs in food supply chains: A review of responsible consumption and production. *Sustainability, 13*(16), 8809.

Ji, G., Gunasekaran, A., & Yang, G. (2014). Constructing sustainable supply chain under double environmental medium regulations. *International Journal of Production Economics, 147*, 211–219.

Julia, W. (2014). The relationship between sustainable supply chain management, stakeholder pressure and corporate sustainability performance. *Journal of Business Ethics, 119*(3), 317–328. https://doi.org/10.1007/s10551-012-1603-0

Karki, S. T., Bennett, A. C., & Mishra, J. L. (2021). Reducing food waste and food insecurity in the UK: The architecture of surplus food distribution supply chain in addressing the sustainable development goals (Goal 2 and Goal 12.3) at a city level. *Industrial Marketing Management, 93*, 563–577. https://doi.org/10.1016/j.indmarman.2020.09.019

Kaur, H. (2019). Modelling internet of things driven sustainable food security system. *Benchmarking: An International Journal, 28*(5), 1740–1760. https://doi.org/10.1108/bij-12-2018-0431

Kawabata, M., Berardo, A., Mattei, P., & de Pee, S. (2020). Food security and nutrition challenges in Tajikistan: Opportunities for a systems approach. *Food Policy, 96*. https://doi.org/10.1016/j.foodpol.2020.101872

Kearney, J. (2010). Food consumption trends and drivers. *Philosophical Transactions of the Royal Society B: Biological Sciences, 365*(1554), 2793–2807.

Kowalewska, M. T., & Kołłajtis-Dołowy, A. (2018). Food, nutrient, and energy waste among school students. *British Food Journal, 120*(8), 1807–1831. https://doi.org/10.1108/bfj-11-2017-0611

Kruijssen, F., Tedesco, I., Ward, A., Pincus, L., Love, D., & Thorne-Lyman, A. L. (2020). Loss and waste in fish value chains: A review of the evidence from low and middle-income countries. *Global Food Security, 26*. https://doi.org/10.1016/j.gfs.2020.100434

Kumar, A., Singh, R. K., & Modgil, S. (2020). Exploring the relationship between ICT, SCM practices and organizational performance in agri-food supply chain. *Benchmarking: An International Journal, 27*(3), 1003–1041. https://doi.org/10.1108/bij-11-2019-0500

Larrea-Gallegos, G., & Vázquez-Rowe, I. (2020). Optimization of the environmental performance of food diets in Peru combining linear programming and life cycle methods. *Science of the Total Environment, 699*, 134231.

Lee, S.-H., Choi, K.-I., Osako, M., & Dong, J.-I. (2007). Evaluation of environmental burdens caused by changes of food waste management systems in Seoul, Korea. *Science of the Total Environment, 387*(1), 42–53. https://doi.org/10.1016/j.scitotenv.2007.06.037

Lillford, P., & Hermansson, A.-M. (2020). Global missions and the critical needs of food science and technology. *Trends in Food Science & Technology, 111*(5), 800–811. https://doi.org/10.1016/j.tifs.2020.04.009

Liu, C., Mao, C., Bunditsakulchai, P., Sasaki, S., & Hotta, Y. (2020). Food waste in Bangkok: Current situation, trends and key challenges. *Resources, Conservation and Recycling, 157*(104779), 1–11. https://doi.org/10.1016/j.resconrec.2020.104779

Magalhães, V. S. M., Ferreira, L. M. D. F., César, A. d. S., Bonfim, R. M., & Silva, C. (2020). Food loss and waste in the Brazilian beef supply chain: An empirical analysis. *The International Journal of Logistics Management, 32*(1), 214–236. https://doi.org/10.1108/ijlm-01-2020-0038

Matzembacher, D. E., Vieira, L. M., & de Barcellos, M. D. (2020). An analysis of multi-stakeholder initiatives to reduce food loss and waste in an emerging country—Brazil. *Industrial Marketing Management, 93*(1), 591–604. https://doi.org/10.1016/j.indmarman.2020.08.016

Michel-Villarreal, R., Vilalta, E. L., & Hingley, M. (2020). Exploring producers' motivations and challenges within a farmers' market. *British Food Journal, 122*(7), 2089–2103. https://doi.org/10.1108/bfj-09-2019-0731

Mir, U. B., Kar, A. K., Dwivedi, Y. K., Gupta, M. P., & Sharma, R. S. (2020). Realizing digital identity in government: Prioritizing design and implementation objectives for Aadhaar in India. *Government Information Quarterly, 37*(2), 101442.

Namany, S., Govindan, R., Alfagih, L., McKay, G., & Al-Ansari, T. (2020). Sustainable food security decision-making: An agent-based modelling approach. *Journal of Cleaner Production, 255*. https://doi.org/10.1016/j.jclepro.2020.120296

Nedelciu, C. E., Ragnarsdottir, K. V., Stjernquist, I., & Schellens, M. K. (2020). Opening access to the black box: The need for reporting on the global phosphorus supply chain. *Ambio, 49*(4), 881–891. https://doi.org/10.1007/s13280-019-01240-8

Paré, G., Trudel, M.-C., Jaana, M., & Kitsiou, S. (2015). Synthesizing information systems knowledge: A typology of literature reviews. *Information & Management, 52*(2), 183–199. https://doi.org/10.1016/j.im.2014.08.008

Pohlmann, C. R., Scavarda, A. J., Alves, M. B., & Korzenowski, A. L. (2020). The role of the focal company in sustainable development goals: A Brazilian food poultry supply chain case study. *Journal of Cleaner Production, 245*, 1–12. https://doi.org/10.1016/j.jclepro.2019.118798

Rapsomanikis, G. (2015). The economic lives of smallholder farmers: An analysis based on household data from nine countries. *Food and Agriculture Organization of the United Nations, Rome.* http://www.fao.org/3/i5251e/i5251e.pdf

Raut, R., & Gardas, B. B. (2018). Sustainable logistics barriers of fruits and vegetables. *Benchmarking: An International Journal, 25*(8), 2589–2610. https://doi.org/10.1108/bij-07-2017-0166

Read, Q. D., Brown, S., Cuellar, A. D., Finn, S. M., Gephart, J. A., Marston, L. T., Meyer, E., Weitz, K. A., & Muth, M. K. (2020). Assessing the environmental impacts of halving food loss and waste along the food supply chain. *Science of the Total Environment, 712*, 136255. https://doi.org/10.1016/j.scitotenv.2019.136255

Rivera, X. C. S., Leadley, C., Potter, L., & Azapagic, A. (2019). Aiding the design of innovative and sustainable food packaging: Integrating techno-environmental and circular economy criteria. *Energy Procedia, 161*, 190–197. https://doi.org/10.1016/j.egypro.2019.02.081

Rockström, J., & Sukhdev, P. (2016). *How food connects all the SDGs.* Stockholm Resilience Centre. https://www.stockholmresilience.org/research/research-news/2016-06-14-how-food-connects-all-the-sdgs.html

Sjauw-Koen-Fa, A. R., Blok, V., & Omta, O. S. W. F. (2018). Exploring the integration of business and CSR perspectives in smallholder souring. *Journal of Agribusiness in Developing and Emerging Economies, 8*(4), 656–677. https://doi.org/10.1108/jadee-06-2017-0064

Suárez II, W. (2018). Cabotage as an external non-tariff measure on the competitiveness on SIDS's agribusinesses: The case of Puerto Rico. *Centro Journal, 30*(3), 172–207.

Thamagasorn, M., & Pharino, C. (2019). An analysis of food waste from a flight catering business for sustainable food waste management: A case study of halal food production process. *Journal of Cleaner Production, 228*, 845–855. https://doi.org/10.1016/j.jclepro.2019.04.312

Thomé, K. M., Cappellesso, G., Ramos, E. L. A., & Duarte, S. C. d. L. (2021). Food supply chains and short food supply chains: Coexistence conceptual framework. *Journal of Cleaner Production, 278*, 1–14. https://doi.org/10.1016/j.jclepro.2020.123207

Thorlakson, T., Hainmueller, J., & Lambin, E. F. (2018). Improving environmental practices in agricultural supply chains: The role of company-led standards. *Global Environmental Change, 48*, 32–42. https://doi.org/10.1016/j.gloenvcha.2017.10.006

Touboulic, A., & Walker, H. (2015). Theories in sustainable supply chain management: A structured literature review. *International Journal of Physical Distribution & Logistics Management, 45*(1/2), 16–42.

Tsolakis, N., Niedenzu, D., Simonetto, M., Dora, M., & Kumar, M. (2020). Supply network design to address United Nations Sustainable Development Goals: A case study of blockchain implementation in Thai fish industry. *Journal of Business Research.* https://doi.org/10.1016/j.jbusres.2020.08.003

Tucho, G. T., & Okoth, T. (2020). Evaluation of neglected bio-wastes potential with food-energy-sanitation nexus. *Journal of Cleaner Production, 242.* https://doi.org/10.1016/j.jclepro.2019.118547

UN. (2015). *Transforming our world: The 2030 agenda for sustainable development.*

UN. (2020). *Zero hunger: Why it matters.* https://www.un.org/sustainabledevelopment/wp-content/uploads/2016/08/2_Why-It-Matters-2020.pdf

UN. (2021). *Food systems summit x SDGs.* https://www.un.org/en/food-systems-summit/sdgs

Wang, L. E., Liu, G., Liu, X., Liu, Y., Gao, J., Zhou, B., Gao, S., & Cheng, S. (2017). The weight of unfinished plate: A survey based characterization of restaurant food waste in Chinese cities. *Waste Management, 66*, 3–12. https://doi.org/10.1016/j.wasman.2017.04.007

Yawar, S. A., & Kauppi, K. (2018). Understanding the adoption of socially responsible supplier development practices using institutional theory: Dairy supply chains in India. *Journal of Purchasing and Supply Management, 24*(2), 164–176.

Yetkin Özbük, R. M., & Coşkun, A. (2020). Factors affecting food waste at the downstream entities of the supply chain: A critical review. *Journal of Cleaner Production, 244*. https://doi.org/10.1016/j.jclepro.2019.118628

Zhu, Q., & Sarkis, J. (2006). An inter-sectoral comparison of green supply chain management in China: Drivers and practices. *Journal of Cleaner Production, 14*(5), 472–486. https://doi.org/10.1016/j.jclepro.2005.01.003

Chapter 11
Carbon Taxes Beyond Emissions' Reduction: Co-benefits and Behavioural Failures in Emerging Markets

Aitor Marcos[iD]**, Patrick Hartmann**[iD]**, Jose M. Barrutia**[iD]**, and Vanessa Apaolaza**[iD]

Abstract Carbon taxes are the preferred structural strategy by economists to reduce carbon emissions. However, the additional costs imposed on emitters and consumers make carbon taxes politically unpopular (particularly in emerging markets) due to the persistence of other unaddressed development challenges affecting institutions, businesses and individuals. Instead of communicating environmental benefits, we argue that developing countries garnering support for carbon taxes could benefit from conveying the idea that carbon taxes contribute to solving development challenges (finance mitigation investments, increase companies' competitiveness and reduce inequality). Nevertheless, carbon taxes can only deliver development co-benefits beyond emissions reduction if their design is optimal (according to the World Bank's FASTER principles) and if stakeholders behave rationally, as modelled. Such assumptions are improbable to hold because the proper functioning of carbon taxes is hindered by frictions between the FASTER principles and different behavioural failures (politically vested interests, self-interested actions and boundedly rational behaviours) attributed to policymakers, companies and consumers. Ultimately, policy implementation experiences could be far from the theoretically optimal carbon tax design because they will be disrupted by agents' behavioural failures. It is yet unclear whether carbon taxes can achieve emissions reduction and development co-benefits simultaneously. Instead of relying solely on carbon taxes, emerging markets could complement their policy mix with non-price instruments (e.g. green procurement and standards) to better navigate behavioural failures.

A. Marcos (✉) · P. Hartmann · J. M. Barrutia · V. Apaolaza
Faculty of Economics and Business Administration, University of the Basque Country
UPV/EHU, Avenida Lehendakari Agirre 83, Bilbao, Spain
e-mail: aitor.marcos@ehu.eus

P. Hartmann
e-mail: patrick.hartmann@ehu.eus

J. M. Barrutia
e-mail: josemaria.barrutia@ehu.eus

V. Apaolaza
e-mail: vanessa.apaolaza@ehu.eus

© The Author(s), under exclusive license to Springer Nature Singapore Pte Ltd. 2022
N. Nguyen et al. (eds.), *Environmental Sustainability in Emerging Markets*,
Approaches to Global Sustainability, Markets, and Governance,
https://doi.org/10.1007/978-981-19-2408-8_11

244 A. Marcos et al.

Keywords Carbon tax · Co-benefits · Bounded rationality · Sustainable
development · Political economy

11.1 Introduction

The most common interventions to encourage pro-environmental behaviour are
informational strategies aimed at influencing knowledge, awareness, norms and
the attitudes of individuals (Steg & de Groot, 2019). Informational strategies are
choice-preserving (i.e. individuals can opt-out without additional costs) and their
implementation features goal setting, commitment, prompting, feedback or other
forms of nudging (Abrahamse & Steg, 2013; Osbaldiston & Schott, 2012).

Despite the relative success of informational strategies (Steg & Vlek, 2009), their
contribution to the environment is difficult to sustain if they are not supported by
structural strategies, namely interventions that alter the costs and benefits of behaving
pro-environmentally. Behavioural researchers have long warned that, without structural strategies (i.e. interventions that change contextual factors such as product
availability and physical infrastructure), the scale of behavioural change needed to
tackle climate change effectively will not be achieved (Corraliza & Berenguer, 2000;
Shove, 2010). As long as polluting is free, its costly consequences will continue to
accumulate in what is known as the 'The biggest market failure the world has ever
seen' (Stern, 2006).

Among the policy instruments able to alter the costs and benefits of behaving pro-
environmentally, carbon taxes are preferred by economists because of their efficiency
(Aldy & Stavins, 2012; Goulder & Parry, 2008; Hook, 2019). Carbon taxes apply the
'polluter pays' principle, which refers to the accepted practice that those who pollute
should bear the costs of managing pollution. By putting a price on carbon emissions,
companies that produce carbon-intensive products will see their costs increased,
which will induce a price increase for consumers unless companies find a low-carbon
alternative to keep producing their products. Besides stimulating innovation, carbon
taxes will also affect consumer behaviour because consumers will respond to price
increases by reducing their consumption of carbon-intensive products or shifting to
low-carbon consumption alternatives (Munnings et al., 2019). Moreover, instead of
drawing on government budgets, carbon taxes will generate revenue that can be used
for public spending on climate change mitigation or on ameliorating the regressive
impacts on consumers (Carbon Pricing Leadership Coalition, 2019).

Pricing pollution via carbon taxes requires policy design, implementation and
monitoring capabilities that may not be within reach for the administrations of many
emerging markets. Nevertheless, it seems highly unlikely that the 2 °C target set in
the Paris Agreement can be reached without pricing carbon in developing countries
(Jakob et al., 2016). The World Bank has focused almost exclusively on promoting the
adoption of carbon pricing (via carbon taxes and cap-and-trade systems) in emerging
markets through its Partnership for Market Readiness (PMR) programme since 2011
(Partnership for Market Readiness, 2017). In addition, the World Bank launched the

Partnership for Market Implementation (PMI) as the successor to the PMR in 2021, with a capitalisation target of USD 250 million in the next 10 years, emphasising carbon pricing instruments as the main structural strategy for emerging markets to mitigate climate change (World Bank, 2021b).

However, the additional costs imposed on emitters and consumers may make carbon taxes politically unpopular (Carattini et al., 2018), particularly in developing countries where the priorities are different (De Gouvello et al., 2020). Compared to rich countries, income inequality is higher in emerging markets, companies innovate less, and government spending on climate change adaptation is scarce due to small budgets. Appealing to emissions reduction has been a successful strategy for carbon tax acceptance in rich countries (Carattini et al., 2017); however, developing countries garnering support for carbon taxes may need to look beyond the environmental benefits of taxation and convey the idea that carbon taxes contribute to development by addressing inherent challenges in emerging markets. Since the tax burden adds to the household's already constrained purchasing power, managing tax aversion in emerging markets requires making the broader benefits of the policy particularly salient.

Consequently, proponents of carbon taxes defend that pricing carbon will generate co-benefits (i.e. positive outcomes alongside emissions reduction) that are especially valuable for emerging markets. Those co-benefits are not only purely environment-related (e.g. decreased soil contamination and acidification, conservation of water resources and health benefits due to better air quality) but also fiscal (e.g. increased government revenue, decreased distortionary taxes and reduced fiscal evasion) and technological (e.g. boosting low-carbon innovation) (Parry et al., 2015; World Bank, 2021a), which are more appealing to voters than emissions reduction alone and hence can reduce public opposition (Maestre-Andrés et al., 2019).

In theory, a well-designed carbon tax and rationally behaving agents could deliver co-benefits for emerging markets beyond emissions reduction. However, due to vested interests or countries' particularities, carbon taxes are often conceived far from the theoretically optimal design (Baranzini & Carattini, 2014). Thus, our first line of enquiry is not whether the characteristics of carbon taxes enable the achievement of relevant development goals (they do, in theory) but whether such co-benefits are still possible when carbon taxes interact with the unpredictable nature of emerging markets. Our second research question challenges the assumption that consumers, firms and governments will behave as modelled (i.e. rational consumers, profit-maximising firms and consistent policymaking). However, if they do not, will emerging markets still be able to reap the co-benefits of carbon taxes? If these concerns are not properly addressed, the case for carbon taxes in emerging markets will weaken, encouraging the consideration of alternative structural strategies to promote environmental sustainability.

The next section describes the theoretical framework used to systematically assess the extent to which carbon taxes might deviate from the ideal design and an agent-based view on the behavioural constraints that hamper the proper functioning of carbon taxes in practice. Drawing on carbon tax design principles and the behavioural dimensions outlined in the theoretical framework, we will examine the merits of carbon taxes to contribute to the development objectives relevant to governments (e.g. expand environmental sustainability-oriented budgets), companies (e.g. increase competitiveness and foster innovation) and individuals (e.g. reduce inequality). Thereafter, we will complete our analysis by focusing on how behavioural failures and practical limitations may hinder the potential co-benefits of carbon taxes in emerging markets. This integrative review contributes to policymakers by identifying incompatibilities between the principles for an optimal carbon pricing design and the practical behavioural challenges carbon taxes face in emerging markets. Besides, we provide future research directions for scholars by outlining the benefits of further investigations on the complementary role carbon taxes and non-price instruments play in the policy mix.

11.2 Theoretical Framework

11.2.1 Principles for Successful Carbon Pricing

Carbon tax design and implementation strategies are as diverse as the realities to which they have to be adapted. Considering such heterogeneity of scenarios, the World Bank and the OCDE identified a set of principles to help policymakers evaluate their different design options: Regardless of the specific circumstances of the jurisdiction, policymakers are encouraged to prioritise and safeguard the FASTER principles for Fairness, Alignment with existing policies, Stability, Transparency, Efficiency and Reliability (World Bank, 2015). The FASTER principles draw on economic literature and practical experience in implementing carbon taxes and cap-and-trade systems (Mooij et al., 2012; Parry et al., 2014) to secure an optimal design for carbon pricing policies.

Each FASTER principle for successful carbon pricing covers a relevant dimension of policy design (Partnership for Market Readiness, 2017): The Fairness principle highlights the importance of equitably distributing the costs and benefits of carbon taxes and avoiding disproportionate burdens on specific segments of the society. The Alignment of policies and objectives principle focuses on harmoniously integrating carbon taxes with the policy mix and ensuring proper interaction with a broader set of climate and non-climate policies. The stability and predictability principle underscores the need for a consistent, credible and strong price signal to influence behaviour in the long term. The transparency principle emphasises that carbon tax designs must be clear from a policymaking standpoint and understandable and regularly communicated to all stakeholders involved. The efficiency and cost-effectiveness principle embodies one of the virtues of carbon taxes: If emissions reductions are to be achieved at the lowest possible cost, affected entities need the flexibility to choose how and when to reduce emissions based on their assessments of costs and benefits. Finally, the reliability and environmental integrity principle reminds policymakers that carbon taxes result in measurable carbon emissions reductions.

Altogether, following the FASTER principles ensures flexibility for policymakers, certainty for companies and investors, and an equitable and understandable effort from consumers (World Bank, 2015). Our holistic approach to carbon taxes' potential in emerging markets will allow us to evaluate the compatibility of FASTER principles with the interferences caused by agents' different behavioural failures.

11.2.2 Dimensions of Behavioural Failure

Designing carbon taxes following the FASTER principles does not guarantee to achieve the modelled environmental and development objectives as predicted. This is because these are also subject to agents' behaviours, which are often boundedly rational and influenced by political and economic concerns. Indeed, the subfield of behavioural-environmental economics urges a review of the assumptions under which pricing instruments work because policy design is often based on a poor representation of individuals' behaviours (Kesternich et al., 2017). Moreover, if agents do not behave as modelled, policy instruments will hardly solve the carbon emissions market failure because the emergence of a new type of failure, a so-called behavioural failure (Shogren & Taylor, 2008), might undercut the rational underpinning of environmental policies.

As the concept was coined, scholars were explicitly asked to incorporate the idea of behavioural failure into the environmental policy's research agenda (Gowdy, 2008; Shogren & Taylor, 2008). Regarding the case of pricing instruments in general and carbon taxes in particular, Stoll and Mehling (2021) recently provided a comprehensive conceptual framework to analyse three dimensions of behavioural failure based on the different manifestations of human behaviour: *Homo Economicus* (i.e. the perfectly rational agent of the standard economic model), *Homo Politicus* (i.e. the political decision maker with specific preferences, perceptions and interests) and *Homo Irrationalis* (i.e. the boundedly rational agent with individual preferences and limitations).

Building on this taxonomy of views, Stoll and Mehling (2021) suggested that carbon pricing might be undermined in situations where, first, Homo Economicus' exclusive pursuit of economic self-interest leads to sub-optimal results in aggregate welfare; second, the institutional barriers or political constraints and interests alter Homo Politicus' rational behaviours, thereby causing sub-optimal results; and third, non-standard beliefs, preferences and decision-making processes in boundedly rational individuals (Homo Irrationalis) generate sub-optimal results. Regarding the last type of behavioural failure, the concept of bounded rationality refers to behaviours not complying with the standard model either because cognitive processes and available information constrain decisions or because individuals have other-regarding preferences (e.g. fairness and reciprocity) or non-standard beliefs (e.g. a particular self-identity) (Gsottbauer & Van Den Bergh, 2011; Stoll & Mehling, 2021).

In the next section, we will review the most salient friction points between the FASTER principles and different behavioural failures (i.e. economic, political and boundedly rational behaviours) of agents that could jeopardise the development of co-benefits promised by carbon taxes in emerging markets.

11.3 Broader Co-benefits and Risks of Carbon Taxes in Emerging Markets

11.3.1 Policymakers

11.3.1.1 Government-Level Co-benefits

The most devastating impacts of climate change are likely to be suffered by developing countries, many of which are rich in biodiversity and yet short of water and food. Developing countries are not only more vulnerable to climate change impacts but also less able to afford its consequences (Gupta, 2008) owing to chronic difficulties in generating revenue to increase public investments. The growth rate of emerging markets hardly translates to increased government revenue due to tax avoidance and the larger share of the informal economy in developing countries (Heine & Black, 2019).

Carbon taxes support governments' revenue collection directly via carbon tax payments and indirectly by taxing the informal economy and limiting tax evasion. The impact on governments' budgets is direct because costs are low and revenue-generating potential is high: In 2020, carbon pricing instruments generated USD 53 billion in revenue globally (World Bank, 2021b). Moreover, compared to other climate change mitigation instruments, such as cap-and-trade systems, the administrative costs of implementing carbon taxes are low because the revenue collection mechanism can be built on the existing fuel tax infrastructure (World Bank, 2021a).

Apart from their revenue-generating potential, carbon taxes are particularly useful in emerging markets because they impact the prices of energy and energy-related products. Experiences from India and China show that shifting the tax base from easily evaded taxes to a carbon tax can substantially increase revenue collection (Liu, 2013). Since oil and gasoline are monitored through a centralised infrastructure, evading carbon taxes is more difficult, settling a prevalent problem in emerging markets (Khlif et al., 2016). Similarly, emerging markets face revenue-generating problems when tax increases in the formal sector further shrink the tax base because some firms and workers shift to the informal sector to avoid paying them. Given that taxing carbon emissions implies taxing the economy as a whole, carbon taxes do not incentivise informality because energy use is ubiquitous in the informal economy too (World Bank, 2021a). Furthermore, the implementation of carbon taxes encourages the reduction of other distortionary taxes (e.g. labour taxes), thus increasing the efficiency of the fiscal system. This may decrease informality as taxes that solely affect the formal economy are reduced and carbon taxes, which are difficult to evade, are introduced.

The ability to reduce distortionary taxes to increase economic output while reducing carbon emissions is known as the 'Double dividend' of the carbon tax (Goulder, 1995). The double dividend hypothesis is contested in developed countries; however, emerging markets can likely increase efficiency by simply limiting tax evasion and reducing the informal economy, although this economic benefit still depends on rational behaviour assumptions (Klein & van den Bergh, 2020). Even if the double dividend hypothesis is proven to be false, there is consensus among experts that carbon taxes are a feasible instrument to generate enough revenue to spur development in emerging markets while limiting the distortionary impacts of taxation on the economy (World Bank, 2021a). As long as emissions reduction goals are met, the reliability and environmental integrity principle is compatible with designing carbon taxes that can reduce tax evasion and the informal economy, or even more ambitious fiscal modifications to improve the efficiency of the whole system.

11.3.1.2 Misalignment of Policy and Objectives

As soon as carbon taxes are effective in curbing carbon emissions, governments will suffer a reduction in their tax base because emissions (i.e. the element of taxation) will decrease. Meanwhile, companies and citizens will incur high costs for paying soaring taxes. Therefore, all stakeholders will have the perverse incentive to avoid that scenario and support ineffective carbon taxes that neither reduce the tax base nor significantly increase prices. Subsequently, the implementation of a carbon tax, yet ineffective, would reduce the pressure on the government to take more climate action. A series of behavioural failures might lead policymakers to implement ineffective carbon taxes and think that further ambition in the broader set of climate policy measures is unnecessary, thus not complying with the Alignment of policy and objectives principle.

From a political economy perspective, the most likely behavioural failure is to set very low-carbon tax rates to gain public acceptability (Haites, 2018; Jenkins, 2014). Carbon tax acceptability depends heavily on the tax rate because citizens tend to perceive carbon taxes as too high, regressive, ineffective and harmful for the wider economy (Carattini et al., 2018). Policymakers around the world have responded to these concerns by simply designing carbon taxes that maximise political acceptability and minimise economic disruption, leading to lower carbon tax rates than planned (Geroe, 2019). The prevalence of this political behavioural failure confirms that pressure on the government hampers the implementation of theoretically optimal carbon taxes (Jenkins, 2014).

Regarding the economic dimension of behavioural failure, governments can only rely temporarily on the revenues associated with carbon taxes to increase public spending (Edenhofer et al., 2021). Governments in emerging markets have small budgets devoted to climate change mitigation and are likely to rely on carbon tax revenues to meet investment needs (Jakob et al., 2016). This opposes the objective of reducing carbon emissions: If current climate pledges are met by the middle of the twenty-first century, governments will see their revenues shrink fast as emissions decrease (Edenhofer et al., 2021). In the long term, maximising the revenue derived from carbon taxes would imply designing taxes that can collect revenue but remain only marginally effective in order to protect the tax base.

Finally, boundedly rational policymakers and voters may consider that carbon tax implementation alone is enough to tackle climate change. A theoretically optimal carbon tax cannot significantly curve emissions if other measures do not support it; however, such additional policy actions might be considered unnecessary after enacting carbon taxes (Ball, 2018). This irrational reaction following policy implementation can be catalogued as 'single-action bias', a phenomenon identified by Weber (1997) referring to the perception that a problem is solved after a single mitigation action is taken, even when further actions would be more beneficial. The single-action bias results in overlooking complementary or superior strategies after an initial measure against climate change has been taken (Weber, 1997). Similarly, governments that successfully implement carbon taxes despite solid public opposition might be tempted to believe that they contributed enough from a policymaking perspective. This perception is likely to be reinforced by single-action biased voters who reduce pressure on the government after the carbon tax is implemented.

11.3.2   Companies

11.3.2.1   Company Level Co-benefits

While emerging markets offer some of the world's best growth opportunities for multinational companies, local businesses often struggle to compete and innovate along the same path. Carbon taxes generate input price increases, which domestic companies fear because taxes presumably imply a worsening of their already constrained competitiveness, leading to a phenomenon known as 'Carbon leakage'. Such a loss of competitiveness is attributed to an asymmetric environmental policy because the implementation of carbon taxes would increase companies' compliance costs and could end up shifting pollution-intensive production towards other markets with less stringent policies where polluting is cheaper (Dechezleprêtre & Sato, 2017). However, carbon leakage seems more likely in the case of multinational companies operating in emerging markets since local businesses would be unable to escape the carbon tax as they have fewer resources to relocate elsewhere. Moreover, exposure to carbon taxes might benefit domestic companies in the medium term because pricing their polluting activities promotes cost-cutting efficiency improvements, which can foster innovation and expand market shares, reducing or even completely offsetting regulatory costs (Dechezleprêtre & Sato, 2017).

Furthermore, a recent study has shown that carbon leakage risks in emerging markets are not as problematic as in the rich world, and they could even benefit developing countries (Qin et al., 2021): The carbon leakage from developed countries to the next 11 emerging markets (Bangladesh, Pakistan, Egypt, South Korea, Indonesia, Philippines, Vietnam, Turkey, Iran, Nigeria and Mexico) easily compensates the potential leakages from these countries to similar developing countries with less stringent environmental regulation (Qin et al., 2021). Nevertheless, carbon leakage risks still need to be monitored in emerging markets, especially in energy-intensive, trade-exposed industries (Peñasco et al., 2021). For instance, recent experience with the Chinese emissions trading system showed that a small carbon leakage in emerging markets occurs through an acceleration of outward foreign direct investment (OFDI) as firms try to relocate their most polluting activities to other countries.

Despite the competitiveness risks posed by carbon taxes, economists argue that carbon pricing is the most efficient way to reduce emissions and foster green innovation, and there is a growing consensus that these co-benefits outweigh carbon leakage risks (Carbon Pricing Leadership Coalition, 2019). First, no structural strategy besides carbon pricing can minimise the overall cost of pollution control for companies (Baranzini et al., 2017): Since polluters from different sectors have different emissions abatement opportunities and costs, it would be unfair and unfeasible to demand the same level of emissions reduction from all companies. Instead, the carbon tax sets a price per additional tonne of carbon emissions emitted, and companies decide whether they would invest in emissions abatement or simply pay the tax, depending on the profitability of each action. Second, the continuous incentive for the adoption and innovation of new low-carbon technologies promotes dynamic efficiency (Baranzini et al., 2017). Practical experience has provided strong evidence that carbon pricing measures, such as carbon taxes, boost productivity and technological innovation (Dechezleprêtre & Sato, 2017), a positive effect that has directly translated into significant increases in patenting (Venmans et al., 2020). Third, carbon taxes can help in obtaining a first-mover advantage when competing with other emerging markets. Real-world experience shows that when a country implements carbon pricing measures, its trade partners follow suit sooner or later, influenced by their trade interdependencies (Steinebach et al., 2020).

Overall, carbon taxes enable a cost-effective transition from a high-carbon economy to a low-carbon economy, providing companies with the flexibility to choose how and when to invest in low-carbon technologies (Carbon Pricing Leadership Coalition, 2019). This flexibility to reduce cost and the continuous incentive to innovate follows the efficiency and cost-effectiveness principle. Finally, although carbon leakage risks also exist in emerging markets, the impacts of carbon taxes seem less relevant than other factors that influence where companies will locate and invest.

11.3.2.2 Unstable and Unpredictable Carbon Tax Rates

Energy-intensive companies are likely to lobby against carbon taxes to delay their implementation or obtain fiscal exemptions, which in turn casts doubts on future carbon tax rate increases. However, if the price signal is not strong enough and if it is subjected to pressure from voters and industries, then companies can hardly make investment plans for long-lived capital assets (key for climate change mitigation) because the lack of policy clarity impedes a proper assessment of future costs and benefits (Carbon Pricing Leadership Coalition, 2019). Moreover, investments in highly polluting projects might speed up as companies anticipate that these activities will be unprofitable once carbon taxes are in place. Ultimately, resistance to carbon tax implementation jeopardises carbon taxes' stability and predictability principle, initiating a succession of behavioural failures that may hinder the low-carbon transition.

The first behavioural failure is political, as opposition to carbon taxes will eventually result in costlier or less flexible abatement measures for polluting firms (Baranzini et al., 2017). Nevertheless, energy-intensive industries have lobbied for delaying carbon taxes by warning policymakers and unions of outward investments and job losses (Mildenberger, 2020). In practice, experiences from South Africa (Rennkamp, 2019) and Mexico (Stevens, 2021) show that emerging markets are especially vulnerable to the vested interests of industry lobbies because they have successfully leveraged unequal power relations to obstruct the implementation of carbon pricing policies. Carbon taxes are often set back or reduced as a result. However, even when they are not, carbon-intensive and trade-exposed industries obtain exemptions that overcompensate for a deliberately exaggerated carbon leakage risk (Martin et al., 2014). Consequently, governments have difficulties credibly committing themselves to predictable carbon price trajectories because carbon tax rates are subject to the inconsistencies resulting from electoral competition and industry pressure (Edenhofer et al., 2021) adding to the unstable nature of policymaking in emerging markets.

Lobbying to reduce or bypass carbon taxes induces an even more prominent behavioural failure in the economic dimension: Industry leaders in emerging markets, whose companies' planning cycles are medium or long term, alert that uncertainty around future carbon tax rates can result in companies deferring mitigation investments (Carbon Pricing Leadership Coalition, 2019). Several years into the future, a predictable carbon tax price signal enables companies to weigh the costs and benefits of reducing emissions, thus facilitating investment decisions (Haites, 2018). In other words, rather than current carbon tax rates, expectations about future prices are important to steer low-carbon innovation opportunities (Jaffe et al., 2005). However, such investments are halted due to the price uncertainty caused by industry lobbies themselves. Therefore, despite the need to decarbonise the economy, delaying green investments from a profit-maximising standpoint makes sense if firms suspect that carbon pricing policies will not endure.

Moreover, from a bounded rationality perspective, energy-intensive industries may overestimate how much the future of the sector will share the same characteristics of today's business-as-usual, prompting short-sighted decisions (i.e. Projection-bias). Foreseeing future carbon tax increases, such companies may accelerate their resource extraction in fear of higher future taxation (van der Ploeg, 2016). This phenomenon, known as the 'Green Paradox', suggests that carbon taxes will not incentivise low-carbon innovation. Conversely, they would divert investments to highly polluting projects (e.g. oil extraction and exploration) before those activities are highly taxed

11 Carbon Taxes Beyond Emissions' Reduction … 253

and consequently become unprofitable (Sinn, 2015). Paradoxically, plans to implement carbon taxes could accelerate global warming because the untapped resources of emerging markets would be depleted faster by short-sighted, profit-maximising companies.

11.3.3 Consumers

11.3.3.1 Taxpayer Level Co-benefits

The most common perception among taxpayers is that carbon taxes will affect poor households more than wealthier ones, especially in markets where there are limited low-carbon options available (Maestre-Andrés et al., 2019). With the difficulties of accessing low-carbon options and the inability to afford the increasing cost of polluting products, consumers believe that most carbon pricing measures exacerbate existing inequalities. Therefore, taxpayers tend to have a strong preference for carbon tax designs that protect low-income households (Baranzini & Carattini, 2017). Such schemes use carbon tax revenues to compensate low-income households that may suffer the regressive impacts of taxation by targeting tax reductions at vulnerable segments of the population or via lump sum redistributions (Klenert et al., 2018).

Consumers understand that direct money transfers or tax cuts have the potential to turn the carbon tax into a progressive policy measure (Carattini et al., 2017), which in turn contributes to reducing income inequality. Lesser known is the trade-off between policy equity and efficiency intrinsic in revenue-use decisions (Rausch et al., 2011): Using revenues to avoid regressive distributional impacts means that less money will be available for climate change mitigation expenses. However, if revenues are used to finance general-purpose tax cuts or to finance emissions reduction projects without assessing their distributional impacts, carbon taxes may favour wealthier citizens. For instance, if governments want to subsidise households willing to adopt renewable energy (e.g. install solar panels on roofs), homeowners would be receiving substantial money transfers, which is not accessible to renters or individuals who cannot afford housing.

Nevertheless, the trade-off between policy equity and efficiency only holds in countries where the impact of carbon taxes is regressive. This is the case for most industrialised countries, where low-income households have carbon-intensive consumption patterns. Conversely, low-income households in developing countries have fewer opportunities to be involved in carbon-intensive consumption, resulting in a smaller tax burden. Moreover, recent research has confirmed the progressive impact of carbon taxes in many developing countries (Dorband et al., 2019) and concluded that reducing carbon emissions, increasing government revenue and reducing economic inequality are not mutually exclusive objectives in emerging markets. Therefore, carbon tax designs can achieve cost-effective climate change mitigation and development co-benefits while still preserving the Fairness principle, as policy equity would be secured.

11.3.3.2 Ambiguity and Lack of Transparency

Carbon taxes are aimed at encouraging pro-environmental consumption by favouring low-carbon products and services over carbon-intensive ones. However, the usual institutional mistrust and poor policy communication in developing countries could make carbon taxes look obscure. This infringement of the transparency principle can result in diverting attention from the objective of reducing carbon emissions. First, consumers could think carbon taxes are a backdoor approach for raising government revenue rather than a measure to mitigate climate change (Klenert et al., 2018). Second, as sceptical individuals could misinterpret the aim of carbon taxes, consumers may still favour carbon-intensive products due to their accessibility and the lack of low-carbon alternatives. Third, the presence of the price signal could eclipse ethical considerations of the purchase decision and distort genuine environmentalists' self-image. As these behavioural failures compound, consumers' reactions to carbon taxes become increasingly uncertain.

Regarding the political dimension of behavioural failure, the rapid urbanisation and economic growth of emerging markets are fuelled by increased energy consumption (Bakirtas & Akpolat, 2018) that carbon taxes aim to curtail. Since carbon taxes discourage carbon-intensive economic activities, individuals in emerging markets might construe carbon pricing as a threat to their growing living standards. Although carbon taxes could also provide several developments co-benefits, in practice, the calculation of the welfare gains of carbon pricing is rather opaque (Kallbekken et al., 2011), and a lack of information could reinforce consumers' perception that they are facing excessive policy risks (Petrovich et al., 2021). Furthermore, the level of trust between citizens and governments is generally low in emerging markets, which undermines carbon tax acceptability because taxpayers do not believe their increased tax burden will be directed towards climate change mitigation (Klenert et al., 2018). Consequently, governments are forced to earmark carbon tax revenues to gain public acceptability, even though other designs would be more efficient (Carattini et al., 2018).

From an economic perspective, individuals could fail to change their consumption patterns either because there are few low-carbon alternatives available or because their demand for carbon-intensive products is more inelastic than previously thought (Heal & Schlenker, 2019). Additionally, boundedly rational individuals could misunderstand the purpose of the price signal and fail to acknowledge that they are expected to reduce consumption. Such reactions occur when structural strategies like carbon taxes affect consumers beyond the instrumental value of money (Reisch & Thøgersen, 2015). As a result, economic incentives to behave pro-environmentally end up changing decision frames, disrupting the process of self-persuasion and interacting with the consumer's self-image.

Drawing on the motivation crowding theory (Frey & Jegen, 2001), carbon taxes can undermine consumers' intrinsic motivation to buy less carbon-intensive products if the carbon tax is perceived as a control mechanism (Nyborg, 2010): The price signal can turn an otherwise ethical decision (i.e. behaving pro-environmentally) into a cost–benefit analysis because the monetary incentive serves as a reminder that there is a trade-off between the size of compensation (paying less carbon taxes) and the effort to shift to low-carbon consumption (Heyman & Ariely, 2004). Furthermore, consumers' self-image may also be affected because the presence of the carbon tax prevents them from attributing their low-carbon consumption decisions solely to their biospheric values (Nyborg, 2010). As a result, even if they choose the low-carbon consumption option, consumers cannot be sure whether their action was driven by genuine care for the environment or simply by economic reasons. This is problematic because attributing past pro-environmental behaviour to oneself also encourages future pro-environmental behaviours (van der Werff et al., 2014), a virtuous circle that carbon taxes could weaken. Similarly, carbon taxes could deprive status-seeking consumers of the self-expressive benefits of behaving pro-environmentally because economic incentives cast doubts on the authenticity of the sacrifice consumers want to signal to others (Reisch & Thøgersen, 2015).

Together, motivation crowding theory and consumers' self-image considerations could explain why demand reductions achieved in practice by carbon pricing instruments are more modest than expected (Lanz et al., 2018; Soregaroli et al., 2021). Moreover, since almost all environmental problems involve some notion of the common good, and this ethical decision is systematically undermined by the mere mention of money (Gowdy, 2008), carbon taxes might not be as effective as expected in encouraging low-carbon consumption.

11.4 Discussion

Governments, companies and consumers in emerging markets can profit from the development co-benefits that an optimally designed carbon tax unlocks. However, such co-benefits seem unlikely when considering the influence of stakeholders' behavioural failures on the proper functioning of the carbon tax. This review has elucidated various incompatibilities between the FASTER principles of optimal carbon pricing design and the practical functioning challenges carbon taxes face in emerging markets. Table 11.1 synthesises our integrative contribution, connecting agents' behavioural failures to their implications and describing each case's (improbable) development co-benefits.

Half of the FASTER principles do not seem to hold in a realistic scenario of carbon tax implementation, and the rest may also be in jeopardy. Unless policymakers manage to meet all design principles, it would be difficult to argue that carbon taxes can achieve the development co-benefits that stakeholders in emerging markets appreciate. Ultimately, if co-benefits do not materialise, carbon taxes will be less acceptable (Baranzini & Carattini, 2017).

Moreover, the prevalence of behavioural failures and deviations from the optimal carbon tax design also casts doubt on its carbon emissions reduction potential. Setting aside the debatable development co-benefits, emissions reduction is not guaranteed; a recent meta-review has only been able to attribute modest emissions reductions to carbon pricing (Green, 2021). Besides, carbon taxes alone cannot meet climate

Table 11.1 Overview of carbon tax co-benefits and behavioural failures by agent

Relevant agents	Development co-benefits	Potential behavioural failures	
		Implications	Dimensions
Policymakers	Increase government revenue to finance mitigation investments (complying with the reliability and environmental integrity principle)	Ineffective carbon taxes: Setting rates too low and displacing other policy measures (not compatible with the alignment of policy and objectives principle)	• *Political*: Maximise the political acceptability of the carbon tax by minimising its impact on prices • *Economic*: Since carbon tax revenues shrink as emissions decrease, governments relying on that money might consider preserving the tax base (i.e. emissions) • *Boundedly rational*: Reduce policy ambition after implementation, thinking that the carbon tax alone is enough to tackle climate change (Single-action bias)
Companies	Despite carbon leakage risks, carbon taxes increase green innovation and competitiveness (complying with the efficiency and cost-effectiveness principle)	Opposition to carbon taxes cast doubts about future price signals, constraining R&D and low-carbon investments (not compatible with the stability and predictability principle)	• *Political*: Companies lobby against carbon taxes even though dispense with them implies using more costly or less flexible policy instruments in the future • *Economic*: Difficulties to assess project profitability paralyse decision-making due to uncertain future carbon tax rates, regardless of the logical argument to invest in carbon emissions abatement • *Boundedly rational:* The announcement of an imminent carbon tax accelerates resource extraction and hence aggravates climate change (Green paradox)

(continued)

11 Carbon Taxes Beyond Emissions' Reduction … 257

Table 11.1 (continued)

Relevant agents	Development co-benefits	Potential behavioural failures	
		Implications	Dimensions
Consumers	Reduce inequality due to progressive impacts and carbon tax revenue redistribution (complying with the fairness principle)	Consumers could misunderstand the purpose of the price signal and fail to acknowledge that they are expected to reduce consumption due to poor policy communication (not compatible with the transparency principle)	• *Political*: Consumers perceive carbon taxes as barriers to growth and, due to the inherent institutional mistrust in emerging markets, they think carbon taxes are not helping the environment but governments' general-purpose budgets • *Economic*: Inelastic demand of carbon-intensive products and few low-carbon alternatives make difficult to change consumption patterns • *Boundedly rational*: Monetary incentives could eclipse ethical considerations of consumption decisions and distort genuine environmentalists' self-image too, reducing the intrinsic motivation to behave pro-environmentally

change mitigation goals because they lack the transformational effectiveness necessary to avoid a lock-in into carbon-intensive technologies and infrastructure (Bertram et al., 2015).

Our analysis focused on carbon taxes, but we could expect similar conclusions for other pricing instruments, such as cap-and-trade systems or emission reduction credits. Essentially, all structural strategies relying on monetary incentives are modelled as agents will behave rationally, an assumption that has been widely questioned in the literature (Gowdy, 2008; Gsottbauer & Van Den Bergh, 2011; Kesternich et al., 2017). Therefore, designing structural policies to solve the carbon emissions market failure without addressing behavioural failures caused by measures such as carbon taxes will be inadequate and insufficient (Shogren & Taylor, 2008). This is especially relevant for policymaking in emerging markets in the next decade, as the research community warns that the post-pandemic era will need a climate change mitigation policy designed to overcome biases to human judgement (Klenert et al., 2020).

Overall, it is unclear whether carbon taxes will achieve emissions reductions, let alone development co-benefits. Behavioural failures affecting policy design, firms' decision-making and individuals' consumption patterns deviate carbon tax's performance from what is theoretically expected. Looking forward, further attempts to investigate other structural strategies beyond carbon pricing instruments could prove quite beneficial in effectively encouraging sustainability, since researchers (Bertram et al., 2015; Haites, 2018) increasingly view carbon taxes as components of a wider portfolio of mitigation policies rather than self-reliant measures.

Moreover, relying only on carbon pricing policies that focus on individual behaviour change may be problematic from a societal standpoint. When deciding to tax carbon emissions, policymakers are implicitly making a choice regarding allocation of responsibility: By attributing global warming to carbon-intensive consumption patterns, the burden of solving the problem is placed on consumer behaviour. We argue that the inclusion of other instruments in the policy mix could underscore the necessary leadership of companies and governments in addressing climate change. Indeed, the low-carbon transition is unlikely to be achieved solely through individual behaviour change but through upstream solutions like government-led interventions (Shove, 2010). Other measures can also be steered by multinational companies operating in emerging markets, such as green supply chain procurement (Grubb et al., 2020), which would harness sustainable practices among domestic companies.

11.5 Conclusion

When carbon taxes are implemented to deal with the carbon emissions market failure, new behavioural failures emerge fuelled by political economy constraints. Given that such political economy constraints are greater in emerging markets than in developed countries, carbon pricing instruments might be less suitable for the former (Finon, 2019). Therefore, effectively reducing carbon emissions and addressing development challenges require a broader set of non-price instruments to support carbon taxes in emerging markets (De Gouvello et al., 2020; Finon, 2019). This view is supported by Bertram et al. (2015), who also concluded that an instrument mix might be a more realistic alternative to an optimal policy based solely on a comprehensive carbon tax.

Structural strategies to promote sustainable behaviours include changing the costs and benefits of behaving pro-environmentally, but that does not necessarily mean that pricing pollution solves the problem. Non-pricing instruments can constitute a feasible structural strategy that can reduce emissions without generating unexpected behavioural failures. Policymakers in emerging markets could benefit from considering carbon taxes as a complement to a broader set of structural strategies to mitigate climate change, such as other market-based instruments (e.g. Allowance trading schemes and green certificates), direct investments (e.g. R&D funding and government procurement to develop low-carbon infrastructure) and efficiency standards and quotas (e.g. Technology phase-out mandates and building codes).

Overall, emerging markets integrating carbon taxes with other non-price instruments in their policy mix could achieve both development co-benefits and emissions reductions while still containing the behavioural failures that pricing instruments may create.

Acknowledgements Financial support from the Basque Government (Grant Number PRE-2020-1-0097) is gratefully acknowledged.

References

Abrahamse, W., & Steg, L. (2013). Social influence approaches to encourage resource conservation: A meta-analysis. *Global Environmental Change, 23*(6), 1773–1785. https://doi.org/10.1016/j.glo envcha.2013.07.029

Aldy, J. E., & Stavins, R. N. (2012). The promise and problems of pricing carbon: Theory and experience. *The Journal of Environment & Development, 21*(2), 152–180. https://doi.org/10.1177/1070496512442508

Bakirtas, T., & Akpolat, A. G. (2018). The relationship between energy consumption, urbanization, and economic growth in new emerging-market countries. *Energy, 147*, 110–121.

Ball, J. (2018). Why carbon pricing isn't working: Good idea in theory, failing in practice. *Foreign Affairs, 97*, 134.

Baranzini, A., & Carattini, S. (2014). Taxation of emissions of greenhouse gases. In B. Freedman (Ed.), *Global environmental change* (pp. 543–560). Springer Netherlands. https://doi.org/10.1007/978-94-007-5784-4_90

Baranzini, A., & Carattini, S. (2017). Effectiveness, earmarking and labeling: Testing the acceptability of carbon taxes with survey data. *Environmental Economics and Policy Studies, 19*(1), 197–227. https://doi.org/10.1007/s10018-016-0144-7

Baranzini, A., et al. (2017). Carbon pricing in climate policy: Seven reasons, complementary instruments, and political economy considerations. *Wiley Interdisciplinary Reviews: Climate Change, 8*(4), e462. https://doi.org/10.1002/wcc.462

Bertram, C., et al. (2015). Complementing carbon prices with technology policies to keep climate targets within reach. *Nature Climate Change, 5*(3), 235–239. https://doi.org/10.1038/nclima te2514

Carattini, S., Carvalho, M., & Fankhauser, S. (2018). Overcoming public resistance to carbon taxes. *Wires Climate Change, 9*(5), e531. https://doi.org/10.1002/wcc.531

Carattini, S., et al. (2017). Green taxes in a post-paris world: Are millions of nays inevitable? *Environmental and Resource Economics, 68*(1), 97–128. https://doi.org/10.1007/s10640-017-0133-8

Coalition, C. P. L. (2019). *Report of the high-level commission on carbon pricing and competitiveness.* World Bank Group.

Corraliza, J. A., & Berenguer, J. (2000). Environmental values, beliefs, and actions: A situational approach. *Environment and Behavior, 32*(6), 832–848. https://doi.org/10.1177/001391600219 72829

De Gouvello, C., Finon, D., & Guigon, P. (2020). *Reconciling carbon pricing and energy policies in developing countries.* World Bank. https://doi.org/10.1596/33490

de Mooij, R. A., Keen, M. M., & Parry, I. W. H. (2012). *Fiscal policy to mitigate climate change: A guide for policymakers*. International Monetary Fund.

Dechezleprêtre, A., & Sato, M. (2017). The impacts of environmental regulations on competitiveness. *Review of Environmental Economics and Policy, 11*(2), 183–206.

Dorband, I. I., et al. (2019). Poverty and distributional effects of carbon pricing in low- and middle-income countries—A global comparative analysis. *World Development, 115*, 246–257. https://doi.org/10.1016/j.worlddev.2018.11.015

Edenhofer, O., Franks, M., & Kalkuhl, M. (2021). Pigou in the 21st century: A tribute on the occasion of the 100th anniversary of the publication of the economics of welfare. *International Tax and Public Finance*. https://doi.org/10.1007/s10797-020-09653-y

Finon, D. (2019). Carbon policy in developing countries: Giving priority to non-price instruments. *Energy Policy, 132*, 38–43. https://doi.org/10.1016/j.enpol.2019.04.046

Frey, B. S., & Jegen, R. (2001). Motivation crowding theory. *Journal of Economic Surveys, 15*(5), 589–611. https://doi.org/10.1111/1467-6419.00150

Geroe, S. (2019). Addressing climate change through a low-cost, high-impact carbon tax. *The Journal of Environment & Development, 28*(1), 3–27. https://doi.org/10.1177/1070496518821152

Goulder, L. H. (1995). Environmental taxation and the double dividend: A reader's guide. *International Tax and Public Finance, 2*(2), 157–183. https://doi.org/10.1007/BF00877495

Goulder, L. H., & Parry, I. W. H. (2008). Instrument Choice in Environmental Policy. *Review of Environmental Economics and Policy, 2*(2), 152–174. https://doi.org/10.1093/reep/ren005

Gowdy, J. M. (2008). Behavioral economics and climate change policy. *Journal of Economic Behavior & Organization, 68*(3–4), 632–644. https://doi.org/10.1016/j.jebo.2008.06.011

Green, J. F. (2021). Does carbon pricing reduce emissions? A review of ex-post analyses. *Environmental Research Letters*. https://doi.org/10.1088/1748-9326/abdae9

Grubb, M., et al. (2020). Consumption-oriented policy instruments for fostering greenhouse gas mitigation. *Climate Policy*, 1–16. https://doi.org/10.1080/14693062.2020.1730151

Gsottbauer, E., & Van Den Bergh, J. C. J. M. (2011). Environmental policy theory given bounded rationality and other-regarding preferences. *Environmental and Resource Economics, 49*(2), 263–304. https://doi.org/10.1007/s10640-010-9433-y

Gupta, J. (2008). *Engaging developing countries in climate change negotiations*. EU Policy Department: Economic and Scientific Policy.

Haites, E. (2018). Carbon taxes and greenhouse gas emissions trading systems: What have we learned? *Climate Policy, 18*(8), 955–966. https://doi.org/10.1080/14693062.2018.1492897

Heal, G., & Schlenker, W. (2019). *Coase, hotelling and Pigou: The incidence of a carbon tax and CO_2 emissions* (Working Paper 26086). National Bureau of Economic Research. https://doi.org/10.3386/w26086

Heine, D., & Black, S. (2019). Benefits beyond climate: Environmental tax reform. In M. Pigato (Ed.), *Fiscal policies for development and climate action* (pp. 1–38). World Bank Group.

Heyman, J., & Ariely, D. (2004). Effort for payment: A tale of two markets. *Psychological Science, 15*(11), 787–793. https://doi.org/10.1111/j.0956-7976.2004.00757.x

Hook, L. (2019, February 17). Surge in US economists' support for carbon tax to tackle emissions. *Financial Times*. Available at: https://www.ft.com/content/fa0815fe-3299-11e9-bd3a-8b2a211d90d5. Accessed 21 July 2021.

Jaffe, A. B., Newell, R. G., & Stavins, R. N. (2005). A tale of two market failures: Technology and environmental policy. *Ecological Economics, 54*(2), 164–174. https://doi.org/10.1016/j.ecolecon.2004.12.027

Jakob, M., et al. (2016). Carbon pricing revenues could close infrastructure access gaps. *World Development, 84*, 254–265. https://doi.org/10.1016/j.worlddev.2016.03.001

Jenkins, J. D. (2014). Political economy constraints on carbon pricing policies: What are the implications for economic efficiency, environmental efficacy, and climate policy design? *Energy Policy, 69*, 467–477. https://doi.org/10.1016/j.enpol.2014.02.003

Kallbekken, S., Kroll, S., & Cherry, T. L. (2011). Do you not like Pigou, or do you not understand him? Tax aversion and revenue recycling in the lab. *Journal of Environmental Economics and Management, 62*(1), 53–64. https://doi.org/10.1016/j.jeem.2010.10.006

Kesternich, M., Reif, C., & Rübbelke, D. (2017). Recent trends in behavioral environmental economics. *Environmental and Resource Economics, 67*(3), 403–411. https://doi.org/10.1007/s10640-017-0162-3

Khlif, H., Guidara, A., & Hussainey, K. (2016). Sustainability level, corruption and tax evasion: A cross-country analysis. *Journal of Financial Crime, 23*(2), 328–348. https://doi.org/10.1108/JFC-09-2014-0041

Klein, F., & van den Bergh, J. (2020). The employment double dividend of environmental tax reforms: Exploring the role of agent behaviour and social interaction. *Journal of Environmental Economics and Policy*, 1–25. https://doi.org/10.1080/21606544.2020.1819433

Klenert, D., et al. (2018). Making carbon pricing work for citizens. *Nature Climate Change, 8*(8), 669–677. https://doi.org/10.1038/s41558-018-0201-2

Klenert, D., et al. (2020). Five lessons from COVID-19 for advancing climate change mitigation. *Environmental and Resource Economics, 76*(4), 751–778.

Lanz, B., et al. (2018). The behavioral effect of Pigovian regulation: Evidence from a field experiment. *Journal of Environmental Economics and Management, 87*, 190–205. https://doi.org/10.1016/j.jeem.2017.06.005

Liu, A. A. (2013). Tax evasion and optimal environmental taxes. *Journal of Environmental Economics and Management, 66*(3), 656–670. https://doi.org/10.1016/j.jeem.2013.06.004

Maestre-Andrés, S., Drews, S., & van den Bergh, J. (2019). Perceived fairness and public acceptability of carbon pricing: A review of the literature. *Climate Policy, 19*(9), 1186–1204. https://doi.org/10.1080/14693062.2019.1639490

Martin, R., et al. (2014). Industry compensation under relocation risk: A firm-level analysis of the EU emissions trading scheme. *American Economic Review, 104*(8), 2482–2508. https://doi.org/10.1257/aer.104.8.2482

Mildenberger, M. (2020). *Carbon captured: How business and labor control climate politics.* MIT Press.

Munnings, C., et al. (2019). Pricing carbon consumption: Synthesizing an emerging trend. *Climate Policy, 19*(1), 92–107. https://doi.org/10.1080/14693062.2018.1457508

Nyborg, K. (2010). Will green taxes undermine moral motivation. *Public Financial Management, 110*(2), 331–351.

Osbaldiston, R., & Schott, J. P. (2012). Environmental sustainability and behavioral science. *Environment and Behavior, 44*(2), 257–299. https://doi.org/10.1177/0013916511402673

Parry, I., Veung, C., & Heine, D. (2015). How much carbon pricing is in countries' own interests? The critical role of co-benefits. *Climate Change Economics, 06*(04), 1550019. https://doi.org/10.1142/S2010007815500190

Parry, I. W. H., et al. (2014). *Getting energy prices right: From principle to practice.* International Monetary Fund.

Partnership for Market Readiness. (2017). *Carbon tax guide: A handbook for policy makers.* World Bank.

Peñasco, C., Anadón, L. D., & Verdolini, E. (2021). Systematic review of the outcomes and trade-offs of ten types of decarbonization policy instruments. *Nature Climate Change, 11*(3), 257–265. https://doi.org/10.1038/s41558-020-00971-x

Petrovich, B., Carattini, S., & Wüstenhagen, R. (2021). The price of risk in residential solar investments. *Ecological Economics, 180*, 106856. https://doi.org/10.1016/j.ecolecon.2020.106856

Qin, L., et al. (2021). The salience of carbon leakage for climate action planning: Evidence from the next eleven countries. *Sustainable Production and Consumption, 27*, 1064–1076. https://doi.org/10.1016/j.spc.2021.02.019

Rausch, S., Metcalf, G. E., & Reilly, J. M. (2011). Distributional impacts of carbon pricing: A general equilibrium approach with micro-data for households. *Energy Economics, 33*, S20–S33. https://doi.org/10.1016/j.eneco.2011.07.023

Reisch, L. A., & Thøgersen, J. (2015). *Handbook of research on sustainable consumption*. Edward Elgar Publishing.

Rennkamp, B. (2019). Power, coalitions and institutional change in South African climate policy. *Climate Policy, 19*(6), 756–770. https://doi.org/10.1080/14693062.2019.1591936

Shogren, J. F., & Taylor, L. O. (2008). On behavioral-environmental economics. *Review of Environmental Economics and Policy, 2*(1), 26–44. https://doi.org/10.1093/reep/rem027

Shove, E. (2010). Beyond the ABC: Climate change policy and theories of social change. *Environment and Planning A: Economy and Space, 42*(6), 1273–1285. https://doi.org/10.1068/a42282

Sinn, H.-W. (2015). Introductory comment-the green paradox: A supply-side view of the climate problem. *Review of Environmental Economics and Policy, 9*(2), 239–245. https://doi.org/10.1093/reep/rev011

Soregaroli, C., et al. (2021). Carbon footprint information, prices, and restaurant wine choices by customers: A natural field experiment. *Ecological Economics, 186*, 107061. https://doi.org/10.1016/j.ecolecon.2021.107061

Steg, L., & de Groot, J. I. M. (Eds.). (2019). *Environmental psychology: An introduction* (2nd ed.). Wiley-Blackwell (BPS textbooks in psychology).

Steg, L., & Vlek, C. (2009). Encouraging pro-environmental behaviour: An integrative review and research agenda. *Journal of Environmental Psychology, 29*(3), 309–317. https://doi.org/10.1016/j.jenvp.2008.10.004

Steinebach, Y., Fernandez-i-Marin, X., & Aschenbrenner, C. (2020). Who puts a price on carbon, why and how? A global empirical analysis of carbon pricing policies. *Climate Policy*, 13. https://doi.org/10.1080/14693062.2020.1824890

Stern, N. (2006). *The economics of climate change: The Stern review*. Cambridge University Press.

Stevens, D. (2021). Institutions and Agency in the making of carbon pricing policies: Evidence from Mexico and directions for Comparative analyses in Latin America. *Journal of Comparative Policy Analysis: Research and Practice, 23*(4), 485–504. https://doi.org/10.1080/13876988.2020.1794754

Stoll, C., & Mehling, M. A. (2021). Climate change and carbon pricing: Overcoming three dimensions of failure. *Energy Research & Social Science, 77*, 102062. https://doi.org/10.1016/j.erss.2021.102062

van der Ploeg, F. (2016). Second-best carbon taxation in the global economy: The Green Paradox and carbon leakage revisited. *Journal of Environmental Economics and Management, 78*, 85–105. https://doi.org/10.1016/j.jeem.2016.02.006

van der Werff, E., Steg, L., & Keizer, K. (2014). Follow the signal: When past pro-environmental actions signal who you are. *Journal of Environmental Psychology, 40*, 273–282. https://doi.org/10.1016/j.jenvp.2014.07.004

Venmans, F., Ellis, J., & Nachtigall, D. (2020). Carbon pricing and competitiveness: Are they at odds? *Climate Policy*, 1–22. https://doi.org/10.1080/14693062.2020.1805291

Weber, E. (1997). Perception and expectation of climate change: Precondition for economic and technological adaptation. In M. Bazerman, D. Messick, A. Tenbrunsel, & K. Wade-Benzoni (Eds.), *Psychological perspectives to environmental and ethical issues in management* (pp. 314–341). Jossey-Bass.

World Bank. (2015). *The FASTER principles for successful carbon pricing: An approach based on initial experience.* http://documents.worldbank.org/curated/en/901041467995665361/The-FASTER-principles-for-successful-carbon-pricing-an-approach-based-on-initial-experience

World Bank. (2021a). *Beyond mitigation: Quantifying the development benefits of carbon pricing.* World Bank (Partnership for Market Readiness). https://doi.org/10.1596/35624

World Bank. (2021b). *State and trends of carbon pricing 2021*. World Bank.